A CELEBRATION
of
ART & CONSCIOUSNESS

KEN BEITTEL
with joan beittel

Cover Art and Book Design
Joan Beittel

Editing
Joan Beittel

*Funding for the printing of this book was
made possible by a special grant from
the College of Arts and Architecture, the
Graduate School, and the Institute for
the Arts and Humanistic Studies of
The Pennsylvania State University*

Library of Congress Catalog Card Number 91-70892
ISBN 0-9628511-1-6

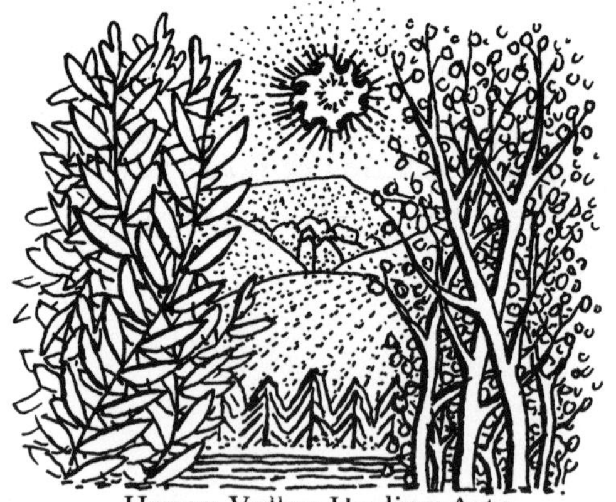

Happy Valley Healing Arts
2014 Pine Cliff Road
State College, PA 16801
814-234-4428

*Our purpose is to offer an alternative to
publishing that increases the healing power
of the arts and of the creative imagination
in the lives of persons of all ages.*

Contents

Permissions

I would like to thank the authors and publishers who so graciously gave me permission to quote from their works.

Excerpts from POETRY, LANGUAGE, THOUGHT BY Martin Heidegger, translated by Albert Hofstadter. Copyright (c) 1971 by Martin Heidegger. Reprinted by permission of HarperCollins, Publishers.

From REMEMBRANCE OF THINGS PAST, VOL. ONE: by Marcel Proust. Translation Copyright (c) 1981 by Random House, Inc. and Chatto & Windus. Reprinted by permission of Random House, Inc.

From THE COLLECTED POEMS OF WALLACE STEVENS by Wallace Stevens, "Anecdote of the Jar." Copyright (c) 1923 and renewed 1951 by Wallace Stevens. Reprinted by permission of Alfred A. Knopf, Inc.

From POETICS OF SPACE by Gaston Bachelard, Copyright (c) 1958 by Presses Universitaires de France, Translation copyright (c) 1964 by The Orion Press. Used by permission of Viking Penguin, a division of Penguin Books USA Inc.

From THE NECESSARY ANGEL by Wallace Stevens, copyright (c) 1942 by Vintage Books. Used by permission of Alfred A. Knopf, Inc.

From COLLECTED POEMS. 1909-1939. Vol I, by William Carlos Williams, copyright (c) 1938 by New Directions Publishing Corporation. Reprinted by permission of New Directions.

From THE POEMS OF W.B. YEATS: A NEW EDITION, edited by Richard J. Finneran. Copyright (c) 1919 by Macmillan Publishing Company, renewed 1947 by Bertha Georgie Yeats. Used by permission of Macmillan Publishing Company.

From FIREFLIES by Rabindranath Tagore. Copyright (c) 1928 by Macmillan Publishing Company, renewed 1955 by Rabindranath Tagore. Used by permission of Macmillan Publishing Company.

From "The Fish" from THE COMPLETE POEMS, 1927-1979 by Elizabeth Bishop. Copyright (c) 1979, 1983 by Alice Helen Methfessel. Reprinted by permission of Farrar, Straus and Giroux, Inc.

"The Clay Jug" by Kabir, translated by Robert Bly and "Archaic Torso of Apollo" by Rilke, translated by Robert Bly, from NEWS OF THE UNIVERSE by Robert Bly, copyright (c) 1980 by Sierra Club Books. Used by permission of Robert Bly.

Excerpts from THE SPECTRUM OF CONSCIOUSNESS, copyright (c) 1977 by Ken Wilber; and from THE ATMAN PROJECT, copyright (c) 1980 by Ken Wilber. Used by permission of The Thesophical Publishing House.

From "Words Rising," from OF SOLITUDE AND SILENCE, Richard Jones and Kate Daniels, editors, copyright (c) 1981 by Poetry East; Beacon Press, 1981. Used by permission of Robert Bly.

Excerpts from A DIFFERENT EXISTENCE by J. H. van den Berg, English translation copyright (c) 1972 by Duquesne University. Used by permission of Duquesne University Press.

In Gratitude

To The Pennsylvania State University for the special support I have received for the printing of this book in the form of a grant through the College of Arts and Architecture, the Graduate School and the Institute for the Arts and Humanistic Studies.

Very special mention is made to Grace Hampton, Vice Provost, for immediately sharing the vision, for her wonderful enthusiasm, warm response and benevolent support for this project; to James Moeser, Dean of the College of Arts and Architecture, who understood the purpose of this work from the outset, for his kind and gracious support and encouragement and for his coordination of University resources; to Charles Hosler, Dean of the Graduate School and Senior Vice President for Research, for his generous support and willing endorsement of the mission behind this work.

To the special Symposium and Conference in my honor at the University of Illinois, which helped kindle the desire to get this manuscript into book form; and to the planning and enterprise of two personal friends, both former students of mine, who made this Conference possible – Dr. George Hardiman, Professor of Art Education at the University of Illinois, and Dr. Marilyn Zermuehlin, Professor of Art Education at the University of Iowa.

To the community of authors whose works helped greatly in clarifying the message. I would like especially to thank Gaston Bachelard, Ken Wilber, Robert Bly, William Carlos Williams, Martin Heidegger, John Senior, Francis Ponge, Martin Buber, Wallace Stevens, and Rabindranath Tagore.

For the climate in art education at Penn State during the 31 years there as Professor of Art Education. The opportunity I had to teach studio classes in pottery, to conduct graduate seminars in theory, research and philosophy, to guide doctoral research, and to engage in basic research of my own – these not only challenged me constantly but allowed me to grow and renew myself throughout my career. Here I must make special mention of the Drawing Lab, a research facility for inquiry into the creative process, for which I received support both from outside sources and internal funding and release of time. The 16 years in which the Drawing Lab was in operation, from 1968 to 1984, were times for constant discovery and wonder about the scope and depth of human creativity in art.

To all my students, teachers and friends, my deepest thanks.

Finally, the reality and form of this book owes very much to the editorial and advisory role played throughout by Joan Beittel. She has been an extraordinary guiding spirit from the very inception of this work.

to
Viktor Lowenfeld
whose radical support for the creative process
was based on the conviction
that art is truly education for higher consciousness

Manji Inoue
one of Japan's Living Intangible Cultural Treasures
my teacher in the Arita Tradition of Porcelain

Joan
islands in the sun
together

my little red Z car
for flying me everywhere I needed to go
while working on this book

and to

Great Spirit

and to

snow flakes

in

the

wine . . .

Crystal and Angie and their castles in the sand... HG, whose sweetness was never wasted on the desert air nor in that restaurant on 7th Street, disguised as my mother but I believe she was a saint... Yi, beloved grandmother and fairy godmother who took me to the theater four times each week and who loved Roy Rogers too... Aunt Maude and Uncle Ed who introduced me to a different way of life, riding horses and milking cows, churning butter and baking bread, fencing bulls and plowing fields, for endless summers and a pantry overflowing with raspberry pies... Ralph and Anna Hoover, who taught me about love and motor boats, racing cars and Doodles Weaver... Richard Winters, because of his irresistable sense of humor and contagious love of life, for his trip to Philadelphia for me and our special friendship... Gerry, mon cher ami, for Paris live... James, wild chef from Kentucky who does flaming brandy coffees spectacularly at midnight by the full moon... Little Nicholas in Germany, Christopher in Toftrees, Cassie, Curt, Jodi and Breanna in Homer City, my very special grandchildren... Richard, Stephen, Kimmerly and Kristianne, my children, for being who they are... Olaf Peterson, for the shared joy of those magical winter wonderlands of childhood in Scandinavia... Nicole, for Saturdays, the San Francisco Ballet and sourdough bread... Virginia, who tried ferociously for nine years to make a concert pianist out of me and who paved the way to Eastman and to Mills... Charles Bailey, world famous heart surgeon at Hahnemann who way back in 1954 opened up new worlds for me as he threw those peanuts on the floor... EV, challenging friend and 81 year old high energy medicine woman from a serenely herbal hillside who makes every moment into a celebration... USAF Capt. Mark McKenzie, my son-in-law, F-15 pilot and great guy, for his courage and compassion... Larry, dear friend, gracious being, and wonderful potter who so beautifully walks the path of the great tradition... NJ at 93, who still shovels snow at 4 in the morning and can't wait to plant his garden this spring, may god bless... Mitsuie, Japanese ichiban deshi, for the experience of the old Miyako in Kyoto and the promise to take me to the Sapporo Ice Festival in Hokkaido... Richard B, for sure as the sun comes up tomorrow there is ecstasy if you know where to find it... Ralph and Deno and their friends... Marc, for his refreshing lightness of being, who knew all along it was 6 am and didn't care at all... Panther, White Bear, Aloha and Great Eagle... the old Halekulani on the beach in Hawaii where dreams really do come true...

and to the spirit that is Greece

thank you
jb

Foreword

This book examines the role of art in the evolution of consciousness. Much of the literature on the evolution of consciousness is either silent on art's contribution or vague about its place and efficacy. Where mention of art does occur, it is often to place its influence on the lower and less evolved of the subtle higher levels where imagery, myth, and imagination are thought to operate most fully.[1] The probability that art functions throughout the spectrum of consciousness has been taken seriously by only a few theorists—by Hegel, for example, in his sweeping statement that "Spirit is artist."[2]

The reason for this neglect and silence is perhaps ascribable to the uncertain appearance of creativity in human affairs, which renders art suspect to systematic thought. This problem is still further complicated in the non-verbal arts. In the case of scriptural revelation, by contrast, a verbal inspired text offers itself for hermeneutics and anagogy, so that even though revelation may appear in poetic or analogical form the translation into shared understanding occurs according to the multilevel meanings within the same medium. Certainly both in its creative and receptive cycles art is one of the truest ways to dwell in the timeless and eternal present—in *the qualitative immediate present* as we might put it in the language of Dewey and Pepper.[3] We find the admission of this state and its meaning in what is called organismic awareness:

> Organismic awareness is what we...ordinarily, but clumsily, refer to as seeing, touching, tasting, smelling, and hearing. But in its purest form, this "sensual awareness" is non-symbolic, non-conceptual, momentary consciousness...In other words, organismic consciousness is properly timeless, and being timeless, it is necessarily spaceless. Just as organismic awareness knows no past or future, it knows no inside or outside, no self or other. Thus pure organismic consciousness participates fully in the non-dual awareness called Absolute Subjectivity.[4]

This organismic awareness, as experienced by itself or as experienced *and* expressed in a medium, is the realm of art *par excellence.*

It is almost impossible to escape the notion that there are clearly differing modes of knowing. Useful to our purposes here is a distinction between knowledge modes made by Eddington:

> We have two kinds of knowledge which I call symbolic
> knowledge and intimate knowledge...[The] more
> customary forms of reasoning have been developed for
> symbolic knowledge only. The intimate knowledge will
> not submit to codification and analysis; or, rather,
> when we attempt to analyze it the intimacy is lost and
> it is replaced by symbolism.[5]

Further, within intimate knowledge we can specify three sub-divisions: the analogical, negative, and injunctive, or what unspeakable reality *is like*, what it *is not*, and what we must do *to reach it*.[6] It should be apparent that art operates as a form of intimate knowledge in all three of these ways.

Schuon speaks about two great subjectivities in man, that of the soul and that of the spirit, which grant us access to the objective unity of the universe. The soul is affective, speaking to the will and to passional man and appearing as beauty. The spirit is intellective, speaking to the intelligence and to contemplative man and appearing as theology.[7] In traditional thought soul is placed hierarchically above mind but below spirit. This is a usage which would situate the province of beauty lower than that of theology. But this order need not be rigorous, for Schuon points out that the soul can include both tendencies. He further states that "psychic and mental consciousness perceives appearances; intellectual or heart consciousness perceives the Essence; but the intermediary consciousness sees the two dimensions at once."[8] We will hold to the view that art is a form of intimate knowledge which probes the highest levels of consciousness, often through its intermediary or multidimensional power, and that it is therefore a primary force in the evolution of human consciousness.

Art, then, remains one of our readiest symbols for intimate knowledge. As we will later explain, art can be seen as horizontal, whereas spiritual sciences appear as vertical. Such a distinction leads one to think that the spiritual sciences and theology might easily fall into the trap of losing intimate knowledge by attempting to engage in codification and analysis. *But both art and spiritual science must be regarded as intimate knowledge, as non-dual, co-equal, the same. The horizontal path and the vertical ascent are the same because the destination is always already there, in that there is neither art nor spiritual science but the eternal, timeless present.* Art then is already as scientific as these sciences, and these sciences are already as artistic as this art. Art is no more a doing than these sciences; these sciences are no more a not-doing than this art. We have only, essentially, the evolution of consciousness to pure and non-dual consciousness, and this union is no more real or unreal as art, or meditation, or drinking tea, for in this state none of these doings or non-doings any longer exists.

This book, then, speaks from the standpoint of intimate knowledge. This form of knowing is much like Maslow's[9] love knowledge, and it is equally "direct and inward knowledge, that of the Heart-Intellect, ...what the Greeks called *gnosis*."[10] It is assuredly not symbolic knowledge of the kind that can be ordered into Cartesian exactitudes. Art speaks directly as a form of intimate knowledge—analogically, negatively, and injunctively. The latter connects art with practice, teaching and discipline. Of such knowledge psychology and philosophy have little to say except as they take their cue from art, love, mysticism and religion themselves and steer clear of reductionism.

Expression lies between heart and head, or soul and spirit. In kundalini symbolism this is between the fourth and sixth chakras, or the heart and brow chakras, and is localized in the fifth or throat chakra. The intermediary and intermediating expressive consciousness is precisely akin to creative imagination. It is not the I speaking nor nature, but one voice which is *simultaneously* the voice of things and our own lost voice. *It is like a pitcher of water set on water itself.* The thing and the word are equiprimordial. The soul and spirit, and both in transcendence of mind toward Mind, of self toward Self, of being toward Being, are held in delicate equilibrium by the music of expression. Art gives us a grasp of the organic unity of self and universe in its microcosmic, concrete expression. "There is nothing in the macrocosm," says Schuon, [11] "that does not derive from the metacosm and cannot be found in the microcosm." All of this is found in the little pure microcosms of art, as pebbles relate to great cliffs and both to the birth of the planet earth.

More concretely, this book will develop in two different but related ways: (1) as a direct celebration of art; and (2) as hermeneutics, the science of interpretation which swings typically through an arc "from naive understanding through explanation to knowledgeable understanding."[12] But the two approaches cannot be neatly separated. Common to both will be a phenomenological attitude, but a phenomenology that centers on the imagination and on the hand of the artist at work.

The artist and the poet have privileged access to the creating stream of consciousness, to how the eye and hand, the mind and spirit, the medium and the image confound and comfort one another in the process of creating. While a critic can talk about a painting, only the painter can bring a participating phenomenological eye to painting itself and to its place in life and culture. Gregory Orr makes this point clear in discussing the art of poetics:

> Poets must write those essays about poetry that only poets can write: those in which blood is mixed with ink.[13]

Poetics demands:

> ...a form of intense, naive enthusiasm. By naive, I simply mean that a poetics must be an unexamined intellectual and emotional energy flowing outward; as such, it is opposed to logical analysis and critical thinking; it cannot be balanced. It's a crystallization in essay form of heart truths. But it's a crystallization: it has form and structure, involves vision and revision just as a poem does.[14]

This is a distinction similar to that which Bachelard[15] makes between reverie and the psychology of the imagination. The first is too unstructured, the latter too pre-structured, whereas *poetic* reverie takes on its own organic form, finds its appropriate words, and, equally important from the view of this book, expands the awareness of the dreamer through interpretations of idiosyncratic and mythic meanings floating over the process and its resultant form.

In art then, poetics and hermeneutics lie side by side, as do therapy and pedagogy insofar as a spiritual discipline is implicated in the practice of art, and our claim is that it is. To proceed:

> Hermeneutics is the science of interpretation, or the determination of the meaning of mental productions (e.g., what is the meaning of *Macbeth*? of last night's dream? of your life?) As such, it is a trans-empirical discipline, for no amount of analytical-empirical-scientific data, no matter how complete, can totally establish meaning (e.g., give me a scientific proof of the meaning of *War and Peace*). Rather, meaning is established, not by sensory data, but by unrestrained communicative inquiry and interpretation.[16]

We will follow as well Wilber's[17] insightful claim that there are relatively clear levels or deep structures of consciousness, one nested inside the other in hierarchical fashion like

Chinese boxes, while on any given level there are many different surface structures—what he likens to different rooms occurring on the same floor of a tall building. Hermeneutics gives us a method and a narrative for describing these different rooms. Further, art has a room on every floor, for we consider it an ultimate and absolute realm symbolic of the edifice of consciousness as a whole.

To the artist the simplest existential act can implicate deep structures of the highest order. Says Baudelaire:[18]

> In certain almost supernatural inner states, the depth of life is entirely revealed in the spectacle, however ordinary, that we have before our eyes, and which becomes the symbol of it.

In cases like this "the exterior spectacle helps intimate grandeur unfold."[19] Artist and mystic begin to lose any imaginary boundary between them.

The *telos* of this book, then, is the revelation of how art is directly engaged, in a privileged sense, in the evolution and celebration of human consciousness. This is all the more important and timely because current works on consciousness largely by-pass the artist, for they are in the grip of what might be termed a *sacrotropism*—a drift toward the super-conscious saint or ascetic mystic as ultimate exemplar. We believe this is because such works have been written by philosophers of saintly bent and saints of philosophic bent—Hegel or Heidegger on the one side; Eastern or Western mystics on the other. The voices of silence—the arts—have not pushed forth their politics nor their words sufficiently in this evolution now beginning to penetrate into the average consciousness.

This book is subdivided into four sections. Though the development of the whole is cumulative, the sections have a certain individual autonomy.

Section I, *Art as Concrete Discipline in Unknowing*, discusses how the addition of creative imagination to the integrated body-mind state characteristic of the practice of art, gives the centaur—a symbol we will use throughout this book for unity of body-mind—its wings. Art is presented as unfolding through a hidden order, as exemplifying dialogue, and as play transformed into structure. The method of the book is described as a special kind of phenomenology of the imagination capable of representing higher states of consciousness as found in art. The unique place of art within the spectrum of consciousness is also explored. Art is seen as operating on all levels of consciousness and also, through the increments of self-awareness it indirectly provides, as participating in the transformational or evolutionary task of moving from lower to higher levels. Art, however, does not fit well into hierarchical spiritual sciences but rather appears to be a horizontal extension of Spirit which comes and goes unpredictably. Metaphysically the artist is seen as a progressive organicist, one who implicates a unity which is not predetermined. Artists are also seen as followers of the esoteric tradition or the perennial philosophy, especially in the sense that they frequently directly invoke or describe *epiphanies* in their works. The artist is called a *verificationist mystic* in the way an intuition of the absolute is verified in matter. Such verificationist mystics synthesize the paths of *love* and *gnosis*, or of *heart* and *third eye* through expression, and they appear to do so without benefit of science or codified method.

Section II, *To the Things Themselves*, begins with an exploration of the concrete imagination, especially as presented in the work of Gaston Bachelard, whose phenomenology of the image methodologically unfolds as a synthesis of direct examples from poetry connected one to the other thematically and through a poetic reverie that becomes the connective tissue between the poetic fragments themselves. We concentrate here on the material imagination as opposed to the formal imagination, or on the silent world and mystery of things. Coleridge's theory of the creative imagination then describes how the imagination plays across the arbitrary boundaries of self-other, mind-matter and conscious-unconscious. This leads to the description of levels of vision, following Blake's twofold, threefold, and fourfold forms of poetic consciousness, or as a hierarchy moving from analogies to archetypes to images and to visions. It is, however, the appearance of the object poem or thing poem, especially as exemplified in the poetry and prose poems or *proemes* of Francis Ponge, that takes us to the *thick of matter* and to the silent voice of things, where ideas and humanistic symbols are set aside for the task of renewing consciousness through direct contact with the forgotten and disenfranchised things of the world. These things turn out, paradoxically, to be forgotten or undiscovered parts of ourselves and symbols for our unity with the cosmos. This

Section ends with exploration of still quieter voices, those from earthen vessels, within the planetary tradition of pottery. This art retains many ties with local traditions, such as Zen, and with atavistic memories and ancient myths, rituals and sacraments. It lends itself as well to communal experience and selfless practice, thus offering a unique discipline toward higher levels of consciousness.

Section III, *The Art of Qualitative Thinking*, lays out and illustrates an expressive-hermeneutic cycle, as a general discipline, which has as its explicit goal the enlargement of consciousness through an understanding of organismic awareness or qualitative experience as found in our own expressions or those of others. The general method superimposes an interpretive process upon a creative process. This leads to an understanding of the deep structure implicated through the expressive act; and it is this understanding of the self-formative aspects of art which leads to an enlargement of consciousness. The art of qualitative thinking is a unified cycle composed of four moments: (1) expressive text, (2) distancing, (3) interpreting, and (4) renewing. *Expressive Texts* are discussed under the following subdivisions: expressive-artistic modes, further subdivided into iconic (non-verbal) and literary versions; and expressive-descriptive modes, further classified into phenomenological and historical versions. Examples of these various modes are presented, and the examples discussed are chosen especially for what they suggest concerning the evolution of consciousness. *Distancing* has a range of meanings, which we first explore through a reverie on the word. It is then related to reduction and expansion and to the paraphrase. Examples of distancing from literature and case histories of expression are given and discussed methodologically. The roles of circumlocution and of digressions in the heart of expression are then taken up, along with dangers implicit in the process of distancing. *Interpreting* shows itself to be a dialectic between explanation and understanding. Rather than think of all texts as distorted, we emphasize the way expressive texts reveal what is hidden. In the Heideggerian sense, interpreting can be a thinking dialogue, and examples of this approach are given. The artist has a unique way of interpreting, and this is one that savors the way the work is done and how it is experienced. Case histories of artistic creation also offer special opportunities for interpretive approaches. Language, in general, and to the degree it departs from an in-depth thinking dialogue or neglects to take wings itself toward expression, is bound to fail in its artistic interpretive mission. This leads to the need for *renewal* and for closure to the cycle of qualitative thinking set in motion originally by experiencing and expressing. Song returns anew within the cycle, and the artist-interpreter is renewed in expression. The art of qualitative thinking, seen as a whole, takes on the image of an esoteric spiritual discipline.

Section IV, *Art as Meditation in Action*, begins with a consideration of how consciousness unfolds through expressive therapy and of how a special role falls upon the artist/therapist in a therapy that attempts to remain open to the entire spectrum of consciousness and to the problems of transformation from one level to another through expressive experience and related self-awareness. Direct examples of self-consciousness and self-transformation in and through artistic expression are presented and discussed, along with the problem of method and developmental levels. Then we present the unique opportunity arising from this book's perspective for constructing an education in and through art for a new age which takes the evolution of consciousness seriously. The artist as special teacher finds his or her own way to relate such an education to the perennial philosophy and to all the local colorations of artistic media and tradition. The creative process and spiritual evolution are seen as related but separate traditions. In terms of method, much hope is seen in the combining of art and the art of qualitative thinking, for the latter begins its cycle toward understanding and enlarged awareness only after experience and expression have occurred. Finally, the book ends in celebration of the renewal of life and consciousness forever found in creating and experiencing art.

References

1. Wilber, K. *The spectrum of consciousness.* Wheaton, Ill.: The Theosophical Publishing House, 1977; pp. 130-131.

2. Hegel, G. W. F. *Phenomenology of spirit.* (A. V. Miller, trans.) Oxford: Clarendon Press, 1977, p. 424.

3. Dewey, J. *Art as experience.* New York: Minton, Balch, 1934. Pepper, S. C. *Concept and quality.* LaSalle, Ill.: Open Court, 1966.

4. Wilbur, K. *Op. cit.,* reference 1 above, pp. 125-126.

5. Commins, S. and Linscott, R. N. (eds.) *Man and the universe, the philosophers of science.* New York: Washington Square Press, 1969, p. 453.

6. Wilber, K. *Op. cit.*, reference 1 above, pp. 56-58.

7. Schuon, F. *Esoterism as principle and as way.* (W. Stoddart, trans.) Pates Manor, Bedfont, Middlesex: Perennial Books, 1981, pp. 32-33.

8. *Ibid.*, p. 34.

9. Maslow, A. H. *The farther reaches of human nature.* New York: Viking Compass Book, 1971.

10. Schuon, F. *Op. cit.*, reference 7 above, p. 18.

11. *Ibid.*, pp. 17-18.

12. Ricoeur, P. *The philosophy of Paul Ricoeur.* Boston: Beacon Press, 1978; p. 154.

13. Orr, G. *The need for poetics: Some thoughts on Robert Bly.* In Jones, R. and Daniels, K. (eds.) *Of solitude and silence.* Boston: Beacon Press, 1981, p. 146.

14. *Ibid.*, p. 148.

15. Bachelard, G. *The poetics of reverie.* (D. Russell, trans.) Boston: Beacon Press, 1971.

16. Wilber, K. *Up from Eden.* Garden City: Anchor Press/Doubleday, 1981; p. 32.

17. Wilber, K. *The Atman project.* Wheaton, Ill.: Theosophical Publishing House, 1980.

18. Baudelaire, C. *Journeaux intimes*, p. 29.

19. Bachelard, G. *The poetics of space.* (M. Jolas, trans.) Boston: Beacon Press, 1969; p. 192.

1

Body-Mind, Earth and World

Shall we go abroad and start anew, O wind,
To build again a better life and song?
— Rabindranath Tagore[1]

Caught up in creative activity, the artist's soul is simultaneously agitated yet calm. In like fashion, the artist's spirit feels drawn upward as though a new vision or a new awareness were granted to the human condition. This new awareness, as a thorough-going organismic state, is experienced like an out-of-time, out-of-space experience. Once the course of creation has ended, the artist becomes self-conscious of this special consciousness that attends the creative imagination and constructive artistic action.

This is how the artist is drawn onward to more and more creative work, for the positive intrinsic rewards of this artistic state of grace far outbalance the burden of difficulties of the workaday mundane world. The desire returns again and again to "go abroad and start anew" with the wind, "to build again a better life and song." Tagore's lines interestingly suggest that the artist's acts are to be equated with the mysterious energy of nature herself and that the artist is in harmony with these forces.

The Winged Centaur

Here arises the image of the centaur: head and upper body, the mental, executive, and spiritual realms are one with the animal nature and earthiness of the lower half. The horse:

> Stroke the withers of this armoire and immediately it has a farway look.
> His skin quivers, irritably tolerating flies, his shoe hammers the ground.
> Ticklish skin, as I was saying...but his natural patience is so profound, that inside his body the parts of his skeleton behave like pebbles in a torrent![2]

But that part of the image cannot take over. The centaur is a symbol of body-mind integration.[3] The human is not a rider of the body, but is one with it. Even St. Francis who, more than anyone in the West, saw the natural and the human and the Divine as one, still referred to his body as "poor brother ass," forgetting that the love of everything in the universe *includes* the body.

But the image goes still further. The creative imagination leads to a timeless organismic awareness, a qualitative immediate present. This shows this integrated body-mind, this centaur, to be one with the universe itself. Here is the spirit-wind with which the poet Tagore goes abroad. The creative imagination gives wings to the centaur. The winged centaur: the artist-mystic, poet-saint, creative visionary who expands consciousness through love of beauty and creative action.

Here is a mythic force which can roam, prance, gallop at will over the valleys and hills of the world. But it can also leap into flight, over the Himalayas, over the oceans, over Parnassus itself, without CBS and mission control in Houston being any the wiser. Poets have repeated images of such flights:

> I live my life in growing orbits
> which move out over the things of the world.
> Perhaps I can never achieve the last,
> But that will be my attempt.
> I am circling around God, around
>   the ancient tower,
> And I have been circling for a
>   thousand years,
> And I still don't know if I am a
>   falcon, or a storm,
> Or a great song.[4]

The *growing orbits* of the poet, as a timeless *circling around God*, are like a great natural energy, so that the poet could equally be *a falcon, or a storm, or a great song*.

When the poet equates creation with nature, we are turned back to the silent world of things, to the timeless cycles and forces, and to that realm where the great chain of being is set spinning so that spirit and matter are one. Up from the seed-bed, the earth, the humid, the dark and the feminine, nature strews before us a cornucopia from which spills "the discontinuous world of symbols."[5] We find that just as surely as one path of enlightenment denies the senses, another enters through them as through a privileged gate. "Liberation by detachment from the world is not mine," says Tagore.[6] In short, it is in evolutionary growing orbits of consciousness that the winged centaur flies around God.

Experiential Foundations

A great wealth of material lies waiting to be integrated toward detailing this basic view. As authors, our experience forms a three part foundation for this task. We are practicing artists. We experience again and again that intimate knowledge of the mystery of vision, imagination and creation that will not yield to symbolic knowledge but yet provides a guiding intuition for all efforts to represent it. Also, we continue to engage in research into the artistic creation of others. In addition, we draw upon philosophical and testimonial literature as these relate to our topic and help with the interpretation of it. Related to the first point concerning intimate knowledge is the desire to show or share intimate knowledge through direct inclusion of art itself, either as poetry or literature or as reproductions of visual art. Such examples as given become the basis for poetic reveries which attempt to remain close to their imaginative source. The intimate knowledge of the artist also leads to poetry and to language of practice in which the creating consciousness reflects on its experience.

Our research[7] for a number of years has focused on the life-world of the artist at work. We have provided a studio environment in which the inquirers and the artist are equally at home. This is an atmosphere where the artist's creative imagination can authentically evolve and where the creative process leaves clues for interpretation. These lead to a sharing of the artist's stream of consciousness. These conditions have enhanced the tendency of the creating consciousness to become self-conscious of its expanding awareness through the unified organismic state common to artistic creation. Our presence as receptive witnesses and co-sharers of the artist's effort binds us to the creating consciousness even as it simultaneously influences it in the sense that modern physics knows and accepts the fact that observation influences that which is observed.

These studies have reinforced our conviction that art plays a primary role in the evolution of consciousness. To begin with, the creative imagination ignores those arbitrary boundaries which split up the world of experience in ordinary thought, logic and language. Even sensuously the artist quickly learns to relax *a priori* expectancies on what things *mean* in perception. The world becomes a visual field where colors and boundaries pay no attention to our habits of seeing discrete objects and verbalized colors attached to them. Instead we experience a world of nuances, interpenetrations and unnamed qualities where seer, seeing and the seen become one unified act of seeing. Under such an attitude, and relaxed from the anxieties and purposes of daily life, the artist approaches a more mystical vision or even experiences an epiphany—a state we will dwell upon at more length later—where everything seems to fall into unity and profundity.

The artist's medium also quickly becomes not just a means toward the representation of some foreign quality, but concrete participation in the earthiness and substance of the voice of things and of the Silence. It relates to and through the artist's body and mind, as these strive to become integrated in spontaneous and concrete imaginative activity. Body-mind and medium then quickly come to symbolize the unity of organism and cosmos, and the winged centaur flies its growing orbits.

The concrete and material imagination, working through art's hidden order, leads inevitably to organismic awareness. The artist experiences and *shows* the mystery and does not just speak *about* it. The artist's work is a form of intimate knowledge ineffably attached to the mystery of things and experience and not just symbolic of them.

Merleau-Ponty[8] thought that art occupied a privileged position *between* perception and reflection. As such, it gives both psychology and philosophy problems: psychology cannot account for it in terms of perception and philosophy cannot begin its reflective analysis of art until art comes mysteriously into existence. Further, art develops through the physical realm of medium and process in and through the body-mind and brute inanimate things, and through a history of interactions along an intentional path which takes on its own purpose and reality in action.

Still further, art represents one of the clearest cases of how self-awareness is enhanced through the conquest of the not-self. Art becomes a prime instrument in the evolution of consciusness, for it leads to the experience of the underlying unity of self and universe and of that non-dual consciousness which is the hallmark of the highest mystical experience. Artists again and again give evidence of an achieved organismic awareness which does not honor the usual boundaries drawn by the mind and by language:

> I see painting as an invitation to the dance of freedom and to the paradox of spontaneity. It appears as a dialogical encounter with the ever-emerging now. In painting there is a synthesis wherein medium, moment and artist are so unified that the "I" disappears, and painting paints. For me the creative act contains a mystery that lies irresistibly and indeterminately inside the continual vacillation of intuition and rationality, so that in painting I search for the I know not what, and for the that which is not yet.[9]

The winged centaur is caught up in a reverie which continually evokes cosmic consciousness. Tangibility and the highest imaginative flight here go together. The artist has a naive and transparent consciousness, believing that if all is well in the about-to-be-created microcosm, all is well in the universe as a whole. A consciousness that is intimate with wholeness is a consciousness that becomes self-conscious of itself as being on a spiritual path.

References

1. Ajaya, Swami (ed.) Quoted in *Living with the Himalayan Masters.* Honesdale, Pa.: Himalayan Institute, 1978; p. 240.

2. Ponge, F. *The voice of things.* (B. Archer, trans.) New York: McGraw-Hill, 1972; p. 133.

3. Wilber, K. *The Atman project.* Wheaton, Ill.: Theosophical Publishing House, 1980.

4. Rilke, M. R. Untitled, translated by Robert Bly, appearing in Summer 1982 catalogue, Omega Institute, Lebanon Springs, N. Y., p. 33.

5. Barthes, R. *Image, music, text.* (Stephen Heath, trans.) New York: Hill and Wang, 1977; p. 51.

6. Quoted in Swami Ajaya (ed.), reference cited in 1 above, p. 236.

7. See Beittel, K. R. *Mind and context in the art of drawing.* New York: Holt, Rinehart & Winston, 1972; and *Alternatives for art education research.* Dubuque, Iowa: William C. Brown, 1973.

   Novosel, J. The structural existentiality of arting: Inquiry into the nature of the creative process. (Doctoral dissertation, The Pennsylvania State University, 1976.) *Dissertation Abstracts International,* 1977, 37.

Novosel-Beittel, J. Inquiry into the qualitative world of creating: The S-E model. *Studies in Art Education,* 20 (1), 1978; pp. 26-36.

8. Crowther, P. Merleau-Ponty: Perception into art. *The British Journal of Aesthetics,* 22 (2), Spring 1982; 138-149. Pp. 146-147.

9. Novosel-Beittel, J. Artist's statement from catalogue of Exhibition, Sloan Gallery, Lock Haven, Pa., 1978.

2

Art's Hidden Order

Overview

The artist's awareness expands through contact with a hidden order. The more visionary an artist becomes, whether painting turnips, crucifixions or abstractions, the more likely it is that a direct intuition of spirit is involved, an involvement which leads to a transformation of consciousness.

These are weighted words, perhaps even paradoxical words. This chapter will underscore how the self of the artist is exceeded in what he or she intentionally creates. It also invokes as illustrative of the art process the analogy to *dialogue* — that process by which dialogue partners find new meaning arising on some subject-matter between them. This chapter also shows the need to complement the dialogue metaphor with that of organism — the analogy which points to how a bud contains the flower. The dialogue of the art process, then, progressively reveals the organism or the art work that was concealed within it from the start.

The discussion will then describe the artist's alienated plight in the modern world, along with the diminution of the meaning of art occurring in general taste which consigns art to its purely aesthetic dimension. Ambivalently, however, the public still would like to find in the artist a *secular savior* to bind up mankind's fractured and fractioned spirit. Following Bachelard, and foreshadowing Section II of this book, we will suggest that the *material imagination* as opposed to the purely *formal imagination*, opens a way for the hidden order and total meaning of art to come forth. Visionary artists of all times have refused the single vision which restricts art to the purely formal and aesthetic; instead they desperately cling to a *two-fold vision* or consciousness which sees beyond the imaginary boundaries between mind and matter, self and not-self, conscious and unconscious processes.

When we ascribe to a phenomenology of the spiritual realms, however, we will have to acknowledge that this is a figurative usage. It will lead us eventually to paradoxical thinking—that is, to mind struggling with spirit, which transcends reason—and to creation and/or *gnosis*—or spirit in the act of creation or in direct intuition.

We will then detail the way Gadamer likens art to a special kind of *game* for this argument will also underscore why we must use both the analogy of dialogue and that of organism for the art process. *Game* is presented as ascendent over the will of the players; how it is that the game which though not serious, seriously wills to be played out. Art is a special kind of game, for its play is a presentation for some one else, and this makes it into a work or transforms it into a structure. The nature of transformation is radical as opposed to mere change, for in the former something literally becomes something else, a new being grows out of the old. Art takes up that which is untransformed—*nature*, *reality*—and by transforming it into a structure, through its hidden order, reveals artistic truth.

Art Exceeds the Artist's Intention

Art can be likened to a crazy game of strategy in which the rules undergo change even while the game is in progress. Though the artist operates autonomously and intentionally, the art process and its fruits conceal in the heart of the work's revelations much more than the artist is aware of.

Ehrenzweig[1] has conceptualized the creative process along this line as a path with unexpected branchings which open up continuously into unforeseen possibilities. To cope with such an activity, the artist must develop special capabilities—for example, something like a cross-eyed *unconscious scanning* ability and engage in a kind of *diffused attention* which leads to *or-or* structures. The latter are disjunctives, dialectical opposites of a qualitative nature, or essentially mutually exclusive variations on a theme in progress which, nevertheless, cannot be rejected in any *a priori* way. *Up* may be *down, large* may be *small.* In one version of Yeat's *Byzantium* poems, for example, the draft contains meanings completely the opposite from those in the final poem.[2]

For Ehrenzweig, art continually exceeds the artist's conscius intentions, for conscious planning and unconscious scanning are linked together in the creating process. In much the same manner Dewey[3] sets forth an organic dialectic between *doing* and *undergoing* as the work progresses, while Kubie link together *cogitation* and *intelligence*:

> Cogitation and intelligence: "cogito" to shake things up, to roll the bones of one's ideas, memories and feelings, to make a great melting-pot of experience: plus the superimposed process of "intelligo": i.e., consciously, self-critically but retrospectively, an after-the-act process of choosing from among unanticipated combinations those patterns which have new significance.[4]

Such theorists prepare us for that which is unexpected within the art process. In fact, we might say that they encourage us to expect the unexpected. The expectation that the unexpected will surface gives the artist an explorer's openness to new experience and the courage to move within the unknown.

In Japanese, the characters for *metaphor* signify *to speak in darkness*. This metaphorical meaning for metaphor, illustrative of an artistic and poetic intelligence at work in Japanese aesthetics in general, parallels the clash of opposites[5] characterizing the creation of art: light comes forth from darkness; meaning comes forth from unintelligible things; the alchemy of the heart transmutes the base metal of experience into the gold of expression.

Jung[6] celebrated responsiveness to the secret hidden order in art by setting up two kinds of artists: the *psychological* and the *visionary*. The psychological type of artist poses no problem for the psychologist, for much of the meaning in his or her works stems directly from conscious life-experience and from the formal imagination. But the visionary artist, *par excellence*, speaks in darkness, by allowing himself or herself to be guided by the unexpressed desire of the times. Such an artist draws upon mythic fragments and archetypes—whatever can help one express what is ineffable.

> The primordial experience is the source of his creativeness; it cannot be fathomed, and therefore requires mythological imagery to give it form. In itself it offers no words or images, for it is a vision seen "as in a glass darkly." It is like a whirlwind that seizes everything within reach and, by carrying it aloft, assumes a visible shape.[7]

This lies toward the deep images Bachelard[8] finds within the material imagination as opened up through poetic reverie: intimations of childhood, the archetypes, the cosmic. Says Jung: "through our feelings we experiencce the known, but our intuitions point to things that are unknown and hidden — that by their very nature are secret."

The hidden order of art that finds expression through the visionary artist is thus one based upon the intuition of *transcendelia*, the data of consciousness which lie beyond reason, which find their source in the light of the ineffable and in the dark spaces of the mind. For the visionary intuitive artist who courts the unexpected and who dares to speak in darkness, the hidden order of art opens one up to a level of experience which transcends self and points toward the transformation of individual consciousness.

The Art Process as Dialogue

Buber[10] has likened the art process to the primary I-thou relationship which signifies dialogue. For him, the dialogue between man and matter is art; between man and man, love; and between man and the mystery, religion. But art, love, and true religion have in common the characteristics associated with dialogue. It might even be said that through dialogue, art, love and religion become one.

The art work and the maker can be likened to dialogue partners engaged about something hidden *in between them* which exceeds the boundaries of each. The dialogue brings into existence new understanding concerning that which lies between the partners.

For Heinrich Ott, "The model and basic structure of every hermeneutical event is the dialogue[11] By *hermeneutical event* Ott means to convey as much as even the whole of our surrounding reality. An existential encounter, a reciprocity, is engaged in all of our apprehensions of meaning.

In making art, the experience of expressing takes priority over the expressing of experience. The artist's beginning intention is not yet the real subject-matter. The latter truly unfolds only within the working dialogue. A dialogue, then, has defining characteristics much as in a game of strategy where one move is determinant of the next. This removes it from one-sided control.

Ott[12] has described some of the defining characteristics revealed through a phenomenology of dialogue. (1) Dialogue demands an explicit or implicit paraphrase that would be acceptable to one's dialogue partner. By successfully paraphrasing, we give evidence of our active understanding. (2) Contradictions can occur insofar as they express a search for a truth binding both together. (3) We understand our dialogue partner to the degree we have a better grasp of the subject matter with which both are concerned. (4) We hold off to the last and the most important words of our partner and take these as the measure of our common understanding. This implies a patience and an allowance for the passing of much that was earlier tentative. (5) Something new can suddenly appear at the end of a dialogue, something which nevertheless was foreshadowed from the start. A dialogue can be creative.

These pointers suggest that understanding concerns something *between* the partners. They imply acceptable seeing, in one's own terms, of each side by the other. Conflict and contradiction can occur on the way to understanding. End moves are to be granted priority over what is tentative and searching. A hidden newness can suddenly emerge.

The Art Process as Dialogue and Organism Simultaneously

If we personify the art process and address it as a *thou*, these pointers become applicable metaphorically. But if we look within them, we find implicit an analogy to *organism* as well. That which is new, appearing at the end, but secretly there from the start suggests a force and a will-to-form somewhat independent of the dialogue partners.

Ott feels that the organism analogy, though seductive, is deficient as compared with dialogue, for the latter incorporates new encounters and impulses coming from outside. In dislogue "...there is no entelechy in the strict sense; the horizon of the future remains open."[13]

We are certainly in accord with the view of the art process as a dialogue with an open horizon. But perhaps *both* metaphors are essential for any account of the art process. By this interpretation, the Pygmalion myth has a "live person" present for the sculptor before and after the creative process, and these "persons" are curiously both autonomous and contingent.

Autonomy engages us in the dialogue analogy; contingency conjures up that of organism. There is a sense in which Pygmalion[1] is the dialogue partner of the artist, but there is also a sense in which that dialogue has Pygmalion[2] as its subject matter. There is a symbolic way in which Pygmalion[2] grows out of Pygmalion[1] without being "caused" by it.

Since metaphors elude direct paraphrase, certainly a doubling up of metaphors will lead us further still into paradox. Let us, therefore, take up another and different approach to the same problem, as set forth in the hermeneutic philosophy of Hans-Georg Gadamer.[14] To do this, we will first turn to the context into which Gadamer places art and the artist.

The Artist in the Modern World

The artist in the modern world, Gadamer says, is projected as free but is also pictured as ambiguous. For the social culture on the one hand expects "only art," meaning here an art that has fallen away from the wholeness it symbolized when there were cohesive religious traditions; but on the other hand the artist is expected to come out of his alienation to become a "secular savior" for an ailing world.[15]

We no longer experience any unity of taste, but rather "a mobile feeling of quality."[16] We have gone through a process of abstraction to arrive at modern *aesthetic experience*, and we have done this by removing from art its original life content and any religious or secular functions which gave it meaning. Gadamer calls this shrinkage of significane through the unconscious process of abstraction *aesthetic differentiation*. All that is left is the aesthetic quality as such, forgetful that the work is also the carrier of extra-aesthetic elements such as its function and purpose and the significance of its content. Thus aesthetic differentiation separates from a work "all elements of content which induce us to take up an attitude towards it, moral or religious, and presents it solely by itself in its aesthetic being."[17]

Gadamer points out that the separatist notion of art removes from the cultural response to it a notion of "artistic truth," the truth that a non-differentiated attitude in times when taste aspired toward cultural universality took for granted. This is seen clearly in the expectancy that a "pure artist" can no longer engage in public commissions, forgetting that this was the norm in the past.[18] Museum, concert-hall, theatre, and the *arts establishment* in general support this decline in the broader public relevancy of art by rendering it into a *quality control* commodity.

Nevertheless, public attraction to art, even under disintegrated taste and under the differentiated partial truth of the exclusive and narrowed aesthetic consciousness, reflects a dim recollection that art serves a larger spiritual and cultural function. Art must be *for* something, we instinctively feel; and it *is*, even under its contemporary guise, but we have short-circuited the larger burden of its artistic truth. When I make a simple cup of native clay, decorate it symbolically and commemoratively with content from my direct experience and life-world, and think of it in terms of the everyday function *and sacrament* of drinking, of "cupping," and all that it connotes at table, hand, mouth, eye, and as passed from person to person, I am engaging in more than "aesthetic differentiation" and the "pure art of pottery." When I take this same cup to museum or gallery, as Dewey[19] also clearly argued, I not only view it differently, I excise it from much of its "truth" and relevance to a "live creature." It becomes merely an aesthetic object.

We are not proposing an argument of content versus form, for that would merely separate the aesthetes from the Philistines. Our concern is no less than *the total thing meant* — image, form, making, and content all rolled together. "The underlying problem is the concept of the art image as aesthetic rather than ontological in the encompassing sense.[20]

Viktor Lowenfeld,[21] a great art educator of the first half of this century, knew that an education or a therapy in and through art could not restrict itself to anything less than a concern for the whole child and whole person. Thus he could not restrict art to only its narrower purely aesthetic dimension.

Such is our function here; to take art away from the distortions of galleries, museums, and, currently, arts establishments and arts managements' political restrictions on its broadest cultural meaning. *Let artistic truth again speak through art's hidden order. And, for our secular time, let art represent not the conquest of mere aesthetic qualities but of self, consciousness and spirit itself, for self transcendence and transformation are among the greatest needs of our time. Art can be, and has been, an illumined path toward these.*

This issue will return in still a different way when we take up Bachelard's[22] distinction between the *formal imagination* and the *material imagination*. The former is more aesthetic, more mental: novelty, picturesqueness, variety, unexpectedness, the free play of forms. The latter, the material imagination, crosses over into the mute depth structures: the elements of permanency present in things, those forms sunk deeply in a substance, forms given in matter and inseparable from it. To Bachelard a phenomenology of the material imagination is not one of the mind but of the soul. In terms of our present discussion, artistic truth, for wholeness of being, demands both the formal and, especially, the material imagination. The latter implicates the deep archetypes of consciousness, especially the anima, and invokes universal childhood and the cosmic.[23].

The arts, much like classical psychology, underwent a decline of scope which first removed the soul and then the head from the body. This decline directly parallels an epistemological and metaphysical shrinkage from a spiritual and hermeneutic to an exclusively scientific perspective. Visionary artists have refused this:

> ...in new creation ... the word is made flesh. We see with
> our own eyes and to see with our own eyes is second
> sight. To see with our own eyes is second sight[24].
> Twofold always may God us keep
> From single vision and Newton's sleep.[25]

The contemporary American poet Robert Bly brings us "news of the universe" in the form of what he calls "poems of twofold consciousness."[26] He presents poems which struggle against the reduction of artistic truth, of the human spirit, to single vision. With the rise of technology we have been so often torn apart that we are forgetful of what interior unity could be:

> High School rips body and mind apart, science rips the
> perceiver and the thing apart, the Industrial Revolu-
> tion rips man and woman apart, rips father and son
> apart, racism rips soul and mind apart, imperialism
> rips the governors and the governed apart, our firm
> houses separate weather from person.[27]

We are not making a case for the "fine arts" in their present cultural condition, but for the promise the broader meaning of art possesses for the transformation of the individual consciousness. This is a call for whole art for whole persons.

To recapitulate, Gadamer's effort to retrieve the question of artistic truth through his principle of the nondifferentiation of aesthetic consciousness, reinstates the experience of art as central to our fullest grasp of body-mind-spirit and to our ontological concern for the meaning of being itself, of consciousness itself. Non-differentiation moves us partially away from the kind of phenomenology proposed by Merleau-Ponty[28] and Dufrenne.[29] Sensitive and insightful though these thinkers be, they grant too much credence to so-called "facts of perception" and to "aesthetic differentiation"—a kind of infiltration from a classical psychology still inclined to separate subject from object. *The magnetic pull of this book is the certain intuition that art is a conquest of awareness leading to a transformation of consciousness.* Perhaps, to be fair to the above writers, it would be more appropriate to say that their usage of phenomenology is "mental-phenomenological inquiry."[30] Useful though this be, their inquiry often stops short of the higher or spiritual realms, for mental-phenomenological thought "is mind (intelligibilia) reflecting on and grounding itself in the world of intelligibilia itself."[31]* We are here concerned with what Wilber calls "transcendelia," represented by "mandalic or paradoxical thinking; ...mind (intelligibilia) attempting to reason about spirit or transcendelia. And gnosis, the eye of contemplation, the trans-symbolic grasp of the trans-symbolic world, spirit's direct knowledge of spirit, the immediate intuition of transcendelia."[32] These are necessary and useful distinctions to guide us in this difficult task, in which we must either exemplify the "voices of silence" of art, in their transcendental aspects, by *words of a certain kind* attempting "to reason about the spirit" or turn directly to the speaking power of these silent voices themselves, through exemplars of poetry or vision. Our partial guide will be phenomenologists of the imagination such as Bachelard and Coleridge, who often lay

---

*In discussing the problem of proofs, Wilber makes an important distinction between kinds of proof representative of epistemological relationships pertaining to various levels of consciousness, thus:[33]

Spirit $\frac{1}{2}$ —————————————————— transcendelia

mind 3 —————————————————— intelligibilia

body $\frac{4}{5}$ —————————————————— sensibilia

out parts of poems themselves as points of access to direct intuition, between which fall their attempts to "reason about the spirit." We will also argue that there is a kind of phenomenology of the imagination *at work within the art process* which allows the artist to speak authentically about the kind of two-fold consciousness operating in creation.

An Interlude Concerning the Phenomenology of Higher States of Consciousness

There is a sense in which Bachelard's term *phenomenology of the imagination* exceeds the bounds of what we usually mean by phenomenology. Bachelard was aware of this extension of meaning, for he pointed out that his was a *phenomenology of the soul*, not of the mind.

To our knowledge, Wilber[34] has laid out the clearest map to the various epistemological relationships that we encounter once we pick up the problem of proof as it plays across the major modes of knowledge: sensory, symbolic, and spiritual. In a prior footnote, we have presented his heirarchical structure, in which *transcendelia* is shorthand for the data for the spiritual level of consciousness, *intelligibilia* for the mental level, and *sensibilia* for the bodily or physical level.

Each of these three modes of knowing has access to experiential data proper to its domain. There are sensible data, intelligible data, and transcendental data. To demand of one domain data inappropriate to it, or to try to reduce the data of one domain to the data of another, is to make a category error.

Each mode, says Wilber, shares with the other modes essentially the same abstract principles of data accumulation and verification. There are three basic strands to valid data accumulation:

> 1. *Instrumental injunction* — which is always of the form, "If you want to know this, *do* this."
> 2. *Intuitive apprehension* — a cognitive grasp, prehension, or immediate experience of the object domain (or aspect of the object domain) addressed by the injunction; i.e., the immediate data-apprehension.
> 3. *Communal confirmation* — a checking of results (apprehension of data) with others who have adequately completed the injunctive and apprehensive strands.[35]

Wilber states that we can use the term *science* in its broadest meaning to refer to "any discipline that conscientiously follows the three strands of data accumulation and verification, whether in the realm of sensibilia, intelligibilia, or transcendelia."[36] The following four sciences then emerge:

(1) Empiric-analytic or monological sciences, based on sensibilia.

(2) Mental-phenomenological, rational, hermeneutical, semiotic or dialogical sciences, based on intelligibilia.

Trans-logical, transcendental, transpersonal, or contemplative sciences, based on transcendelia. There are two divisions here.

(3) Mandalic sciences, where the mind attempts to deal, however inadequately, with the data of transcendelia. The knowledgeable use of this mode admits that the mind's efforts are here inadequate and that they lead to paradoxical thinking.

(4) Noumenological or gnostic sciences, where there is *direct* and intuitive apprehension of spirit and noumenon.[37]

Of these four sciences, levels 2, 3, and 4 come under what Dilthey[38] called *Geisteswissenschaften* (the mental and spiritual sciences). Dilthey pointed out that the mind and spirit, through their objectifications (their expressions), do form and inform, mold and alter, the objective world of sensibilia. In other words:

> Geist (mind and spirit) everywhere objectifies itself, and part of geist-science is not only dealing with the higher realms in and as themselves, but also in grasping and understanding the meaning and intent of their particular objectifications in their junior realms, the intermediate realms of culture and history, and the lower realms of nature and physical material.[39]

Dilthey felt the geist-sciences had as their foundation the relation of *lived-experience, expression,* and *understanding.*[40] *Spirit, then, can be grasped through understanding its external expressions.* We have here the mirror image of the expressive act, as a movement from inside to outside, which understanding reverses as a movement from the outside to the inside. This understanding constitutes "a vision-insight given only by the mental and/or contemplative eye."

> The point is that the higher realms everywhere leave their footprints in the lower. The higher realms form and inform, create and mold, produce and alter, all manner of forms in the lower realms. But these productions cannot be grasped by the lower realms nor reduced to them. And it is that double understanding—the

> higher as higher and the higher as objectified, express-
> ed, and embodied in the lower – that will announce the
> new and truly higher sciences.[41]

In this context, we remain with a carefully conceived *phenomenology of the imagination and of the soul,* following Bachelard's lead, but with the cautions and qualifications arising from the insights of Dilthey and Wilber. For ours is a phenomenology that moves farther and farther from standard phenomenological methodology. Because in art and poetry we experience, in creation and response, expression and understanding, the *objectification* of mind *and* spirit, there is a phenomenological contact, but it is always one in touch with spirit as well as mind. Thus it is not reducible to mind alone. We are therefore forced "upward" on the hierarchy of consciousness to an understanding of objectified traces of transcendelia. *Our language, then, tends to be paradoxical or poetic, or both.* To go any further we would have to become the equivalent of Zen masters, who in their writings for their disciples can only leave behind a map for the territory, or a menu for the meal. The disciple would be deluded who tried to eat the menu. *Art is a similar esoteric spiritual discipline*, but there is little in the way of concensus about its practice.

Art as Play Transformed into Structure

Following the above necessary enlargement and qualification of our view and method, let us pick up an insight developed by Gadamer which states why the metaphors of *dialogue* and *organism* are both essential for an ontological grasp of the meaning of the art process as it relates to the evolution of consciousness.

Gadamer builds his understanding of art through an analogy to *game* or *play*, but by the latter he does not mean what so-called "play theories of art" mean. Let us follow his argument.

Though a game is not "serious" but "only a game," it becomes deadly serious in the playing of it. The game is spoiled if the player fails to take it seriously. "A game is only a game as it comes to pass, yet while it is being playing it is master." Possessed of its own momentum and dynamics, transcending the players, the game "wills to be played out."[42]

But an important distinction creeps into art which is not there for a game. A game is not intended to be a show, to be a representation for another. This is true even in sports, where the game can lose its true character as play by becoming a show. In football, for example, the vicarious flavor of contemporary life becomes evident, as 90,000 or more spectators live through a small number of players that commitment toward play they themselves cannot directly realize. In contrast, "artistic presentation, by its nature, exists for someone, even if there is no one who listens or watches only."[43]

Gadamer calls this development "in which play finds its true perfection in being art, 'the transformation into structure.'" At this point play becomes idealized, expressed, objectified. It becomes detached from the players and takes on "the pure appearance of what they are playing." It becomes permanent, repeatable. "It has the character of a work, of an ergon and not only of energeia."[46]

This transformation is much more than change, for the latter retains sameness of character even where there is great change. "But transformation means that something is suddenly and as a whole something else, that this other transformed thing that it has become is its true being, in comparison with which its earlier being is nothing." It also implies:

> ...that what now exists, what represents itself in the play of art, is what is lasting and true...the concept of transformation characterizes the independent and superior mode of being of...structures. From this viewpoint "reality" is defined as what is untransformed, and art as the raising up of this reality into its truth.

To go back to our earlier argument, Pygmalion[1] becomes, rather *transforms into,* Pygmalion[2]. The dialogue of making becomes its truth through transformation into organism, the structure of the work; and, for the latter, "its actual being cannot be detached from its representation" for in its "representation the unity and identity of a structure emerge."[46] This work, however, is purely existential or temporal in a historical sense, yet paradoxically "eternal," for

> ...it is its own original essence always to be something different (even when celebrated in exactly the same way). An entity that exists only by always being something different is temporal in a more radical sense than everything that belongs to history. It has its being only in becoming and in return.[47]

Art, so seen, becomes an esoteric spiritual discipline, but one resisting codification. In the experience of art "...what matters is to see the appearance as the reality of presence in its essential origin," for then "...man, as the message-bearer of the message of the two-fold's unconcealment, would also be he who walks the boundary of the boundless."[48]

So said, expression and appearance belong together. In an everyday example, I am on the path through a small woods on the way from one building to another on a university campus. I am suddenly stopped by the way a pine gestures and throws its point heavenward, illuminated singly by a ray of sunlight, in a small clearing, beneath giant oaks which vault together five trees higher than that pine, even though the latter seems already to be piercing the sky. Thus a rhythm of upward thrusts is set up in my experience. I quickly make a sketch on the back of the official envelope I am carrying to remind me of what I saw. The sketch is made while looking up. It is as though appearing, expressing and the very ground for these come forward at once. I pick up my path and errand anew, but that simple experience which my sketch renews is what I recall of that day. In such simple ways is consciousness expanded by art as well. To recapitulate, as structure appears transformatively within the play of art, the consciousness of artist or contemplator is likewise opened up for transformation. It is common talk among artists to say that the block carves the sculptor just as the sculptor carves the block. This saying is not merely figurative. *Just as, on the vital level, giving birth transforms a woman into a mother, so giving birth to the work of art radically transforms the artist's consciousness.* To account for this process, we need to invoke both the dislogue-like play within the making of art, with its "serious" choices and to-and-fro movement, *and* its transformation into structure, where a new being comes forth from the hidden order of art.

The Zen potter meditates *before* working; but he also meditates *while* working. *This active meditation allows the hidden order to emerge,* and as that transforms into structure, the unmistakable print of spirit is left on the work, the artist, and the contemplator. Simply put, art is an esoteric discipline in unknowing, a gnosis, a ground for the direct intuitive apprehension of spirit. This is a transformative vision.

References

1. Ehrenzweig, A. Conscious planning and unconscious scanning. *In Education of vision*. Kepes, G. (ed.) N.Y.: George Braziller, 1965.

2. Bradford, C. Yeats' Byzantium poems: A study of their development. *PMLA*, 75 (March 1960); 110-125.

3. Dewey, J. *Art as experience.* N.Y.: Minton, Balch, 1934.

4. Kubie, L. S. *Neurotic distortion of the creative process.* Lawrence: University of Kansas Press, 1959; pp. 50-51.

5. Novosel-Beittel, J. Inquiry into the qualitative world of creating: The S-E model. *Studies in Art Education*, 1, 1978; 26-36.

6. Jung, C. G. *Modern man in search of a soul.* N.Y.: Harcourt, Brace & World, 1933.

7. *Ibid.*, p. 164.

8. Bachelard, G. *The poetics of space.* (M. Jolas, trans.) Boston: Beacon Press, 1969.

9. Jung, C. G. *Op. cit.*, reference 6 above; p. 162.

10. Buber, M. *I and thou.* (W. Kaufmann, trans.) N.Y.: Charles Scribner's Sons, 1970.

11. Ott, H. Hermeneutics and personhood. In Hopper, S. R., and Miller, D. L. (eds.) *Interpretation: The poetry of meaning.* N.Y.: Harcourt, Brace & World, 1967; p. 15.

12. *Ibid.*, p. 23-32.

13. *Ibid.*, p. 19.

14. Gadamer, H-G. *Truth and method.* N.Y.: Seabury Press, 1975.

15. *Ibid.*, p. 79.

16. *Ibid.*, p. 78.

17. *Ibid.*, pp. 76-77.

18. *Ibid.*, pp. 78-79.

19. Dewey, J. *Op. cit.*, reference 3 above.

20. Palmer, R. E. *Hermeneutics.* Evanston: Northwestern University Press, 1969; p. 170.

21. Lowenfeld, V. *The nature of creative activity.* N.Y.: Harcourt, Brace, Jovanovich, 1939.
Lowenfeld, V. *Creative and mental growth.* N.Y.: Macmillan, 1947.

22. Bachelard, G. *Op. cit.*, reference 8 above.

23. Bachelard, G. *The poetics of reverie.* (D. Russell, trans.) Boston: Beacon Press, 1971.

24. Brown, N. O. Apocalypse: The place of mystery in the life of the mind. In Hopper, S. R., and Miller, D. L. (eds.) *Interpretation: The poetry of meaning.* N.Y.: Harcourt, Brace & World, 1967; p. 12.

25. Blake, W. *Letters.* (G. Keynes, ed.) N.Y.: Macmillan, 1956; p. 79.

26. Bly, R. *News of the universe.* San Francisco: Sierra Club Books, 1980.

27. *Ibid.,* p. 5.

28. Merleau-Ponty, M. *The primacy of perception.* Evanston: Northwestern University Press, 1964.

29. Dufrenne, M. *The phenomenology of aesthetic experience.* Evanston: Northwestern University Press, 1973.

30. Wilber, K. The problem of proof. *ReVision, 5.* (1), Spring 1982, pp. 80-100; p. 84.

31. *Ibid.,* pp. 93-94.

32. *Ibid.,* pp. 93-94.

33. *Ibid.,* p. 93.

34. *Ibid.,* pp. 80-100.

35. *Ibid.,* pp. 82-83.

36. *Ibid.,* p. 96.

37. *Ibid.,* p. 96.

38. Palmer, R. E. *Op. cit.,* reference 20 above, pp. 103-106.

39. Wilber, K. *Op. cit.,* reference 30 above, p. 99.

40. Palmer, R. E. *Op. cit.,* reference 20 above, pp. 106-115.

41. Wilber, K. *Op. cit.,* reference 30 above, p. 100.

42. Palmer, R. E. *Op. cit.,* reference 20 above, p. 172.

43. Gadamer, H. G. *Op. cit.,* reference 14 above, p. 99.

44. *Ibid.,* p. 99.

45. *Ibid.,* pp. 100-102.

46. *Ibid.,* p. 109.

47. *Ibid.,* p. 110.

48. Heidegger, M. *On the way to language.* (P. D. Hertz, trans.) N.Y.: Harper & Row, 1971; pp. 40-41.

3

Art Within the Great Chain of Being

Spirit is Artist. Hegel[1]

To attain to Knowledge wish alone is not sufficient, there must also be Method: That is why, under the emblems of the bell and the *Dorje*, or sacred sceptre, which every lama wields, these two, Method and Knowledge, are represented as an eternally inseparable pair, and are said to be "married." So we, dwellers under the veil of Form, make use of ritual or art, a part of Method: it is a most useful instrument for Form to use, in the attempt to pierce a loophole and look out towards Non-form.

Pallis[2]

Every artist who works with feeling knows how suddenly the right form comes. Bocklin said that a true work of art must be a grand improvisation; that is, meditation and composition should be steps to a goal which the artist will glimpse unawares.

Kandinsky[3]

...this is the Light of all lights, the light of pure Consciousness...lighting up every object in the world, from sun and stars, from unconscious mind and conscious reason, to...the Omega, and even the apparent darkness of the avayakta [unknown].

The Upanishads

Art as Operating at All Levels of Consciousness

Most of us have accepted the idea that consciousness evolves in both meanings: that of humankind as a whole and that of the whole life of the individual. Both as a species and as individuals, we also usually grant that this process is incomplete, partial, opening up always anew toward that next higher step.

But there is also an intuition that art does not "evolve" in this same sense. Picasso bristled under queries concerning the evolution of his art—even though critics and historians, after the fact, classify periods and progressions within his oeuvre. Picasso said: "To me there is no past or future in art. If a work of art cannot live always in the present it must not be considered at all."[4]

Yet, the coincidence between art and spirit and between consciousness and spirit is such that the common term, *spirit*, directly implicates art within the evolution of consciousness. But how? Certainly artists and writers on art have been vocal concerning this relationship. Consider, for example, Kandinsky's *Concerning the Spiritual in Art*,[5] or Faure's fifth volume to his history of art entitled *The Spirit of the Forms*,[6] or Focillon's *The Life of Forms in Art*.[7]

It often happens, however, that writers on consciousness make little or no reference to art. The four published volumes of Wilber,[8] for example, have provided us with the best and broadest available synthesis of the varying schools and traditions touching on consciousness and its development. Here we have a solid, even structural base, unifying diverse esoteric strands into a single tradition of planetary scope, a modern grasp comparable to the system built by Hegel[9] earlier, and to the great religious systems of the ancient East. But in this modern system there is no mention of art and poetry and, only by indirection, is there mention of creative imagination. In like fashion, saints and sages of philosophic bent have produced and continue to produce spiritual maps of the territory of consciousness, but seem, quite often, suspicious of the artist.

This absence of reference and ambivalence must signify some problem of inclusion.

> ...in the Alhambra I heard that the first Sultan to occupy it said in wonder, "If this is earth, what must heaven be?" Is this life the true state of affairs? – Then man creates in his vision of the eternal an image of his own creativity. And we are back to a threadbare debate, did God make man in his likeness, or vice versa? Believers and doubters, perhaps this man is surer when authority is external and that man when it is internal.[10]

The argument is indeed convoluted and paradoxical. The "great chain of being," appearing again and again in esoteric tradition and in the perennial philosophy,[11] connects, within a circle, matter-body-mind-soul-spirit, and projects consciousness as moving around it in one direction in development – from subpersonal to personal to transpersonal (or pre-self, to self, to Self) – and in the opposite direction in a devolution or involution, from the All down to the level of simple matter. Wilber presents a clear model of the great chain of being and of its coordination with levels of consciousness applicable to both the human species and to the individual.[12]

But forming, the instinct to form, to express and to create is then implicit in that "Light of all lights, the light of pure Consciousness" mentioned in the quotation from The Upanishads at the head of this chapter. This instinct, then, appears within all colors of the spectrum of consciousness as that blinding white light, the source, is refracted into its parts. The turn of the Wheel of Being brings extremes together, as part of the one great Light, or the ground unconscious, or the Self.

> There is a constant interchange between the material of the world, which we immediately transform into spirit the moment it touches us, and the spirit that we immediately represent as matter the moment we are touched by it.[13].
> ...as the "spiritual technique" is essentially the art of concentration, the traditional ideology favors art, which in origin was the imitation of the divine act or the analogy used by revelation for exegesis, "as direct aid to spontaneity"; "the spiritual efficacy of aesthetic supports is in the very nature of things," for "...the efficacy of art is to be found in the unifying power of aesthetic experience."[14]

These quotations reciprocally link spirit and matter, and the Light of all lights with the light of artistic intuition as effected through revelation. It is for this reason we can say that consciousness evolves though art does not, but add that art, paradoxically, "as direct aid to spontaneity," nevertheless is an undeniable guide to the evolution of consciousness. The paths to illumination appear to be four-fold: ascetic, ritualistic, magical, and spontaneous.[15] Art undoubtedly leans towards the spontaneous path and contributes this spontaneity as spiritual aid to the contemplative eye. Blake, for example:

> ...rejected asceticism. It smacked of the Mosaic stones. Ritual was mechanical...But Blake had spontaneous illuminations; he refers to himself as prophet, as seer, who has been granted the power to see into eternity without any particular discipline on his part.[16]

We will later, however, grant that art may find its spontaneous illuminations through means closer to asceticism, ritual, and magic as well.

Art as a Horizontal Extension of Spirit

While similarity attracts, it is difference, as Ponge[17] well knew, the difficult naming of "the differential quality," which constitutes real purpose and progress, whether in poetry or thought. Thus it has been instructive to find resistances at the same time we are affirming a general "yes" in our reading of Wilber's great synthesis. Sometimes the clue comes from his writing itself. In an article on *The Problem of Proof*, Wilber[18] discusses the question of what to do with the *para-sciences* within his structure. Such sciences differ from the transcendental sciences (systematic methodologies like Zen or yoga) because in psychic events "the mind and senses are not *vertically transcended*, they are simply *horizontally extended*, by mechanism(s) as yet unclear."[19] Such events, he feels, work with "para-sensibilia" and "para-intelligibilia" (outside-sensibilia sensibilia and outside-intelligibilia intelligibilia) but not with trans-mental transcendelia. He does not say why he excludes the combination para-transcendelia (outside-transcendelia transcendelia), although logically we might conclude that nothing can be outside the direct intuition of the All. But we are left wondering why we cannot envision horizontal extension of spirit as well as of matter and mind. The gist of his exclusion seems to relate to the non-orderly unfolding or sequencing of such phenomena, such that they cannot be systematized even into the maps and menus of yoga and Zen. In other words, such events reside on the plane of the spontaneous, the exceptional. Also, he says, since he is discussing sciences and problems of proof, one cannot make repeated demonstrations of such phenomena because "psychic events, like creativity, seem to come and go."[20]

But shall we exclude from knowledge what seems to come and go, like creativity? Perhaps the eye of flesh, the eye of mind and the eye of contemplation are all simultaneously involved in the experience of art, so that the great wheel of Being is, as it were, set spinning. Perhaps there is an instrumental injunction, an intuitive apprehension and a communal confirmation appropriate to art knowledge or love knowledge. These are the three strands of proof Wilber sets forth as common to all sciences.

Like the scriptures, art is an emanation from the One. It is against their nature, and ours, for us to work at codifying them or forcing them within hierarchies. Yet scriptures often give birth to hierarchical disciplines. Intellectually I understand the beauty of hierarchical structures. As an artist, something in me strongly resists them.

In art, as a paradoxical discipline of unknowing issuing from a hidden order, we can refer to revelation as "method" where there can be no talk of method. *Knowledge* and *method are indeed the wedded spirits entwined on the spiritual sceptre mentioned earlier, but that sceptre merely symbolizes what takes form beyond method* and *knowledge.* Art knows this and has always known this from ancient times even perhaps better than religion. Or rather, esoteric religion and whole art have been as one in this realization. *The Tao which can be spoken is not the Tao.* Thus Cezanne, forgetful, leaves his painting in the field; the ailing Monet drags his body to his huge canvases; Beethoven collects timeless silence into sound in his C Sharp Minor String Quartet.

But since this is a phenomenon of horizontal extension of the All, this happens in humbler ways as well. In the Drawing Lab we found that the creative is a spontaneous emergence wherever one intends to act as pure artist. This emergence over time foreshadows a superordinate myth of artistic development which is a path parallel to that of the development of consciousness.

Though spontaneity and revelation are the primary evidences of that horizontal extension from "the Light of all lights, the light of pure consciousness," we feel that ritual and tradition can add dignity and community to the artistic enterprise. Freedom, however, remains essential to art. "The artist," says Kandinsky, "is not only justified in using, but is under a moral obligation to use, only those forms which fulfill his *own need.* Absolute freedom from anatomy or anything else of the kind must be given to the artist in his choice of means. Such spiritual freedom is as necessary in art as it is in life. This absolute liberty must be based on internal necessity, which might be called honesty."[21]

In this sense, we cannot be *beyond* human dignity and freedom. That is why I teach pottery as an esoteric planetary discipline, as a dialectic between Western freedom and Eastern dignity. In this way, the making of a simple pot can become an invitation for a "spirit vessel" to freely come into being. Method here, as spiritual discipline and practice, becomes a kind of gnosticism, a horizontal extension, a clearing where creative form may appear.

The *art of qualitative* thinking, as later developed, will present a hermeneutic of the expressive act and simultaneously a hermeneutic of the creating self. In this way knowledge and method take on a depth connotation in their contact with expressive form, and we make a tentative map for a discipline based on revelation and spontaneity which nevertheless feeds directly into the evolution of individual consciousness according to hierarchical levels. All art experience adumbrates this potential so that, to repeat an important point, while art may not evolve, the artist's consciousness may truly be said to do so insofar as the "internal necessity" of which Kandinsky spoke is maintained.

Art as Revelation

Schuon offers an insight which suggests why the sage, the saint or the evolved consciousness may give little attention to art. Scriptures, anagogy (mysterious interpretation of scriptures), and art, says he, all come from *revelation*. Of these, "art constitutes...the extreme limit or material shell of the tradition and thus, by virtue of the law that extremes meet, rejoins what is most inward in it, so that art is itself inseparable from inspiration."[22] Scriptural revelation, then, according to him, has anagogy on its one side—as "its inspired and indispensable commentary"—and this is the inward path essential for contemplative men, whereas art constitutes its other side and is external and indispensable for people in general, even for the elite since in the final analysis they are dependent "on the whole collectivity." "For the sage," he continues, "there is no common measure between the commentary on Scripture and art; he may even do without the latter provided he replaces it by an emptiness or by virgin nature and not by a falsified art."[23]

To our interpretation, this is like saying that the sage, secure in his discipline and hierarchic structure, oriented toward the formlessness surrounding "the Light of all lights," sees no need to turn toward the emanations of that Light in the varying colors of the spectrum of consciousness as these are played upon through creative expression in art. All is perhaps art to that transcendental eye, but then we can see no need to turn away from art just because it refuses mapmaking. We will pick up this issue later, suggesting it to be possibly a final problem in philosophy and theology, a confounding of the revealed map—an expressive form par excellence — with the territory, of which art is one horizontal extension or stratum.

Here, however, we would like to further discuss the way revelation and spontaneity manifest themselves out of the hidden order of art and why art can therefore be thought of as one of the highest forms of gnosis. Senior, [24] in his valuable book on Symbolist poetry and the occult Tradition suggests that there are two ways in which this happens in art: through the recording of *epiphanies* and through symbolism directly, wherein the "poet tries to create the experience on the page."[25] We will take up these two approaches, but first it is necessary to lay out some notion of what this occult tradition, this perennial philosophy or esoteric tradition, stands for as it comes into poetry and art, as it inevitably does by our definition of whole art.

Senior begins his book with a historical survey ranging from Babylonia and Egypt to India and Greece, to hermetics, cabalists, alchemists, and astrologers, and to modern occultists from Swedenborg to Blavatsky. He then presents a detailed list of twenty-one related notions which occultists tend to believe and act upon.[26] It is tempting to quote this useful list, but instead we will be content to present the three points summarizing Yeats' credo. Yeats believed:

> (1) That the borders of the mind are ever shifting, and
> that many minds can flow into one another, as it were,
> and create or reveal a single mind, a simple energy.
> (2) That the borders of our memories are a part of one
> great memory, the memory of Nature herself.
> (3) That this great mind and great memory can be
> evoked by symbols.[27]

While these three beliefs cannot do full justice to the twenty-one items of Senior's list, they can stand before us as a representative and economical surrogate for that list. If we add to Yeats' three beliefs his further elucidation of the role of imagination, we have a firm basis for relating art, *whole art*, to perennial philosophy:

> In imagination only we find a Human Faculty that
> touches nature at one side, and spirit on the other. Imagination may be described as that which is sent bringing spirit to nature, entering into nature, and seemingly losing its spirit, that nature being revealed as symbol may lose the power to delude.[28]

This description foreshadows the content of a latter discussion of the concrete imagination. But for now, let us return to our discussion of two ways in which art directly functions within the esoteric tradition.

Art Within the Esoteric Tradition: Epiphany and Symbolism

An *epiphany* is "a spiritual event in which the essence of a given object of manifestation appears to the subject, as in a sudden flash of recognition; a revelatory manifestation of a divine being."[29] Senior picked up the usage of this term for application to literary passages through Joyce's Stephen Dedalus, where it points to "a significant moment in the consciousness of a character, a moment when the usually meaningless ebb and flow of ideas and perceptions...suddenly makes a kind of sense."[30] The constant appearance of epiphanies in literature suggests that they are much more than a literary device. As symbolizing revelation — the sudden breakthrough of the Light of all lights, of the oneness of God, universe, and man — epiphanies reflect the world view of the old, old tradition known as the perennial philosophy or the esoteric tradition. Novelists often base the depth structure of a character, a life, on the ineffable quality of the epiphany, the sudden appearance of mystical experience and unity. We will later refer to some of these as examples of the experiential-expressive base, or text for the cycle and the discipline we are calling *the art of qualitative thinking*. Proust is a modern novelist who readily comes to mind for his repeated use of the epiphany. The taste of a cake dipped in tea, the feel of uneven paving stones beneath his feet, the sight of three trees on the bend of a country road while on a carriage ride with an aging countess — these exemplify much more than "the remembrance of times past." They signify the eternity of time — the *nunc stans* as opposed to *nunc fluens* — which erases all memory of clock time in a mystical experience spreading from full immersion in the boundarylessness of the qualitative immediate present.

Such revelations open up a deep structure within experience which comes as an oracular intuition that what has happened means to instruct one about self, life, eternity, and vocation. Thus art, linked directly with scriptures and anagogy in revelation, is itself an epiphany. As such, it comes to instruct as well. Caught up within the serious play of art and its self-transforming transformation into structure, the artist develops by giving up all idea of self-development. "Music — like dancing — is the art of bringing terrestrial shadows back to celestial vibrations and divine archetypes."[31] We are drawn to whole art for this epiphany-like instruction, for we find in it "something in which the conscious and unconscious meet in a kind of passive activity, and it is this element to which the lofty and easy language of art speaks. The language is lofty because of the spiritual symbolism of its form and the nobility of its style; it is easy because of the aesthetic mode of assimilation."[32]

> Leger et profond! It is the secret of all art...What is good is easy; everything divine runs with light feet.[33]

We might say that art has a very special role in the evolution of consciousness because it instructs us in epiphany-like experience, an easy and profound revelation of the divine in matter, body, mind, soul, and spirit — that is, across and through the entire great chain of Being. So seen, we might as well say that art is a *yantra*, in the sense that all of the aids to practice in yoga, for example, may be called yantras. The word literally means *an instrument for giving the mind control.* As such, some of the rituals and repetitions in the practice of pottery can be seen as concentration or meditation devices in preparation for throwing a pot on the potter's wheel.

> The Yantra, the instrument by which...[the] absolute is grasped, must be constructed so that sets of opposites will be contained and yet remain opposite. Thus a process shown as evolving must at the same time be shown ad devolving — and at the same time be static, that is transcendent, "a simultaneity of antagonistic aspects in the one and only essence."[34]

Seen as a yantra, the function of symbolic art is religious. If that word is too loaded for Western ears, habituated to hearing only its traditional meaning, we can say that its function is consciousness expanding or consciousness developing. Yeats had two ways of approaching the symbolic in poetry. A symbol

> ...should be the invocation — or evocation — of higher consciousness...The poet can take a symbol from occult tradition which has proven efficacious for others and, by concentrating on it, hope to extend his own and his reader's unconscious powers. Or, by meditation he can stir his unconscious until a symbol floats to its surface.[35]

These then, are foremost of the ways in which art takes on its revelatory mode: by recording epiphanies and by indirectly or directly gaining access to archetypes and the unconscious. As revelation, art is a yantra, which "insulates [the absolute] in a symbolical envelope so that eyes, which cannot look upon its naked intensity, may gradually become fortified through constant contemplation of the symbol, even to bearing the sight of the thing symbolized."[36]

While there is great structural logic and order to the way Hegel, Wilber, and Eastern esoteric disciplines outline the path to at-one-ment with the universal consciousness, on the existential plane it does not seem that our developmental problems come in any clear order. One can be intuitively aware of the eternal present from childhood on but still have mind-chatter and mental-egoic hang-ups intruding into, and holding one within, the passing present.

We sense that structural hierarchies of consciusness are not exclusively true, but only for the most part. While the notion of hierarchical development fits most great artists and thinkers, it fits some better than others. It fits Beethoven and Heidegger, for example, better than Bach and Plato. The ultimate ground in spiritual hierarchies is only, or rather, completely, the ground itself: the ground of all grounds, the top rung and the entire ladder at once, the center of the wheel and every point on the circumference simultaneously. And THAT can erupt at any time, symbolically, in revelation, in epiphany, in satori; or, since words by their very nature cannot say these things, it can suck all the parts back and show no other—as though the earth could swallow all the trees, cities, mountains, and beings to show it is purely earth offering itself up to the heavens as pure horizon for the ultimate marriage of earth and sky.

Even so, as a young boy sitting in my father's church where he was the pastor, the eternal present often broke through, and does now, as though "my father's church" were everywhere, everytime. Even though my pilgrimage is on the earth plane, my existential path and plight thrusts me forth like a *persona* in a play where all the acts of an unfolding drama take place. In art, the solution is profoundly simple. In Suzuki's words, the secret is always to be a beginner.[37] But that is indeed a *horizontal extension*, an unruly datum for structure. It is the invitation to the wind to go abroad "to build again a better life and song."[38]

Quite possibly for the artist at least, too much attention to spiritual hierarchies might lead to a progress anxiety comparable to that which overtook science in the modern world. It is fascinating to see that a good fit can be made between Beethoven's compositions, ranged along a time line, and the best codifications of spiritual and consciousness hierarchies.[39] It may even be possible that Beethoven transferred to the spiritual realm something of the progress anxiety of the cognitive realm inherited from the Enlightenment.

In the contemplative and mystical sense, we "know" the data of art to be transcendelia, in child art as well as in Beethoven's late quartets. It is a breakthrough, an eruption of the spirit at any level of consciousness or at any level of skill, at all beginner's minds. The symbol of a winged centaur deals with the objectification of spirit in all colors of the spectrum of consciousness. Only a mythic animal-human-god organism can thus fly and prance within and across all levels and domains. It appears, then, as an esoteric spiritual discipline but not as an esoteric spiritual science, since no concensus can be established concerning that discipline. It is radically historical in a unique way in its every appearing without orderly placement in our mental schemas.

As light and profound, art can represent simultaneously an esoteric and exoteric tradition. As mummified by museum and professor, it becomes exoteric, ontic, and historical in the dry sense. *But as an art of qualitative experience, the new artist, the epiphany, the yantra break through—a free, non-institutionalized esoteric tradition of the way surfaces. In the latter sense, art is not chained to the great chain of Being in any precise way, nor to hierarchies of consciousness, nor to specific epistemologies and metaphysical systems. It is parahierarchical, outside the hierarchies.* No wonder that a mental-egoic, single-visioned, technological age cannot admit that art has revelatory power, absolute freedom, and pure imagination as its ideal parameters. Art then, alas, seems precariously perched between the reductionistic, materialistic world and the hierarchical world of spiritual sciences.

Developmentally, educationally, and therapetically there are specific art-life connections and interactions that are natural correlates of whole or nondifferentiated art. But art itself will not confine itself to those functions to which it may be put. We may intend its usage for X, but it may affect also Y and Z.

Two simple, personal examples of how art operates as revelation through epiphany and symbolism may here be in order. Recently, on a walk through the campus where I taught, I passed by a tree, or cluster of small trees, where I and my students sat daily to share tea and conversation during a summer class in advanced pottery. We concentrated on the throwing of porcelain according to the tradition I had earlier learned in Arita, Japan. I learned it from a Jananese master potter who is the world's leading maker of pure white porcelain. That summer had been from the start unusual because of the close communal feeling developing in the class, unified as we were by purpose, vision, and the practice of the Japanese porcelain tradition. I had written my Japanese friends about this special summer class, but I was hardly prepared for the next event: I received a wire from my Japanese master saying, "I come Penn State. Help Teach Arita Method." Barely preceded by his telegram, he came to live with us for several weeks, taking up residence hourly, daily in the pottery classroom. Our sessions continued twenty-four hours a day two entire weeks beyond the official close of the Summer Session schedule. Students lived in the studio day and night. The photograph reproduced shows my class and me at tea break. When I recently passed this same

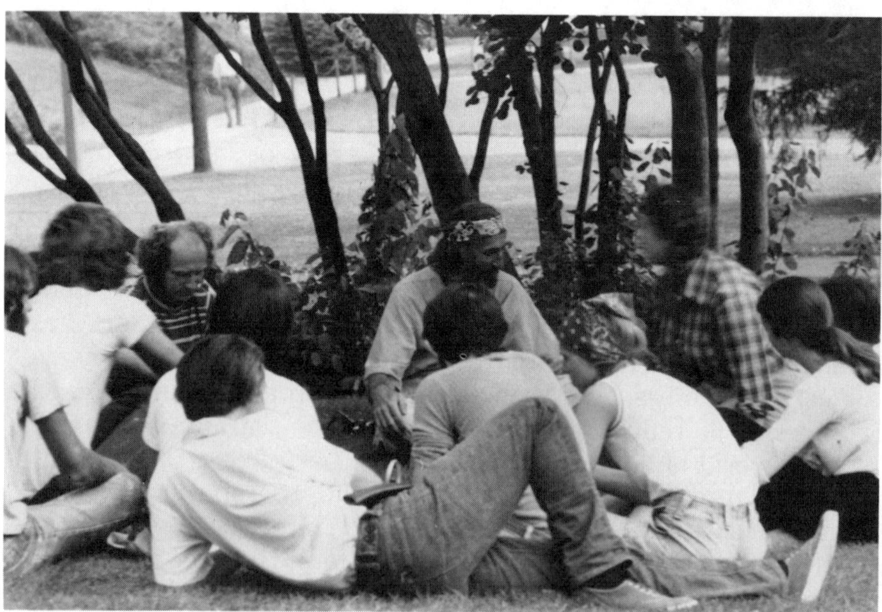

Communal Tea Break.
Author's advanced pottery class.

spot, alone, the class was both there and not there. I walked to where I sat and commemorated my feelings simply:

> Seven summers since I sat
> Beneath this tree, cross-legged,
> In smock and red bandana,
> A spirit son at my right hand,
> The class encircling round for communal tea,
> Passing the quiet bowl hand to hand,
>   mouth to mouth, eye to eye.
> We have much in common tree:
> Seven annual rings of the eternal present.

Secondly, I have included a pen and ink drawing made some years ago. After I finished it, I was invited to exhibit several pieces of my work in a campus exhibition relating religion and art and asked to submit a brief statement with each piece. I wrote the following on the drawing reproduced:

> Osmosis of Silence
> This drawing in its making—the mood, the simple
> means, the unhurried tempo—matched the experience

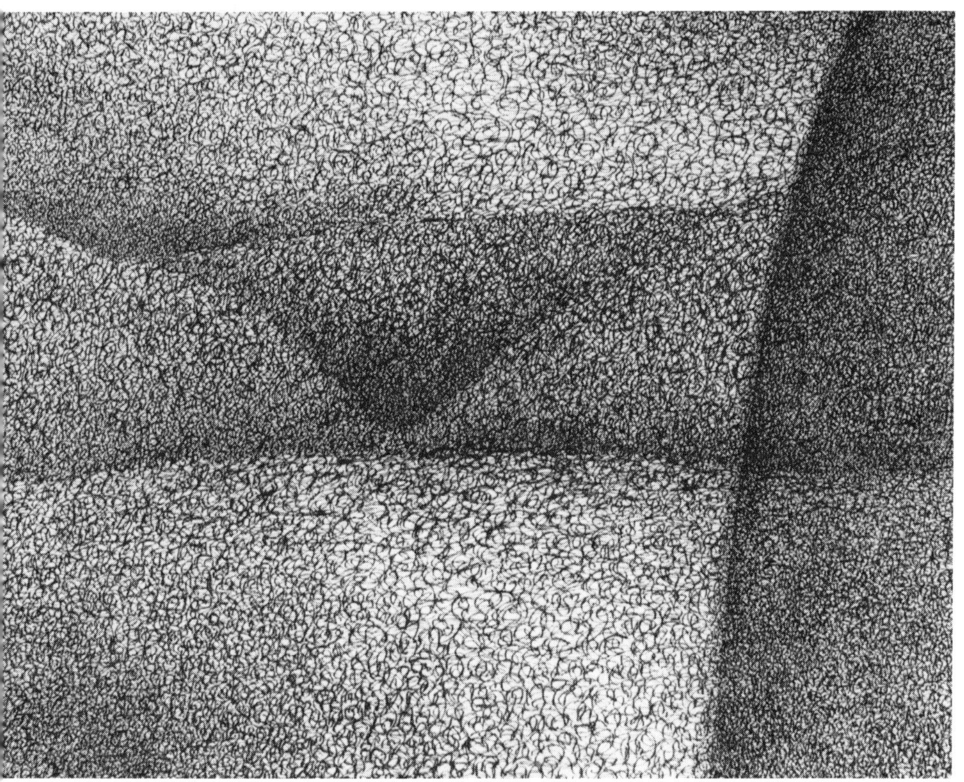

Osmosis of Silence.
Pen and ink. By the author.

> that it came to express. Both were meditative, still, contentless. I say contentless even though I had in mind a mountain gap backed by another mountain, approached across an unobstructed plain. This was the elemental theme upon which the light, the air, the muted tones of dusk or dawn could play—even as the pen played, rhythmically, roundly, within and across all the forms. There were to be no real contours, only approximate boundaries, like zones of passage which could be here and there lost altogether—a place for the osmosis of silence to occur. The moving edge of light or shade came in later, as the passing of time, and, curiously, thereby connoted timelessness. It is a drawn meditation, or a meditative drawing.

These are humble examples meant to symbolize what I have always known—that art can be a form of gnosticism. I guess I have not been up to now as explicit about this as the time and purpose of this book now allows me to be.

Schuon has said: "There is no science of the soul without a meta-physical basis to it and without spiritual remedies at its disposal." While we have not seen fit to call art a "science of the soul," nevertheless it has been one of the chief revelatory arms of almost all such "sciences." But, as creators of art as well as thinkers about it, we do feel that there is a kind of clarity to the metaphysical basis best fitting the artistic and spiritual enterprise: what has been called *organicism*.

Organicism is the metaphysics which most artists unselfconsciously and intuitively espouse. Some artists and thinkers achieve highly spirit-full organic creations early in their careers—e.g., Hegel's *Phenomenology of Spirit* or Buber's *I and Thou*. In some way they never come up to them again, and they intuitively know not to edit or revise these inspired works later in life. Nor can they be adequately paraphrased, for they are as much poetry as philosophy.

If we leave aside artists like Mozart and Keats who die young, we find many examples of artists who constantly renew their vision and perhaps do not so much change as become their most organic selves in spirit-full and cosmic works late in life: Titian, Rembrandt, Monet, Rubens, Renoir, Bonnard. Visual artists seem to find their visionary unity and stride later in life than in the other arts. They seem to peak later and continue to peak, to flower, to transcend.

The Artist as Progressive Organicist

The organicist mode of seeing begins holistically, where

every detail becomes a fragment of an intuited whole which is more than the sum of its parts. Many years ago I made sketches and wrote organicist notes as I walked along the banks of the wide Susquehanna River in Harrisburg, Pennsylvania. I grew up there and would often take daily walks over the same territory. Here are examples of organicist vision as I described my feelings at the River:

> Fragment 1: In walking down here to the River, I noticed that the smallest thing, the most ungainly twig or brush or pitiful porch step, was not in fact ill-designed as our training may have tried to suggest, but possessed of a larger unity the whole of which was not a mere summation of its parts. This configuration, my spring—for my consciousness in this time and place are also mere elements of the total—rules all...A glimpse up an alleyway from the River was moving indeed, with its banded shadows, depth and varied life and renewed variation on a theme my eyes must always hear. A dog, and a girl on a bicycle moved slowly, attached to a solid band of shadow.

> Fragment 2: A white cherry, darker-more-intense than turgid water's moving plane; a blossom's snow of flight through air and path aligned.
> The far shore leans more clearly toward the heart, and pits itself against the watery break of distance and of mind. The light more dazzles there—the hills drop off on unknown thoughts.

> Fragment 3: The lights of windows over River become mere playful sparks that form innumerably anew. The shadows loosely lie along the structured street, whose rigid immobility steps back for the aimless movement of a few people placed as if for composition's sake. All chance things now form a higher order, seen against this transformed monotony, where light and shade and season cancel all complaints. So River, tree, window, yard, well known, become the background for my chance delight. Like this, that chilling wind near warmth of spring, that cloud of white across the water plane, that sound of bell, that girl in spreading tan spring outfit, all completed...
> Some people come to walk their dog, for habit or no clear reason—I, to walk my mind, to stalk my past and future.

> Fragment 4: The late glow on balustraded porch burns like a phrase, or like the loved one near. Closer harmonies are matters of the intellect. This time of day remains "my light"—corny by modern standards, or at least Venetian, it is the light of autumns and of late afternoons, warm, slanting, banding long shadows; and it is like the squares of colored glass around the windows in my parents' old house, which first showed me, under feeling, that things change when seen under slightly changed conditions.

> ...The river dances and shimmers; its infinitesimal sparks go on and off by thousands. And nature's feeling is of multiplicity and unity. Here (across the river) one has the distance that is needed for contemplation. The incomprehensibility of the real (perception) far transcends our fantasies. There is always an air of movement here. A man walks through shadow stripes and gapes. The near trees are architectural, the distance poetic, the cars black beetles with high gloss. The lights, the neutrals, are the river, the street and pavement, the sky. The sun-drenched arbor, the cloud-strewn street.
>
> Fragment 5: Times and places are inextricably bound together, and their tie is often based on the flimsiest or most erratic of sensations, or the most subjective and even subconscious of motivations. The truth of an interplay of lights and shadows upon forms of seeming stability, is that the instability and changes of these seemingly solid forms—changes in nature and in ourselves and in the very structure of each, changes of the real and the abstract, the fantastic and the formal, the past and the present, modern and traditional, material and mystical, the possible and the ineffable—all of these paradoxes are expressible through an active interplay of light and shade itself...

These on-the-spot fragments written in sketchbooks, old envelopes, on paper bags, while standing along the sidewalk or sitting on a park bench, are like slow-burning epiphanies—minor mysteries of an organicist artistic disposition unknowingly already under the esoteric tradition, probably under the indirect influence of my father's more inspired sermons or my mother's lived religion. They are presented not as art but as tangible examples of what pure thought makes too quickly abstract. Walt Whitman even more concisely and directly states the organicist world view of the artist and suggests that it is one with the esoteric tradition:

> I will not make poems with reference
>   to parts,
> But I will make poems, songs, thoughts
>   with reference to Ensemble,
> And I will not sing with reference to a day,
>   but with reference to all days,
> And I will not make a poem nor the least
>   part of a poem but has reference
>   to the soul.
> Because having looked at the objects
>   of the Universe,
> I find there is no one nor any particle
>   of one but has reference to the soul.[40]

Such examples as the above show the interaction and even the necessary contradiction of the progressive and ideal categories of the organicist world-view.

Objective or idealistic organicism is anathema to the artist. Though end as *idea*, even as *unifying image*, may be known from the start of an art process, the actual integration of materials in terms of feelings is something that must be worked out step by step in the thick of feelings and materials. The artist is a progressive organicist working from a hidden order. Metaphysically the dialogue metaphor which we used for the give and take, the serious play of art, is like a blend of contextualism and organicism: the immediate apprehension and gradual incarnation of a variety of vivid values is what the artist is after. This dialectical process is very present-minded. Says Matisse:

> If upon a white canvas I jot down some sensations of blue, of green, of red—every new brush stroke diminishes the importance of the proceding ones. Suppose I set out to paint an interior: I have before me a cupboard; it gives me a sensation of bright red—and I put down a red that satisfies me; immediately a relation is established between this red and the white of the canvas. If I put a green near the red; if I paint in a yellow floor, there must still be between this green, this yellow, and the white of the canvas a relation that will be satisfactory to me. But these several tones mutually weaken one another. It is necessary, therefore, that the various elements that I use be balanced that they do not destroy one another...
>
> I am forced to transpose until my picture may seem completely changed when, after successive modifications, the red has succeeded the green as the dominant color...I must interpret nature and submit it to the spirit of the picture—when I have found the relationship of all the tones the result must be a living harmony of tones, a harmony not unlike that of a musical composition.[41]

Yet it is not contradictory to say at the same time that there is a telos to the process that is implicit from the start; and this is what we called transformation into structure, or more simply, we used the organism metaphor.

This is the way it appears from the artist's side. But the *progressive organicist* and the *idealist organicist* are at odds over the meaning of process. Esoteric spiritual "sciences" gravitate toward idealistic organicism for only thus can levels and transitions be seen as fragments falling off from an *a priori* unified whole. Even advanced physics seems to have caught on to the necessary unbroken wholeness of the universel in order to make sense of the paradoxes otherwise everywhere confronting it.[42] To that extent, advanced physicists are ideal or objective organicists.

The view from the path and the view from the top are different. The artist is on the path with visions of the summit guiding him or her but will not presume beforehand what these visions signify. In fact, what these visions signify is what cannot be said or symbolized. That there is a remarkable similarity to the symbols used by visionaries[43] is procedurally beside the point. An idea-heavy philosophic poet may report an epiphany, but a symbolic one must make us feel it physically, mentally and spiritually. The *vibrations* between material, human, mental and spiritual realms must match.

So the artist knows through *fragments* — parts foreshadowing wholeness — which lead to *nexuses* or similarities, and on into *conflict* between the various nexuses, demanding a specific *integration* fitting to only these concrete fragments, nexuses, and their conflicts, falling within this unique presentational context we will soon call a work of art. The vibrations from the idea or ideal site are worthless if they do not set up unexpected resonances and reverberations in us through matter itself.

To further clarify the world view of organicism it would be useful to name the categories which Pepper says are found within any organic process and its achievement. These are:

> (1) *fragments* of experience which appear with (2) *nexuses* or connections or implications, which spontaneously lead as a result of the aggravation of (3) *contradictions*, gaps, oppositions, or counteractions to resolution in (4) an *organic whole*, which is found to have been (5) *implicit* in the fragments, and to (6) *transcend* the previous contradictions by means of a coherent totality, which (7) *economizes*, saves, preserves all the original fragments of experience without any loss. The fourth category is the pivotal point of the system and should be included in both the progressive and ideal sets. It is the goal and final stage of the progressive categories and it is the field for the specification of the ideal categories.[44]

Pepper goes on to say that the progressive categories are often called *appearance*, whereas the ideal categories are called *reality*.[45] But a contradiction exists between the progressive and ideal categories which is an ineradicable characteristic of this world view. The artist, for example, has his or her being within the progressive categories, but his or her achievement is in the ideal ones. We have represented the paradoxical necessity of this conflict by our insistence on the dialogue-into-organism argument, which we believe is the way art's hidden order manifests itself. It is art's way of turning appearance into reality. Malraux says:

> To the eyes of the artist things are primarily what they may come to be within that privileged domain where they "put on immortality..."
>
> The artist's voice owes its power to the fact that it arises from a pregnant solitude that conjures up the universe so as to impose on it a human accent.[46]

In short, the artist is intuiting reality through appearance by moving through the heart of illusion.

The Artist as a Verificationist Mystic

The artist is something like a combined contextualist and organicist while at work. In search of pure imagination, she or he nevertheless evades classification into any pure type. Since, however, the artist's role is one of revelation, we must not assume that the artist does not know what she or he is doing for want of an idealized, from-the-top-down explanation. This was Socrates' error in deriding poets for not being able to explain discursively what their poetry already explained in purely poetic terms. By a curious reversal, it usually turns out that the artist's *appearance* is often more *real* than the verbal *reality* propounded by idealist organicists. The artist lives out and heals the contradictions the idealist organicist will not countenance. The artist works toward the absolute in the realm of time, change, and finitude — terms which must be dropped from the vantage point of the absolute.[47] Organicism would be important enough if only because it has given us the doctrine of the creative imagination — especially as represented in the thought of Coleridge[48] — and here we pay homage to our human ability to thread a way through the contradictions and arbitrary boundaries besetting our existential path.

But we deal not only with organicism but with mysticism. It is Pepper's limit that he excludes mysticism because it is not a cognitively adequate world view. In this his view is only partially right. Once we equate cognitive adequacy with dependence exclusively on the data of *intelligibilia* and point out that the data of mystical world views consists of *transcendelia*, then Pepper's view becomes reductionistic. From Pepper's perspective, the artist's abode in progressive organicism would be called mystical and labelled as cognitively inadequate, for it depends on intuitive certitude of a *beyond*. But if that certitude be seen from the realm of transcendelia, then that charge of mysticism loses its pejorative ring.

> Mysticism is not regression in service of the ego, but
> evolution in transcendence of the ego.[49]

Furthermore, the artist may be said to verify his or her intuition in matter. *Painters may talk about painting, says Malraux, but in practice must paint only what they can.*[50] The rift which the charge of mysticism has caused between art and thought can now be healed. It was already being healed by the art of hermeneutics as applied to the objectifications of the human spirit of which Dilthey spoke. The term *science* is a strong one to apply to matters spiritual, but the case made by Wilber and Schuon is such that the direction begun by Dilthey nears fulfillment. It may not help matters to say that there is spiritual science on the one hand but only artistic mysticism on the other, but that seems to be where our thought comes to rest. The artist is an active mystic, a believer in meditation in action, and as such, out of the hidden order of art finds ways to verify intuitions of certitude.

The Artist Synthesizes Love and Gnosis, Heart and Third Eye

In the fuller version where Blake speaks of two-fold or double vision, he also refers to threefold and fourfold vision. Senior likens the four levels of vision to the steps of yoga, in which the yogi progressively strips away from the self the senses, the body, the mind and the emotions. In twofold vision the world is a fantasy, a metaphor, "a garden of ripe analogies." In threefold vision the *reality* behind the illusory appearance of the world is grasped. Things are seen as images. "God makes up the whole world instantly by his poetic act of the imagination." Finally, fourfold image is delight, bliss and enlightenment. "It is becoming God, like the

Chinese painter who could paint seeds so that grass sprang up from them."[51]

Blake represents a synthesis of that which usually appears separate. In the orderliness of spiritual science the initiate in yoga is told by the master to concentrate in meditation either on the heart chakra, that golden center where lower energies are transmuted into higher, the seat of universal love, *or* on the tiny circle between the two eyebrow winged by two petals, in the center of which burns steadily the white flame of pure consciousness. But the initiate is not to shift from one to the other. The difference is that *the artist of vision sees with the heart and with the eye of contemplation*—not either/or, but both.

In a similar way, we have the path of love and the path of knowledge, or *bhakti* and *jnana.*

> ...for the "volitional" or "affective" man...God is "He" and the *ego* is "I," whereas for the "gnostic" or "intellective" man...God is "I"—or "Self"—and the *ego* is "he" or "other."
>
> In spiritual life, he who says "to will" says "to will Good"; "to will Good" is "to will well," that is to say to "will through the good," or "through God"; instead of "to will" one could also say "to love" and instead of "the Good" one could say "the Beautiful." On the other hand, he who says "to know" says "to know that which is"; he who says "to know that which is," says, in a final analysis, "to be that which knows": the Self.[52]

Blake combines through his twofold, threefold, and fourfold vision these extremes—"to love the Beautiful" with "to be that which knows: the Self."

Spirit Is Artist

We began this chapter with Hegel's all encompassing statements, "Spirit is artist." In Hegel's thought, the foremost role of the self was to reveal itself to itself, for it is in so doing that the self becomes realized and can know itself as self. Art is at the center of this enterprise as the only means that produces change continually while its process remains the same. The objectifications of spirit of which Dilthey spoke mirror spirit back to itself through art. These objectifications of spirit in art, then, give us a world and a self to know. Philosophy, reflection and systematic thought in this way depend on such expressions of self and world for their critique to begin.

Spirit can work with itself at any level of consciousness through art. This extremely important insight has guided our research in the Drawing Lab and it will guide our later reflections on therapy and education. Under the intention to make art, even "the single vision," to which Blake refers, gives way to "twofold vision," as fantasy and metaphor begin to illumine matter-of-fact perception with the poetry of consciousness as an origin becoming aware of itself. Vision is then born.

> The condition of vision is universal, from the primitive who marshals mana to the modern theosophist who marshals astral light. First the visionary feels heat and sees light, and then he perceives the universe as the single living – "animate" – substance of which all separate things living and dead are forms.[53]

The Visionary Artist and the Leading Edge of Consciousness

From the earliest human origins, visionary artists have symbolized the leading edge of consciousness, of spirit, of the numinous. Similarly Langer claims that this tendency is innate since an infant can engage in *symbolic transformation* before the development of speech.[54] And Wilber[55] in his fascinating account of the evolution of the average state of consciousness gives example after example of symbolic depictions from art, magic and religion. At first these were undifferentiated one from the other. They appeared as the mysterious serpent, on brass shields from Africa, in Coptic woodcuts, as symbols of the kundalini, and as the entwined snakes of the caduceus. Later came the half-man half-snake or half-animal typhon found in cave drawings and on totem poles. Then followed the early temples of the mythic-membership periods. And then the great mother of paleolithic Venus sculptures, and Cretan serpent goddesses. Still later came the great goddess of medieval manuscripts, the Buddhist goddess of compassion, and the great goddess Kali of India. Finally the slaying of the typhon, the killing of the dragon, and up to and including the symbolic warfare of present day fooball. In the evolution of consciousness in the human species art has always played a visionary, revelatory and symbolical role on the leading edge of conscousness. In the sense of spirit othering itself to become more purely spirit, art plays exactly the same role at the leading edge of the individual consciousness.

The artist, then, as a visionary participates in a hidden process with a secret order dependent on revelation. The artist does not, however, evolve in a way completely acceptable to idealist organicists. For outside their maps and paths and ladders, all but the greatest of saints and sages can be dogmatic in their exclusions. We happen to believe that a Blake, a Giotto, a Whitman, or a St. Francis is in no way inferior to a Patanjali; and believe that a Lao Tsu, a Buddha or a Christ would understand this. It would seem rather uncharitable to so discriminate against artists for being disorderly when they give us our clearest symbols of order.

Summary

When then can we say about the place of art within the great chain of Being? To begin with, art operates on every level or link of the chain and in the transformational, evolutionary task of moving from one level or link to another. Also art does not fit well into hierarchical spiritual sciences — or mental ones either — seeming as it does to be a horizontal extension of spirit which comes and goes unpredictably. Further, art is revelation as surely as are scriptures and anagogy, and these serve each other, even though the sage or saint may feel no personal need for art. The artist, in addition, is a born organicist, not of the ideal or objective kind but rather a progressive organicist working out of a hidden order, embodying paradoxically both dialogue and organism metaphors within the art process. Again the artist is a mystic who verifies an intuition of the absolute in matter. It also appears that many, many artists have worked, consciously or not, within the esoteric tradition, invoking it through epiphanies and through deliberate resuscitation of past myths and archetypes and through direct emergences from their own conscious/unconscious processes. We have also shown that the artist, as a verificationist mystic paradoxically synthesizes the paths of love and gnosis, of heart and third eye, without benefit of science. And finally, *spirit* itself is artist, and thus the way of being of the artist provides us a model of models in the purity of its uncodified method as a spiritual discipline for revelation and for the evolution of consciousness.

This is a heavy burden to lay self-consciously on the shoulders of the artist in hopes that he or she will become a kind of secular priest for an unbelieving time. Artists may best do all these things indirectly. It is time to leave the more philosophical side of our discussion and to look at how the artist functions closer to the things themselves.

References

1. Hegel, G. W. F. *Phenomenology of spirit.* (A. V. Miller, trans.) Oxford: Clarendon Press, 1977; p. 424.

2. Pallis, M. *Peaks and Lamas.* London: A. A. Knopf, 1940; pp. 373-374.

3. Kandinsky, W. *Concerning the spiritual in art.* New York: Wittenborn, 1955; p. 75.

4. Picasso, P. Quoted in Goldwater, R. and Treves, M. (eds.) *Artists on art.* New York: Pantheon Books, 1945; p. 418.

5. Kandinsky, W. *Op. cit.* reference 3 above.

6. Faure, E. *History of art.* Vol. V. *The Spirit of the forms.* (W. Pach, trans.) New York: Harper & Brothers, 1930.

7. Focillon, H. *The life of forms in art.* (C. B. Hogan and G. Kubler trans.) New Haven: Yale University Press, 1942.

8. Wilber, K. *The spectrum of consciousness.* Wheaton, Illinois: Theosophical Publishing House, 1977.
   . *No boundary.* Los Angeles: Center Publications, 1979.
   . *The Atman project.* Wheaton, Illinois: Theosophical Publishing House, 1980.
   . *Up from Eden.* Garden City, N.Y.: Anchor Press/Doubleday, 1981.

9. Hegel, G. W. F. *Op. cit.*, reference 1 above.

10. Gibson, W. *A season in heaven.* New York: Atheneum Publishers (Bantam Book Edition), 1975; p. 122.

11. See Wilber, K. *Op. cit.,* reference 8 above.
    Also, Lovejoy, A. O. *The great chain of being.* Cambridge: Harvard University Press, 1936.
    Also, Huxley, A. *The perennial philosophy.* New York: Harper, 1970.
    Also, Senior, J. *The way down and out.* New York: Greenwood Press, 1968.

12. Wilber, K. *Up from Eden,* p. 9; see reference 8 above.

13. Faure, E. *Op. cit.,* p. 265, reference 6 above.

14. Schuon, F. *Language of the self.* (M. Pallis and M. Matheson trans.) Madras, India: Ganesh, 1959; p. XIV.

15. Senior, J. *Op. cit.,* p. 62, reference 11 above.

16. *Ibid.,* p. 62.

17. Ponge, F. *The voice of things.* (B. Archer, trans.) New York: McGraw Hill, 1972; p. 107.

18. Wilber, K. The problem of proof. *ReVision,* 5 (1), Spring, 1982; 80-100.

19. *Ibid.*, p. 96.

20. *Ibid.*, p. 97.

21. Kandinsky, W. *Op. cit.*, p. 74, reference 3 above.

22. Schuon, F. *Op. cit.*, p. 109, reference 14 above.

23. *Ibid.*, p. 110.

24. Senior, J. *Op. cit.*, reference 11 above.

25. Senior, J. *Op. cit.*, p. 51, reference 11 above.

26. *Ibid.*, pp. 39-41.

27. Yeats, W. B. *The collected works.* Stratford-on-avon: Chapman & Hall, 1908. vol. VI, *Ideas of good and evil*; p. 23.

28. Ellis, E. J. and Yeats, W. B. (eds.) *The works of William Blake*, London, 1893; p. XII.

29. Morris, W. (ed.) *The American heritage dictionary of the English language.* New York: Houghton Mifflin, 1969.

30. Senior, J. *Op. cit.*, p. XII, reference 11 above.

31. Schuon, F. *Op. cit.*, p. 244, reference 14 above.

32. *Ibid.*, p. 39.

33. Read, H. *Reason and romanticism.* New York: Russell & Russell, 1963; p. 150.

34. Senior, J. *Op. cit.*, p. 19; see reference 11 above.

35. *Ibid.*, p. 164.

36. Pallis, M. *Op. cit.*, p. 375; see reference 2 above.

37. Suzuki, S. *Zen mind, beginner's mind.* New York: Weatherhill, 1970.

38. Tagore, R. Poem cited in reference 1, Chapter 1.

39. Funk, J. Beethoven: A transpersonal analysis. *ReVision*, 5 (1), Spring 1982; 29-41.

40. Whitman, W. *Leaves of grass.* Philadelphia: David McKay, 1891-1892.

41. Matisse, H. Quoted in Goldwater and Treves (eds.), p. 44; see reference 4 above.

42. Capra, F. The *Tao of physics*, Boulder: Shambhala, 1975 and, Zukav, G. *The dancing WuLi masters.* New York: Bantam Books, 1980.

43. Senior, J. *Op. cit.*, p. 56; see reference 11 above.

44. Pepper, S. C. *World hypotheses.* Berkeley: University of California Press, 1970, p. 283.

45. *Ibid.*, p. 282.

46. Maraux, A. *The voices of silence.* (S. Gilbert, trans.) Garden City, N.Y.: Doubleday, 1953; p. 275, p. 630.

47. Pepper, S. C. *Op. cit.,* p. 314; see reference 44 above.

48. Lowes, J. L. *The road to Xanodu.* New York: Houghton Mifflin, 1930.

49. Wilber, K. *Op. cit.,* see reference 18 above.

50. Malraux, A. *Op. cit.,* see reference 46 above.

51. Senior, J. *Op. cit.,* pp. 59-60; see reference 11 above.

52. Schuon, F. *Op. cit.,* p. 231; see reference 14 above.

53. Senior, J. *Op. cit.,* pp. 2-3; see reference 11 above.

54. Langer, S. K. *Philosophy in a new key.* Baltimore: Penguin Books, 1948.

55. Wilber, K. *Up from Eden.* See reference 8 above.

4

The Concrete Imagination

If a man could pass through Paradise in a dream, and have a flower presented to him as a pledge that his soul had really been there, and if he found that flower in his hand when he awoke—Ay! and what then?
Samuel Taylor Coleridge[1]

One of the paradoxes of the imagination: while thinkers who reconstruct a world retrace a long path of reflections, *the cosmic image is immediate*. It gives us the whole before the parts. In its exuberance, it believes it is telling the whole of the Whole.
Gaston Bachelard[2]

Presence before order. Where this priority is lost, it is always at the expence of visionary art.
Theodore Roszak[3]

The Decline of Vision

Those who see visions have either dwindled in number or have not expressed their visions. When visions dwindle or are not expressed, the role of art in revelation correspondingly shrinks. In religious terms this condition parallels the lessening experience of the *kerygma*—that is, the hearing of the word or the scriptures directly.

Vision, inspiration, imagination—this signifies a sequence that might be seen on the one hand as a diminishing of intensity and power. On the other however, it signifies a change in the locus of the experience. Vision and inspiration seem to come from outside, whereas imagination seems to have an internal locus. We are *possessed* by visions and inspirations and we *participate* in the life of imagination. In terms of consciousness therefore, the transition to imagination may be construed as an advance. Certainly it is an advance in awareness and comparatively speaking, in control. Imagination leads to slower-burning epiphanies, but for that very reason it may also lead to greater self-consciousness and to greater self-transformation.

In the imaginative life, epiphanies, visions and inspirations still make their appearance, but we have prepared an environment and context for them.

Barfield[4] suggests that what we now call imagination includes that which transcends it and which still needs to be called inspiration, but without the suggestion of mania or possession. It is rather a transformed and interiorized inspiration which is the successor to imagination. In the state where inspiration reappears, we see a reaching out beyond the confines of art as currently conceived toward that nondifferentiated aesthetic or whole art which concerns us and our consciousness in all possible dimensions of being. In literature, Barfield sees such inspiration speaking in a direct tensile language. He hazards the prophency that:

> ...if imagination advances towards transformed inspiration, it will be accompanied by something like a transition from metaphor to transformed personification and from myth and symbol to transformed allegory.[5]

The kind of language to which Barfield points is a language which at a higher level of consciousness lets the "gods" back in, as it were. In terms of the evolution of consciousness, an interiorized inspiration adds a forward step to *The Origin of Consciousness in the Breakdown of the Bicameral Mind.*[6] As such, the *voices* are now from a much different source and have a new function. Instead of slaying the ancient gods to come to a mental-egoic state, such inspiration now helps slay the ego to move toward a transpersonal state where consciousness is no longer in the hold of nature nor the mind, but in harmony with the universe. We then have art as a leading voice toward a new ethic which Roszak[7] calls the person/planet ratio. He says that if we reassert the human scale we can subvert bigness and save the planet. Human scale would especially mean that developing the art-life-consciousness connection simultaneously opens up within each of us the fullest evolution of our consciousness. The interiorized inspiration that works through imagination is therefore seen not as a decline nor a hunger for the old times, but as an advance toward self-transformation to higher levels of consciousness.

Holism of the Imagination

The artist, the winged centaur, the verificationist mystic who believes in love and gnosis, has been presented as a progressive organicist. He acts ideally, says Collingwood,[8] as though pure imagination were possible. It is the imaginative function which binds together feelings, sensations, attention and thoughts into one organic whole.

> Everything which imagination presents to itself is a here, a now; something complete in itself, absolutely self-contained, unconnected with anything else by the relations between what is and what it is not, what it is and that because of which it is what it is, what it is and what it might have been, what it is and what it ought to be. If any of these distinctions are imported into the object of imagination, it absorbs them; the duality of terms with a relation between them disappears, and leaves only a trace of itself in the shape of a modification of the whole...What I imagine, however complex it may be, is imagined as a simple whole, where relations between the parts are present simply as qualities of the whole.[9]

Thus imagination to Collingwood is a basic kind of thought—primary thought we might call it—in which attention and therefore consciousness are brought to bear upon the flux existing through sensa and feelings. Its mobile unity deserves special mention. The imaginative faculty, especially as engaged in the art process, is one of the strongest and clearest ways in which we can learn to dwell within *the qualitative immediate present*[10], within kairotic as opposed to chronotic time, or within the eternal present—*nunc stans* rather than *nunc fluens*. When it so functions and spreads, art is clearly a meditative state and an arm of revelation and consciousness expansion. The ego is temporarily forgotten through the fullness of absorption in the imaginative-expressive state, which can also be thought of as a condition of the integrated body-mind in touch with otherness.

> Imagination is the home of intentionality and fantasy one of its languages. I use fantasy here not meaning something unreal to which we escape, but in its original meaning of *phantasitikous*, "able to represent," "to make visible." Fantasy is the language of the total self.[11]

The imagination is complex, varied, integrative and evolving under our participation yet with its own autonomy. Jung feels that the inner image expresses unconscious and conscious influences simultaneously, so that any intepretation we may give to it must take into account their reciprocal relations.[12] This double base to imagination underscores the intuition that there is a hidden voice within the holistic out-of-time operation of the imagination.

Bachelard: Phenomenologist of the Image and Poetic Gnostic

Countering the notion of Cassirer's that we perceive conceptually, we have the contribution of Cantril and Dewey, of Sartre and Bachelard. These clearly point to the affective side of perception. Dewey and Cantril say we perceive socially. But Bachelard insists that we perceive imaginatively.[13]

> In the case of the thing...we not only excise the thing from its surroundings, in the act of perceiving, through our prior assumption which stipulates that it must be conceived as isolated; we also endow it imaginatively with all sorts of other properties.[14]

Bachelard is the explorer of all those other properties with which we imaginatively endow the thing. We will follow the special way in which he sets out on this exploration.

Though I have read Bachelard's *Poetics of Space* and his *Poetics of Reverie* three times — he tells the reader that by the third leisurely reading the reader finally understands the author — I find it impossible to reduce him to a set of *ideas*. I take this to be to his credit and to that of his method. Such ideas as can be separated out are more in the nature of insights, specific conclusions, commemorations, celebrations, elations, footnotes on images and reveries, or attacks on those who psychologize and scientize — that is, on all who attempt to submit the work of art to a reductive analysis.

Rather than philosophize at length, Bachelard catches images on the wing and holds them for a flitting moment apart from the poem or literary work of which they are a pregnant fragment. He then turns them loose. His language is not overly paradoxical. It is not overly reasoned. It is as though he knows instinctively that reason and even impassioned purple paradoxical prose will not work. The poetic fragments with which Bachelard constructs his poetics of space and reverie are transcendelia pure and simple. They are data for gnosis, for the eye of contemplation, for the trans-symbolic grasp of the trans-symbolic world, spirit's direct knowledge of spirit.[15]

Bachelard picks up and classifies poetic fragments for spiritual understanding much as a geologist might treat rock samples for geological understanding of the earth's surface. To love both concepts and images is, for Bachelard, to "love the psychic forces of different types of love...[which] are the masculine and feminine poles of the Psyche."[16] These are no other than reason and imagination, and they develop, he says, "on two divergent planes of the spiritual life."[17] He continues:

> ...neither will it be I who, telling my faithful love for images, will study them with great support from concepts. Intellectualist criticism of poetry will never lead to the source (foyer) where poetic images take form. One must keep from giving commands to the image as a mesmerizer gives commands to the somnambulist. In order to know the success of images, it is better to follow the somnambulistic reverie, to listen...to the dreamer's somniloquy. The image can only be studied through the image, by dreaming images as they gather in reverie. It is a non-sense to claim to study imagination objectively since one really receives the image only if he admires it. Already in comparing one image to another, one runs the risk of losing participation in its individuality.[18]

Here is a genuine credo for the phenomenology of the imagination. As Bachelard uses the word *phenomenology* I am inclined to let it stand, for it is a direct and not a figurative usage. The poetic fragments he holds up are a kind of phenomenology of poetic transcendelia not requiring paradoxical or mandalic reasoning. Admittedly Bachelard steps in and out of paradoxical thinking, but this is merely connective tissue between the real images. And indeed it may take three readings for the reader to arrive at the kind of *dreaming observation* which Bachelard says allows us to receive, in admiration and in reverie, poetic images directly and intuitively.[19] In a way, it is a show-and-tell game with much more showing than telling.

The work of the phenomenologist in this sphere is something like spiritual classification, where archetypes and recurrent themes, the similarities between visions and images, can accumulate by contiguity and correspondence, where family resemblances enrich, and through repeated variation of similar experiences give us a distancing and clarifying effect simultaneously—Dewey[20] would say allow for *funding* when we come back to each unique image and fragment.

To Bachelard the poetic image is an absolute origin of consciousness and as such it points legitimately to a phenomenology. Further "the poetic image is under the sign of a new being. This new being is happy man."[21] As an origin of consciousness, it is bad form and an error to seek antecedents to an image once we are in touch with it, for that would be "a sign of inveterate psychologism."[22] As pointed out above, this direct product of the imagination is only approachable through *admiration, poetic reverie,* and *dreaming observation.*

To know the self, even the Self, through the poetic image and through poetic reverie is to be a poetic gnostic. Again we see the same synthesis of what reason shows as separate: love and gnosis come together. Perhaps in Hegelian fashion, it would be preferable to call them two moments of one process—the love leads to gnosis. The way is through matter, senses and body-mind directly to spirit. Admiration and poetic reverie in the presence of the poetic image is an ideal setting for demonstrating that Spirit is artist. There is a curious way in which Bachelard's reasoning is equivalent to anagogy, as the inspired mysterious interpretation of revelation through poetry. Join together art and anagogy and one enters into an esoteric spiritual discipline.

The Image as a Variational and Radiating Phenomenon

We start with the image already there, an absolute origin of consciousness before us in fullbodied presence. It means something, but we neither know nor care at this point what. A flick of our minds or a flutter of our emotions is absorbed into its autonomous history. Phenomenologically—and this I consider a revolutionary insight of Bachelard's—the image reveals itself to us not as direct objects of perception usually do through the way they are constituted in our minds, but through its vital life of variation.[23] Wave lengths exceed photography, but images exceed wave lengths. The life of an image, like a slow, slow meteor moving across the sky, resembles the work of art in Langer's[24] felicitous construction, *a whole held together only by activity.* It maintains itself through a life of shifting change under a simple qualitative impetus, or throbbingly spins in place almost numinously radiating from a center. Thus in the artistic image the painter is not a reflector but a producer of lights, "the light that an inner vision knows and expresses in the world of brilliant colors, in the world of sunlight, so that a veritable reversal of psychological perspectives is demanded."[25]

An image need not be fleeting. An artistic image can be sustained so that it guides an entire creative process eventuating in a work. Let me give an example. It is early Spring. Like Picasso,

I catch what he calls a "green sickness" out in the early spring landscape. It is as though one large amount of green matrix could be mixed up and, apart from the sky, the whole universe painted from it. I mix up chrome green stains and slips (colored clays) for decorating some of my stoneware spheres. These pieces are already tooled and scrubbed with overlapping layers of white slip into a textured *hakeme*, a visually palpable surface that renews the formism of my rather exact tooling, bringing the surface back into material away from the sheer appearance of form. The image of spring-green and its many parts, a *unity in multeity* as Coleridge put it, is already in me, in my medium, in the world around me everywhere, and even anticipated in the transformative fire of the future. But there is no hurry with a deep image.

I drive through the countryside and walk along old paths. I see how the black-black tree trunks and branches, along with the green-black of firs and pines, is part of the dialectics of the spring green. Now I discern parts of this whole: how the maple in its branching sphere—visually now a circle—is tinged with substantial green only at the edge of its outline; how apple orchards writhe and color differently from cherry and peach orchards and how they bloom on a different schedule; how pear trees pile up their masses of blossoms in the shape of an upright pear; how the oaks hold back or hint at pink and yellow like a mist; how sheep and geese stand forth like baroque pearls on the velvety pasture; how the white-blossomed tree has the sense to appear on the ground of a green hill in front of sap-green leaves behind the black-green firs; how the yielding soft blue of the sky, with the contradictory warm and cool hues of an overglazed corner of a Poussin classical landscape, bounces off the roof of the farmhouse. I see Grandma Moses and Henri Rousseau paintings in all their innocent realism. I hear music and bits of poems. A continuing reverberation has been set up.

It has been said that the artist thinks in material media, but I could as easily say that media think in the artist's life-world. The artist's mind is not just laying cunning traps of *techne*. There is also the *praxis* and *poesis* of the artist in the *polis*—unfettered communication between tradition and the cosmos.

All of this is but the first cycle of the artistic image guiding this spring-pot-medium context. In the next cycle, hand, eye, medium and image become still more subtly interfused as the life world of the art, not the artist, beings to take over. Now spring-greens, brush strokes, scratchings, fusings, spontaneous details and sub-images, and fired transformations of these in the mind's eye begin to arise. Now the art dreams the artist. The present becomes, as Van den Berg[26] puts it, an invitation from out of the future for the conquest of by-gone times. The work becomes personified as a presence with its own political and legal rights—it owns itself, is its own actor, pays its own taxes (or avoids them). At first it is too much; it works its will on me as I was earlier inclined to try to dominate it. But then we back off for another close encounter, will to will, eye to eye, about this image that has fallen between us.

Note that the initial experience and the pervasive image arising from it, and the artistic image, coalesce, and that neither are a general image. It was fed by particulars of experience, medium and tradition. I became aware, for example, that a certain barn had a cross for its floor plan only as I painted and scratched it onto the pot's surface. I sensed at work the reduction that art always works on experience and image as the hills on the sphere took on a life and form different from hills in nature. I folded back trees and shrubs and houses and clusterings of these on the special ground laid down by these hills-on-sphere enclosures.

This is a concrete material imagination at work within a process with a tradition and life of its own. My pots lead a double or even a triple existence. Between forming and firing comes decorating, independent but related. This is what Langer[27] means when she says: "The immediate effect of good decoration is to make the surface, somehow, more visible." More broadly, throwing is decorating, tooling is decorating, decorating is decorating, and firing is decorating. The sphere, especially the sphere wider than high that is lifted up on a sturdy foot hidden in its shadow, is a kinesthetic discipline of the body-mind meditating on the evolution of formative essence from an instinctual attitude toward material—as the British potter Hans Coper[28] put it, "like a demented piano tuner straining for a phantom pitch."

This personal example is meant to particularize our abstract discussion. In all its variations over time, a single qualitative whole was maintained despite all the problems, interruptions and exigencies. A radiating center lit all of these up and accepted them into a continuing unity.

The Material and the Formal Imagination

According to Lipman:

> ...at the core of our response to the intelligible object of art is the response to the brute, unintelligible thing. And similarly in creation, the "instinct of workmanship" is not more primary than the "instinctual" attitude towards the material.[27]

And since we address the brute, unintelligible thing through a material medium as body-dispositions, as minds, as body-minds and as spirits, we implicate all of these as we explicate the *thing*. It therefore turns out that a rhetoric appropriate to the thing is also appropriate to our human condition. According to these characteristics the function of poetry becomes clearer:

> It is to nourish the spirit of man by giving him the cosmos to suckle. We have only to lower our standard of dominating nature and to raise our standard of participating in it in order to make the reconciliation take place. When man becomes proud to be not just the site where ideas and feelings are produced, but also the crossroad where they divide and mingle, he will be ready to be saved. Hope therefore lies in a poetry through which the world so invades the spirit of man that he becomes almost speechless, and later reinvents a language.[28].

When the cosmos nourishes us, when the world invades us, when we become the crossroad or confluence of cosmic energies, then interiorized inspiration will arise from its center in imagination and speak as spirit, as revelation, not through grandious themes but rather the simplest of things. The ends of the great chain will come together: matter into spirit and spirit into matter.

This is what Bachelard calls concrete metaphysics and the material imagination. A distinction needs to be made here between the *formal* and the *material imagination*. Philosophers and aestheticians have paid much attention to formal imagination, because it is more mental and can be described more easily. Novelty, picturesqueness, variety, unexpectedness and the play of free forms—these are the formal imagination's artistic stock-in-trade. The material imagination, however, crosses over to the mute side of the fence: the elements of permanency present in things, those forms sunk deeply *in* a substance, forms given in matter and inseparable from it, and the primordial aspects of the elements and of natural rhythms. These two forms of imagination represent a *yang* and a *yin* principle of aesthetics. The yang principle, the purely formal, more mental and more masculine orientation is in popular ascendency. But we are witnessing a slow shift as the need for a more pervasive feminine consciousness is breaking through.

To repeat, a phenomenology of the material imagination is not one of the mind but of the soul. Starting from the most concrete sources, the art work works through a reverberation which sets up a multiplicity of resonances issuing from that reverberation's unity of being,[31] and just as the poetic image "places us at the origin of the speaking being," so the artistic image places us at the origin of the seeing being, for "...it is at once a becoming of expression, and a becoming of our being. Here expression creates being."[32] We are back to Hegel's grand theme: "Spirit is artist."

Insofar as one can specify, within the confines of the material imagination, this cycle may be said to exist in visual art: image/medium/form/medium/image. In the beginning and at the end is the image—the same and yet not the same image—not as begun but as lived through in its life cycle as a unity within development. In the visual arts the work itself is a *thing*. But it is a thing with both brute thingness and cultural history—that is, as Heidegger[33] would say, that exists as both *earth* and *world*.

A pot, for example, often exists for me as a medium-process-image in relation to some idea-form at its inception, with the instinctual attitude toward the material and its future in the fire at the hand's-mind's-eye as surfaced through the total body-mind: from the physical feel and involvement with wedging (kneading), centering, kicking (the kick wheel), raising and lowering the clay, forming, tooling, etc. When I dig clay from the living earth and use it directly, the process extends still further into mute material origins. Then, as artist-spectator, we experience a similar history in a movement from earth to world to earth to world, i.e., from the brute unintelligible thing into cultural history and novel intelligibility then back into the unintelligible earth again with the element of fire, again into the world as we deploy art-thing and body-mind to relate to one another, whether in home, gallery, museum, or tea-ceremony. Art thus participates in a rhythmic movement in and out of the mute, the silent, the dark into the revealed, the bright, not unlike the reciprocity between conscious and unconscious influences which Jung[34] said characterizes our understanding of the inner image.

Still, I would not want to mislead the reader into thinking that the things of art must be small and commonplace, waiting, as it were, to be irradiated by spirit. Within the poetics of space, as Bachelard explores this theme, we have a range of topics: "the house, from cellar to garret, and the significance of the hut; house and universe; drawers, chests, and wardrobes; nests; shells; corners; miniatures; intimate immensity; the dialectics of outside and inside; and the phenomenology of roundness."[35] Each of these topics is a complex within which are to be found myriad poetic and artistic images. Within intimate immensity, for example, we could extend Bachelard through Taoist landscapes which:

> ...externalise a metaphysic and a contemplative state: they spring, not from space, but from the "void"; their theme is essentially "mountain and water" and with this they combine cosmological and metaphysical aims. Here is one of the most powerfully original forms of sacred art.[36]

In such art the correspondence between the immensity of world space and the depth of inner space is demonstrated, [37] and this correspondence is expressed by a sure interaction between thing-medium-spirit and by the forms organically emerging from the hidden order of art.

The material world and the material imagination exist because the poet and the artist are not locked inside their own body. We earlier quoted Tagore's statement that his way was not one of liberation by detachment from the world. Gnosis comes through love for the artist. While I am working on these abstract topics, even while surrounded by a number of books on improvised shelves, I find it essential to be writing in my pottery studio where pots in various stages, raw clay and the tools of my art are within arm's length. My eye of contemplation must remain connected with the eye of the heart. The artist and the poet engage creative imagination and material imagination simultaneously. The poet's imagination must be free to roam at will everywhere. Listen to Keats' description of himself:

> As to the poetical character itself...it is not like itself—it has no self. It is everything and nothing—it enjoys light and shade; it lives in gusto, be it fair or

foul, high or low, rich or poor, mean or elevated. It has as much delight in conceiving an Iago as an Imogene. What shocks the virtuous philosopher delights the chameleon poet. It does not harm from its relish for the dark side of things, any more than from its taste for the bright one, because they both end in speculation. A poet is the most unpoetical of anything in existence, because he has no identity—he is continually in and for, and filling some other body...When I am in a room with people, if I am ever free from speculations on creations of my own brain, then, not myself goes home to myself, but the identity of every one in the room begins to press upon me, so that I am in a very little time annihilated—not only among men; it would be the same in a nursery of children.[38]

Coleridge and the No Boundary Condition

Lionni[39] has written a delightful book on *Parallel Botany* which, in addition to being a spoof on scientism, is an absorbing adventure with "the plants on the other side of the fence." Here we find plants that keep equidistant from us when we attempt to approach. Others will not register on photographic plates. The humor in this book rests on the mistaken carry-over into an alien domain of attitudes appropriate only within their user's original domain. An epistemological category error is involved.

Wherever boundaries are drawn territorial disputes and skirmishes along the frontiers spring up. A no man's land, a buffer zone, a neutral strip—these are among the ineffective means through which we attempt to solve border disputes. The same problems arise with mental boundaries.[40]

The imagination continually approaches a threshold between what is *self* and what is *not self*, between what is *conscious* and what is *unconscious*, between what is *mind* and what is *matter*. To tell the truth, the imagination is drawn more to the "parallel botany" or strange side of the fence: to the not-self, to the unconscious, to matter. These are almost definers of the concrete imagination. Actually, the artist and the poet work both sides of the fence, largely ignoring it. We who wish to investigate this human power must bring our minds to bear on both sides of the threshold and on the relation between the two sides.[41] Here is a problem because our words are biased to the near side of the fence. Barfield says that "imagination and a faculty of 'double vision' seem...to be almost inseparable."[42] One way out is what Senior's book [43] is about, namely, to take "the way down and out," to move into and through the other side and to seek gnosis through love and risk. This is the artist's and the poet's way. And it is the way we recommend. The way *down* is the way *out* much as a *downer* in depression, foreshadows an *upper.* A death or a self-immolation, a transcendence or a transformation—these are all part of the *way down* that is part of the *way out.* Similarly shamans lie down in a trance and symbolically die before their visions transform them into a new being.

Coleridge provides us with a clue to the problem of boundaries. He says that imagination is charged with preserving a right relation between self and not self, between conscious and unconscious, and between mind and matter. The mind can be rendered intuitive of the indwelling spirit.[44] To Coleridge this is a form of knowledge won only with the help of the imagination. This he called *superindividual reason* (which we would call *transpersonal consciousness*), which is also the unconscious. The term *unconscious* remains a problem. What we call *unconscious* is nevertheless something which can be revealed and even known, but not at the time by the person for whom it exists as unconscious.[45] What is important here is that a transfer can be effected from the unknowable to something specifically knowable through this special intuition. For this, nothing short of the imaginative disciplines of art or the meditative disciplines of the East would seem to qualify.

Coleridge's insight is that there is a *telos* or a goal to consciousness which transcends the boundary conditions experienced everywhere. This consciousness is already there intuitively, ready to transcend our mental-egoic hang-ups. The artist yearns for pure imagination and lives within the hidden order of art.

Analogies, Archetypes, Images, and Visions

Visionary artists not only repudiate single vision in favor of twofold, but they also urge us on toward threefold and fourfold vision. This creates a new visionary hierarchy. We could say facetiously that single vision will get us to Tokyo and back, but fourfold vision will get us to eternity and back. Blake himself, when asked whether he did not see something round like a coin when looking at the sun, replied: "Oh no, no, no, but an immeasurable Company of the Heavenly Host crying Holy, Holy, Holy is the Lord God Almight." This sure shows that Blake took his imagination seriously!

If we look at the art of our time coldly, we find efforts to self-consciously approach four-fold vision surprisingly unconvincing, but still many people would rather see Hollywood extras walking about in white robes enacting poorly constructed Biblical narratives than come face to face with some of the greatest religious art of the West. Likewise, the visual art that often appears around meditation centers seems like pale renderings of visions *never seen*. And certainly not as revelation. In fact, apart from an inspired teacher, roshi or swami in residence, the scriptures themselves often fall silent. I am reminded of Swami Rama's insistence to his initiates that actual experience is much greater than the scriptures.[46]

Lowes, in his fascinating work *The Road to Xanadu*,[47] draws some conclusions from his detailed study of Coleridge. These he means to apply to imaginative life and creation generally. *Chaos* and *the deep well* precede the poet's work of forming. The deep *well* figuratively symbolizes that the chaos of images, memories and associations, odd bits and tatters from everywhere and everytime can be stored and even fed by clear filtering springs. When imaginative creation occurs three factors reciprocally interplay: the *well*, the *vision*, and the *will*.

> Without the Vision, the chaos of elements remains a chaos, and the Form sleeps forever in the vast chambers of unborn designs. Yet in that chaos only could creative Vision ever see this Form. Nor without the cooperant Will, obedient to the Vision, may the pattern perceived in the huddle attain objective reality. Yet manifold through the ways of the creative faculty may be, the upshot is one; from the empire of chaos a new trait of cosmos has been retrieved; a nebula has been compacted—it may be!—into a star.[48]

Again the thesis argued by Senior[49] that "the way down is the way out" is partially supported by Lowes. We say partially because it is *vision* and *will* that brings forth *form* from chaos and the *well*. The pivotal force of the triad is *vision*, the mediator between the *well* and the *will*. What is this visionary power that can bring back a real flower from a dreamt image? And does this *vision* operate on a hierarchical scale?

Perhaps the eventuating forms can provide an answer. But form, even when appearing as a new star, bears its unique history within it—*that* chaos into *this* form. In his work on *The Life of Forms in Art*, Focillon[50] does follow a kind of organizational hierarchy. First he explores the realm of space, then that of matter, followed by mind and time. He moves from the palpable and substantial to the rarefied and immaterial. But as artists we cannot say that this is a spiritual advance. In fact for our time we could more cogently argue the opposite. Locked in the mental, we really are "out of touch."

Bachelard likewise roughly leads us in his *Poetics of Space*[51] from the close and tiny to the immense and abstract—from The House, Nests, Shells, etc. to Intimate Immensity, The Dialectics of Outside and Inside, and the Phenomenology of Roundness. Even more insightful is the route vision takes in a later book, *The Poetics of Reverie.*[52] Here he begins with Reveries on Reverie. First, he speaks as a *Word Dreamer*, then he picks up *Archetypes* (animus-anima). Following these, he unfolds *Reveries toward Childhood* and, after an excursion into the special *Cogito of the Dreamer*, ends with *Reverie and Cosmos.*

Here we have more substance to argue for a kind of spiritual triangle, like Kandinsky,[53] the apex of which is the most rarified and spiritual, the base the most accessible and popular. But we wonder then whether we have not inherited again the mentalistic twist of the philosophical imagination as opposed to the creative and artistic imagination. In like manner, for all Scheler's[54] sensitivity to forms of sympathy and love, we cannot follow him in his hierarchies because he moves from an ethics where vital love is not honored as equal to cultural, cosmic and metaphysical love.

Perhaps we fall back once more to the differing perspectives between the way of love and gnosis. The gnostic is a believer of triangles and aspires to stand at their apex. The follower of the way of love finds the apex everywhere—and again we come upon the horizontal extensionality of art as opposed to the verticality of spiritual science. Vision, then, could be seen in art, as operant at any point or level of the triangle, the whole of which is Spirit.

We have here two usages of vision. Vision[1] is artistic vision generally, that which mediates between *well* and *will* to create *form*. Vision[2] is the vision of the visionary, the fourfold vision which penetrates eternity. Our thought remains confounded nevertheless, and our intuition moves toward paradoxical speech. Then the *way down* appears as not only the *way out* but the *way up*. And indeed this is our general thesis. It is not a matter of primary and secondary processes or of regression in the service of the ego. But rather "Spirit as artist" gives the means for expanding our consciousness through the creation and knowledge of what is other.

In *I and Thou* Buber[55] gives an example of dialogue that is an encounter with a tree. The tree it turns out can be approached through any mode of vision—onefold to fourfold—and seen in all its complexity as "its form and its mechanics, its color and its chemistry, its conversation with the elements and its conversation with the stars." Further, no suppression of one for the other is necessary. "There is nothing that I must not see in order to see, and there is no knowledge that I must forget."

> But it can also happen, if will and grace are joined, that as I contemplate the tree I am drawn into a relation, and the tree ceases to be an it. The power of exclusiveness has seized me...The tree is no impression, no play of my imagination, no aspect of a mood; it confronts me bodily and has to deal with me as I must deal with it—only differently. One shoul not try to dilute the meaning of the relation: relation is reciprocity.[56]

Here we see how artistic vision operates over the entire spectrum, from analogy to the vision of visionaries. This varying radiating quality that characterizes the image is that necessary ingredient upon which artistic freedom is based. As Lowenfeld was fond of saying: "It is not the subject matter but our relationship to the subject matter that changes.[57]

We could hazard the guess that as art more closely serves gnosis and religion then it is inclined to interpose some hierarchical notion of spirit. Purely in terms of subject matter an oyster is as good as a crucifixion; purely in terms of imagery a surface decoration as good as a *yantra*; for all art is spiritual, all art is like a yantra for the eye of contemplation and for direct spiritual intuition.

But the very material of art permits its easy annexation into spiritual and mental hierarchies. Artists have played at such reasoning as well. Consider a few passages from Kandinsky:

> ...white...is a symbol of world from which all colors as material attributes have disappeared. This world is too far above us for its structure to touch our souls. There comes a great silence which materially represented is like a cold, indestructible wall going on into the infinite. White, therefore, acts upon our psyche as a great, absolute silence, like the pauses in music that temporarily break the melody. It is not a dead silence, but one pregant with possibilities. White has the appeal of the nothingness that is before birth, of the world in the ice age.[58]

Kandinsky gives similar symbolic interpretations of black and of all the colors. Light warm red for example, "is a sound of trumpets, strong, harsh and ringing," whereas a cool, light red "contains a very distinct bodily or material element, but it is always pure, like the fresh beauty of a young girl's face. The singing notes of a violin exactly express this in music."[59] And, to make the connection to our topic still more manifest, consider this, also from Kandinsky:

> As in a great circle, a serpent biting its own tail (the symbol of eternity, of something without end), appear the six colors that make up the three main antitheses. And to the right and left stand the two great possibilities of silence—death and birth.[60]

Kandinsky is a visionary artist writing *concerning the spiritual in art.*

Writers on esoteric disciplines make similar claims, showing for example, how in symbolism, poetry, music and art certain objects, sound and colors correspond to certain inner states.[61] The holy mantra *OM* is said to be a seed sound containing all sounds much as white light contains all colors. In its sounding as *AUM*, the *A* signifies the outer world, the *U* the inner, and the *M* their oneness.

And to be fair to the great traditions of spiritual science, the leftist branch of Tantra yoga even acknowledges that there can be a way down and out and up. Here the eating of meat, the drinking of alcohol, and sexual relationships are part of self-exploration and spiritual development.[62] A late Indian guru even went against tradition by offering as a meditative discipline what he called *chaotic meditation* which:

> ...consists of five ten minute stages. The first is deep, fast, chaotic breathing to awaken the energy within. The second stage is a catharsis, a release of suppressions that have been made conscious by the breathing process. This is followed by a third stage: the vigorous repetition of the sound *hoo*, a sound that strikes the sex center and moves the energy upward. Then, ten or fifteen minutes of silence and stillness (the meditation); and ten or fifteen minutes of celebration, expressing the bliss that has been felt in the fourth stage, and, in gratitude, returning it to the universe.[63]

It is generally held however, that higher levels depend on the successful exploration and integration of infantile identifications, of primary processes, and of the personal unconscius. A *living through* is implied. This is equivalent to Emerson's advice to "give all to love" but to be prepared to learn that "when the half-gods go, the true gods arrive."[64] Existentially the artist will always dance away, for the artist's way is rarely ascetic, but rather ritualistic, magical or spontaneous.

Thus we cannot consign what has been called *vision-imagery* merely to a transformational role which leads from the mental-egoic and the personal to the transpersonal through integration of body-mind which dimly grasps its organic relatedness to the universe.[65] This is indeed a role which vision-imagery *can* serve, but it is not its only or even primary role. Here vision-imagery is linked more narrowly with imaginative processes which are stirred up and refracted before they subside again into their true origin as white light.

To spiritual adepts, the state of vision-imagery is a noisy one. *Vision* for them is not the mediator between the chaos of the *well* and the *will* that leads toward *form* as *revelation*. Rather it is on the way toward the formless silence, the white light of pure consciousness. Physiologically this is the Alpha-Theta brain wave state, that image-filled space between practical and conventionalized Beta thinking and non-conscious or deep sleep. Somewhere in this center state we also make contact with the regulative wellness function ascribed in general to meditation and positive imagery. As Elmer Green of the Menninger Clinic puts it: "It seems increasingly certain that healing and creativity are different pieces of a single picture."[66] His research offers further verification of the clear imagery associated with Theta waves. He says:

> Pictures or ideas...spring full-blown into consciousness without the person being aware of their creation. The Theta reverie, as we began to call it, was definitely different from a daydreaming state, and much to our surprise, it seemed to correspond with descriptions given by geniuses of the past of the state of consciousness they experienced while being their most creative.[67]

What is fascinating here is the insight that the artist does not go from this state directly to *the silence* but to the dislogue between *vision* and *will* that produces *form. The radical newness of a created form may be for the artist indeed what Samadhi is for the spiritual adept.* To wrest form out of nature and self is not easy. Like the physical mother the artist brings forth newness through his or her own body and life-world. The artist's role is revelation as surely as is the saint's.

The saint is God-like, withdrawing into the Holy of Holies. The artist is Christ-like, moving through love into incarnation. Otherwise, both are the same, as regards Revelation. In the artist, a devolution or involution is implicated, the function of which, however, is just as surely the evolution of our consciousness as is any other path. It is the creators of myths, the poets, who play the role of the greatest importance in the moral universe, since they bind the universal dead illusion to the universal illusion which is being born through a chain of personal illusions to which they consent to sacrifice their rest.[68]

Image-Work and Self-Work

Much of Jung's work was devoted to the study of the relationship between imagery and *individuation*, the term he used for the process of psychological development. He discovered: "first, that images serve to compensate for the limited perspective of our conscious awareness; second, that there is a patterned series of images which parallel the individuation process; third, that cultivating and attending to these images can facilitate the process of individuation."[69] His first discovery points to our general conclusion concerning the imagination, namely, that it does not honor the boundaries drawn by ego or culture. His second finding is also supportive of our view, for images tend to progress from analogies to archetypes to symbols of unification, and this is precisely the visual path which corresponds to the process of individuation. The third point says what this section discusses: *image-work is also self-work.*

Jung also developed a hermeneutic treatment or method for helping his clients find meaning and direction from their imaginative work.

> Hermeneutic treatment of imaginative ideas leads to the synthesis of the individual and the collective psyche...As soon as ever we begin to map out the lines of advance that are symbolically indicated, the patient must begin to proceed along them...He is in truth obliged to take the way of individual life which is revealed to him, and to persist in it until and unless an unmistakable reaction from his unconscious warns him that he is on the wrong track.[70]

How this is done is also spelled out by Jung. His explanatory approach "...consists in making successive additions of other analogies to the analogy given in the symbol."[71] Apparently the first analogy or interpretation is to be given by the patient. Then the analyst and patient together search for objective analogies in the history of symbols and archetypes. He cautions: "Even the best attempts at explanation are only more or less successful translations into another metaphorical language...the most we can do is dream the myth onwards and give it a modern dress."[72]

Though Jung worked with literary and artistic productions of his patients, he mostly concentrated on the *dream series*, treating it much as we treated the *artistic serial* in the Drawing Lab. Important in the present discussion as well is Jung's sensitivity to his patient's own imaginative productions and dreams as possible clues from the unconscious that the patient is on the wrong track. In other words, interpretations are *reductions* only by way of *extensions*, that is, by gathering together symbols, analogies, archetypes and images meaningful to the patient. Images, in short, are approachable only through admiration, dreaming observation, and a kind of symbolic contagion, for what is involved in the relationship between image-work and self-work is a translation across unnecessary barriers in order that integration and transformation may occur. Bachelard confirms that this effect is not limited to Jungian analysis. In using the phenomenological method to examine poetic images, Bachelard says, "...it has seemed to us that we were being automatically psychoanalyzed."[74]

The idea of othering the self through the other of the work of imagination runs like a thread through Bachelard's writings:

> Poetic reverie gives us the world of worlds. Poetic reverie is a cosmic reverie. It is an opening to a beautiful world, to beautiful worlds. It gives the I a non-I which belongs to the I: my non-I. It is this "my non-I" which enchants the I of the dreamer and which poets help us share. For my "I-dreamer" it is this "my non-I" which lets me live my secret of being in the world.[74]

It is because poetic reverie is self-directed and creative that its force is augmentative and self-formative. Poetic reverie operates opposite the reality function through what Bachelard calls an essential "...irreality function which keeps the human psyche on the fringe of all the brutality of a hostile and foreign non-self."[75] An evolution in a spiritual direction is also implied by both Jung and Bachelard. For Bachelard: "Reverie sacralizes its object. From the beloved familiar object to the sacred personal object is only a step. Soon the object is an amulet which protects us in life."[76]

Archetypes are symbolic personifications and messengers from the silent side of self and cosmos and are directly evoked in image work:

> ...the being projected by our reverie – for our I-dreamer is a projected being – is double as we ourselves are, and is, like ourselves, *animus* and *anima*. Here we are at the knot of all our paradoxes: the "*double*" is the double of a double being...In order to analyze all the psychological potentialities offered to the solitary person in reverie, it will be necessary to start then from the motto: I am alone, so there are four of us. The solitary dreamer copes with quadripolar situations...The idealized being starts talking with the idealizing being. He talks as a function of his own duality. A concert for four voices begins in the reverie of the solitary dreamer.[77]

Bachelard extends through his phenomenology of the imagination the work of Coleridge and Jung, thus in the present context making it more possible to dream the self-formative myth onward. What is pertinent to our present and following discussions is that he finds this image work best studied and centered in the *material imagination* and in a *concrete metaphysics*.

Art as image-work, directly or indirectly intended, can indeed mesh nicely into self-work schedules and specific therapies. It can be put to such usages insofar as it is *whole art*, for under a non-differentiated aesthetic art-life connections maintain their organic relationship to whatever else the art work does and can signify. Art can, for example, help with integrating the *shadow* (or repressed parts of the self) with ego, with integrating body and mind, with integrating body-mind with the universe, and with integrating the self with the Self or with superconsciousness. It can do so because all of these applications demand a transformation from a lower to a higher level of consciousness through the breaking of unnecessary boundaries or illusions set up within the self by the self.[78] Art can do this by giving symbolic form to what consciousness only dimly perceives as the next necessary step forward. Spirit here is indeed artist, for in *othering* itself consciousness can heal itself, knowing and understanding itself in terms of its own evolution. It can play harmoniously across all the therapies, since these therapies need not be seen as contradictory but as appropriate to the different stages and problems of consciousness to which they are addressed.[79] To use Lowes' terms,[80] it could be said that *vision* and *will* can consign a specific art event to such therapeutic roles, but the *well* and the *form* remain free and greater than any context to which they may be temporarily related. If our identifications do not become frozen, *vision* and *will* will forever find new *form* issuing from the *well*. The mystery is that the universe can symbolically arise out of the individual *well*.

Summary. We began our discussion of the concrete imagination with a commentary on the decline of vision in our times, also tracing the shift in the locus of inspiration to within, interiorized under the guidance of the imagination. Imagination itself is a holistic mobile phenomenon which assimilates all it touches into its one grand pervasive quality. As such, imagination is also claimed to be language of the total self. Bachelard, whom we present as a phenomenologist of the imagination and also as a poetic gnostic, insists that our very perception is imaginative. Dwelling close to images themselves, Bachelard resists any attempts to summarize his thoughts, for he works through direct example, through contagion, admiration, and dreaming observation. He himself insists on the complete separation of image from concept. One cannot come to conclusions with images for comparisons fail and psychologizing sends them flying. His is a phenomenology of poetic transcendelia given to consciousness for the direct intuitive apprehension of spirit. Still, he says, the self is revealed to the self through poetic image and poetic reverie, so that his work takes on the form of poetic gnosticism. Bachelard's reasoning bears kinship to anagogy, as an inspired and mysterious interpretation of "sacred" texts. The image is an absolute origin of consciousness for him. It reveals itself through a life of shifting change, through variations around a single qualitative base, or by radiation from a dynamic center. This means that we can take flight with an image or bask in the warmth of its radiating light. While Bachelard specializes in the fleeting and dancing quality of images, an artistic image guiding creation can be sustained over great time periods and changing external conditions.

There is a clear distinction between the formal and the material imagination. In the latter, more *anima* inspired kind, we lower or evade the boundaries between self and nature. The things which nourish us can be as miniscule as thimbles, boxes, nests and shells. They can be as grand as deserts and oceans, or as artistically elemental as Taoist landscapes. The artist's path to gnosis is through love for all the cosmos, its 10,000 things *and* the void.

It was Coleridge who clearly explored the role of the creative imagination in transcending the inherited boundaries between self and other, conscious and unconscious, and mind and matter. By a special imaginative intuition consciousness can transcend these boundary conditions to apprehend the spiritual.

The question remains whether vision is hierarchical in nature. It is possible that those who think on such topics—whether it be varieties of love or religious experience, forms in art, or the poetics of space and reverie—fall into a discursive inheritance of pseudologic which rank orders the varius kinds of visions by some grand conceptual dimension. We can make some sense of hierarchical schemes if we follow Kandinsky's analogy of a spiritual triangle where he moves from a popular base to a rarified apex; but a suspicion creeps in that he has merely shifted from creative imagination to philosophical imagination and that qualitatively and experientially the claim would become less certain.

We suspect that the difference again is between the way of love and the way of gnosis. Art is an engagement on the path of love, though it indirectly serves gnosis. Art is a chameleon. As it more closely serves religion, gnosis and spiritual science, it *appears* to be more hierarchical. But in fact we are more likely speaking of cabbages and Kings and of their potential imaginative equality.

Much the same can be said for the fascinating linkages between image-work and self-work: they are possible and under certain conditions more than likely, but they are not necessary. Expressive therapy through art, therefore, remains broader than any of the uses to which it may be put. To be sure, through Jung's hermeneutic extension of the symbols of image-work, and Bachelard's four voices in the reverie of the solitary dreamer, we have the opportunity to establish important relationships between image-work, life-world, and self-work.

Now it is time to thicken up our description of the role played in art by the things themselves.

References

1. Coleridge, S. T. Quoted in Lowes, J. L. *The road to Xanadu*, N.Y.: Houghton Mifflin, 1930.

2. Bachelard, G. *The poetics of reverie.* (D. Russell, trans.) Boston: Beacon Press, 1971.

3. Roszak, T. *Person/planet.* N.Y.: Anchor Press, 1979.

4. Barfield, O. Imagination and inspiration. In Hopper, S. R., and Miller, D. L. (Eds.). *Interpretation: The poetry of meaning.* N.Y.: Harcourt, Brace & World, 1967; pp. 54-76; p. 74.

5. *Ibid.*, p. 75.

6. Jaynes, J. *The origin of consciousness in the breakdown of the bicameral mind.* Boston: Houghton Mifflin, 1976.

7. Roszak, T. *Person/planet.* N.Y.: Anchor Press, 1979.

8. Collingwood, R. G. *The idea of history.* N.Y.: Oxford University Press, 1946; p. 314.

9. Collingwood, R. G. *The principles of art.* London: Oxford University Press, 1958; pp. 252-253.

10. Pepper, S. C. *Concept and quality.* La Salle, Illinois: Open Court Publishing Co., 1966; p. 356.

11. May, Rollo. *Love and will.* N.Y.: Norton, 1969.

12. Jung, C. G. *The basic writings of C. G. Jung.* (V. 5, De Laszlo, ed.) N.Y.: Modern Library, 1953.

13. Lipman, M. *What happens in art.* N.Y.: Appleton-Century-Crofts, 1967; p. 52.

14. *Ibid,* p. 52.

15. Wilber, K. The problem of proof. *ReVision*, 5 (1), Spring 1982, pp. 80-100; p. 94.

16. Bachelard G. *Op. cit.*, reference 2 above, p. 53.

17. *Ibid.*, p. 52.

18. *Ibid.*, p. 53.

19. *Ibid.*, p. 69.

20. Dewey, J. *Art as experience.* N.Y.: Minton, Balch, 1934.

21. Bachelard, G. *The poetics of space.* (M. Jolas, trans.) Boston: Beacon Press, 1969; p. xxx.

22. *Ibid.*, p. xxv.

23. *Ibid.*, p. xv.

24. Langer, S. K. *Mind: An essay on human feeling.* Baltimore: The John Hopkins University Press, 1967.

25. Bachelard, G. *Op. cit.*, reference 21 above, p. xviii.

26. Van den Berg, J. H. *A different existence.* Pittsburgh: Duquesne University Press, 1972; pp. 91-92.

27. Langer, S. K. *Feeling and form.* N.Y.: Charles Scribner's Sons, 1953; p. 208.

28. Coper, H. *Collingwood/Coper.* Catalogue for joint exhibition. London: Victoria and Albert Museum, 1969.

29. Lipman, M. *Op. cit.,* reference 13 above, p. 66.

30. Ponge, F. *The voice of things.* (B. Archer, trans.) N.Y.: McGraw-Hill, 1972, p. 109.

31. Bachelard, G. *Op. cit.,* reference 21 above, p. xix.

32. *Ibid.,* p. xix.

33. Heidegger, M. *Poetry, language, thought.* N.Y.: Harper & Row, 1971.

34. Jung, C. G. *Op. cit.,* reference 12 above.

35. Bachelard, G. *Op. cit.,* reference 21 above, Table of Contents.

36. Schuon, F. *Language of thought.* (M. Pallis, M. Matheson, trans.) Madras: Ganesh & Co., 1959, p. 116.

37. Bachelard, G. *Op. cit.,* reference 21 above, p. 205.

38. Dewey, J. *Op. cit.,* reference 20 above, quoted on p. 257.

39. Lionni, L. (P. Creagh, trans.) *Parallel botany.* N.Y.: Knopf, 1977.

40. Wilber, K. *No boundary.* Los Angeles: Center Publications, 1979.

41. Barfield, O. *Op. cit.,* reference 4 above, p. 67.

42. *Ibid.,* p. 68.

43. Senior, J. *The way down and out.* N.Y.: Greenwood Press, 1968.

44. Barfield, O. *Op. cit.,* reference 4 above, quoted on p. 71.

45. Van den Berg, J. H. *Op. cit.,* reference 26 above.

46. Swami Rama and Swami Ajaya. *Emotion to enlightenment.* Honesdale, Pa.: Himalayan Institute of Yoga Science and Philosophy, 1976; p. 53.

47. Lowes, J. L. *The road to Xanadu.* N.Y.: Houghton Mifflin, 1930.

48. *Ibid.,* p. 432.

49. Senior, J. *Op. cit.,* reference 43 above.

50. Focillon, H. *The life of forms in art.* (C.B. Hogan, and A. Kubler, trans.) New Haven; Yale University Press, 1942.

51. Bachelard, G. *Op. cit.,* reference 21 above.

52. Bachelard, G. *Op. cit.,* reference 2 above.

53. Kandinsky, W. *Concerning the spiritual in art.* N.Y.: Wittenborn, 1955; p. 27.

54. Scheler, M. *The nature of sympathy. Hamden, Connecticut: Archon Books, 1970.*

55. *Buber, M. I and thou.* (W. Kaufman, trans.) N.Y.: Charles Scribner's Sons, 1970; p. 58.

56. *Ibid.*, p. 58.

57. Lowenfeld, V. *Creative and mental growth.* N.Y.: Macmillan, 1947.

58. Kandinsky, W. *Op. cit.*, reference 53 above, pp. 59-60.

59. *Ibid.*, p. 63.

60. *Ibid.*, p. 63.

61. Swami Rama; Ballentine, R. and Swami Ajaya. *Yoga and psychotherapy.* Glenview, Ill.: Himalayan Institute, 1976; p. 225.

62. *Ibid.*, p. 235.

63. Bhagwam Shree Rajneesh. *Meditation: The art of ecstasy.* N.Y.: Harper & Row, 1976.

64. Emerson, R. W. (E. L. Masters, ed.) *The living thoughts of Emerson,* N.Y.: Longmans, Green, 1940; p. 157.

65. Wilber, K. *The Atman project.* Wheaton, Ill.: Theosophical Publishing House, 1980; pp. 144-147.

66. Stearn, J. *The power of alpha-thinking.* N.Y.: Signet Books, 1977; p. 143.

67. *Ibid.*, p. 138.

68. Faure, E. *History of art. Vol. V The spirit of forms.* (W. Pach, trans.) N.Y.: Harper & Brothers, 1930; p. 473.

69. Battista, J. R. *Images of individuation: A Jungian approach to the psychology of imagery. ReVision, 3* (1), Spring 1980, pp. 3-11; p. 3.

70. Philipson, M. *Outline of a Jungian aesthetics.* Champaign: Northwestern University Press, 1963; quoted on p. 66.

71. *Ibid.*, p. 65.

72. *Ibid.*, p. 62.

73. Bachelard, G. *Op. cit.*, reference 2 above, p. 3.

74. *Ibid.*, p. 13.

75. *Ibid.*, p. 13.

76. *Ibid.*, p. 36.

77. *Ibid.*, p. 80-81.

78. Wilber, K. *Op. cit.*, reference 40 above.

79. Wilber, K. *The spectrum of consciousness.* Wheaton, Ill.: The Theosophical Publishing House, 1977.

80. Lowes, J. L. *Op. cit.*, reference 47 above.

5

The Thick of the Matter

O infinite resources of the thickness of things, brought out by the infinite resources of the semantical thickness of words.

Francis Ponge

The Politics of Things

We come now directly to the thing: to *matter*, which in the diagram of the great chain of being lies closest to spirit. It might not be so bad that we humans have been "thingafied" by modern life, were it not for the fact that the statement reveals our low notion of things, how they have become disenfranchised bits of a fractioned universe.

Standing still, walking, running, cycling, driving, flying, rocketing—here is a continum that progressively blurs all things, much as an additive color wheel spins and fuses the separate particles into a single hue. How do we position ourselves anymore to see a sunset, here and now, apart from the travel brochure, apart from the tour which already turns places into pictures in a book?

What is lacking, said Whitehead,[1] is an *immediate apprehension of a variety of vivid values with a minimum of eviscerating analysis.* Such an appreciative grasp of what is unified and whole, he felt, might well underlie social progress itself. Where and how do we contact the silent world which Ponge[2] thinks is our only homeland? The ascetic spiritual path seems more and more appealing, burned out as we are in body and mind, beset by too many blurred and manufactured pseudo-things. The quieter path of gnosis toward bliss consciousness seems more and more like a drop-out's way *up* and *out*, away from the cacophony of unloved and unknown things and from thoughts and images not even our own.

If we cannot *feel* and *sense* things, what is being said will seem like romantic non-sense. In our great technological and commercial rage to control everything toward some adstract and predetermined end, we consign things and humans to a great *standing reserve*, as Heidegger[3] called it, waiting for processing—whether current or projected.

I am reminded of a story told by a therapist who daringly made contact with a catatonic schizophrenic who was in the habit of endlessly propelling his arms. The therapist suddenly thrust a large lump of clay into the catatonic's hand. The tangible reality of wet clay threw off his kinaesthetic balance to such an extent that he forgot his withdrawal behavior long enough to examine the clay and even make something with it.

So might one of our contemporaries be thrown off-balance by a real encounter with a "thing" during the usual course of conditioned daily routine. Many of us know summer mostly through the medium of the power lawn mower, which takes away the grassiness of grass in exchange for a socially approved green uniformity. We rarely see grass high enough to dream on its soft mysterious edges that shift between sun and shade. Ordinary grasses will bloom and seed and grow five or more feet high—on undeveloped land, that is.

It has often been said that our brain has three levels—a hindbrain or serpentine brain; a midbrain or animal brain; and a cerebral cortex[4]—and that these correspond to successive stages of our evolution. Even our recent brain has hemispheres which differentially function, the left linearly more like a digital computer and the right more intuitively like an analog computer.[5] All of these brain functions remain with us even though culture conspires against some of them and even though thinking of some of them makes us uneasy, as though fearful of some dire regression.

> ...art is perhaps a product of the archaic part of our nature and may retain its vitality only as it draws its sustenance there and only as we ourselves maintain some tie to that part of us.[6]

If this is so, when we are out of touch with matter and nature, with the feminine and the unconscious, we have then removed ourselves from imagination and inspiration—that is from art itself.

Advanced physics, in disintegrating things into wavicles and particles, in doing away with the separation of space and time, in equating mass with energy, and in showing that the observer is actually a participant, has shaken any certainty we might have had about appearance and perception. The effect has been to still further lock us into the Cartesian split between self and nature, subject and object. We dwell on our perceptions as purely subjective, as locked within the self and body. Thus we accept with a vengeance Kant's statement that we cannot know things in themselves—to the degree that we do not know things at all.

Stepping within the thickness of matter, we will not have to wear wide gum boots like the senile physicist who was afraid he would fall through matter. We may even be surprised to find that the path to salvation lies in a *reversal* of the proposed hierarchies of vision—in a return to the innocence of single vision. This is the way out of Newton's dilemma into a poetic and imaginative universe where things again gain the right to free speech.

Blake could scarcely repress twofold vision:

> For double the vision my Eyes do see,
> And a double vision is always with me.
> With my inward Eye, 'tis an old Man grey,
> With my outward, a Thistle across my way.[7]

But it now seems too hasty and overly poetic to call a thistle "an old Man grey." Does not this rob the thistle of its proper rights, its dignity? A reverse sentiment sets in here. Today fourfold vision may require a renewed single vision. This lets evolution unwind as involution so that matter and world can be in-spirited again. In each moment, with each breath.

Perhaps these two views are one. Anti-symbolists hold out against too easy an extension into the hermeneutics of symbols, claiming that we will be overwhelmed by dead sentiment. We live in the present, says Laing, in terms of the past. "Sometimes it seems that it is not possible to do more than reflect the decay around and within us, than sing sad and bitter songs of disillusion and defeat."[8] This view reflects tired resignation and points to a crisis of will and imagination. "The needs of the planet are the needs of the person. The rights of the person are the rights of the planet."[9]

With all respect to Blake, let us give the thistle its due. *Things* are never what they *seem*. With Bachelard we can say that perception is imaginative. We can also say that it is phenomenological in that a pre-reflective, *natural* attitude is necessary. As Heidegger and Gadamer would insist, we cannot bracket out our historical consciousness nor our linguisticality.[10] Then face to face with the thistle we can recover an optimistic present. We can then see the moment "as an invitation from out of the future to conquer bygone times."[11] If we allow the thistle to speak and if we can listen to what it says we will find originary speech and fresh imagery within us. *Art then becomes a discipline in unknowing. Revelation then comes out of the hidden order of art.*

> If God created things by naming them, it is rather by taking their name away or by giving them a new one that the artist re-creates them.[12]

The Japanese traditional house blends natural materials and hand work into a harmonious setting where clean lines and quiet spaces permit nature and dwelling to flow together. But behind the Shoji screen nowadays are piles of "world things" in the line of "conspicuous consumption"—Yves St. Laurent, Givenchy, Pierre Cardin and Christian Dior. And the signed box lid seems more important than the contents of the box. What is inside has shrivelled into a formal nod in the direction of the original, for the name's sake. Were he now alive, Basho would brush in some angry haikus on the departure of the "thing gods" from the Japanese landscape. The "things" of unknown craftsmen are disappearing. Tokyo entrepreneurs buy up sight unseen the entire contents of wood-fired kilns in the little mountain pottery village of Onda. So it is that the honest and simple pickling, miso and grain jars made there are excised from their cultural meaning.

> Real singing is a different breath. A breath for nothing.
> A wafting in the god. A wind.[13]

An art work as an honest thing of earth and world comes from and can return us to the things themselves. What happens when an art work is placed back in nature? What are the reciprocal influences? As a potter I have often felt that a good pot should seem equally at home in nature and in the museum—if anything is *at home* in a museum. Wallace Stevens beautifully symbolizes this reciprocity in his *Anecodote of the Jar.*

> I placed a jar in Tennessee,
> And round it was, upon a hill.
> It made the slovenly wilderness
> Surround that hill.
>
> The wilderness rose up to it,
> And sprawled around, no longer wild.
> The jar was round upon the ground
> And tall and of a port in air.

> It took dominion everywhere.
> The jar was gray and bare.
> It did not give of bird or bush,
> Like nothing else in Tennessee.[14]

The work of art lets "that which shows itself be seen from itself in the very way in which it shows itself from itself."[15] Returning the jar of an unknown potter to the landscape, we may also see things in nature in the very way in which they show themselves from themselves. This is single vision comparable to that one-pointed concentration which cancels out the figure-groundness of the universe, letting it come forward as an unbroken unity. To do this requires a kind of slaying of our cultural inheritance but without stepping outside our tradition. What it takes is more like the conquest of bygone times through full and innocent immersion in the eternal qualitative present. As no longer alienated, we will no longer be aliens.

Imagination, then, allows the thing to speak without the interfering and clamoring *I*. Instead of taking the thing as object, the thing takes *us* as object. Now both I and the thing occur as one event. And then something like reciprocity occurs. For though the thing speaks, *language* is ours, so a forgotten voice situated somewhere in between is heard again.

The contemporary poet Robert Bly asks again and again: "how much consciousness is the poet willing to grant to trees or hills or living creatures not a part of his own species?"[16] We live in a time, he says, when we place emphasis on perception—"what Kant calls the noumena—rather than on the object that has drawn forth the perception."[17] Rilke wrote a poem which urges us "to leave the house," that is, to depart from our locked-in perception. "Rilke's poem says that if you make the effort to see one tree, you've essentially granted the whole world its being."[18] Where this fails, we have the *past-dominated, I-fixated poem*, the locked-in perceptions which imprison sexual and spiritual energy within the body. To Bly, consciousness is meant to be a "desire energy" that metaphorically shoots out from the eyes.[19]

One of Ponge's major books *Le Parti Pris des Choses*, roughly translated as "taking the side of things," has a double meaning: "(1) the poet's option for things over ideas, and (2) the will expressed by the things themselves."[20] On the will expressed by things themselves, Beth Archer says:

> Snails, trees, flowers, pebbles, the sea, all express an indomitable will, a striving for self-perfection, a single-minded purpose, that assumes heroic proportions combining the excesses and self-mastery characteristic of the noblest of mythological heroes. The wrathful fury of a Hercules or an Ajax is echoed by the tree's rage for expression as it floods the world with more and more leaves, the snail's proud drivel that remains stamped on everything, the rose's excessive petals, the shrimp's persistent return to the same places. Yet in their weakness, their extravagent expressions of self, lie the makings of their greatness...Conquering the apparent futility of their acts, their vulnerability, their mortality, by continuing their efforts, they brave destiny by becoming more of what they are.[21]

Ponge, himself, is less high-sounding:

> Merely by wanting to account for the *total content of ideas* about them, I am drawn *by objects* away from traditional humanism, away from current man, and drawn ahead of him. I add to man the new qualities I name.
>> There you have *Taking the Side of Things*.
>> *Taking Account of Words* does the rest.[22]

By renaming the world and adding the new qualities that are named, we become directly involved with the politics of things. We move away from a tired humanism toward a new poetic Genesis where the world again acts as a nurturant mother. Spirit and matter meet. The ends of the chain join. The *well* is not just the human unconscious but the collective unconscious. For if our consciousness is one with the universe, then our unconscious must also be one with the universe. Then we and things are one, whether in concealment or in revelation.

Matters of Import

How shall I name the things of earth and sky anew? The only way is to speak through poetic fragments or as a poet myself.

It is mid-July now. If I go to a favorite field or a nearby woods, I can *experience* what I need to express. Once I am there, nature, weather and I interfuse. Indeed I seem like only the confluence of natural forces. Consider Van den Berg's statement.

> We see things within their context and in connection with ourselves: a unity which can be broken only to the detriment of the parts. A significant unity. We might say that we see the significance things have for us. If we don't see the significance, we don't see anything at

> all...Our world is our home, a realization of subjectivi-
> ty. If we want to understand man's existence, we must
> listen to the language of objects.[23]

There would be no reason to ask me to introspect about what is going on here. It would be much more to the point to get me to describe the things I experience. Here is a Hegelian switch: as we describe *out there* we directly describe *in here*. It is not a question of *projection* since it is impossible to see objects without participation. We usually use *projection* unthinkingly to apply to some one whose world is not taken to be as *real* or *stable* as ours.[24]

No clearer indication of the relationship between self and object can be seen than in the art of the child. Lowenfeld[25] was able to describe phenomenologically how the child's world is reflected in "exaggerations of value," where important things and personages loom large. Proportions themselves refer to value and not to "fact." When a depiction shows an arm reaching out for something important, for example, it wil stretch through space as far as it needs to go to get there.

But back to the fields and woods. My fields and woods must be untended, but always have a path. The path humanizes the wildness and hidden order of nature. A path *in* is also a path *out*, for paths of this kind are reversible. These fields and woods are wildernesses in miniature. They have a natural ecology all of their own. Here all manner of growing things, of natural forces, and of plant and animal communities have come to agreement and rest. There is a special quality to each miniature wilderness — something idiosyncratic and unique about it. In one field I know there are aspens, daisies, crown vetch, buttercups, evening primroses, blackberries, currant bushes, butterfly weed, sweet white clover, grasses tipped with red flowers, sumac, oaks, several firs there where an old foundation is barely visible, teasels, milkweed, goldenrod, wild roses, and so forth. In a nearby woods the path winds over a stream through more open hardwoods. Here are many old oaks. The one that was blasted open by lightning is still growing among the hickories, maples, and wild cherries. Then the path loops back through dark woods of hemlock and white pine with rhododendron and laurel tangled underneath. The rocks are wet on their surface and surrounded by moss gardens. Worlds within worlds occur in the field and woods, even though the field is just a step off a manicured golf course, and the woods are a short distance from a mountain road.

In passing, it is worthy of reflection on the isolation-into-uniqueness context of these miniature wildernesses. The process I have in mind is more clearly seen in isolated islands:

> ...Sometimes on...desert islands there has been a great evolutionary proliferation amongst the flora and fauna that remain. Strange shapes, exotic growths which, on the mainland, would have been quickly strangled by formidable enemies, here spring up readily. Sometimes the rare, the beautiful can only emerge in isolation.[26]

Stalking things of import in this way is often a matter of solitude, the state also of poetic reverie and creation. Virginia Woolf expresses this well:

> It was odd, she thought, how, if one was alone, one leant to things, inanimate things; trees, streams, flowers; felt they knew one, in a sense were one; felt an irrational tenderness thus (she looked at that long steady light) as for oneself.[27]

Such walks, then, may be hopeful of epiphanies.

But solitude is not essential. "The person with us is not another isolated individual, next to us, who throws words in our ear and who remains foreign to the objects around us. He is the person who is either with us or not with us and who makes the degree of togetherness or distance visible in objects, concretely and in reality."[28] When lovers walk together nature is seen directly as poetry. When there is a true community among people common objects are sacralized and simple acts take on the character of ritual.

The poet and artist in each of us can regain that wonder that the child has in the midst of things.

> The poem of matter saturates our flesh to such a point that, to follow its unfolding in a work of art, it would be necessary to begin with one's mother's milk, when a liquid matter models our very form, touch upon all the contacts which the education of our senses (food, clothing, lodging, play) imposes upon that form, and end with the amorous embrace...[29]

And indeed the dreamer goes as far as to believe "that between him and the world, there is an exchange of looks, as in the double look from the loved man to the loved woman."[30]

> Whoever goes to the bottom of reverie rediscovers natural reverie, a reverie of the original cosmos and the original dreamer. The world is no longer mute. Poetic

> reverie revives the world of original words. All the be-
> ings of the world begin to speak by the name they bear.
> Who has named them? The names are so well chosen
> that they seem to have named themselves. One word
> leads to another. The words of the world want to make
> sentences.[33]

And they also want to make paintings, pots, and poems. But we do not imitate forms *out there*. We get to the forms of nature halfway between them and us. Faure rhapsodically celebrates the poetic presence of nature:

> This stag's horn is like a wing or a flame. These roots
> like greedy fingers that clutch their prey to feed on it.
> These leaves spread out in search of their fluid nourish-
> ment like lungs or fish-gills. The sap of plants, like the
> blood of animals, circulates through the veins. The hide
> of elephants, of rhinoceroses, or hippopotami, of
> crocodiles, resembles the bark of trees, or the rugged
> and mossy surface of rocks. The skin, the flesh of
> women, resemble the flesh of fruits, the down of
> flowers. Certain corollas or shells are like sex organs.
> These furry coats, variegated, speckled, spotted,
> striped, these reddish-brown wing shells, cannot be
> perceived in the jungle grasses because they blend
> there with the gold and red, with the velvet of the
> petals, stalks and leaves...The desert quivers like a sea,
> and breaks into foam in the manner of waves. Gulfs,
> promontories, estuaries, seem embraced by the water,
> that great plastic matter that wears stone at its
> pleasure, washes away gravel and sand, slowly changes
> the profiles of the earth by alluvial deposit or slow ero-
> sion, and is indefatigably persistent in striking, falling,
> or dripping in the same spot.[32]

But we can hardly inventory the world's variety nor the way things appear like other things. Besides, such inventories are not specific enough to a given dreamer, a given thing or a given context. In a less passionate time we feel more drawn to poetic phenomenology, as in Elizabeth Bishop's *The Fish*:

> I looked into his eyes
> which were far larger than mine
> but shallower, and yellowed,
> the irises backed and packed
> with tarnished tinfoil
> seen through the lenses
> of old scratched isinglass.
> They shifted a little, but not
> to return my stare.
> — It was more like the tipping
> of an object toward the light.[33]

Anything of the world is a matter of import or can be. Some, however, like *threshold* or *door* are loaded in readiness whenever we dream on them. The door is "an entire cosmos of the Half-open."

> On May nights, when so many doors are closed, there
> is one that is just barely ajar. We have only to
> give it a very slight push! The hinges have been
> well oiled, and our fate becomes visible.[34]

There are also "doors of hesitation." Bachelard quotes a line by Jean Pellerin: "The door scents me, it hesitatates."[35] Doors connect with thresholds, and ever since ancient times thresholds have been considered sacred. This sacred nature is ritualized by the custom of removing footwear at the threshold of a Japanese home before walking and sitting on their revered tatami, or rice-straw mats.

Then there is Ponge's "The Pleasures of the Door":

> Kings do not touch doors.
> They know nothing of this pleasure: pushing before
> one gently or brusquely one of those large familiar
> panels, then turning back to replace it—holding a door
> in one's arms.
> ...The pleasure of grabbing the midriff of one of those
> tall obstacles to a room by its porcelain node; that short
> clinch during which movement stops, the eye widens, and
> the whole body adjusts to its new surrounding.
> With a friendly hand one still holds on to it, before clos-
> ing it decisively and shutting oneself in—which the click
> of the tight but well-oiled spring pleasantly conforms.[36]

When object and imagination join, things have no more dominion over us than we over them, for the event where these are joined together is an indivisible unity. There is no need for exotic objects although every dreamer may have treasured memories of far away places—favorite haunts, special landscapes, certain regions of the world. We are drawn again and again, for example, to the South Pacific where the soft colors, the air and almost transparent light, the flowers with fragrance everywhere, create an atmosphere where you don't breathe—rather it breathes you.

One more example, this time a visual one. I am in my pottery studio on a wintry sunny day, following a magical nighttime snow. As I look out the window I am struck by the timeless pattern made by a wooden sunscreen and its shadow across the drifted snow. There is a small fir tree nearby. I look around and find a large stoneware plate I just made. It's already been tooled and its inner field is scrubbed with white clay. This circle of fixation becomes at once the fixated snow field against whose roundness the pattern before my eyes plays. I translate what I see and feel almost eidetically into black slip clay, into scratches, into resist and brush strokes. I do not think of Japanese pottery, although my study in Japan and my admiration for its traditions prepares me for the translation of nature onto ceramic surface. I know it will require care in glazing and firing, plus a lot of luck or what the French call *le part de Dieu*. The result, in its good time, commemorates, symbolizes and transcends the event of its origin and making. It is a minor epiphany, for something was revealed to me at that instant which fortunately I was able to represent through my readiness and that of my materials and tradition.

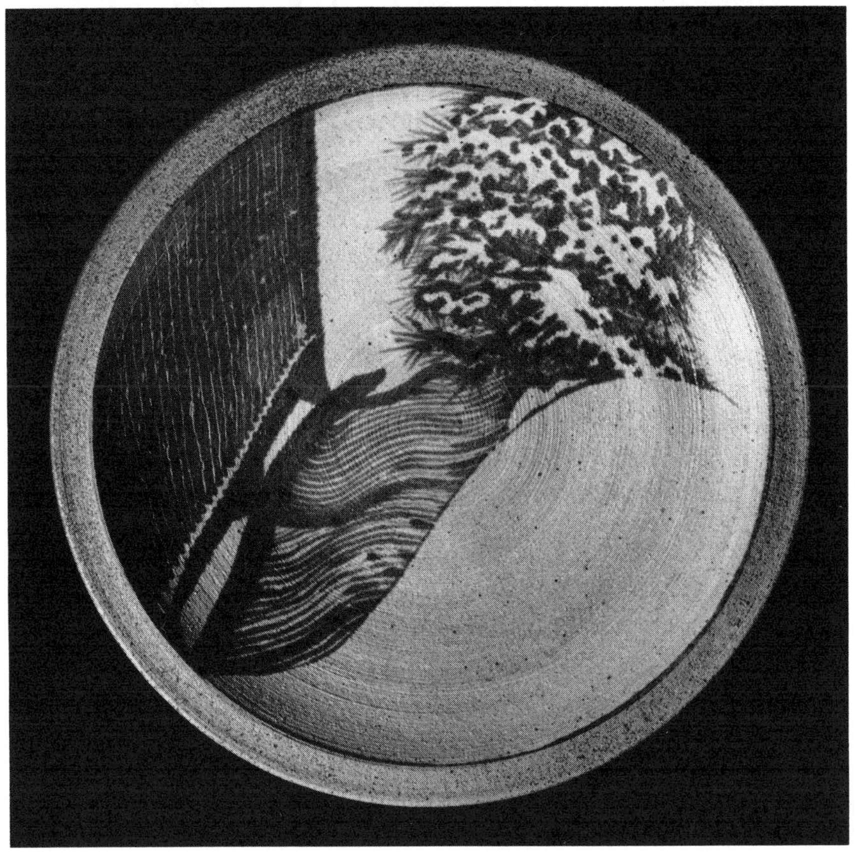

Winter Sunscreen Plate.
Stoneware. By the author.

One is merely the confluence of such events. The best decorations come unsought.

> Suddenly an image situates itself in the center of our imaginary being. It retains us; it engages us. It infuses us with being. The *cogito* is conquered through an object of the world, an object which, all by itself, represents the world. The imagined detail is a sharp point which penetrates the dreamer; it excites in him a concrete meditation. Its being is at the same time being of the image and being of adherence to the image which is astonishing. The image brings us an illustration of our astonishment...In a reverie which is dreaming on a simply object, we know a polyvalence of our dreaming being.[37]

The simplest and commonest of objects have this potential. "Thanks to a fruit, the whole being of the dreamer becomes round. Thanks to a flower, the whole being of the dreamer relaxes...The flower born in poetic reverie...is the very being of the dreamer, his flowering being."[38] In his *Sonnets to Orpheus*, Rilke has one poem which begins "Dare to speak what you call apple" and another with "Dance the orange."[39]

We come back to where we started: matter has import to us, and we might say, we to it. The *well*, the *vision*, and the *will*, though uniquely known to us as *individuals*, might equally be said to be the Well, the Vision, and the Will of the *universe*.

I doubt if there could be a clearer welling up of all these connections than the answer Usharbudh Arya, doctor of literature, yoga scholar and disciple of Swami Rama of the Himalayas, gave to what must have seemed to its speaker a simple question:

> People ask, "Should I take a shower before my hatha yoga or after my hatha yoga?" And they expect to have a prescribed law. But what is a shower? If you cannot revive the concept that all waters are mother waters, that going to the water is going to the womb, taking a dip in the primeval, cosmic coean, that taking a daily shower is Jesus being baptized in the river Jordan, that taking a shower is an act of reunciation, an act of washing off the dirt of the body and of the mind; if that attitude is not there, whether you take a shower before or after isn't going to do too much good. It's going to keep your body clean and that's all. But its overall psychological impact is being missed, because you have demolished mythology, because you have killed Milton, because you have murdered Dante, because you have destroyed the anicent Greeks' culture, because you have cut off your connec-

tions of individual mind from the cosmic mind, because you're ashamed to recite poetry in school. Because of all these collective, cultural murders, entering a shower for you is only washing the dirt and sweat from the body, and the psychological satisfaction, the spiritual satisfaction, the ritual satisfaction, the washing of the mind, changing the overall pattern of thought—that is missing. That is where the basic psychological problems of the modern man are; the objects are just objects and have no psychic connections. There is nothing from the subtle body flowing between you and the mother waters.[40]

Matters of Expression

Though wood, clay and stone may be said to *speak*, their message is only heard fully by the artist who feels powerfully drawn to one of these and takes it on as a medium for expression. Standing within an artistic tradition the artist can use properties of matter as a medium where the discovered and displayed characteristics of the physical thing can act contextually and organizationally as a uniquely *ad hoc* set of signs.[41] Following Dewey, we might say that inferior potters apply clay *to* their forms or ideas. Some other material might have done as well. But the genuine potter makes forms *out of clay, in* clay.[42] The long apprenticeship of the potter within the Japanese traditions is such that the raw matter, clay, is physically, technically, ritualistically and spiritually absorbed. Thought within it seems automatic. Too automatic if the Zen spiritual side of the discipleship is lacking.

The medium is physically matter of the earth. When an art work is buried and rediscovered, this connectedness is exaggerated. An old pot of clay, for example, becomes "so stamped with the mark of the damp earth, by dark stains and livid lines, that it seems a fragment of it, thrown up from its volcanoes, sleeping under its crust with lava and coal."[43]

Tool and tradition seem, in fact, to follow the lines laid down in matter itself.

> Why should not wood, which is so soft and can be cut in all directions without being chipped, give to the German or the Polynesian who attacks it and whose knife pierces it all the will of his sensual and sentimental impulses, a taste for the complications of winding lines, for picturesque irregularities on the surfaces, for scrolls, volutes, and rhythmic repetitions?[44]

Rhythm can also be that of the moving hand and body that creates. The calligraphic line which brush and arm automatically fall into can become like a dance which parallels the dancing images of field grasses in the wind. In a poetic and abstract way an affinity between dancing artist, dancing medium and dancing nature is established, for medium is matter mediated toward expression through not only the tool but the entire body of the artist, as in this example from a *fields series*.

Field Series, IV: Winter's Spring.
Painting. By Joan Beittel.

With experience comes the power to do more with less. As a potter, I use only a few clays, slips, and glazes. For my clay, there is one which I come back to again and again. It is a clay which I dig in the woods about twenty miles from my studio. I have used it for about twenty-five years. It has many of the characteristics of the clay used in Bizen (now Inbe) in Japan: a quiet, earthy clay capable of all the colors within a hemlock woods, able to withstand high temperatures despite all of the iron in it, responding to simplicity and directness of throwing and decorating. It is especially suited to the slow build-up of glaze from the fly-ash of a long wood fire that is stoked rhythmically for days and burns in cycles much like breathing in and out as the dry pine wood bursts into flame. Pieces made from this clay resemble the woods where the clay was dug: dark, deep, greenish-orangish-brownish-purplish-- blackish; sometimes speckled like a fallen rhododendron leaf. Place a jar from this clay back where it came from and it will become part of nature itself.

Beginning potters think that expression will be enhanced by the use of many clays, many glazes, many techniques. Therefore they will change restlessly from one combination to another, always searching for something outside. *For knowledge, it has been said, add one new item daily; but for wisdom, give up something each day.* The medium represents a reduction, a narrowing down for the sake of intensity and clarity. It is therefore closer to wisdom and intuition, to the unity of imagination, than to knowledge and technique, or to the mind's formal play. This is why studying with a master in a tradition is never a case of knowledge or isolated technique, but of developing an intuitive, holistic, body-mind feel for medium and working process. Watching the whole and effortless actions of the master is—with the added virtues of patience, zeal, and humility—the chief mode of learning in the master-apprentice relationship.

Artists personify their medium. Since the medium *speaks*, they may be excused for answering and carrying on dialogues. Bachelard, who calls himself a *word dreamer*, imagines that words are little houses.

> ...each with its cellar and garret. Common-sense lives on the ground floor, always ready to engage in "foreign commerce", on the same level as the others, as the passers-by, who are never dreamers. To go upstairs in the word house, is to withdraw, step by step; while to go down to the cellar is to dream, it is losing oneself in the distant corridors of an obscure etymology, looking for treasures that cannot be found in words. To mount and descend in the words themselves—this is a poet's life. To mount too high or descend too low, is allowed in the case of poets, who bring earth and sky together.[45]

One might say that the labyrinthine spaces and open potential found by poets within words allow them to celebrate the world opened up by the object, to find that these two worlds are really one:

> ...the poet shows us that flowers are already coordinating generalized images in reverie. Not simply perceptual images, colors and fragrances, but images of man, of the delicacies of feeling, of warmths of memory, of temptations to make an offering, everything that can flower in a human soul.[46]

And what can "flower in a human soul" will, for the poet, flower in words.

Bly sees the *content* of a poem as *inside the chest*, drawing its life from the heart and lungs of that which is deeply private. *Meaning* is close to the chest but floats outside it a bit, *between the chest and the human community*. Meaning suggests the hidden tradition, the poet's allusion to an unteachable love-gnosis. *Form* is still further from the chest, and it includes the conflicting energies of a *successful animal that endures*.[47]

> So when we speak of form as a wildness, and consider a poem's form as drawn from the careful economy of nature, we then can imagine the poem as a being that moves fast, can leap in the air, escape from tigers or professors, and live for generations, even during lean times.[48]

The image of the poem as a successful wild animal integrates the separate strands which are represented by *well, vision, will,* and *form*.

The French poet Francis Ponge works at the problem of recovering and renewing the poet's medium. He does not even call himself a poet at times, and he refers to his works as *proemes* — a halfway house between prose and poem. He arrives at a rhetoric and poetic clarity also by a process of reduction and simplification for the sake of increased intensity. He says that he uses *poetic magma*, but without any intention to make poems. He approaches what is idiosyncratically human through an examination of the non-human.

> The richest of propositions contained in the smallest object is so great, that I do not yet conceive the possibility of taking into consideration anything other than the most simple: a stone, a grass, the fire, a piece of wood, a piece of meat.[49]

> For an individual who has a contemplative disposition,
> the whole secret of happiness is not to cosider *as an evil*
> the invasion of his personality by objects. In order for
> that experience to avoid becoming a mystical one, it is
> necessary (1) to arrive at a precise inventory of each
> thing that one has made the object of one's contempla-
> tion: (2) to change objects of contemplation rather fre-
> quently to assure a degree of equilibrium. But for a
> contemplative individual, what is most important is
> the progressive *nomination* of all the qualities that he
> discovers; those *qualities* that TRANSPORT him
> should not transport him further than their measured
> and exact meaning.[50]

In our discussion of how art may lead the way toward an evolution of consciousness, it might be inferred that we point toward a metaphysically abstract vision and language, when what we mean is much closer to Ponge's attitude and to Bachelard's *concrete metaphysics*. The quote of Ponge's at the start of this chapter says directly what we mean: the infinite resources of the thickness of things is *brought out* by the infinite resources of the thickness of the medium.[51] There is a fit and a reciprocity between the expressive thickness of medium and the unintelligible things of the earth lying outside our medium. The wonder of it all is that in times of grace we catch sight of these as lying in each other's arms.

But those times of grace are rarer and rarer in our present culture. Bachelard and Ponge are on a secret mission—a secret teaching that could save men and women and themselves from annihilation. This is "because they find that *others* own too large a share of them."[52] This idea is clearly presented in one of Ponge's proemes on Paris where he lays out the monstrous attack the overpopulated city makes on our very being:

> Unfortunately, to cap this horror, *within ourselves*, the
> same sordid order speaks, because we have no other
> words at our disposal, no high sounding words (or
> sentences, that is to say, ideas) except those that have
> been, and from the beginning of time, prostituted on a
> daily basis in this crass world. We are like painters
> who, from as far back as can be remembered, would all
> have to dip their brushes in the same immense can in
> order to thin out their paints.[53]

The methods used by Bachelard and Ponge to get us into the thickness of things and the thickness of medium differ but support each other. Bachelard, more in the feminine anima-inspired spirit, gets to salvation through poetic reverie and directed dreaming. He uses things and themes of the tangible world as they echo the intangible spirit. To do so, he engages endlessly in a poetic reverie on poetic fragments, so that by contagion and celebration the image expands through ripples as wide as the universe and the dreamer's oneness with it. We will call this a *reduction by expansion and extension*—a welcoming to a community of kindred spirits. The method is one of similarity.

Ponge, on the other hand, moves toward culture by retreating from it. Instead of an initial move toward inclusion, there is one toward exclusion. This initial move first takes the side of things, the side of the life and will of things, towards them and away from ideas. *Then* under their guidance, once they have invaded his personality, to stop from drifting into mysticism he begins to inventory the thing by entering into "the progressive *nomination* of all the qualities he discovers." But he watches lest these qualities transport him away from "their measured and exact meanings." Bachelard in his more receptive reverie state courts mysticism and yearns to dream on universal childhood, the archetypes and the entire cosmos. Ponge and Bachelard thus complement one another in the differing scope and intensity of their material imagination. But both keep us in the thick of things and in the thick of the medium, for that is where the matter of expression resides.

As we have hinted, Ponge works from differences rather than similarities. His is a reduction through distancing:

> ...When I say that the inside of a walnut is similar to a praline, it is interesting. But even more interesting is their difference. To make one feel analogies, that is something. To name the differential quality of the walnut, that is purpose, that is progress.[54]

It is for such an approach that we have reversed the directionality of fourfold vision. The thistle needs to be seen anew, quietly, meditatively, through itself and through any medium that can mediate what we can say to one another. That will include enough of tradition since, as he says, "everything written moralizes," even though his purpose is not to moralize. The medium turns out to be more tyrannizing than the things, so Ponge tips the scales toward things. It is an art of contradictions.

He admits he "uses poetic magma" but hastily adds, "only to get rid of it." Just as he insists that "ideas are not my forte," yet ideas spring out of each page in dizzying profusion. And everything points to man—his formidable capacity for renewal, the glory of his mind and soul, albeit in a non-religious yet strongly metaphysical context. "The veneration of matter: what can be worthier of the spirit? Whereas the spirit venerating spirit..."[55]

Here we touch on an interesting issue: though both saint and artist are part of the universe, their orientations are complementary, not similar. Ponge's veiled unfinished remarks on the spirit venerating the spirit as opposed to venerating matter suggests Fuerback who

> ...said, and saw, that man was emptying himself into
> the absolute—that the absolute is a loss of substance.
> The task of man is to reappropriate his own substance,
> to stop this bleeding of substance into the sacred.[56]

That suggests the artist's way: to allow the thickness of things and the thickness of medium to come together through the life and body of the artist so that new beings can celebrate that worthy veneration of matter by spirit.

Interestingly enough, Ponge and Bachelard meet in their veneration of the circle. "If there is any graphic symbol to characterize Ponge, it would be the circle—the cycle of the seasons, the sea-rounded pebble, the orange, the plate—but above all the circularity of his technique."[57] In Bachelard's summation:

> ...images of full roundness help us to collect ourselves,
> permit us to confer an initial constitution on ourselves,
> and to confirm our being intimately, inside. For when it
> is experienced from the inside, devoid of all exterior
> features, being cannot be otherwise than round.[58]

The Voice of Things: The Thing Poem

Our book celebrates the winged centaur as a creature liberating consciousness through a work of love-gnosis. This means that the voice of the art-things must be allowed to speak directly. Since our medium is words, based on a phenomenology of art-fragments and images, it seems wise to spend some time with examples in the word medium of which books and poems are made.

When Rilke was Rodin's secretary for a brief period, the sculptor gave him *seeing* assignments. The advice paid off, for Rilke did several hundred *seeing poems*. Rodin's advice took Rilke away from self contemplation toward what Novalis called "genuine observation outward — spontaneous, sober observation of the external world."[59]

Here is Rilke's "Archaic Torso of Appolo."

> We have no idea what his fantastic head
> was like, where the eyeballs were slowly swelling. But
> his body now is glowing like a lamp
> whose inner eyes, only turned down a little,
>
> hold their flame, shine. If there weren't light, the curve
> of the breast wouldn't blind you, and in the swerve
> of the thighs a smile wouldn't keep on going
> toward the place where the seeds are.
>
> If there weren't light, this stone would look cut off
> where it drops so clearly from the shoulders,
> its skin wouldn't gleam like the fur of a wild animal,
>
> and the body wouldn't send out light from every edge
> as a star does...for there is no place at all
> that isn't looking at you. You must change your life.
>> Rainer Maria Rilke
>> Translated by Robert Bly[60]

Here is Rilke's celebration of the apple:

> Dare to speak what you call apple.
> That softness which first condenses
> In order, with a softness set up in the taste,
>
> to reach clarity, alertness, transparency,
> to become a thing of this place which means
> both the sun and the earth —
>
>> Rainer Maria Rilke[61]

Bly says: "We all use our senses, but if the senses are called upon only to embody intuitions about ourselves, they die. The senses long to experience objects and things on their own; they don't want to be slaves of our intuition."[62] In *A Dream of What is Missing,* he reveals his intuitions about the gnostic and the thinker, a sense of imbalances and yearnings pertinent to our inquiry into the role of art in the evolution of consciousness:

> Last night such glad powerful dreams, each tile laid
> down of luminous glazed clay...The dream said that
> The One Who sees the Whole does not have the senses,
> but the longing for the senes. That longing is terrible,
> and terrifying — the herd of gazelles running over the
> savannah — and intense and divine, and I saw it lying
> over the dark floor...in layers there. The one who thinks

does not have feelings, but the longing for feeling—that longing makes the lines of force at the bottom of Joseph's well. In the dream I saw the lumps of dirt that heal the humpbacked, what rolls slowly upward from the water, and prowls around the rocky edges of the desert, keeping the hermit inside his own chest...[63]

In this prose poem we hear an echo of Jung's opposed functions: intuition-sensation; thinking-feeling. And we find that concern with the *shadow*, the inferior or repressed side of these opposite pairs and of all that which the conscious ego doesn't want to own, which so characterizes Bly's poetry. We also hear an indictment not just of sage or saint but of our times: the mechanistic blend and Cartesian split which produces *sensate thinkers* lacking intuition and feeling and curiously separated between body and mind. *Our mythical winged centaur liberates thinking from its strangehold under mechanism through a unity of sensation and intuition and feeling.* If Jung is right, the repressed feeling and intuitive functions would help most in this recovery. Ponge's directive to abandon ideas and even poetry in order to inventory the qualities of the thing provides a method and a solution to our mental-egoic hang-ups. In describing a simple object: "Something surpising happens often during the writing. It is as if the object itself, a stump or an orange, has links with the human psyche, and the unconscious provides material it would not give if asked directly. The unconscious passes into the object and returns."[64]

Fire

Fire has a system: first all the flowers move in one direction...

(One can only compare the gait of fire to that of an animal: it must first leave one place before occupying another; it moves like an amoeba and a giraffe at the same time, its neck lurching, its foot dragging)...

Then, while the substances consumed with method collapse, the escaping gasses are subsequently transformed into one long flight of butterflies.

Francis Ponge[65]

Bread

The surface of a crusty bread is marvelous, first because of the almost panoramic impression it makes: as though one had the Alps, the Taurus, or the Andes at one's fingertips.

It so happened that an amorphous mass about to explode was slid into the celestial oven for us where it hardened and formed valleys, summits, rolling hills, crevasses... And from then on, all those planes so neatly joined, those fine slabs where light carefully beds down its rays—without a thought for the unspeakable mush underneath.

That cold flaccid substratum is made up of sponge-like tissue: leaves or flowers like Siamese twins soldered together elbow to elbow. When bread grows stale, these flowers fade and wither; they fall away from each other and the mass becomes crumbly...

But now let's break it up: for in our mouths bread should be less an object of respect than one of consumption.

Francis Ponge[66]

"Ponge doesn't try to be cool, distant, or objective, nor 'let the object speak for itself.' His poems are funny, his vocabulary immense, his personality full of quirks, and yet the poem remains somewhere in the place where the senses join the object."[67]

The Butterfly

When the sugar prepared in the stem rises to the bottom of the flower, like a badly washed cup—a great event takes place on the ground where butterflies suddenly take off.

Because each caterpillar had its head blinded and blackened, and its torso shortened by the veritable explosion from which its symmetrical wings flamed—

From then on the erratic butterfly no longer alights except by chance of route, or just about.

A flying match, its flame is not contagious. Furthermore, it arrives too late and can only acknowledge the flowers' blooming. Never mind; in the role of lamplighter, it checks the oil supply in each one, places on top of the flower the atrophied cocoon it carries, and so avenges its long, amorphous humiliation as a caterpillar at the stem's foot.

Miniscule airborne sailboat abused by the wind mistaking it for a twice-spawned petal, it gallivants around the garden.

Francis Ponge[68]

It is surprising how such ordinary objects seen in a manner far from passionate—unless it be the passion for seeing—become such arresting images. Ponge has written as to how this occurs:

> Superiority of poets over philosophers: they
> know what they are expressing in their own terms.
> From the specific to the general:
> The specific in the external world;
> a rhetoric for each object;
> it is always toward the proverbial
> that language tends.[69]

So it is that "the very form of the poem must in some way be determined by its subject." And this has to do "with a word given to the object which should express its mute character, its lesson, in almost moral terms. (There has to be a bit of everything in it: definition, description, morality.)[70]

Here it appears that the word-house of which Bachelard spoke gives way to an object-house. But if there is a rhetoric for each object, it is more likely that there is a half-way house in which both object and word take up habitation.

> Watery syllables come welling up.
> Anger that barked and howled in the cave,
> The luminous head of barley
> The priest holds up, growls
> from under fur, none of the sounds are lost!
> The old earth fragrance remains
> in the word "and." We experience
> "the," in its lonely suffering.
>
> We are bees then; honey is language.
> Honey lies stored in caves
> beneath us, and the sounds of words
> carry what we do not.
>
> Robert Bly, from
> "Words Rising"[71]

"The poet gives the real object its imaginary double, its idealized double. This idealized double is immediately idealizing, and it is thus that a universe is born from an expanding image."[72] This expansion is all the more striking as it arises from a thing poem, a proeme. For Ponge unmistakalby "constructs a cosmogony which turns out to be an account not of the origin, but of the agony of the cosmos—an agony of joy as well as an agony of death. One has the feeling of eternal resurgence and surprise,...each text a fresh attempt to seize a fragment of the universe."[73] And these are the artist's, the progressive organicist's fragments—those which lead on through a hidden order. They work desperately against the "bleeding of substance into the sacred"; they heal the longing for the senses of "The One Who Sees the Whole."

Matters Beyond Mind and Matter

It should not be assumed, Socrates notwithstanding, that poets are completely unaware of the many overtones playing above, below and through these poems. Since we have drawn much from Ponge, let him be the one to speak of ways in which creating a poem and expanding one's consciousness relate:

> The relationship between Eros and Thanatos is evident, and death in this sense is part of life. I have often insisted on the fact that it is necessary in some way to die in order to give birth to something, or someone, and I am not the first to have seen that the birth of a text can only occur through the death of the author. The sex act, the act of reproduction, also requires the presence of another. The two must die, more or less, for the third person, in this case the text, to be born. The second person for me is the thing, the object that provoked the desire and that also dies in the process of giving birth to the text. There is thus, at the same time, the death of the author and the death of the object of the desire—the thing, the pre-text.[74]

This language of a contest between Eros and Thanatos is equivalent in all details to the language used to speak of the symbolic death which precedes transformation to a higher level of consciousness. The object poem directs this curious traffic between what is conscious and what is just barely arriving on the horizon of consciousness. "The seat of the soul is where the inner world and the outer world meet, and where they overlap, it is in every point of the overlap," said Novalis.[75] The object poem seems to be a down-staged stage where this overlap can be lightly *and* seriously played out. The Westerner, Bly says, after centuries of successful planning," loses touch with nature so much that he loses touch with her dark side also. The fear of nature, which both men and women have, becomes unconscious, and spreads to include all women, the feminine, dreams, all 'lower races' and 'lower things.' "[76] When art and poetry help to light up and lighten up this irrational fear, to show that it is part of us and of the universe with which we are one, then we have a primary role in the evolution of human consciousness. The voice of things is both the voice of the planet and our own voice. Carry the overlap of which Novalis spoke far enough and it becomes obvious that the inner world and the outer world are one. Then we may be ready to go as far as Whitman: "Clear and sweet is my soul, and clear and sweet is all that is not my soul."[77] Or, "Is it lucky to be born? It is just as lucky to die."[78]

> Thou hast O Nature! elements! utterance to my
>   heart beyond the rest — and this is of them...
> Thou art spiritual, Godly, most of all known
>   to my sense,
> Minister to speak to me, here and now, what
>   word has never told, and cannot tell,
> Art thou not universal, concrete's distillation?[79]

The saint or the sage turns within to reunite the sundered world. When the spirit outpours we speak of e-volution. The artist turns outward to reunite the sundered inner world. When the spirit inpours we speak of in-volution. The two meet: *the way up is the way down, and the way down is the way up.* In samadhi, inner universe and outer universe are the same, no matter which path is taken to complete this union.

The way of the poet is not worse, nor better, but it *is* different.

> In every dreamer there lives a child, a child whom reverie magnifies and stabilizes. Reverie tears it away from history, sets it outside time, makes it foreign to time. One more reverie and this permanent, magnified child is a god.[80]

References

1. Whitehead, A. N. *Science and the modern world.* N.Y.: The Free Press, 1967 edition; p. 199.

2. Ponge, F. *The voice of things.* (B. Archer, trans.) N.Y.; McGraw-Hill, 1972; p. 108.

3. Heidegger, M. The question concerning technology. In *The question concerning technology*, pp. 3-35. (Translated by W. Lovitt) N.Y.: Garland Publishing Co., 1977.

4. Sagan, C. *The dragons of Eden.* N.Y.: Ballantine, 1977; p. 55.

5. Sagan, C. *Ibid.*, p. 169.

6. Barrett, W. *Time of need.* N.Y.: Harper Torchbooks, 1973.

7. Sampson, J. (Ed.). *Blake's poetical works.* Oxford: Oxford University Press, 1947; p. 306.

8. Laing, R.D. *The politics of experience.* N.Y.: Ballantine Books, 1967; p. 11.

9. Roszak, T. *Person/planet.* N.Y.: Anchor Press, 1979.

10. Palmer, R. E. *Hermeneutics.* Evanston: Northwestern University Press, 1969.

11. Van den Berg, J. H. *A different existence.* Pittsburgh: Duquesne University Press, 1972; pp. 91-92.

12. Proust, M. *A L'ombre des jeunes filles en fleurs.* V. 3. Paris: Gallimard, 1923-27; p. 98.

13. Rilke, M. R. *Sonnets to Orphens* (M. P. Herter, trans.) N.Y.: W.W. Norton, 1952; p. 21.

14. Stevens, W. *The collected poems of Wallace Stevens.* N.Y.: Alfred A. Knopf, 1954; p. 26.

15. Heidegger, M. *Being and time.* (J. Macquarrie and E. Robinson, trans.) London: SCM Press, 1962; p. 58.

16. Bly, R. *News of the universe.* San Francisco: Sierra Club Books, 1980; p. 250.

17. *Ibid.*, p. 250.

18. *Ibid.*, p. 251.

19. *Ibid.*, p. 288.

20. Ponge, F. *Op. cit.*, reference 2 above, p. 11.

21. *Ibid.*, p. 11.

22. *Ibid.*, p. 107.

23. Van den Berg, J. H. *Op. cit.*, reference 11 above, pp. 37-38, 40.

24. *Ibid.*, p. 20.

25. Lowenfeld, V. *The nature of creative activity.* N.Y.: Harcourt, Brace, Jovanovich, 1939.

26. Eisely, L. *The mind as nature.* N.Y.: Harper & Row, 1962; p. 29.

27. Woolf, V. *To the lighthouse.* Paris: The Albatross, 1948; p. 76.

28. Van den Berg, J. H. *Op. cit.* reference 11 above, p. 65.

29. Faure, E. *History of art.* Vol. V. *The spirit of the forms.* (W. Pach, trans.) N.Y.: Harper & Brothers, 1930; p. 272.

30. Bachelard, G. *The poetics of reverie.* (D. Russel, trans.) Boston: Beacon Press, 1971; p. 185.

31. *Ibid.,* p. 188.

32. Faure, E. *Op. cit.,* reference 29 above, p. 321.

33. Bishop, E. Poem anthologized by Bly, R. *Op. cit.,* reference 16 above, p. 234.

34. Bachelard, G. *The poetics of space.* (M. Jolas, trans.) Boston: Beacon Press, 1969; pp. 222-223.

35. *Ibid.,* p. 223.

36. Ponge, F. *Op. cit.,* reference 2 above, p. 38.

37. Bachelard, G. *Op. cit.,* reference 30 above, pp. 153-154.

38. *Ibid.,* p. 154.

39. *Ibid.,* pp. 155-156.

40. Arya, U. *Philosophy of hatha yoga.* Honesdale, Pa.: The Himalayan Institute of Yoga Science and Philosophy, 1977; pp. 68-69.

41. Beardsley, M. C. Review of *What happens in art,* by Matthew Lipman. *Journal of Aesthetics and Art Curiticism,* 26 (3), Spring 1968; pp. 411-412.

42. Dewey, J. *Art as experience.* N.Y.: Minton, Balch, 1934; p. 200.

43. Faure, E. *Op. cit.,* reference 29 above, p. 322.

44. *Ibid.,* p. 268.

45. Bachelard, G. *Op. cit.,* reference 34 above, p. 147.

46. Bachelard, G. *Op. cit.,* reference 30 above, p. 157.

47. Jones, R. and Daniels, K. (Eds.) *Of solitude and silence.* Boston: Beacon Press, 1981; pp. 23-24.

48. *Ibid.,* p. 25.

49. Ponge, F. *Proemes.* Paris: Gallimard, 1948; p. 137.

50. Ponge, F. *The power of language.* (L. Gavronsky, trans.) Berkeley; University of California Press, 1979; p. 79.

51. *Ibid.,* p. 79.

52. *Ibid.,* p. 73.

53. *Ibid.,* p. 69.

54. Ponge, F. *Op. cit.,* reference 2 above, p. 107.

55. *Ibid.*, p. 24 (B. Archer's Introduction).

56. Ricoeur, P. *The philosophy of Paul Ricoeur.* (C. E. Reagan and D. Stewart, eds.) Boston: Beacon Press, 1978; p. 216.

57. Ponge, F. Op. cit., reference 2 above, p. 25 (B. Archer's Introduction).

58. Bachelard, G. *Op. cit.*, reference 34 above, p. 234.

59. Bly, R. *Op. cit.*, reference 16 above, p. 210.

60. *Ibid.*, p. 245.

61. Bachelard, G. *Op. cit.*, reference 30 above, p. 155.

62. Bly, R. *Op. cit.*, reference 16 above, p. 211.

63. Bly, R. This body is made of camphor and gopherwood. N.Y.: Harper & Row, 1977; p. 27.

64. Bly, R. *Op. cit.*, reference 16 above, pp. 212-213.

65. Ponge, F. *Op. cit.*, reference 2 above, p. 40.

66. Ibid., p. 39.

67. Bly, R. *Op. cit.*, reference 16 above, pp. 213-214.

68. Ponge, F. *Op. cit.*, reference 2 above, p. 46.

69. *Ibid.*, p. 104.

70. *Ibid.*, p. 102.

71. Jones, R. and Daniels, K. (Eds.). *Op. cit.*, reference 47 above, p. 3.

72. Bachelard, G. *Op. cit.*, reference 30 above, p. 176.

73. Ponge, F. *Op. cit.*, reference 2 above, from B. Archer's Introduction, p. 25.

74. Ponge, F. *Entretiens de Francis Ponge avec Philippe Sollers.* Paris: Gallimard/Seuil, 1970; p. 171.

75. Bly, R. *Op. cit.*, reference 16 above, quotation from Novalis, p. 214.

76. *Ibid.*, pp. 284-285.

77. Whitman, W. *Leaves of grass.* Philadelphia: David McKay, 1891-1892; p. 22.

78. *Ibid.*, p. 34.

79. *Ibid.*, p. 414.

80. Bachelard, G. *Op. cit.*, reference 30 above, p. 133.

6

The Poetic Thing: Voices from Vessels

Inside this clay jug are canyons and
  pine mountains,
and the maker of canyons and pine
  mountains!
All seven oceans are inside, and hundreds
  of millions of stars.
The acid that tests gold is there, and the
  one who judges jewels.
And the music from the strings that no
  one touches, and the source of all water.

If you want the truth, I will tell you the truth:
Friend, listen: the God whom I love
  is inside.

Kabir[1]

My concern is with extracting essence rather than with experiment and exploration...Concentrating on continuous variations of simple themes I become part of the process; I am learning to operate a sensitive instrument which may be resonant to my experience of existence now—in this fantastic century...Practising a craft with ambiguous reference to purpose and function one has occasion to face absurdity. More than anything, somewhat like a demented piano-tuner, one is trying to approximate a phantom pitch. One is apt to take refuge in pseudo-principles which crumble. Still, the routine of work remains. One deals with facts.

British potter Hans Coper[2]

The Expressive Thickness of Clay

Here I speak as a potter about the meaning of immersion in a living tradition and about a marriage of East and West in this art that I call the *Great Tradition*. Since I have taught pottery for over forty years, and since I have studied in Japan with a potter who is now one of Japan's national living cultural treasures, I will be speaking of *discipleship* and *discipline* as well.

Pottery is an extremely physical art. The clay that I know you don't buy at the bookstore. It has to be either mixed from raw materials (clays, feldspars, flint or sand) or dug up out of the ground. When I go out in the woods to dig clay I need a couple of shovels, a pick and some large buckets as well as the stamina and will to engage in plain hard labor. Clay is earth *plus* water — and is usually found far from the road. So over the years I've developed my own weight training routine. And when I wedge or knead a 30 pound ball of clay 300 turns to get it ready for the wheel, I feel as though I've already done my aerobics for the day. Potters always remind me of farmers in that there is just no end to the sheer physical basis of their work. Digging, carrying, mixing, kneading, shaping, finishing, decorating, glazing, firing — all of these are just a part of what goes into making a simple pot or a most sophisticated work of art.

One of the things that excited me when I first got interested in clay years ago was the discovery that I needed no money to begin making pots. Clay can be found virtually anywhere. It results from the breakdown of igneous rocks through pressure, time, and water. I merely had to locate a good natural source and dig it up. Once that was done I could form simple bricks, build a fire to bake them, and then use the clay bricks to build a primitive kiln — and I could start making pots. Later I learned that still more simply I could dig a kiln into a clay bank and make it permanent as I fired it. Some early Japanese *hole kilns*, or *anagamas*, were made this way. All this gave me the insight that potters have been guardians of earth and fire since the earliest of times. *So I saw the natural ecology implicit in pottery: stones transform into clay through the elements, and through fire and air they transform back into stones — stones of use and stones of beauty.*

A pot is a poetic earth thing having much in common with nuts, bark, eggs, fruits, and shells. *Its inside contains a god, a void, a darkness — a yin nothingness.* Sculptors who have to peel off many layers to get to a solid core that is the center of their transformative process often cannot understand the Tao of pottery, the empty center that determines its use and form. For a vessel is a curtain of earth wrapped on pure air. That air flows inside and outside and all around it everywhere. It is the definer of the form of the clay vessel.

It is almost certain that pottery does not evolve. By this I do not mean that all of the good things have already been made or that I am conscious of imitating the past, but rather that an earth-honest and fire-honest piece of 3000 B.C. has more in common than not with an earth-honest, fire-honest contemporary one. And when it comes to the everyday sacraments of eating and drinking and the ritualistic aspects of daily activities, these have as much to do with the shape of hand and body now as they did then. Even the transcendence of these into ritual objects and talismans remains important to this day.

> A pre-dynastic Egyptian pot, roughly egg-shaped, the size of my hand: made thousands of years ago, possibly by a slave, it has survived in more than one sense. A humble, passive somehow absurd object—yet potent, mysterious, sensuous. It conveys no comment, no self-expression, but seems to contain and reflect its maker and the human world it inhabits, to contribute its minute quantum of energy—and homage. An object of complete economy made by MAN; Giacometti man; Buckminster Fuller man. A constant. This is the only pot which has really fascinated me. It was not the cause for my making pots, but it gave me a glimpse of what man is.[3]

I said that potting is physical. Many times I have gone to dig clay from my favorite source. Then I have pinched and examined that clay, moist and pliable from the ground. I have beat it into sheets and worked through it for bits of roots or an occasional small stone. I have wet it down enough to fuse these sheets and started the slow kneading process that prepares it for the kick-wheel. There simple shapes bud out from this malleable, pliable and tough gold clay. From the earth to a formed piece can happen in the same day. During this process my mind is quieted and uninterrupted by a thousand thoughts—even poetic ones—as it usually is in drawing or painting. Its physical, kinaesthetic and tactile reality keeps the vessel a poetic thing and also an earth thing.

We become simplified in such art-work. A quiet takes over, an active meditation of stillness, of center. It is like the enchanted place at the top of the forest. "We can go there at any time. It's not far away; it's not hard to find. Just take the path to Nothing, and go Nowhere until you reach it. Because the Enchanted Place is right where you are..."[4] But a potter must learn to be selfless to get there, and that is not easy.

Sometimes I throw a wide base on the potter's wheel as the lower section of the bottom wall for a large jar. Then after this has slightly stiffened I add a large coil of clay to this base. Once this is fused and pinched roughly into a smooth and thinner wall, I slowly and rhythmically begin a process of cir-

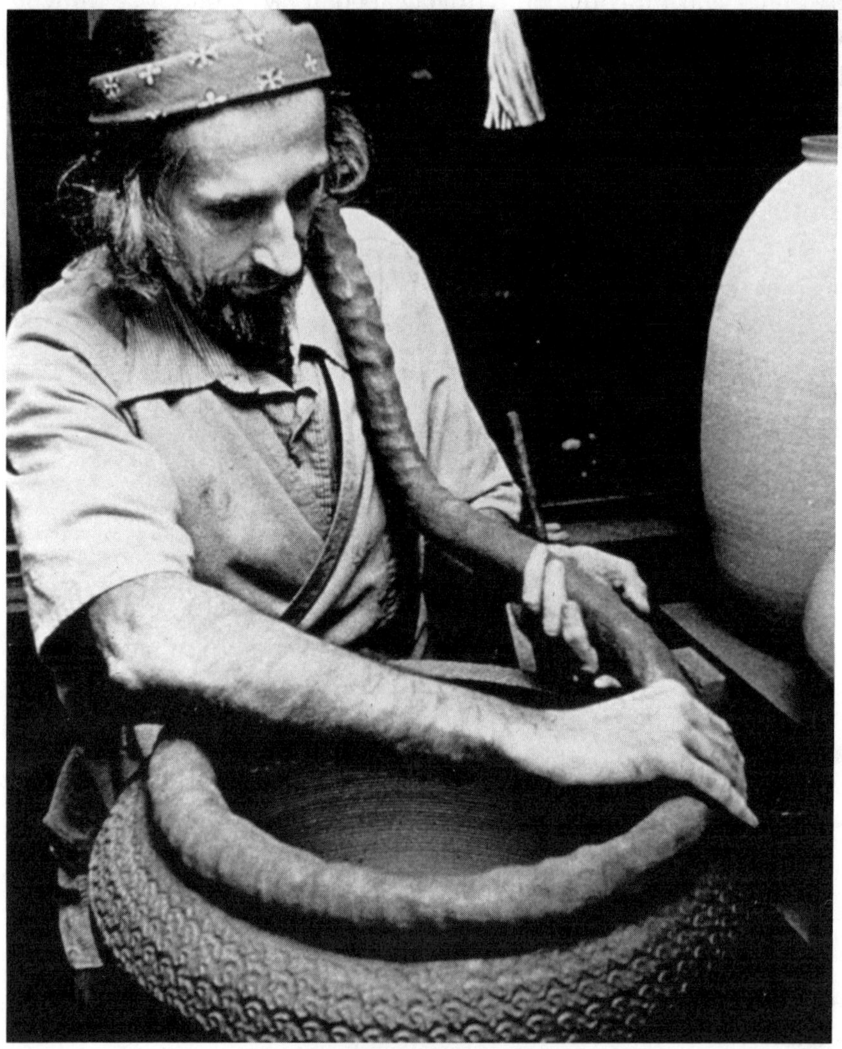

The Author Forming a Large Jar by Coiling,
Pinching, and Stamping, with a Bisque Stamp.

cular pinching and stamping, pressing hard from the inside
with the tips of my fingers while on the outside pressing firmly with a bisque stamp. This process leaves its clear impress,
one stamping overlapping the next. This coil-pinch-stamp
method makes an extremely tough, thin wall—very much
alive. My fingers know every part of it. It's not like throwing
when the wet slip and the spinning wheel carry all those same
points in rapid fire beyond the touch. In coiling-pinching-
stamping the potter feels like a primordial architect fashion-

ing habitations out of unprocessed raw material. Since waiting for stiffening is necessary, great patience is also required. The bottom of the jar may be bone dry while work is still going on at the top — such is the time span of the process. Though incremental, the build-up is thoroughly organic. The

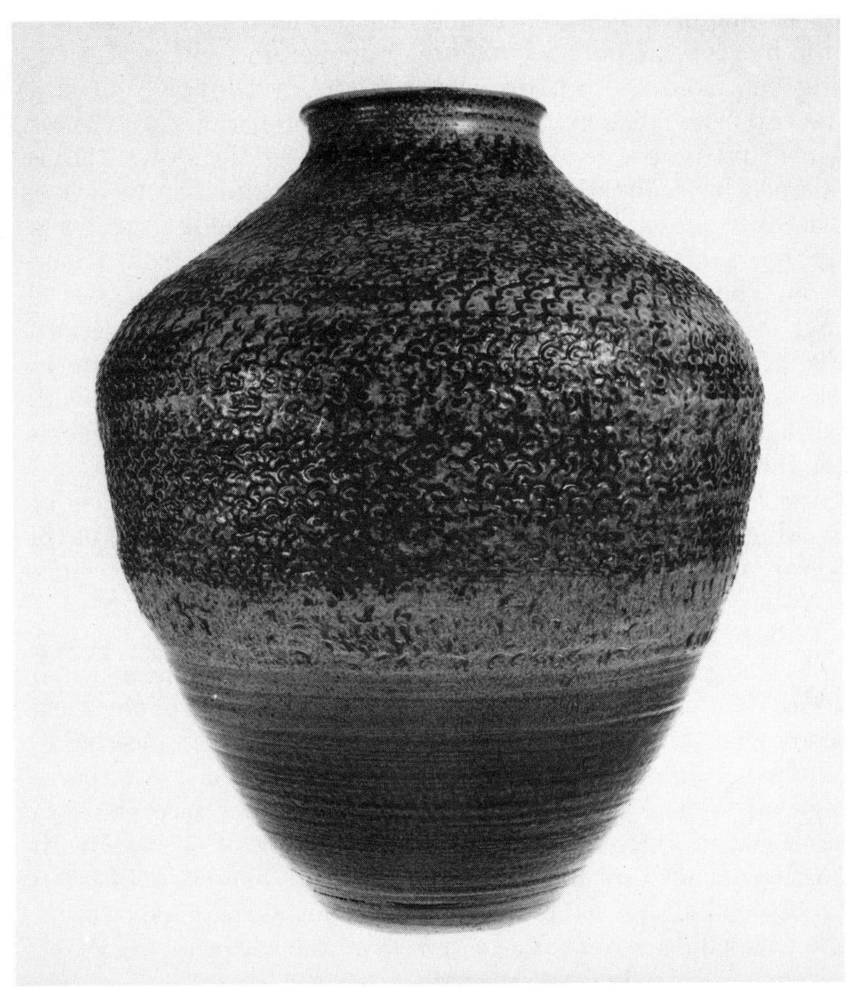

Gathering of the Ancients.
Stoneware. By the author.

whole surface retains a local malleability and spring in the region of recent work. This means that shaping is possible through gentle pushing in and out or hammering with a rounded rock or a paddle. The surface becomes animated, textured, hide-like and landscape-like. Finally the top coil is added and thrown. This repeats the exact center which began the piece at the bottom. It verifies that through all those surface undulations and natural imprints *center was never lost.*

In still a different forming process a clay dance is performed by one of my students who has an affinity to the spiritual in clay. Here the potter rotates—instead of the wheel—around a solid watermelon's worth of clay set on a low stool. The clay is pinched and scraped into a crude hollow; step by step the hole becomes ever deeper and wider. The clay dug out from the bottom is deposited rhythmically around the top. The walls thin as the form becomes taller and taller. Then rhythmic arcs of the inside hand begin the slow swelling process from foot to lip as the outside hand firmly braces wherever the inside hand presses out. The swelling grows as though a giant caterpillar is pushing to escape from its cocoon. The off-center balance must be carefully monitored so that a thrust here moves against a counter-thrust there. Fissures and splits, crevasses and stretchings now form on the swelling and ripening skin of the outside, while the inside remains smooth and unbroken. The swell reaches full season, the landscape solidifies into its permanent geological formations, and the top closes in to complete the puffed out feeling of full growth. It is like a giant puff ball just before all of the spores escape in a cloud—a great natural swelling up stopped at fullest inspiration.

I discuss these two methods in some detail to illustrate something of the expressiveness of clay as a medium which almost repeats the infinite resources of the things of the earth itself. The spin of the wheel and the press of hand and tool do much the same in the throwing of a large sphere. The expanding wall of the large sphere becomes so sensitive that the push of the inner hand against the support of the following fingers of the outer hand is like a gentle, relaxed exhalation of breath. If being itself is round, and if method is often circular, then we could say that *the spherical pot is the being of the essence of roundness.*

Pots show that works which cut through the leading edge of consciousness do not have to be epiphanies of cosmic scope to none the less be cosmic. *Pots are like cosmic events in themselves.* The clear-eyed phenomenological poem speaks with a similar voice—neither of the object nor of the subject, nor even of the inbetween, but almost like the voice of the *event* itself. Here, for example, is a poem which is a *successful animal* in a double sense:

As the cat
climbed over
the top of

the jamcloset
first the right
forefoot

carefully
then the hind
stepped down

into the pit of
the empty
flowerpot

        — *Poem*, William Carlos Williams[5]

Or consider the same poet's *The Locust Tree in Flower*:

Among
of
green

stiff
old
bright

broken
branch
come

white
sweet
May

again

        — William Carlos Williams[6]

Simplicity and profoundity lie close together:

Between Walls

the back wings
of the

hospital where
nothing

will grow lie
cinders

in which shine
the broken

pieces of a green
bottle

        — William Carlos Williams[7]

Here the poet's phenomenological brilliance is turned toward
the human condition:

To a Poor Old Woman

munching a plum on
the street a paper bag
of them in her hand

They taste good to her
They taste good
to her. They taste
good to her

You can see it by
the way she gives herself
to the one half
sucked out in her hand

Comforted
a solace of ripe plums
seeming to fill the air
They taste good to her

—William Carlos Williams[8]

And here an *event* concerning a *thing* becomes incredibly
alive:

The Term

A rumpled sheet
of brown apper
about the length

and apparent bulk
of a man was
rolling with the

wind slowly over
and over in
the street as

a car drove down
upon it and
crushed it to

the ground. Unlike
a man it rose
again rolling

with the wind over
and over to be as
it was before.

—William Carlos Williams[9]

We turn to these *simple* poems of William Carlos Williams as
the printed equivalent of placing in the reader's hands a *simple*
woodfired sphere of native clay. In Williams we get an

American light and shadow like the tones of a local clay. Williams saw American shadow "reflected everywhere, in trash, in broken chips of glass, in the bums, even in the dog-droppings of the Rutherford and Passaic Streets—the sense of inadequacy, of failure, the holes in our being. Williams doesn't turn away from this ugliness; rather, he embraces it."[10]

But he also had a sense for the feminine, for the earth as nourishing what no one can see. Williams was in touch with his *anima*, and with "the twists and turns and leaps of his anima. To be in touch with the anima is to listen to one's own heartbeat... Williams really meant that each of us had to find the pulse of his or her own work without falling back on a dead tradition."[11] In Williams' own words:

> The female principle of the world
> is my appeal
> in the extremity
>
> to which I have come.
> *O clemens! O pia! O dolces!*
> *Maria!*
> —from *For Eleanor and Bill Monahan*[12]

Williams' struggle is much the same as that of the potter. In his words, the struggle is

> the virtual impossibility of lifting to the imagination those things which lie under the direct scrutiny of the senses, close to the nose. It is this difficulty that sets a value upon all works of art and makes them a necessity.
> —*Prologue* to *Kora in Hell*[13]

Close to the nose but *lifted to the imagination* is also close to the sensate formative work of the potter in touch with the feminine, in touch with the earthy expressiveness of clay.

Close to the nose suggests the timeless memory with fragrances evoke; and that is a parallel for the timeless images evoked by pinching, stroking, pulling, and pressing the clay.

> ...the odor is a root of the world,
> a truth of childhood. The odor
> gives us the universes of childhood
> in expansion...
>
> The fragrance of paths
> hemmed with mint
> dances in my childhood.
>
> ...Henri Bosco says that he breathed
> "the odor of roses and salt" of a
> childhood snow. That is the very odor

> of vivifying cold. [Elsewhere he says]
> "I was raised in the odor of the earth,
> the wheat and the new wine. When I
> think about it, a vivid vapor of
> joy and youth still comes back to me."[14]

Bachelard himself reminisces about *wheaten bread*:

> ...an odor of warm bread invaded a house
> of my youth. The custard (*flan*) and round
> loaf returned to my table. Festive occasions
> are associated with this domestic bread. The
> world was in joy for the celebration of the warm
> bread. Two cocks on a single spit were cooking
> before the scarlet hearth. "A well-buttered sun
> was roasting in the blue sky."
> In days of happiness, the world is edible.
> And when the great odors which were preparing
> feasts return to me in memory, it seems to me,
> Baudelarian that I was, that "I eat my memories."
> Suddenly I am taken by the urge to collect all the
> warm bread to be found in poetry. How they
> would help me give to memory the great
> odors of the celebration begun again, of a life
> which one would take up again, swearing gratitude
> for the original joys.[15]

In speaking of pots as *poetic things* I did not realize that it would be through poetry in part that I would try to establish the very physical, tactile, light and profound earthiness of this art and craft and of all the sensate qualities and memories evoked by it. Williams and Bachelard, along with Ponge's *bread* which we sense *and* eat, come close to the all-accepting, ativistic, odor-like and event-like character of the *clay act*, or of *claying* and of the *clay dance*. Note that we also evoke a self-less and child-like attitude through these affinities, and a unity with the things and places of our environment. I am saying that *claying* has the simplicity and yet the concealed event-like character that we find in Williams' poems, and that it also has the ability to tap timeless memories, childhood, and earth-and-anima-nurtured forces similar to those that smells evoke. In short, the expressive thickness of clay as a medium effectively quiets, centers, and grounds the clay-worker in a timeless, meditative reverie and earth rhythm.

What Is Pottery?

Pottery is the humblest and most speechless of man's arts. Even before it became metaphor, pottery brought

Earth to shine forth in man's World. It is best when it is most earth honest; that includes process-honest, fire-honest, honesty-of-being itself. Often a beginning potter will hone a simple bowl down to where it breaks through, and he will learn that a pot is made of nothing – and earth. A potter's labor is consumed within the work; his craft within the art. His mere expressiveness has no depth compared with rocks and mountains, sand and sea, which speak of being and presence, not of expression. His forms innovate through subtle differences of individually within the world's infinite and pervasive Roundness. The shape of Nothing and of Space is curved. The movement of hand and arm, head and trunk, body and mind is curved.

A cup is he sacrament of drink, a bowl the benevolent nurturance of sustenance. We have commerce with cupping and bowling, not with objects at rest. The potter constructs a begging bowl for being, sees the bursting bud of the June rhododendron in his black December clay, and creates a vast storage jar for Big Spirit in a day when even children forget their animism.

But this is all too poetic unless, we see the Sacred as the Everyday. For then again, the potter thinks not, but dances Zorba-like in every wedging, he meditates on the nothingness of all forms at each centering; he dies and is born again at each trial by flame. A young potter is like a determined oak, an old one like a flowing willow. His works are at rest in fields and woods and beaches, and contain themselves patiently in museums. Pots play the range of the Everyday-Sacred, reflecting the vitality of children-at-play as well as the silence of a Holy Day. They are All. And Zen Nothing.

But actually, a pot's a pot: Earth come to stand as World to man. It is the humblest and most speechless of man's arts.[16]

Zen and the Art of Pottery

In 1967 I spent a sabbatical leave from teaching in studying with a master potter in Arita, Japan, the porcelain pottery capital of the world. Arita now has over 100 kilns in operation, all engaged in the production of porcelain pottery. The area became a concentration for porcelain over 300 years ago when a Korean potter named Ri Sampei discovered porcelian stone there. The mountain of *jiki* (porcelain stone) is now only a picturesque shell with pines growing out of the remaining parts of it, looking like the irregular peaks and rocks of Chinese Taoist landscapes.

The man with whom I studied, Manji Inoue, is the world's leading artist producing porcelain on the potter's wheel today. He is the third in line of recent masters who developed the art of making large porcelains on the wheel. He has, for example, a finished jar over five feet in height which now resides in the new wing of the Emperor's palace in Tokyo. Just recently he has been named a living national cultural treasure.

It was not my intention to study porcelain, but that was where my opportunity fell by unexpected coincidences. Japanese pottery has influenced me since the mid-forties when I read the English potter Bernard Leach's *A Potter's Book*. Leach had spent years in Japan before settling and establishing his own pottery studio at St. Ives, England. He had also formed a life-long friendship with another world reknown potter, Shoji Hamada of Mashiko, Japan. (Hamada had invited me to spend two years with him, but at the time I could not go because of my university commitments.) Both men were active in the Japanese *Mingei* or the folk-art movement.

Though Leach's standard of excellence was the Sung Dynasty of China, he was the first to open my eyes to the great range of styles and local traditions (some now centuries old) to be found in modern Japan: Hagi, Shigaraki, Tamba, Bizen, Seto, Oribe, Shino, Satsuma, Imari (Arita), Kutani, Mashiko, Onda. In each of these places, usually small country villages, local clays and local ways have combined to produce a distinctive ware. The tradition is kept alive by a master-apprentice lineage stretching far back in time. In Arita for example, the fourteenth generation Kakiemon is now at work in the production of the world-famous Kakiemon ware, and the thirteenth generation Immaemon carries on the Nabeshima tradition. I was to get to know both of these artists. I have acquired works of theirs, and they of mine.

I still largely work in stoneware since I find its earthy naturalness close to my liking. But there is a vast keyboard of clays ranging from the native stoneware I dig to the pure white porcelain stone of Arita—*from the cruddy to the sublime* as I often put itt. That range in itself is very important to me. I have often found a balancing dynamism at work: as my thought approaches one or the other end of such a continum from of the earth earthy to the rarified white light, my pottery will seek out the other end. If my thought plays the whole keyboard, so does my pottery.

I have envisioned a planetary tradition of pottery, a Great Tradition, as I call it, both East and West, of all workers of clay of *all* times, from the Pre-Dynastic Egyptian potter of whom Hans Coper spoke, from the American Indian potter, the

Nigerian potter, to Leach, Hamada, Inoue, and those now working, like myself, in the effort to discipline and unite hearts, hands, and beings in the making of simple vessels of clay. As the sun now rises outside my pottery studio, it strikes the stack of my stoneware kiln, and I am set dreaming of the high fire I want soon to have, to see if some of the large jars I made and decorated this year will survive that final test.

All of the forty years I have been a potter have been devoted to the search for the core of this Great Tradition. It was, however, through the chance I had to apprentice myself to a specific tradition in Artia, Japan, that my search took on a different kind of depth and selflessness than might have been possible had I remained in America and studied the world's pots only in books and museums.

When I went to study in Japan, I vaguely knew there was much more involved than picking up a few techniques. *My own teaching of pottery to beginners had taught me what a total art of body-mind and life-world pottery means to be.* I already knew something of the paradoxical intentionality associated with the practice of any art:

> No matter how we rehearse our intention, the performance has its own accidents. And though we may prefer indeterminacy, we are determined in our preference and find that we are surprising almost nobody with our surprises. Because of the law of polarity, if we devote ourselves too exclusively to one pole, our world will tend to go flat. It is not a formula we are involved in, but a mystery.[17]

But I was still not thoroughly prepared for the Zen-like attitude with which the practice of a traditional art is associated by the Japanese. A classical statement of this is Herrigel's *Zen and the Art of Archery.*[18] Reading Herrigel and actually learning a traditional art in Japan are, however, very different realities! I have told this story anew from the standpoint of my own pottery experiences in Japan in my recent book *Zen and the Art of Pottery.*[19]

We of the West, with our pride in freedom and individuality, do not emotionally comprehend the selflessness taken on by an initiate or a disciple within an Eastern tradition, nor how this is mediated through a guru or master. The master stands in a long line of masters. It is the tradition that this lineage represents that the master embodies. His *right answers* are not just his own. He is like a judge who must come to a modern interpretation of a law *and* its long history.

In India where spiritual disciplines are practiced according to a number of established traditions, a guru is a master well along on the path, perhaps himself an initiate from earliest childhood. Pandit Arya has recently talked to Americans as an initiate himself, on *What is a Guru?*

> The *guru*, that focus of the great God, great Self, great *shakti*, supreme transcendental energy, is very powerful. That person is one in whom this field is very intense. Do you know the story of Christ and the robe? "Who is touching my robe?" He said, "I see my power passing." This is not a myth. It happens in the great yoga tradition too.
>
> ...initiation is the one and only secret of yoga science. It involves a different dimension of the mind, a linking of minds. I know, for instance, that my *guru* protects me. I know that whatever I'm doing is known to him because there is this link. I know, too, that I am less aware of this link than he is; that is why I am the disciple and he is the master.
>
> A guru will never place a disciple in a situation that he cannot handle, but the disciple has to handle it to the maximum of his capacity. The *guru* brings you to your limits. That's how he trains you to rise, to elevate yourself. No laziness is allowed. No laziness of mind is allowed. And that is what is known as teaching. It is not lecturing; that is nothing.
>
> When you become an initiate, then, what is your relationship with the *guru*?...The relationship from the guru's side can be total, but normally it varies according to the degree you feel the relationship—and "feel" here does not mean an emotional need. It is something much purer than that. In means, how much of your life can you give to the *guru*, for example? Go as far as you can go, and that is your relationship. Again: meditation, service and purity of life. The farther you go in that, the more your relationship with the *guru* develops. Come closer. Your aspiration, then, is lifted upward. It is said, "If you walk one step toward the *guru*, the *guru* walks four steps toward you."[20]

We in the West have no tradition culturally and historically established quite comparable to this. It is important to note as well that this is an oral tradition, an *act-centered one*, not one dependent on the atrophying authority of the printed word alone. Although the *guru* may engage in anagogy, revelation is directly experienced by him. *The voice or the silence of the guru addresses a part of our mind that cannot,* like even the scriptures, *be put back on the shelf.*

My teacher, whom I will call *Sensei* in the Japanese manner, was referred to as "a four hundred year old freak" by one of my students when Sensei came to American during the summer of 1976 to help mediate the Arita tradition to my advanced pottery class concentrating on porcelain throwing. It was an apt description, for Sensei stood on the shoulders of many other potters who stood on the shoulders of still many others in an unbroken chain stretching undoubtedly back through Korea to China.

I learned that in working on the porcelain I was indirectly working on myself. I learned that my breathing, my body, my thoughts all had to come to terms with a selfless immersion in practice: *right attitude, right mind, right practice. See yourself, know yourself, free yourself*—through this discipleship, this discipline. There is also something here in common with Bachelard's and Ponge's attitude: if we can see well and dream well, we can write well. These are not completely new notions. Many of them can be found in Christian writings or in those of Western mystics as well. But I had the opportunity to experience them as applied directly to the simple acts of wedging clay, throwing and tooling pots, and decorating and firing. It even included the ritual of sweeping out the studio. This was new to me, and it came at the right time in both my life and in that of my teacher.

But I intuitively had known all of these things beforehand. I had moved to the woods, set up a pottery partnership, built kilns and had my own studio ten years before going to Japan. *My students and I were already in search of tradition* and of the unity of life and work undergirding a sense of genuine community and of relatedness to nature. It is a small step from this attitude to that expressed in the Bhagavad Gita:

> The world is imprisoned in its own activity, except when actions are performed as worship of God. Therefore, you must perform every action sacramentally (as if it were *yajna*, the sacrifice that, in its divine Logos-essence, is identical with the Godhead to whom it is offered), and be free from all attachment to results.[21]

The Fading of Tradition

Though I learned that this attitude *can* be embodied in the practice of a traditional art in Japan, over the intervening years I also learned that it is becoming an endangered species in Japan itself, for socio-cultural reasons beyond the scope of this work to analyze. So it has been that the spiritual burden of my discipleship to this specific tradition, that of Arita, has been elevated to one of more planetary scope, in truth a Great Tradition. This *Tradition* is embodied in the *esoteric tradition* or the *perennial philosophy* as it is appropriate to art. This means *not* as a spiritual science under some guru, but rather, as *an act of love in the service of the evolution of consciousness through the sacramental performance of that art.*

After a return visit to Japan in 1980 for several exhibitions of my pottery there, I came to some new and even painful insights. The spirit which Japan had helped me search for was diminishing at its source, so that I sometimes felt that in my own way I was reminding them of their own roots.

In travelling back and forth from America to Japan, the question arose whether our collective future might not indeed be somewhat beyond human freedom and dignity. Most frightening of all, we might not even know the difference.

Already Japan seems to be beyond freedom and America beyond dignity. Nowhere can this be seen more clearly than in art: Japan is all *a priori* form, control and skill; America is all shock, anti-structure and surface novelty. By the negational principle a movement of freedom in Japan stands out pure and clear; in America human dignity has all but vanished from the fast-moving pace of daily life.

In America, *A Bureau of Appreciation* might be set up where citizens could go to be valued and heard with no judgment or end in mind. There, as in Heidegger's definition of language and its origin, we would enter a clearing where the peal of stillness preceding the coming of being can yet be heard. All the dignity of our potential would come forth.

In Japan, in the *Office of Free Acts*, citizens would gather to express intrusive spontaneity and to allow emotion to surface without aid of *sake* and forgetfulness. Love and creativeness would receive state sanction.

Were these pseudo-bureaucratic novel institutions to be found side by side in a neutral place half Japanese and half American, and were a Japanese and an American to leave them simultaneously and meet halfway, an East-West dialogue might occur on the theme of "the human spirit and its evolution."

So unsettling might such a meeting be that the bewildered dialogue partners, blinded by the light of a true transcultural relation, would probably re-enter the wrong institution and come out in comfortable reaction formation all the more confirmed—Japanese here, American there, much as before. The passing light of that dialogue would not then be able to sustain itself beyond a barely conscious trace, like a dream residue all but crowded out at mid-day.

But why should tradition fade at all? I pick up a humble Karatsu tea bowl several hundred years old. It is smaller than modern ones—maybe hands were smaller then. But it fits beautifully into my hand. This tea bowl departs from symmetry just slightly. A quiet unobtrusive gray color, it has glaze drippings of a sudden dip into the liquid ash glaze, and there are marks where the fingers held it then. Inside, one careless spiral brush stroke of hakeme white slip (a thick white clay painted on with a coarse broomstraw brush) winds its way from bottom center to upper rim. In the cradle of the bowl there are also three irregular unglazed spots where the brown sandy clay shows through. Here clay balls held another bowl inside this one during the firing. This beautiful ceremonial piece inspired me to write:

Karatsu Tea Bowl

It floats off-center in hands cupping the
patient air into ritual as
   everyman's fingers dance across that
timeless gate of fire...while
   the farmer's chopsticks shovel in
noon rice, uncovering clouds spiralling
   off into infinity—
   how did a careless pinch of elegance
settle into pearls and ashes this way?

K.B.

Actually tradition never really fades at all. It is passionately alive for all those who can hear:

The temple bell stops
But the sound keeps coming
Out of the flowers.[22]

Hieratic Presences and Kiln Gods

Pottery has always drawn me toward that place in experience where new rituals and sacraments come into being. Revelation, divination and sacred possession have in common the idea that the divine and the human have interpenetrated. The numinous is just as much around the corner of my kiln as in the hands of a priestess at the great oracle of Delphi or flowing through a healer at Epidauros.[23]

Myth is that which takes over the night spaces of the mind. It exists even for us today, as though there were a vestigial native or folk wisdom more bred in the marrow bone than in the brain. Our dreams and reveries are permeated by archetypes and intuitive premonitions. We miss our natural innocence. We long to stand alone before the ocean or lost deep in a virgin forest near the sacred mountain.[24]

There is a community of work which arises spontaneously in an open environment where pottery is practiced in the spirit of the Great Tradition. There we become stimulated by a spectrum of less than conscious mythogenic forces. We stand between earth and sky, half gods and half human, in dialogue with elemental natural forces.[25]

It feels good to respond to these urges openly and playfully. When I taught pottery, my students and I would unselfconsciously pick up a piece of clay to fashion special *kiln gods* as a supplication to the unknown forces of fire. We would crowd the projection of the kiln door with spectacular new kiln gods before each firing. Those from the previous firing often disappeared into a cavern under the kiln chamber floor, to become permanently fired. Then later they took their place in an anonymous collection of used but not depotentized kiln gods encircling the high rafters of the kiln shed.[26].

Kiln gods want to be made without preconception. They stand *completely* outside aesthetic criticism. They clean out the mind through searching fingers at work according to an ancient urge. They deploy and damp any hubris which presumes that we control fire. They can be playful, terrifying, childlike, simplified or stylized, actual gods and mythic beings, griffons, gargoyles, centaurs, typhons, elements, pure textures and geometric forms — no limit can invade their symbolic and formal range.[27]

What we do in throwing, tooling, decorating, glazing, and firing *is not to be taken lightly*. It has all the seriousness *and* naturalness of divine play. It is indeed a *self-formative as well as a self-transformative process.*[28]

The shapes of pottery are pure and simple: cylinders, spheres, sections of spheres, and variants and combinations of these. They are fundamentally anthropomorphic: lips, shoulders, necks, bellies, feet, ears, arms. Each unique piece exhibits a fused physiognomy and gesture all of its own. Some pieces seem to be at the top of a cycle of full inhalation.

Others squat low, all *hara* or belly like a fat unshakable Buddha. What is not seen infuses what is: the other side of the piece, the bottom, and most mysteriously the dark interior continuous with the nothingness from which it came.[29]

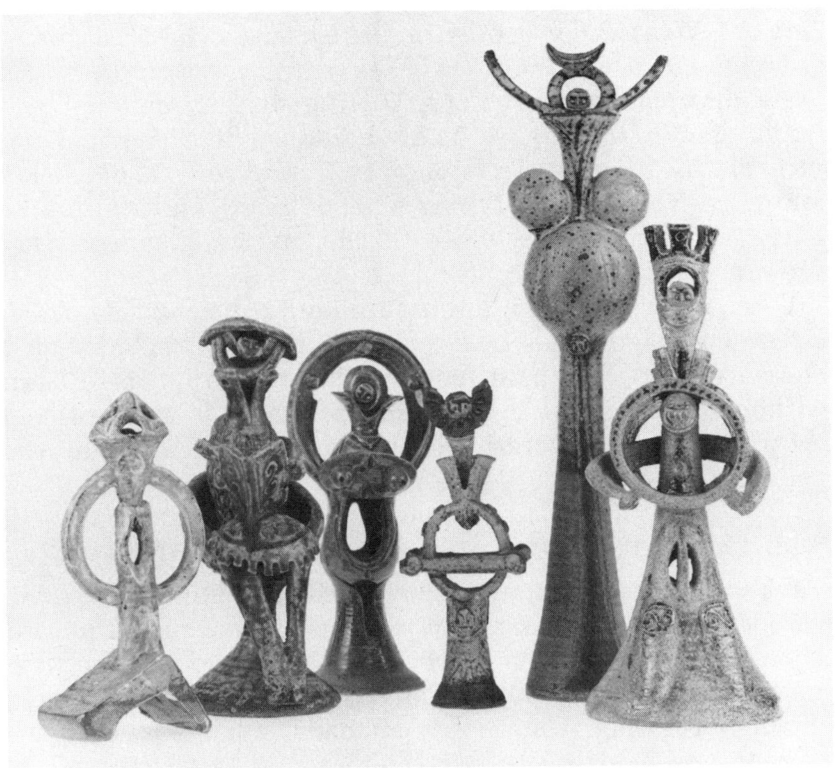

Hieratic Clay Presences.
Stoneware. By the author.

Over the years as potter I have fashioned hieratic and primitive clay presences. These have something in common with kiln gods but they are more sustained, more based in dreams, more overladen with an archetypal archaeology of symbols. Often they are primal mothers, earth goddesses, valley spirits, and in general personifications of the feminine principle, of the fecund mystery of life. At other times they personify nature directly: the river spirit, the tree of life, the ocean, the mountain, and the arc of the sky. They can even fuse into a complete environment or landscape, a micro-universe of the universal.[30]

As a wheel potter I have gradually learned the structure of forms in clay, so that formation and expression are always one — neither clay nor idea running wild. These personages and gods are not premeditated in detail. They have their own guiding images. But they are constructed as a rule from a *clay bank* in which scores of pre-thrown cylinders, cones, spheres, necks, and parts of these are kept in a damp but firm state appropriate to joinery, cutting, fitting, shaping and building. *With care*, such a clay bank can be active and serviceable for months. Thus one can improvise without delay and deep forethought, taking what is ready and waiting as both stimulus and response to the mythic dream of clay presence.[31]

When I walk through a museum under the attitude of the Great Tradition, I see how diversely this mythogenic spirit has surfaced throughout history. There is so much to learn without any desire for imitation. I belong to an unbroken brotherhood and sisterhood in clay of which I am the youngest sibling.[32]

Decoration as Disciplined Spontaneity

Like the professional musician, dancer, and athlete, the practitioner of a traditional art in the East is *disciplined toward trained spontaneity*. A reciprocity is inculcated in which the hand finds the form in moving, and the form moves the hand in coming into being. That is why Hamada could paint the same ostensive decoration for decades, for each performance deserved a standing ovation. The brush selflessly moved of its own volition, perfect for the piece and the occasion.[33]

The story is told of an Eastern master painter who sent his apprentice away from the studio into a grove of bamboo trees, telling him not to come back until he felt as one with the bamboo. Days went by, and the student failed to return. The master finally found him swaying with the bamboos in the summer wind. "Go away," said the apprentice, "I am absorbing the sun and swaying with the wind." "Come," said the master. "Now it is time to paint."

Decoration thus evokes the image of relaxed concentration and of serious play. In origin, the words *decorate, decorative, and decoration* retain their connotations of wholeness in their root meanings: *to be fitting and acceptable; grace, elegance, beauty, seemliness,* and to my surprise these link up with *to learn, to be a disciple,* and *discipline.*

We also need to set off taste from *fashion* in trying to delimit the true meanings of decorating. Simply put, taste and decoration are not subservient to *ruling fashion.* Taste projects an ideal community. It "...makes an act of knowledge...which cannot be separated from the concrete situation on which it operates and cannot be reduced to rules and concepts."[34]

Thus one cannot *demonstrate* decoration; one can only decorate. The act and its meaning are one, and the thought or image prior to the act is not the act but only the first moment of the act.

Accidents are not decorative unless they *fall toward* the event of decorating—to use the original meaning of *accident.* Kiln accidents such as in a wood-firing where flame and fly-ash leave their mark are decorative because they are directly linked to the spontaneity of the firing process. Whenever pots are fired to a high temperature with active flame in the chamber they receive degrees of accidental or natural decoration. *It is as though the clay speaks the first word, the potter the second, and the kiln the last.*[35]

The natural accidents of natural decoration are the truth criterion for our attitude toward all decoration. They are like the decoration of true character, where a thing appears as what it really is. Some potters settle for the subtlety of accidental, natural decoration alone. This is the humblest decoration path to follow. In Bizen ware of Japan for example, some dozen clearly different fire and fly-ash patterns are categorized and cultivated.

But decoration in pottery rarely stops with natural, accidental decoration. Usually these intensify and mystify intentional decoration. In the earliest pieces I can find the scratch of a twig, the mark of the finger, the pinched coil, the effigy on the rim of a jar, legs that are modeled like feet, spouts which are beaks of birds, and handles turning into branches, snakes, and dragons. This is a second level of decoration springing organically from the process of forming itself. At this level, decoration is relatively unselfconscious. In the method I described at the beginning of this chapter where I constructed a jar by a combination of throwing, coiling, and pinching with fingers and bisque-clay stamp, forming and decorating were one.[36]

The third level arrives when I pick up brush or carving tool and face the blank pot, much in the spirit that the painter addresses the canvas. It is the least accidental and process-related of all decoration. But it is worth all risk of ruined pots, for here I can play harmoniously or contrapuntally with the other two levels of decoration. A great pot somehow fuses all three.[37]

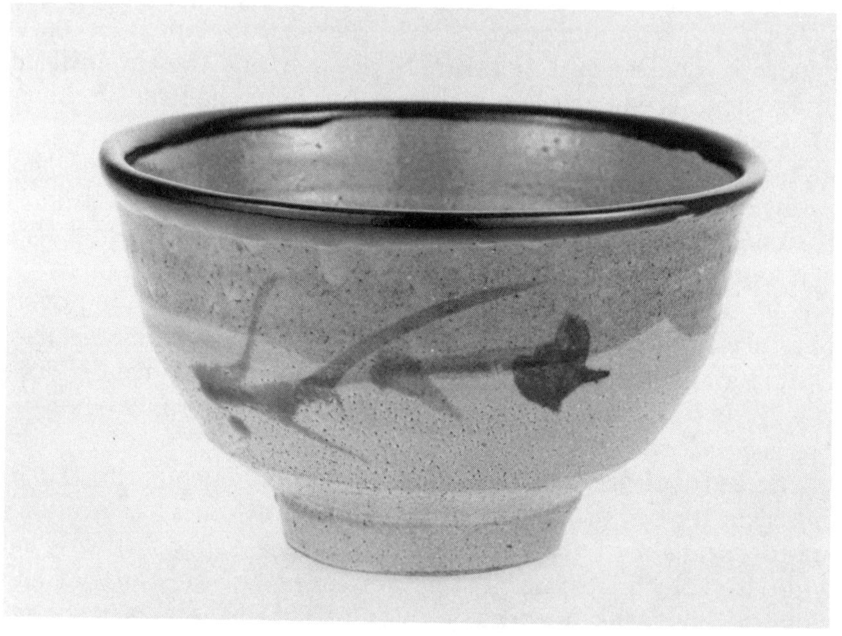

Bowl by Hamada Shoji.
Stoneware. Collection, Rochester Institute of Technology. Gift of the author.

I pick up a simple bowl of Hamada's. Fire and glaze, forming and tooling, slipping and decorating have all become one, an integration even further enhanced by its living weight and surface, its balance in relation to my eye and body. Were I to use it in the daily ritual of eating—for it "functionally" functions as well—I would erase any taint it might acquire of object fetishism as an art object by a famous potter. What comes through is the *vitality*, the *genial spirit*, and the *paradoxical nature of the man himself*, which somehow is yet transcended in this piece that has its own presence.[38] The 14th century Chinese scholar T'ang Hou perfectly caught what I feel:

> Set forth your heart, without reserve,
> And your brush will be inspired.

> Writing and painting serve a single aim,
> The revelation of inner character.
> Here are two companions,
> An old tree and tall bamboo,
> Metamorphosed by his unreined hand,
> Finished in an instant.
> The embodiment of a single moment
> Is the treaure of a hundred ages,
> And one feels, unrolling it, a fondness,
> As if seeing the man himself.

Spontaneous decoration is learned through discipline, native vitality and exuberance, playfulness and risk. *And especially by connecting to one's life-world.* Decoration celebrates and commemorates a direct art-life connection.[39] It hangs a medal on the event. When we bought a new truck I carved it on a pot that showed it roaming through time and space, conquering miles and linking together faraway places. And after returning from the islands of Tahiti I couldn't get that special tropical magic out of my mind. The fragrance of those incredible flowers, that warm balmy air, turquoise water so blue and so green like no other islands anywhere on earth, their fiery music and native dancing—all lingered in my mind for weeks and weeks. Part of me was still there. So when I threw a particularly pregnant sphere that was wet and extremely sensous, I was again transported back to that magical land, and I began carving a memory pot in honor of the time spent there.

Such decorations are very obvious and direct. The event and the decoration are almost one. But the content and the affection with which it is remembered have a forming energy all of their own. Easterners have still another advantage through their pictographic language, through the ambiance surrounding each character, and in their training in brushwork and calligraphy which makes their writing naturally poetic and spontaneous. Still, whatever the motif or image, that which is painted, scratched, modelled, or carved on pots is never painting, graphics, sculpture, or architecture; and it must, in addition to itself, establish its relationship to fire and forming as well.

I am sensitive to two large modes of decorating. One of these is lyrical, intense and direct. I call it *spontaneity-with-containment.* The other is symphonic, expansive and architectonic. I call it *spontaneity-with-dispersion.* These should be seen as tendencies, not as pure or mutually exclusive; but it is true that they are not often found together.

A single pot is a universe all of its own. It can as well be seen as a symbol for the cosmos which receptively awaits one or the other of these modes to reveal some aspect of its endless complexity, never repeated but falling toward simpler patterns within that infinite variety. In spontaneity-with-containment the universe is reflected as a space which is deep, astral and oceanic: the space of ultimate quietness that becomes the ground for the piercing song of a bird. In the case of spontaneity-with-dispersion, I sense all the structural articulations which complicate sensate space: the interwoven lushness of a landscape painted by Rubens or Bonnard in their late years, where the ten thousand things are caught up in a sweeping organic unity.

Assuredly the decoration of pots can reveal all that we as humans can be. The first mode moves into being like a sudden revelation. It is an act of possession, the gesture of a hero. The scales are delicate. Everything—the brush, the form, the moment—must be *precisely* right. One mis-stroke and the whole thing must be rebegun.[40]

Here is an example of the spirit of this kind of spontaneity. A broad house painter's brush loaded with molten wax breaks

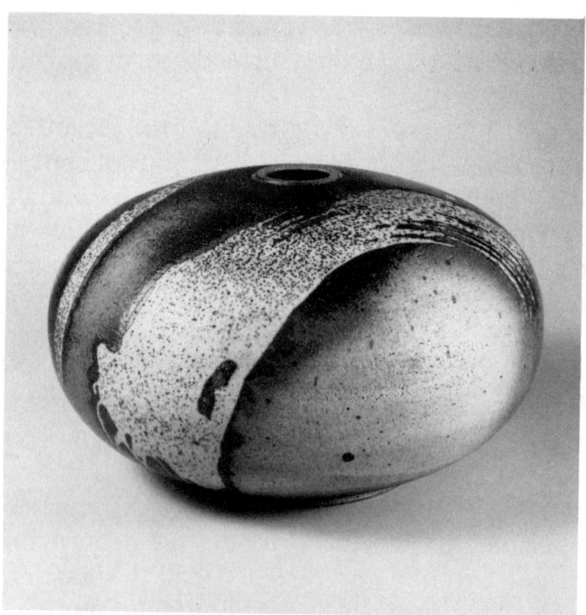

Homage to Hokusai.
Stoneware. By the author. Collection, Masashi Sakaida (Kakiemon), Arita, Japan.

upon the white ground of a wide sphere like a wave just beyond its crest. The natural force of the gesture is forever captured in the runs, the gaps, and the reaching out and fading foam furthest from the point of impact. Black stain blown upon the wax resist accents the organic textures left behind by the splash of the cooling wax, and the whole is unified by further colored oversprays and a simple wood-ash glaze.

The other mode, spontaneity-by-dispersion, has a different pace about it. The quality of the present moment is drawn out

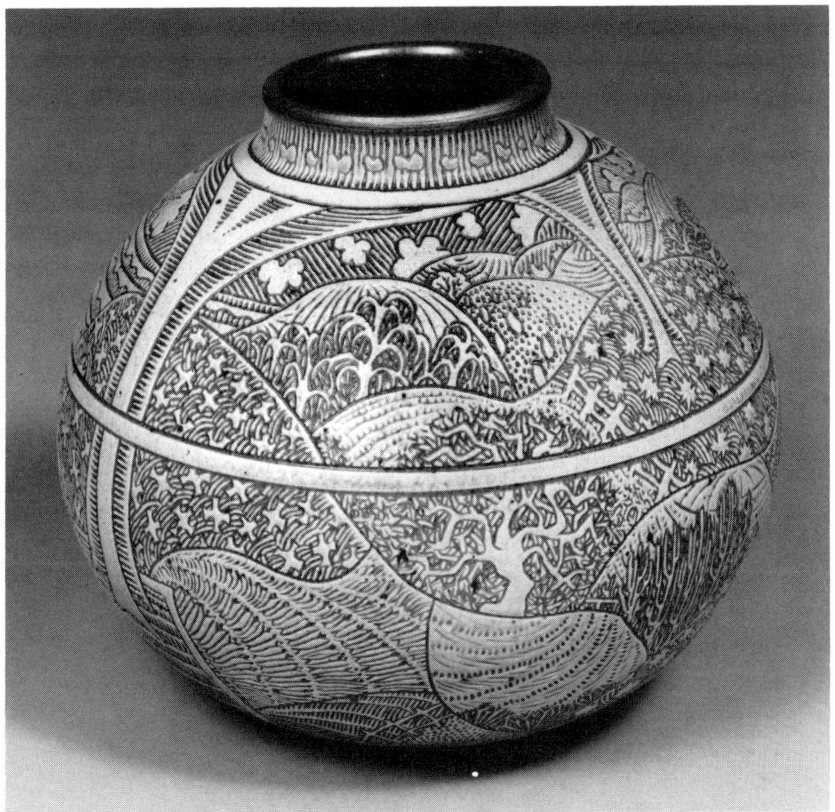

Hills by the Sea.
Stoneware. By the author. Collection, Institute of the Arts and Humanistic Studies, Penn State. Gift of the author.

patiently, lovingly. Why hurry? What's the urgency? Why settle for one lyrical passage? The mode is nurturant and trusting. There is time to explore in detail every aspect of a theme.[41] A complex network of carvings spreads over the white ground of a large sphere. Fields of flowers, forests, tilled land, fence rows, sky, clouds and ocean in endless variety find expression within the many structural subdivisions of this round jar. (See *Hills by the Sea.*)

Decoration then, is one with the wholeness of pottery itself. It doesn't even end with the firing, but seeks to live on in the right environment and relationship. And the best decorations are like divine play working through a creative channel, surfacing in a way surprising to me as artist as well.

One time I had in my studio three or four large jars, tooled and covered with light colored slip clay, waiting patiently for

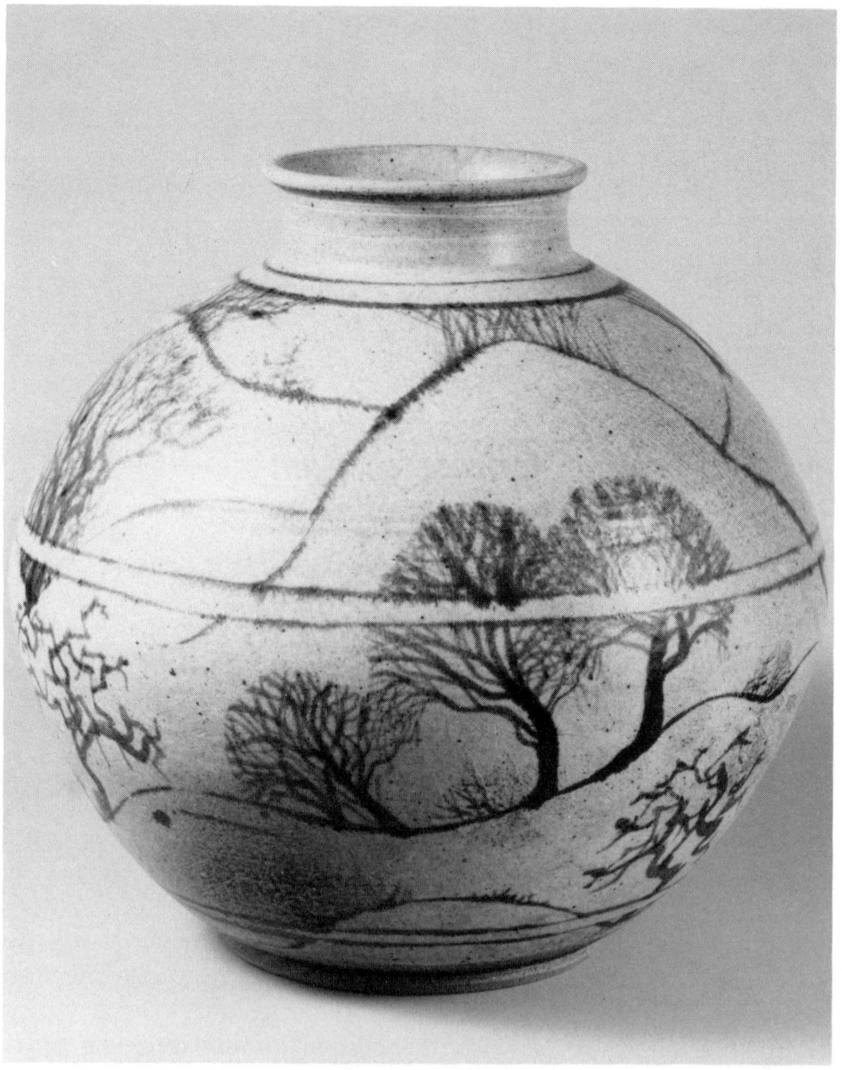

Trees on Winter Fields.
Stoneware. By the author. Collection, Palmer Museum of Art, Penn State.
Gift of Joan Beittel.

decoration. We drove through the countryside right after a fresh snow. Upon our return, the image of the divided field rows and the stark purity of the tree forms set against them seemed to paint themselves on one of the waiting spherical jars. The occasion, the form in readiness, and my agency as artist fused into one unified act of celebration which inundated me with both playful and sacred feelings. (See *Trees on Winter Fields*.)

When a sphere is divided, it sets up its own harmonics. In sacred geometry such as that used in the lay-out of temples in ancient times, even numbered divisions were thought to be

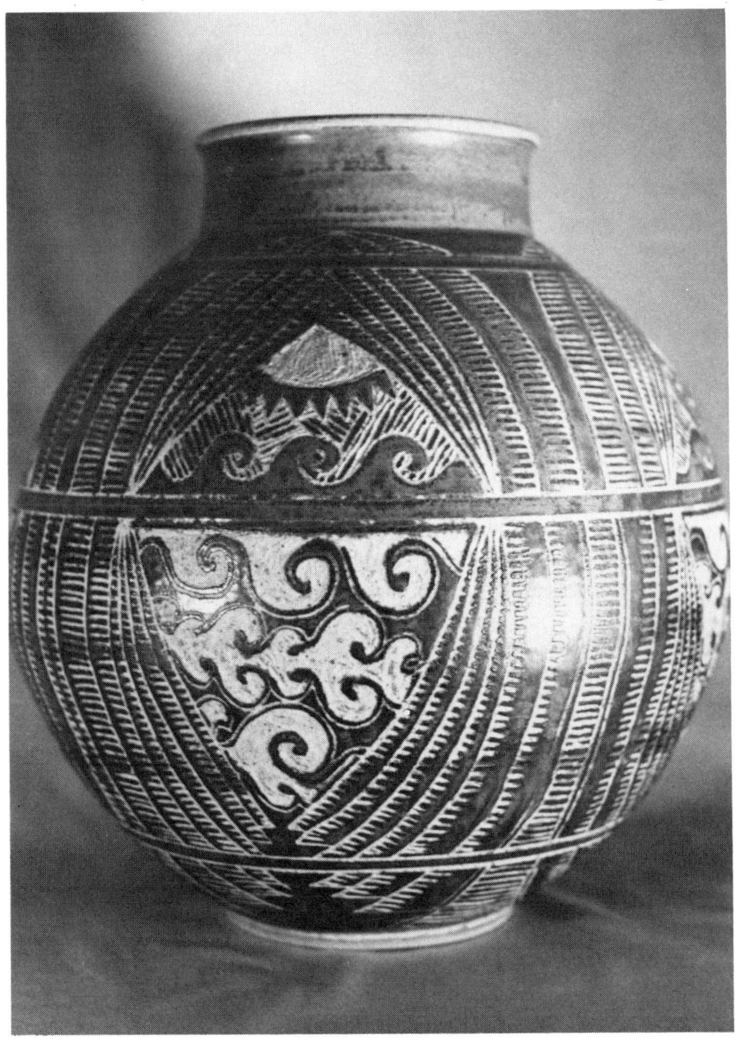

Pago Pago Rainmaker.
Stoneware. By the author.

celestial, while odd numbered ones were called *terrestrial.* I tend to divide spheres in even numbers although lately I have used more and more a division into six basic parts to escape from the more common regularity of 4, 8, 16, and so on. Seen from the top, a sphere regularly divided into major segments which contain the decorative elements appears like a *yantra* or visual mandala used as an aid to meditation. More than once such decorations have led me to circular drawings as well.

In another large jar a simple fourfold division from the top created four arches. These were intensified by a series of receding arches clustered around the four central piers. The result is much like an architectural construction, and it is well suited to the pure geometry of pots themselves. Here the receding arches come to a point at both the top and mid-way down the sphere so that they draw back like deeply folded curtains encircling an open window. In the "windows" sun and wave motifs appear, changing their figure-ground relationships above and below a middle band. All of this must be carved through the slipped surface—in this case black—while the jar is still damp.

Decoration is just not what is fitting to the whole. Decoration *is* the whole. There is a true ecology of decoration—not merely just a set of techniques.

Selflessness, Tradition and Community in the Art of Pottery

Pottery practiced as a discipleship within an alive tradition, whether it be a specific one like that of Arita or a Great Tradition of planetary scope such as I have envisioned, soon raises the image of selflessness, selfless practice, or selfless service. There is a connotation that the notion of a separate self is even an illusion. In the religious sense this meaning is relatively clear: it is not the ego self but the divinity within one which we choose to engage. "Rooted in Being," says the Bhagavad Gita, "proceed into right action."

> "Internally" every religion is the doctrine of the one Self and its earthly manifestation, as also the way leading to the abolition of the false self or the way of the mysterious reintegration of our "personality" in the celestial Prototype.[42]

Clearly, from the viewpoint of a vital tradition or from within a true community, the false self would give way to the true self of the tradition or community. There the shared values and goals would define the ideal prototype, and the communal spirit itself would affirm its truest expression. This is why, when Sensei came first to America to teach with me in 1969, his reaction to a "fine arts" display of pottery was so strong that he said: "Expression only. No depth." Now these words are upsetting to Americans, but they can be easily understood when heard from within a long tradition. We forget that from the viewpoint of tradition, as in much of the world's art over many centuries, art has been defined by nobility of content, exactness of symbolism, and purity of style.[43] Further, clay as an art material has its own objective qualities, its own find of cosmic significance, which no amount of experiment and innovation can gainsay. From this point of view the modern retreat from the intrinsic qualities of art materials is but another sign of our being *out of touch* with *spirit in matter*. Within tradition a *communal gathering together of potters values clay as clay, fire as fire, and the varied labor and work connected with these as worthy and honorable in all their many forms.*

Though the West seems more rootless in these matters, nevertheless there is a clear selflessness in Ponge's openness to being *invaded* by things, or to Keats' becoming all that he experiences. There is also the widespread realization that the state of artistic creation is an out of self, almost out of body-and-mind state.

In considering the evolution of consciousness and in seeing growth as a realization of progressively higher levels, we conceive of the death of the self of a lower level as leading to transformation to a higher level, as on the way to the Self *celestial prototype*. In this sense the beginning level of consciousness which is in reality a false self is disengaged and transcended – a process which is often lengthy and painful. Substitute gratifications are even said to order themselves according to the Great Chain: "material/food/money, sex, power, belongingness, conceptual knowledge, self-esteem, self-actualization, subtle transcendence, ultimate enlightenment."[44] But that's only if we opt for hierarchies, for even ultimate enligtenment can become a *substitute gratification.*

But we do not wish to commit the artist to the same task and method as an initiate within an esoteric spiritual science, though much overlap can and does occur. It is humbler to say that "the poet is successful in proportion to his ability to find means for holding a vision in his art. This kind of alchemy is difficult and dangerous..."[45] What we are saying here is that the vision and the alchemy for holding to it in art are often rooted in selfless discipleship as practiced within a vital tradition.

In my own teaching of pottery I make use symbolically of many aspects of the Arita tradition. I feel that collective and communal ways with clay can provide a discipline of the total body-mind in excess of ego-centered or even personal and idiosyncratic beginnings. At the very least, the inclusion of such methods, rituals and attitudes sets up a dialogue between East and West which in itself expands parochial awareness. At its very best, the spiritual dimensions of a planetary Great Tradition uniting the vast community of workers in clay is powerfully evoked. Nobility of content, exactness of symbolism and purity of style are never finished matters even within a strict tradition, but are achieved in the presence of the worthy lineage. Also by beginning my classes in this way I hope to suggest something of the selflessness and self-study an honest search for tradition transmits.

I have also been priviledged to see the communal nature of clay-working expand into true community, where dialogue

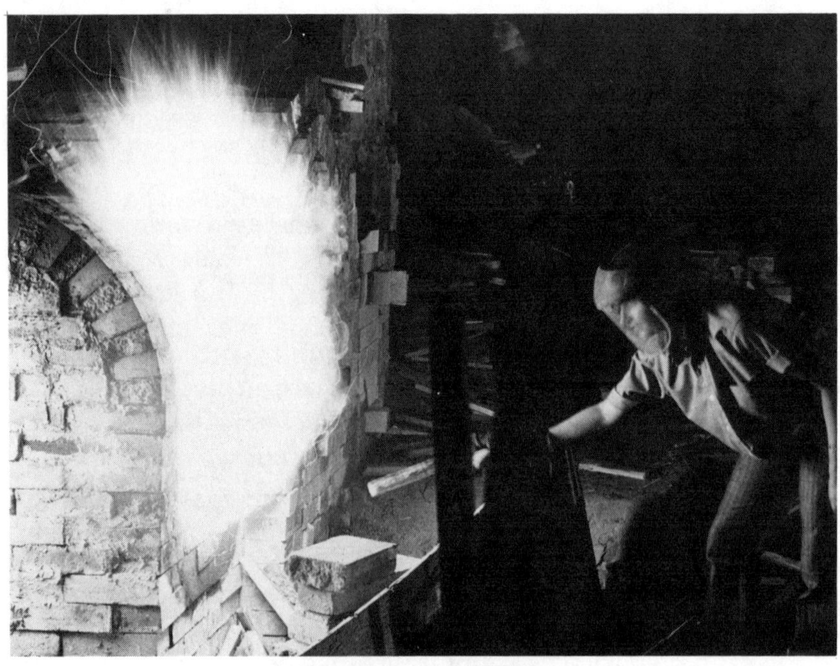

Communal Wood-Firing.
Author's advanced pottery class.

reverberates throughout and where sacrament, ritual and common goal organically arise. Among the specific instances of these I will point here to three: (1) a summer in which anonymous collaboration was practiced where nobody *owned* a pot, where the artistic work was often collaborative – where different persons threw, tooled and decorated the same piece; (2) several summer classes where the building of high fire wood kilns was the common goal; and (3) many instances where we dug native clay and communally prepared it by trampling it with bare feet. Selflessness, self-study and self-discovery were natural correlates of these communal ventures. As one of the students in the first summer's efforts to build a climbing wood-fired hill kiln, in the way of the Japanese *noborigama*, put it:

> I wasn't prepared for what really happened but fortunately no preparation was necessary. It is difficult to explain what really did happen – it was more an evolution than a happening. The core element to this evolution was people – people doing something together in a very natural way. People standing in sloppy sticky goo and being excited about its change in color and purity. Jobs being done by people who weren't asked to do them – whose only payments were blisters, sunburn, insect bites, sore muscles and a feeling of satisfaction.
>
> The wonder is that though this effort led to failure this group of people failed with more enthusiasm than others do in succeeding. Failure did not disorganize this group but instead tended to unite them even more.
>
> The above is a rather superficial report of what a group of people did and how they outwardly reacted (or seemed to react to me). There was, however, some mysterious element in the clay, bricks, wood, fire and air that motivated these people and it is beyond me to explain. As a member of the group, you understand what I mean but others (outsiders) might never understand.[46]

Within tradition and within community selflessness is a natural way to enlarged selfhood. There is no strain to be *original* – for this is an error of the *technical theory of art* which presumes to control means to predetermined ends.[47] *"In traditional art the masterpiece is most often an anonymous culmination of a series of replicas; a work of genius is almost always the resultant of a long collective elaboration.* For example, many Chinese masterpieces are copies of which the models are unknown."[48] We might say that to the degree art retains the sense of living community and tradition, so it also opens up the opportunity of participating in spiritual growth. This thus could be called the communal pole of selflessness just as matter and the common thing constituted the more solitary pole of selflessness working through the material or concrete imagination. Both approaches lead through death of the lesser self to progressively higher levels of consciousness.

Within tradition and community we find a drawing together of artistic and religious modes of being. This is not to say that the religious way cannot be infused with an artistic orientation toward every act and thought as a consummate *art of being*; nor that the artistic cannot be infused with a spiritual orientation that finds the divine manifested everywhere and in all creation. It was the philosopher Charles Morris who suggested that art and religion are basically different *universes of discourse*, art being essentially appraisive-valuative, while religion is essentially *prescriptive-incitive* in the sense that ideal character is *prescribed* and we are then *incited* to achieve it.[49]

Insofar as there is community and deep vital tradition as the milieu in which art functions, to that degree there is a direct rapprochement between the religious and artistic universes of discourse. Then there can be revelation through art in the religious sense as well. In other words the appraisive-valuative mode of the artist would then have as its direct concern the prescriptive-incitive mode of community and tradition. Then there would be a natural kinship between the artist's progressive organicism and the saint's idealist organicism. The hidden order of art celebrates over and over again the revealed character of the holy. This requires saints and sages who welcome art as genuine revelation of the truth of Being, equally as important as the scriptures themselves. It also requires artists who can make the ultimate sacrifice of their *self-full-ness* so that in their *self-less-ness* they may dwell in grace and receive the *vision*. The *well* then is the *whole*, so that *vision* and *will* can lead to holy *form*. *The ultimate realm of art and the ultimate realm of the Ultimate then coalesce.* Needless to say the conditions for this rapprochement are largely wanting in contemporary culture, as rare as the existence of genuine tradition and community that embraces the artist. The fear projected on the artist may well represent one of the last faults of saint and sage, for it is simultaneously a fear of the free becoming of Being through the creative. The *whole* as a *creation* signifies a hidden order and unfinished character as an organizing principle within the *whole* itself, for which a *Divine hermeneutics* forever hidden from even "God-realized" mortals would be required.

References

1. Bly, R. *News of the universe.* San Francisco: Sierra Club Books, 1980; p. 272.

2. Coper, H. *Collingwood/Coper.* London: Victoria and Albert Museum, 1969 (catalogue).

3. Coper, H. *Ibid.*

4. *Hoff, B. The Tao of Pooh.* N.Y.: Penguin Books, 1983; p. 153.

5. Williams, W. C. *The selected poems of William Carlos Williams.* N.Y.: New Directions, 1968; p. 54.

6. *Ibid.,* p. 68.

7. *Ibid.,* p. 84.

8. *Ibid.,* pp. 67-68.

9. *Ibid.,* pp. 91-92.

10. Jones, R. and Daniels, K. (eds.) *Of solitude and silence,* Boston: Beacon Press, 1981; p. 138.

11. *Ibid.,* pp. 136-137.

12. *Ibid.,* p. 133.

13. *Ibid.,* p. 134.

14. Bachelard, G. *The poetics of reverie.* (D. Russel, trans.) Boston: Beacon Press, 1971; pp. 138, 139, 140.

15. *Ibid.,* p. 141.

16. Beittel, K. *Kenneth Beittel.* Everson Museum of Art Catalogue for exhibition, Syracuse, N.Y.; Aug. 25-Sept. 12, 1978.

17. Richards, M. C. *Centering.* Middletown, Conn.: Wesleyan University Press, 1969; p. 116.

18. Herrigel, E. *Zen in the art of archery.* N.Y.: Vintage BOoks, 1971.

19. Beittel, K. *Zen and the art of pottery.* Tokyo: John Weatherhill, 1989.

20. Arya, U. What is a guru? *Himalayan News,* Nov. 1979, pp. 3,6; p. 6.

21. Huxley, A. *The perennial philosophy.* N.Y.: Harper and Row, 1970; p. 272.

22. Bly, R. *Op. cit.,* reference 1 above, p. 256; poem by Basho.

23. Beittel, K. *Op. cit.,* reference 19 above, p. 32.

24. *Ibid.,* p. 32.

25. *Ibid.,* p. 32.

26. *Ibid.,* p. 32-33.

27. *Ibid.*, p. 33.

28. *Ibid.*, p. 33.

29. *Ibid.*, p. 33.

30. *Ibid.*, pp. 33-34.

31. *Ibid.*, p. 34.

32. *Ibid.*, p. 34.

33. *Ibid.*, p. 87.

34. Gadamer, H. G. *Truth and method.* N.Y.: The Seabury Press, 1975; p. 36.

35. Beittel, K. *Op. cit.*, reference 19 above, p. 86.

36. *Ibid.*, p. 86.

37. *Ibid.*, pp. 86-87.

38. *Ibid.*, p. 87.

39. *Ibid.*, pp. 87-88.

40. *Ibid.*, p. 88.

41. *Ibid.*, p. 89.

42. Schuon, F. *Language of the self.* (M. Pallis and M. Matheson trans.) Madras, India: Ganesh, 1959; p. 234.

43. *Ibid.*, p. 122.

44. Wilber, K. *Up from Eden.* Garden City, N.Y.: Anchor Press/Doubleday, 1981; p. 308.

45. Senior, J. *The way down and out.* N.Y.: Greenwood Press, 1968; p. 63.

46. Anonymous student evaluation from a 1971 summer course in advanced ceramics taught by K. Beittel at The Pennsylvania State University.

47. Collingwood, R. G. *The principles of art.* London: Oxford University Press, 1958.

48. Schuon, F. *Op. cit.*, reference 42 above, p. 127.

49. Morris, C. W. *Signs, language and behavior.* N.Y.: Prentice-Hall, 1946.

7

Qualitative Experiencing

as Expressing

I stretched out
alongside beings and things
Pen in hand, my writing table
(a blank page) on my knees.

Francis Ponge[1]

*We cannot love water, fire, the tree without putting a
love into them, a friendship which goes back to our
childhood.
...childhood remains within us a principle of deep life, of
life always in harmony with the possibilities of new
beginnings. Everything that begins in us with the
distinctness of a beginning is a madness of life.*

Gaston Bachelard[2]

I touch God in my song
as the hill touches the far-away sea
with its waterfall.

Rabindranath Tagore[3]

Overview of the Art of Qualitative Thinking

Dilthey[4] emphasized lived experience, expression, and understanding as the foundation for the "geist sciences." *Geist*, happily refers to both mind and spirit. Dilthey's formulation of the dependency of that experience on expression—on objectifications of mind and spirit, that is—provides the ground for envisioning a combined expressive-hermeneutic art which I call *the art of qualitative thinking*.

Qualitative thinking is put forth here as an *art*. That art is further linked to the hermeneutic enterprise which takes upon itself the contact between shared norms and values and the hidden inner structure of texts and works which we need and wish to understand. The *hermeneutic circle* means that just as works come out of mind, life and spirit, so it is through mind, life and spirit that they are understood. We stand within tradition in expression and in understanding. A clash of time zones is implicated, for though understanding centers within the present it reaches out for what has issued from the past. Further, the linguisticality, historicality, and finitude of the interpreter are essential aspects of understanding, as is the meaning and application of what is understood to the interpreter's on-going life.[5]

The title of this chapter has the important word *as* between qualitative experiencing and expressing. This is the same *as* that Dewey held to in his organicist art theory—perhaps organicist-contextualistic art theory—in his classic work *Art as Experience*[6]. While all experience might not be thought of as art, what Dewey called *an* experience, organizes itself *as* art does and remains the model for a vital conceptualization of art itself. In like manner, all experiencing might not be thought of as expressing, but *qualitative experiencing* is meant to be the equivalent to Dewey's usage and in addition, to connote that it provide us, through expression, with an invaluable text for understanding the deeper meaning of that experience itself. This is what I refer to as an *art of qualitative thinking*. The qualifier "qualitative" to "thinking" is meant to raise thinking above the limits of mind and of its data, intelligibilia, to include spirit and its data, transcendelia. Thus the art of qualitative thinking is a geist (mind-spirit) science or discipline in which certain broad steps lead to progressively higher orders of self-insight and self-understanding and therefore to self-transcendence and self-transformation—in short, *to the evolution of consciousness*. This remains, nevertheless, a love-gnosis, an art-full discipline compatible with the esoteric tradition and the perennial philosophy, but without the local colorations of specific traditions within these. It thus stands in a generalized relationship to them, even as envisioning a planetary Great Tradition in pottery stands in relation to specific traditions, such as that of Arita, Japan.

The art of qualitative thinking superimposes an interpretive process upon a creative process, leading to understanding of the deep structure adumbrated through the expressive act. It bears some relationship to the inquiries in the Drawing Lab, earlier described, in the sense that the influencing inquiries, in accepting the general autonomy and personal meaning of the intentionality to engage in creating art, *produce an open traditionless tradition for art gnosis.* The self-formative process of the artist becomes the eventual focus of these inquiries, and the task of those inquiring becomes that of a depth hermeneutic of the artist's self-formative process. If that depth hermeneutic were to be shared with the artist in a defensible way, it would have to be according to a shared tradition that over-arches both inquirer and artist. At that point, the depth hermeneutic would encompass, in addition to a therapeutic and pedagogic dimension, a critical reflective philosophical one, the interest of which is toward liberation from the limits of thought itself, by acknowledging and speculating upon those limits.[7]

Unlike various therapeutic methods—for example, Progoff's use of the journal as a tool for neo-Jungian self-analysis—the Drawing Lab and the art of qualitative thinking do not directly explore the *shadow*, archetypes, complexes, past traumas, and the like, but rather *actively engage the wholeness of the person in expression*, whatever psychological problems or levels of functioning may be present. The art of qualitative thinking is like a generalized Drawing Lab, extended beyond place and medium to include potentially all media and forms of expression. Wholeness through expression is taken to be the best basis for wholeness of interpretation and understanding toward increments of self-awareness implicated by the deep structure of qualitative experiencing *as* expressing, toward higher and higher levels of consciousness. Something similar is indeed done through a realized guru or a master working within a specific esoteric discipline or tradition: the quality of experience is the route toward interpretation, self-knowledge, understanding, and self-renewal or spiritual progress.

Since gurus, masters, and vital specific traditions are in short supply, considering our planetary need for greater spiritual enlightenment and wider expansion of consciousness, it is my belief that a generalized creative art process combined with a generalized hermeneutics has much to offer toward these ends. Insofar as we are *othered* through making art and through doing hermeneutics, and insofar as both processes reveal the self by departing from the self, this combination constitutes a powerful means of spiritual progress within the reach of solitary or communal involvement in an *art* of qualitative thinking.

The General Structure of the Art of Qualitative Thinking

Quality, consciousness, and experience are separate words for inseparable lived-processes. Current metaphors for consciousness tend toward the dialogue analogy, away from the earlier container-and-contents metaphor, and the still earlier wax-and-stamp metaphor.[8] Our reality, as qualitatively experienced, is dynamically interactive and two-fold from the start. The witnessing effect of consciousness during our most *in-volved* participative states and the way we become addressed by our own expressions point to a constantly reflexive and self-formative process ongoing within us. There is a natural, organic, and æsthetic unity in our experiencing when it has most presence and vitality for us; and this is what Dewey[9] describes as an experience—one with a beginning, middle, and end, like a good drama. It is a rounded out, eventfull and consumatory whole. Poets, artists, saints and sages have all learned to extend the qualitative immediate present, or the eternal present, through special practices that lead to states of bliss and grace.

William James has given a number of images for consciousness. He called it a stream to get at its change with continuity. It became a sculptor finding a single figure in a stone to accentuate the way consciousness has both selectivity and unity. Still again, to show the tender care and authorship the mind has for its thoughts, he spoke of it as a herdsman herding his sheep.[10]

Here we see how James gravitates to imagery and metaphor to remain in touch with an elusive quality. By doing so he creates an expressive symbol which mediates that quality. We will use the word *text* for this symbolic surrogate in what follows, especially in reference to expressions symbolic of the pervasive quality of *an* experience, whether it be of a simple thing, as in a proeme by Ponge, or of some more outright or expansive epiphany as in Blake. Further, there is a functional distinction between the *originary quality* and *dependent quality* of texts, a shift from the more restricted meaning usually held to in hermeneutics. *Originary* simply means that no text exists as the start for our hermeneutic art of qualitative thinking, so that we have to *express* one. A focus on the originary quality of the text sets it off from the dependent quality of those already realized cultural objectifications called works and texts. The latter inspire a consumer's mentality which evoke differing political, academic and language problems than do texts of originary quality. Still, the distinction is largely functional and didactic.

In what follows, the art work—or its qualitative equivalent—as text for an art of qualitative thinking, is presented as a part of a dialectical and cyclical process composed of four moments: (1) *expressive text;* (2) *distancing* or distantiation as the start of an analytical-interpretive effort; (3) *interpreting* as itself a dialectic between explanation and understanding; and (4) *renewing* as a process where mental forces reach their limit and subside, so that evaluation, speculation, and, especially, expressive return can occur. It seems important to concentrate here on the nature of expressive texts.

Expessive Text

This is undoubtedly the most important of the four moments of this art. Unless we imaginatively enlarge our capacities to create and respond, we will not be able to open ourselves to the profundity and potential for meaning of our lived experience. Unless the pool from which we draw is wide and deep, we will have less yield for the remaining three moments, and thus less opportunity for expanding our consciousness through a process of interpretation and self-discovery. Put as a maxim, we could say: the more we move *from* in order to move *to*, the less there is to move *towards*. It is extremely important to develop a discipline of playful immediacy, spontaneity, and imagery toward fullness of expression at the text level.

We will adopt the following operational schema for distinguishing between various kinds of related expressive texts:

1. Expressive-Artistic Modes
   a. Iconic (non-verbal)
   b. Literary
2. Expressive-Descriptive Modes
   a. Phenomenological
   b. Historical

Further reflection on this schema suggests that the expressive-artistic modes are closer to the experiential event—are in fact *themselves* such an event; are depth symbolic — or presymbolic of deep structure; are more risk-taking in their intensity; are more omnivorous of the remaining moments or stages — that is, they tend to absorb distancing, interpretation, and renewal into themselves as one grand qualitative whole, or art; and they give the impression that experience and expression are likewise one whole. In this regard, the expressive-artistic modes are closest to the hidden trope or figure of speech called metaphor in classical rhetoric, where whole-to-whole relationships predominate.

The expressive-descriptive modes, in contrast, give the impression of already starting more distanced from the experiential event or of seemingly allowing a gap to appear between experience and expressing — we say "seemingly," because we are considering qualitative experiencing *as* expressing from the start. These modes also seem to be more reflective or receptive of deep structure than directly symbolic of it. They are more prone, as more self-conscious, to acknowledge from the start the separation of expressive description from distancing, interpretation, and renewal — and with renewal, they are apt to be more inclined toward evaluation, application, or speculation than toward artistic expression. In short, they are more verbal, more intellectual, closer to a hermeneutics dependent on intelligibilia instead of straining to encompass that paradoxical or intuitive thought drawn toward transcendelia — which is where the artistic-expressive modes gravitate. In terms of the classical literary tropes or figures of rhetoric, the expressive-descriptive modes are akin to metonymy, synecdoche, and irony — that is, to part-part, part-whole, or a distanced meta-view that is self aware and quite sophisticated. In an era when scientism and technology enjoy center stage, expressive-descriptive modes often take on a pseudo-scientific language and attitude, or, more generously, admit to a proto-scientific interest ready to be abandoned when "true science" appears.

Artistic-expressive modes are thus more holistic, richer, more profound, but harder to tame toward the other three moments or stages; whereas expressive-descriptive modes move more easily into reduction, analysis, and interpretation, but have less to reduce and interpret within them. The oracular and the revelatory do not yield gracefully to the clarity of a cooler knowing, for "all positivity makes the superlative fall back upon the comparative."[11] Still, as we are presenting these modes, *all* of them are expressive *of* and *as* qualitative experiencing. And even though the mind is of course involved in qualitative thinking, nevertheless it does not forget that its thinking is here treated as an art; and to the degree that it is an art, thinking is imaginative.

> ...the mind that imagines follows the opposite path of the mind that observes; the imagination does not want to end in a diagram that summarizes acquired learning. It seeks a pretext to multiply images...[12]

It is indeed the addition of *qualitative* to *thinking* and the ascription of both to *art* that changes the meaning of thought. Thinking in touch with quality is under the pervasive spell of the latter and cannot bring impurities and reason into the whole further than the notion of pervasiveness permits. It is our belief that the intelligence in art is intrinsic, not derivative. "Art activity may be deemed intelligent if it involves the purposive organization of means to ends, or of parts to wholes. By either criterion, art qualifies as a species of human intelligence."[13] An art of qualitative thinking which begins with an originary expressive-artistic text will reflect throughout its cycle the pervasive qualitative experience that launched it into the world.

Dewey in his essay on *Qualitative Thought*,[14] warns us of the objectifying imperialism of language in the presence of qualitative experience. Subject-predicate logic hypostasizes and freezes qualities into definable *whatnesses*. Things become not individual entities or even types, but containers for their categorized characteristics. The context of a live speaker drops out and leaves behind frozen conceptual schemas. "Honey is sweet" replaces "honey sweetens" which replaces my direct experience of the taste of a particular honey on a specific occasion.

If, however, thought becomes what Heidegger[15] calls *meditative thinking*, then we learn to embrace openness to the mystery "and releasement unto the things themselves." Similarly, the followers of Langeveld's pedagogical phenomenology sent their students out for "the gathering of life-experience material."[16] Under both, language reverts to its original, poetic and phenomenological role of bringing an experiential world into being, rather than pushing it away for calculating control. An art of qualitative thinking based on such origins is life-affirming. Such an art turns life back on itself, telling us that within its inscrutable presence everything we can know is simultaneously revealed and concealed, so that the mystery of consciousness itself comes forward. *Behind life,* said Dilthey, *we cannot go.*[17]

This is an art which is expressively cyclical. It moves from expression through qualitative thinking to expression again. "The being of man is an unsettled being which all expression unsettles. In the reign of the imagination, an expression is hardly *proposed*, before being needs another expression, before it must be the being of another expression."[18]

Science as we know it has progressed by means of a ruthless severance of any bonds bewtween image and concept (although this separation seems less certain in advanced physics). The art we are proposing here bears some resemblance to alchemy, where a mixed comprehension was courted which would welcome images and ideas, contemplations and experiences at the same time. Still—and we are drawing upon Bachelard here—"...from all this past of culture, it remains true...that the images of substances are touched by a polemic between imagination and thought."[19] Even more so will this be true of our focus on experiencing quality: *the existential and the ideational set up a dialectic.* This is precisely what hermeneutics as the science of meaning and understanding sets out to study.

Expressive-Artistic Texts

The following examples of artistic-expressive texts may be helpful here. It is believed that the art of qualitative thinking is an organic one in which what has been separated for discussion's sake occurs naturally and integrally in clear instances of artistic expression. Consider a literary excerpt from Proust's *Within a Budding Grove.* In the example, the first person narrator, Proust, is on a carriage ride in the country with an aging countess called Mme. de Villeparisis. At a turn in the road he sees three trees at what appears to be the entrance to a country lane. All of a sudden he is overwhelmed with a happiness that poignantly echoes feelings of joy from his childhood. This feeling is so real that it cancels out *everything* else around him. The three trees seem to express to him *all* there is of reality. They beckon to him and become omens of a deep meaning he feels he must grasp. He longs to be alone, to stop the carriage so that he can probe further into his overwhelming pleasure. As the three trees begin to withdraw into the distance he searches frantically for some connection from the past to help unravel the mystery before him:

> Was I to suppose, then, that they came from years already so remote in my life that the landscape which accompanied them had been entirely obliterated from my memory, and that, like the pages which, with sudden emotion, we recognize in a book which we imagined that we had never read, they surged up by themselves out of the forgotten chapter of my earliest infancy? Were they not rather to be numbered among those dream landscapes, always the same, at least for me in whom their unfamiliar aspect was but the objectivation in my dreams of the effort that I had been making while awake either to penetrate the mystery of a place beneath the outward appearance of which I was dimly conscious of there being something more, as had so often happened to me on the Guermantes way, or to succeed in bringing mystery back to a place which I had longed to know and which, from the day on which I had come to know it, had seemed to me to be wholly superficial, like Balbec? Or were they but an image freshly extracted from a dream of the night before, but already so worn, so altered that it seemed to me to come from somewhere far more distant? Or had I indeed never seen them before; did they conceal beneath their surface, like the trees, like the tufts of grass that I had seen beside the Guermantes way, a meaning as obscure, as hard to grasp as is a distant past, so that, whereas they were pleading with me that I would master a new idea, I imagined that I had to identify something in my memory? Or again were they concealing no hidden thought, and was it simply my strained vision that made me see them double in time as one occasionally sees things double in space? I could not tell...I chose rather to believe that they were phantoms of the past, dear companions of my childhood, vanished friends who recalled our common memories. Like ghosts they seemed to be appealing to me to take them with me, to bring them back to life. In their simple, passionate gesticulation I could discern the helpless anguish of a beloved person who has lost the power of speech, and feels that he will never be able to say to us what he wishes to say and we can never guess...
>
> I watched the trees gradually withdraw, waving their despairing arms, seeming to say to me: "What you fail to learn from us to-day, you will never know. If you allow us to drop back into the hollow of this road from which we sought to raise outselves up to you, a whole part of yourself which we were bringing to you will fall forever into the abyss." And indeed if, in the course of time, I did discover the kind of pleasure and of disturbance which I had just been feeling once again, and if one evening – too late, but then for all time – I fastened myself to it, of those trees themselves I was never to

> know what they had been trying to give me nor where
> else I had seen them. And when, the road having forked
> and the carriage with it, I turned my back on them and
> ceased to see them, with Mme. de Villeparisis asking
> me what I was dreaming about, I was as wretched as
> though I had just lost a friend, had died myself, had
> broken faith with the dead or had denied my God.[20]

In this one example can be found most of the rounded out art of qualitative thinking. Perhaps all that is missing is the stage of renewal, but that may be a literary device to move readers on through Proust's active search for deep structure in the remembered past.

This is far from ordinary perception. The experience of the three trees takes on the character of an epiphany — "a significant moment in the consciousness...a moment when the usually meaningless ebb and flow of ideas and perceptions... suddenly makes a kind of sense."[21] To repeat, the use of the epiphany is not a mere literary device but the expression of the world view of the perennial philosophy which leads to revelation of spirit in the world and in experience.[22] *It is a movement towards transpersonal consciousness.*

The narrator sees the three trees "double in time" and senses that they are concealing something extremely meaningful for him. The trees are not just a remembered image or a trace of some association from the past. They cut through all that. They bracket out everything else as being unreal.

First-person narration establishes the scope and depth of a qualitative event in its context. With scarcely a pause a distancing movement and a search for interpretation sets in. What can these three trees signify? The narrator searches within and comes up with six possibilities: (1) they were from the remote and nearly forgotten past; (2) they belonged to repetitive dream landscapes; (3) they brought mystery back to a place that knowledge had denuded of meaning; (4) they were a simple dream residue from the night before; (5) they hid a meaning so obscure that the narrator searches in the past when the idea is actually a new, a present one; and (6) they had no concealed thought or message from the narrator. Then comes a movement into interpretation: "*I chose rather to believe* that they were phantoms of the past, dear companions of my childhood, vanished friends who recalled our common memories." (Italics added.) But this interpretation, profound though it may be, is reductive, not renewing. It will take Proust seven volumes to round out his research into the vanished past, wherein he seems fated to place the rich golden vein of significance.

A postponed evaluation and renewing liberation occurs, however, as he suggests to the reader that he will eventually succeed in penetrating farther into this kind of mystery in what lies ahead, but, he laments "...of those trees themselves I was never to know what they had been trying to give me nor where else I had seen them." Hence Proust returns to the mystery unfulfilled, partially because of his linkage of meaning with a memory trace which he cannot find. This is a perfect literary device to move the reader on with him. And the slippage of solution from his hands is painful: "...I was as wretched as though I had just lost a friend, had died myself, had broken faith with the dead or had denied my God."

We have here a *text within an artistic-expressive text*. The example has aspects of a phenomenological-expressive text in its method as well, but it is foremost artistic. There is an inner *text* also, *and it reveals that the passage is grounded in epiphany, art, spirit and consciousness. The artistic-expressive text itself takes us out of time into the fullness of qualitative immediacy. We feel as though we know these three trees. Do they not recall the mystery of Rembrandt's etching of Three Trees?* As so often happens art here conceals and reveals simultaneously.

Had Proust allowed the narrator to remain within the suchness of the three trees as suddenly grasped in the eternal present, enlightenment or satori would have resulted and the long search of Proust's volumes would have ended. The drama of a life is not so easily solved, as we know when we witness the long journey and many unending paths of spiritual disciplines. Still, it is instructive to linger with the meaning of the inner text of our example. Krishnamurti said:

> The real is near, you do not have to search for it; and a man who seeks truth will never find it. Truth is in what *is* — and that is the beauty of it. But the moment you conceive it, the moment you seek it, you begin to struggle; and a man who struggles cannot understand. That is why we have to be still, observant, passively aware.[23]

This is a condition of grace, a meditative openness to the mystery, a releasement unto the things. Wilber has abstracted from voluminous examples the essence of how this state seems to occur. There are three factors. First, *ac-*

tive attention, as "attention-authorization to what is Now, watching inside and outside with equal eye." This is akin to the *witness* in beginning stages of meditation. Secondly, *stopping*, as "the suspension of thought, of conceptualization, of objectification, of mental chatter...It is a suspension of space, time, form, and dualism, and in this condition an utter mental Silence prevails. *This is remaining with what is.*" Third, and cumulatively, *passive awareness*, as "a special seeing that is *seeing into nothing*...it is pure timeless awareness without the primary dualism of subject vs. object...It operates above space-time in the absolute Now, pointing to nothing beyond itself and seeing nothing beyond itself."[24] This is gnosis, the eye of contemplation, the immediate intuition of transcendelia.

In the example there is clearly a kind of hermeneutics occurring. The narrator is "attempting to reason about spirit or transcendelia."[25] Such thinking is paradoxical, always coming up to the limit of thought. In this case, the narrator actually begins to retreat to the level of mind alone — to the data of intelligibilia, and in a search for direct linkages to prior experience. Krishnamurti, however, is saying that when memories and images arise, if you

> give complete attention at that moment, then you will see
> that there is no image, and having no image there is then
> no division between the observor and the observed.[26]

Curiously enough the excerpt from Proust can supply just this kind of experience. We are held within the lower limits of the realm of spirit and the upper limits of the realm of mind. We experience qualitatively an extended present as the narrator explores the meaning of the three trees. We vacillate with him between the self-conscious conceptual mind and the intuitive mind of cosmic consciousness.[27]

It is important for our study of the role of art in such affairs to distinguish between *image* as used in the above quote and as we and Bachelard are using it. The former implies seeing the present through an existing or preconceived image, whereas we refer to the artistic image as an absolute origin independent of a definite external referent. In Blake's system, threefold vision is equivalent to the direct vision of the thing as image and symbol joined. Thus its suchness is not in question. And its meaning is exponential, exfoliating out into the vastness of the cosmic, the eternal and the ineffable. It appears therefore in the lower reaches of revelation, incarnate as timeless beauty. Thing and the eternal fuse in one direct symbol of the ineffable. This is why the simplest poetic or artistic image, in the form of a poem or a humble pot, can be, as Yeats called it, a "dancing master to the soul."

The overarching purpose of the art of qualitative thinking is to express, describe, and lead to epiphany, so that through its hermeneutic-expessive cycle consciousness becomes self-conscious of its expansion and can evolve. It moves from one expression to a still deeper one. The purpose of its cycle, as one large art process, is to extend qualitative time, to extend depth interpretation, to extend expression.

It is no accident that Heidegger in his late works turned toward art in order to meditate on "the free becoming of being."[28] He sought out poets like Rilke, Trakl, and Holderlin— especially Holderlin—because these poets talked poetically about the very issues of Heidegger's meditation. Their poems, as in the example from Proust, had a hidden text within their artistic-expressive one. Here is an excerpt from a late poem by Holderlin which forms the basis for Heidegger's essay "...Poetically Man Dwells..."[29]

> May, if life is sheer toil, a man
> Lift his eyes and say: so
> I too wish to be? Yes. As long as Kindness,
> The Pure, still stays with his heart, man
> Not unhappily measures himself
> Against the godhead. Is God unknown?
> Is he manifest like the sky? I'd sooner
> Believe the latter. It's the measure of man.
> Full of merit, yet poetically, man
> Dwells on this earth. But no purer
> Is the shade of the starry night,
> If I might put it so, than
> Man, who's called an image of the godhead.[30]

The poet finds God not unknown but manifest like the sky—or chooses to believe so. In that choice we have a clear distinction between artist and saint or mystic, still allowing for all of the degrees of combinations which we do in fact find. For "poetic images are imaginings in a distinctive sense: not mere fancies and illusions but imaginings that are visible inclusions of the alien in the sight of the familiar...The measure taken by poetry yields, imparts itself—as the foreign element in which the invisible one preserves his presence—to what is familiar in the sights of the sky."[31]

To the artist, the eternal is "manifest like the sky." The three trees are either a direct image of that manifestation and lead toward union with the eternal, *or* they become through slippage, it seems, archetype or analogy, *or* slipping still further, associative memory-linked ties of a seer who dualistically now separates self and seeing from the seen.

What Pepper[32] calls the *qualitative immediate present* is the artist's form of the eternal present. It is the *now* that has no space—that has no time. It is a state where the artist brings into being that which is manifest like the sky and that which is divine simultaneously.

> I take it that, in considering the relative and the absolute, man and God, we are no longer talking about some geography external to the human mind. If the creative is truly our essence, what deeper eye in us would we call on when speculating about the mystery we are born into?—And it would not be improbable to find the artist's creativity in the archetype and pattern for all cosmology.[33]

This last is an artist speaking. The point is similar to Holderlin's: in the state of creation we not unhappily, as poetically full of merit, dwell on this earth and measure ourselves against the godhead, finding God manifest like the sky. Holderlin says, and we say, that these are choices between the artistic version of the esoteric tradition and the more commonly espoused one of spiritual science.

The hidden purpose of the artistic-expressive text is to extend the qualitative immediate present as far as possible, for that will also thicken up to be as deep as possible. A depth hermeneutic then opens up this text for an expanding consciusness. This further leads toward understanding of what is manifested from the science and eventuates in renewed expression.

The examples in this chapter are meant to be few and intensive. For the artistic-expressive modes we will stop with the few examples chosen from literature. The iconic modes are harder to present directly in book form, although that was the intent behind presenting the art of pottery in the previous chapter. Music would be a perfect medium for our purposes, but we cannot mediate it even indirectly here. "Sound agitates directly, as a commotion of the organism itself...[for] the ear is the emotional sense."[34] To further contrast the iconic qualities of art and music: "Architecture is to mountains what music is to the sea."[35] Here we engage the elemental, the cosmic, and the timeless through the voices of silence and through wordless voices.

The discussion so far has drawn from existing texts. But the art of qualitative thinking is most valuable for the evolution of consciousness when the one doing the interpreting is also the one engaged in expression from the start. Then personal evolution is more powerfully and directly implicated. Where art and the evolution of consciousness are jointly concerned, expressing *is* superior to responding. One must also receive to create, but the reception is that of the God become manifest, as vision, revelation, form. We are very aware of these also in a receptive hermeneutics — of all the great manifestations human kind has brought forth from the well through vision and will to form. Spirit is *spirit* and *is*. A true understanding is always also *new and true* to the objectification which drew it forth. But if we exclusively exercise only our performing and interpreting faculties, creation, beings and world tend to congeal, the kerygma fails, and revelation withdraws. Therefore we stress qualitative experiencing *as* expressing, well knowing the arguments that a true understanding of a great work is superior to a humble creation doubtlessly destined for oblivion. But a true understanding and creative action need to be linked together, even as *poetic* reverie always dreams with a pen in hand. It is in that simple writing out of a received insight that the deep structure of one's own evolution is indirectly but potently implicated.

Expressive-Descriptive Texts

We will first take up phenomenological description as an expressive-descriptive mode. This mode implies a certain suspicion of expressive closeness, but it also simultaneously claims closeness to qualities and events as ongoing experiences. In that it calls into question our all too ready or easy inclination to symbolize and interpret the meaning of qualitative experience, it works toward undercutting any purely surface impetus to engage in poetry or narrative.

But which is more *natural*, the *natural attitude* praised as the starting point of phenomenology, or *the dance of the live creature? "All we know of any situation is what it does to and with us: that* is *its* nature."[36] Any *a priori* claim to lay bare the objective thinghood and essence of an object or event must be called into question from the point of view of an art of qualitative thinking. A phenomenological positivism is just as noxious as logical positivism, for while the latter wishes to reduce everything to the status of physical matter, to sensibilia, the former wishes to reduce everything to intelligibilia. Our problem becomes that of how to use language in relation to our qualitative experience. Dewey cautioned:

> Language comes infinitely short of paralleling the variegated surface of nature. Yet words as practical devices are the agencies by which the ineffable diversity of natural existence as it operates in human experience is reduced to orders, ranks, and classes that can be managed. Not only is it impossible that language should duplicate the infinite variety of individualized qualities that exist, but it is wholly undesirable and unneeded that it should do so. The unique quality of a quality is found in experience itself; it is there and sufficiently there not to need reduplication in language. The latter serves its scientific or its intellectual purpose as it gives directions as to how to come upon these qualities in experience. The more generalized and simple the direction the better. The more uselessly detailed they are, the more they confuse instead of guiding. But words serve their poetic purpose in the degree in which they summon and evoke into active operation the vital responses that are present whenever we experience qualities.[37]

This passage endorses the guiding function of simple, generalized language pointing to how to come upon qualities in experience; but it likewise suggests that there must be something expressive and evocative, something poetic, in all of the texts forming the first moment of an art of qualitative thinking. Thus we have called all texts expressive, for the end of this art is that of summoning and evoking into active operation that human vitality which dwells within the fullness of qualitative experiencing, so that we may understand it, renew it, and enlarge our developing consciousness. The expressive-descriptive modes merely allow for the range and varied colorations involved in the poetic element.

Followers of Langeveld, in what is called the Utrecht School of phenomenological pedagogy, are urged to begin a phenomenological description thus:

> Describe a personal, simple experience as much as possible in life-world language; watch out for interpretations and causalities in the description, and do not get lost in factual details. The important point is the "lived" aspect of it.[38]

Topics such as *the sickbed, fear of the dark, waking up, stealing apples, driving a car,* and the like are typical beginning points. These are approached in a manner generally congruent with the phenomenological attitude: one emphasizing pretheoretical, prereflective experience; as free as possible from presuppositions, unexamined preconceptions, causual explanations, and factual details. The tie to the experiential, personal life-world acknowledges that our consciousness of phenomena is intentional, purposive, appetitive, and existential. The *facts* one attends to are the *given* ones. "This is the basic principle of all phenomenology: *the investigator remains true to the facts as they are happening.*"[39]

The Dutch phenomenologist J. H. Van den Berg, in his book *A Different Existence,* [40] sets forth the principles of phenomenological psychopathology. He organizes his presentation under these topics: man and world; man and body; man and fellowman, communication; man and time, life history. This is a progression interestingly paralleling that of the great chain of being: relationships with matter; body; group membership; mind, soul and spirit. An example from his book as a kind of expressive-descriptive phenomenological text illustrates the point here for our purposes.

> It is winter. Evening is falling, and I get up to switch on the light. Looking outside, I see that it has started to snow. Everything is covered by glittering snow, falling down silently out of a heavy sky. People are moving soundlessly past my window. I hear someone stamping the snow from his feet. I rub my hands and look forward to the evening, for a few days ago I telephoned a friend to ask him if he could spend this evening with me. In an hour he will be standing before my door. The snow outside seems to make his visit even more pleasant. Yesterday, I bought a bottle of good wine, which I put at the proper distance from the fire.
>
> I sit down at my desk to answer some mail. After a half-hour, the telephone rings. My friend is calling to say that he cannot come. We exchange a few words and make another appointment. When I put down the receiver, the stillness of my room has become slightly more pronounced. The hours to come seem longer and emptier. I put a log on the fire and return to my desk. A few moments later, I am absorbed in a book. The evening slips away slowly.
>
> When I look up a moment to think over a passage that refuses to become clear, the bottle by the fire catches my eye. Once more, I realize that my friend will not come, and I return to my book.[41]

Thus far, we have the basic phenomenological text; but somewhat in the manner of the example from Proust, the text continues directly into distancing and interpretation:

> Reviewing this episode taken from everyday life, I notice that there is a continuous interaction between me, the subject, and the things around me, the objects. I am expecting my friend; this subjective condition is visible to me through the objects in my room. I light the fire, arrange cigarettes and let the wine get to the proper temperature. Even to another, my subjective condition (at this point) is quite apparent; coming in unexpectedly, one would say: "I see that you are expecting company." Then, it snows; this objective condition appears capable of adding to my subjective expectation. When the telephone puts an end to this expectation, the silence of the room is more pronounced. When, later on, I see the bottle, this objective actuality tells me that my subjective expectation is cancelled.
>
> An interaction. Now the question as to the nature of this interaction. To find the answer, I concentrate on the last observation; I see the bottle of wine and I realize that my friend will not come. What happens at this moment? Or, more precisely: What do I see when I observe the bottle of wine? The question seems trivial and the answer is accordingly simple. I see a green bottle with a white label, on which is printed a mark.
>
> At closer examination, I can read the printed words. It is a bottle of Medoc. The bottle is corked and sealed with a lead capsule. I could go on in this way and sum up all the details of the bottle. But it becomes obvious to me that, writing down these facts, I don't get any nearer to that which I was observing when, looking up, I saw the bottle. What I was seeing then was not a green bottle, with a white label, with a lead capsule, and things like that. What I was really seeing was something like the disappointment about the fact that my friend would not come or about the loneliness of my evening. Of course, I did see a bottle with a green label, a capsule, etc., but my seing these things meant that I jumped over the object, bottle, to the value this bottle had acquired for me this evening.[42]

We see through this example how close the relationship really is between human beings and their world. There is no pure subject any more than there is a pure object. We follow the narrator here because we share the same human existence which he describes. Such writing is not based on a clear theory or method, but rather gives us a plausible insight.[43] Van den Berg says that a behavioristic psychologist would say that he is contaminating his observation with "poetry" and the projection of his lonely, disappointed condition. But no description can be neutral, least of all the reductionistic psychologist's, since he presumes to restrict and eliminate what we naturally feel to belong to our everyday experience. Would a survey of one's feelings directly through introspection not help? No, says van den Berg:

> As soon as I ask myself, by introspection, that is, by leaving out everything that is outside myself to investigate my feelings, I don't know what to do. I'm standing in front of a blind wall. Every effort, purely by myself, to summon my loneliness results in a realization of what is there: my room, the fire, the bottle and, within all this, my absent friend.[44]

We can now see why such phenomenological expressively descriptive texts are useful beginnings for the art of qualitative thinking, for we have here that first stage of the mystical experience which Wilber called *active attention* — as "attention-authorization to what is Now, watching inside and outside with equal eye."[45] The subject-object dualism here is suspended as we watch the interplay between ourselves and the world. We *witness* the *way things are*. Not only are such descriptions a firm basis for ourselves in context in the ongoing event, but they can also lead us to the condition of *stopping, where we learn not to disturb things,* where we still further suspend all dualism and mental chatter through *remaining with what is.* From this point it is a short step to that *passive awareness* that holds us timelessly in the absolute.[46] The seer, seeing, and the seen then collapse into *pure seeing*, and epiphany, vision, revelation or cosmic consciousness spontaneously may occur.

But whether our beginning through active attention and expressive phenomenological description takes us this far or not, *our consciousness begins to expand through this non-judgmental attitude* of watching inside and outside as events unfurl. The very quality of the experienced event becomes faithfully expressed and commemorated at the same time so that we can interpret it and learn what significance and guidance it possesses for us. For underlying all existential and hermeneutic phenomenology is the assumption that a deep structure is implicated in our descriptions and that an analysis and interpretation of these will provide us with understanding and a guide to action. This guide to action is taken to be adumbrated in the concrete situation or event we are trying to express through our phenomenological descriptions.[47]

But here we are attempting to get the flavor of expressive-descriptive texts. These can be lighter and more playful as well, as is this one, done as an expressive-descriptive sketch of a personal qualitative experience for a graduate seminar:

Casing Up Mail and Running the Route

I usually arrive at the post office at about 7:15 and put down 7:30 on my time sheet, since they don't like to pay me extra. The regular starting time is 7:45.

I get my half-cup of coffee, hang up my hat and coat and get into high gear. On RD-5 I have about 492 customers. Each of them receives an average of about 3 pieces of mail a day. Milory Davis, Olin Construction, the Game Commission and Swanger's Supply usually have about 20 pieces, including flats and packages. WBPZ Lock Haven plays its sad songs and I try not to fall into the blues. Then Henninger's Lumber comes on sponsoring a local fire, with full details as to location and the companies responding. Then they play an old Hank Williams tune, Dolly Parton, Waylon Jennings, Freddie Fender, and it's time for the news. I can never hear the news because the big fan seems to always come on at that time. I sort James Taylor-211, Robert Wagner-32, Gary Powers-332, Wayne Johns 228-Z, Milton Brogelzuber-21, and Helen Mook lives up Lucas Lane with those other two women in 45.

Robert Thomas isn't going to get his mail if his dog is loose again today. Doyle Trill is the last customer on this route., Michael MacVinter moved from 450 to 314-A, and Richard Pragonuschi resides next to Em-maleen Resides. I have two Hosterfuses and two Zooks, they're Amish. Philip Riser lives on that rise in Schreffler Terrace. Rev. Trueby and Rev. Fatal have lots of mail. They work the missions.

While I ply my part of Centre County, every person in the country gets mail once each day, and a letter from Alaska costs about ½ the price of a candy bar — yuk!, and I'm convinced that communication is something so vital and quite unspoiled. With my rear shocks gone, I feel like a pony express rider bouncing down the dirt roads in the noonday sun. And the world of anxiety is not out here in the country, where rabbits get run over sometimes and dogs chase my car and kids come to get the mail. I see the seasons change in the mountains and follow the crows.

What bothers me is the Mossers and the Barnards and the Martins; large extended farm families who sold off part of their land to their offsprings over the years. So now I have mail for James Martin, James C. Martin, P. James Martin, John Paul Martin, Curtis Martin and Michael James Martin; and they all live near each other, and they seldom use box numbers. They tell people just to address mail RD 5 Bellefonte. "It'll get here." And they complain if their mail is in someone else's box. The regular mailman recently retired after 25 years. He knew them all.

So around 11 AM, 2 half-cups of coffee; getting my packages, registered and certified mail, etc. in order, and all the mail strapped into bundles, packed into my little car, and I'm on the road. I like that best. It goes like clockwork; I know the boxes and I watch the weather changes; eat fruit, shift gears, listen to music, and watch my right hand doing the pay work. And if any mail is out of place, I bring it back. No trouble. Only 44 miles to go, and my car knows the road. Maybe some nice lady will leave cookies in a box, along with a request for a book of stamps, and the change lying loose on her letters.[47]

So such descriptions need not be epiphanies to be insightful. In this case it created good feeling between the writer and the rest of us in the seminar who shared his life-world as part-time rural mailman. The distancing of the everyday is a healthful act in such writing, allowing us to see with pleasure, humor and concern the care and the trials of simple situations and something of the worlds of others crossing with ours.

Descriptions need not be of live situations in the here and now. They can be imaginative ones or incidents from the past. Here is another example done by a student in a similar graduate seminar:

A Childhood Reverie

Creak...Bump-Creak, the murmur and occasional roar of other conversations. Images flash by with an undecipherable rhythm before I really understand what they are. A trail of lights on a bridge zips and, one by one, extinguish themselves on the frame of the window. My eyes become aware of another layer of conversation within the frame. Against the darkness of night my own image is cast on the glass. A tired, somewhat lonely but good natured face stares at the window. A severe face stares back with hollows for eyes, hollows for cheeks and a line where the lips should be. Is this me? How did this come to be? Someone lights a cigarette and the smoke curls around a light. Its first scent comes to me and I go...through the window shattering the image cast there, out into the night, not tonight but nights and days spent long ago...

The smell of clean white sheets rubs against my nose. I pull them closer around me as a soft breeze comes through the open window; a welcome breeze for the days are warm and sunny.

The curtains have been pinned in front of the window so no wind could blow on me directly (and no reflected image can be seen through them). Well hey, I know what I look like anyway! The salt air pushes the cur-

> tains into a balloon. Then they fall away creating the rough rhythm of breath. My father coughs. He coughs a lot, more and more it seems, but it doesn't bother me, in fact I kind of like it. I know he's there when he coughs. I don't have to get up out of bed to check and see. I accept his cough's reassurance and so he coughs a kind of lullaby, an invitation to sleep.
>
> If I do lean a little out of bed...Creak...Bump Creak...I can see half his face concentrating on a page of his book. The waves lap on the night beach twenty feet away...and Dad turns a page (about forty-five laps to a page)...lap...lap...turn a page in rhythm, then cough...flick...a cigarette is lit, and smoke curls around the light. The first scent comes to me and I feel secure...lap...lap...turn. I snuggle down more in the covers. Dad coughs in the blue, curling smoke. o o o o o! I felt so secure...o o o o o o o! – a fog horn mourns its warning to deaf ears...a night ahead of the one it mourns. But the smoke is too thick and too many nights lie between in the darkness. I'm asleep... o o o o o o o o...[49]

Were the reader to learn that the young man who wrote this goes to a cottage on a Cape Cod beach every summer with his family and that he had a year before lost his father, then it becomes easy to understand something of the significance this mixture of time zones and this dream toward place, security, and childhood expresses. The autobiographical element is important in these texts, even when it may cloud the literary quality, more narrowly taken, for we are talking about *a total art, one of qualitative thinking*, of which such texts are one of four moments.

In a certain sense perhaps everything of significance to us is dreamed first or encountered in reverie and in imagination – whatever its status in the so-called "real world." Julien Green said: "It is a bizarre disposition of my mind to believe a thing only if I have dreamed it. By believing, I do not mean simply possessing a certainty, but retaining it within oneself in such a way that the being finds itself modified because of it."[50] Artistic and descriptive expressive texts, when they are of originary quality, where the *I* speaks directly or indirectly, get at the deep structure of *beliefs* that modify the expressing and dreaming being.

This is a delicate realm, and all of our experiences with artists in the Drawing Lab and with qualitative thinkers in our seminars underscore this fact. A nurturant, non-critical attitude seems best on the whole, although once we are admitted to the artist's or the dreamer's world, even direct confrontation drawn forth by intuition *in support of that world* can be likewise helpful. On the whole however, a receptive, appreciative ear and mind seem to liberate an inner dynamism and directionality intrinsic to these worlds. Thus, curiously, an art of *qualitative thinking* begins without an emphasis on thought. The feeling, expressing and dreaming being has its own *cogito*, says Bachelard:

> The dreamer's *cogito* is less lively than the thinker's *cogito*. The dreamer's *cogito* is less sure than the philosopher's *cogito*. The dreamer's being is a diffuse being. But on the other hand, this diffuse being is the being of a diffusion. It escapes the punctualization of the *hic* and of the *nunc*. The dreamer's being invades what it touches, diffuses into the world. Thanks to shadows, the intermediary region which separates man from world is a full region, of a light density fullness. This intermediary region deadens the dialectic between being and non-being. The imagination does not know non-being.[51]

The dreamer's *cogito* is a special kind of *active attention*, paying perhaps more attention to inner than outer, but nevertheless always dreaming of something *other* than the self. The boundaries between human kind and world are relaxed. A kind of *stopping* and *passive awareness* are involved as the dream dreams itself forward. It is not the Silence that is entered—unless it be the silence imposed on all that is not of the dream. Yet, the ineffable Silence is implicated by the numinous quality of the dream for the dreamer. Poetic reverie becomes a form of *active* meditation just as surely as does throwing on the potter's wheel or drawing a bow in the art of archery.

Artists dream on the *things* of their medium. Here is a delightful description of Kandinsky's colorful world:

> On my palette sit high, round raindrops, puckishly flirting with each other, swaying and trembling. Unexpectedly they unite and suddenly become thin, shy threads which disappear in amongst the colors, and roguishly skip about and creep up the sleeves of my coat...It is not only the stars which show me faces. The stub of a cigarette lying in an ash-tray, a patient, staring white button lying amidst the litter of the street, a willing, pliable bit of bark—all these have physiognomies for me...As a thirteen- or fourteen-year-old boy I bought a box of oil colors with pennies slowly and painfully saved. To this day I can still see those colors coming out of the tubes. One press of my fingers and jubilantly, festively, or grave and dreamy, or turned thoughtfully within themselves, the colors came forth. Or wild with spor-

> tiveness, with a deep sigh of liberation, with the deep tone
> of sorrow, with splendid strength and fortitude, with
> yielding softness and resignation, with stubborn self-
> mastery, with a delicate uncertainty of mood—out they
> came, these curious, lovely things that are called colors.[52]

Artists not only think in their medium, but dream in it. Here is a qualitative description of the quality of the artist's palette. The artist's raw materials mediate even before they become a medium.

Where the autobiographical element is not present in an originary expressive descriptive text, there can be a sensitive indirect representation of that in special case histories. These occurred in our work in the Drawing Lab, [53] where a nurturant environment—a place an artist could call home—was established. This became a community made up of the artist working there and of us who were sharing participants in the artist's unfolding series of works. We have had artists who have worked as long as two and one-half years under this relationship. We immediately became the keeper's of the artist's history of creation in the Drawing Lab setting. *We did not study the artist as an object* but took the *text* of our interactions with him or her—in the form of transcripts of recorded dialogues of stimulated recall of working processes, of shared ideas and feelings—as the basis for a *case history* to be interpreted and understood. The artist while working was left undisturbed. Our sharing inquiries and *listening* occurred before and after the working sessions. These inquiries were prompted by the actual art works and by in-process photographs we took as the artist drew or painted.

Thus we had the raw material—this included the iconic mute evidence of the art works and the in-process photographs, our *field notes* or *lab notes*, and the transcriptions of stimulated recall process dialogues—all as a source for a *very special artistic case history*. In fact the transcribed dialogues constituted an originary descriptive-expressive text in themselves. They included our dialogues with the artist as well as all the events that occurred during the entire creative process. They adumbrated what we have called *the artist's superordinate artistic myth*—that dreaming and directing coherence that floats *above* the serial of the artist's work *over an extended time period.* Certainly here we have good reason to feel the *deep structure* and the *consciousness-expanding function of continuing immersion in art activity.*

Space does not permit the inclusion of full case histories or full dialogue-transcriptions as special historical, descriptive and expressive texts. The reader will note that these histories have a strong phenomenological ingredient as well, because they strive to be true to events as they occurred, and, as their authors, we strive to approach these events prereflectively or at least to be as aware as possible of our preconceptions so that we can disconfirm them or bracket them out. To give the reader the flavor of such *texts*, we have chosen the following examples that vary greatly in complexity and in intensity.

Here is a discussion of a sudden change occurring in the work of a young artist whom we'll call Larry, a change which occurred during the seventh weekly session of his first ten week period in the Drawing Lab:

> The transformation of Larry's series occurred the session (week 7) after the all-talk session with W (week 6). When Larry came into the lab (for week 7), he was greeted but pretty well left along—a kind of tacit understanding that he'd draw because the session before was all talk.
>
> Larry didn't know what he was going to draw. He looked at the complex still-life, set on a cart with wheels, that was always present if the artist wanted it. He focused on the broken screen of the still-life, the moire effect of its double fold, and the shape of the whole as an abstract form. He worked out "pen figures," as he called them, to signify the light and dark pattern (using two symbols ---- and ####). He placed these units carefully on the page. First he put in all the light units, then all the dark ones. He varied the marks in both darkness and density. He deliberately gave no setting which would identify the drawing as "screen" or "landscape" or whatever. He later connected his desire to leave it open and ambiguous to the feeling he got at the Flavin (light) exhibition and the Montenegro (3-D and painted) exhibition. When questioned at the close of the session, Larry saw virtue in this ambiguity. It led to "interest." He also saw his approach now as under a different attitude, not bringing to bear as many rules and technical requirements before the process, and relaxing his "first the tools and then the building" theory. In an interview the following week, further corroboration of a changed attitude occurred:
>
> R: Was this drawing a conscious effort?
> L: I did it after seeing those two displays.
> R: The Montenegro and the light show?
> L: It's different. Before what I was building up for was so I could get realistic—make a face or something; show a mood or something like that.
> R: You're implying two things: the technique and the feeling.

L: The reasoning behind it. This is different in that there's no attempt to be realistic.

Then there followed a discussion comparing literature and visual art, in which it came out that, to Larry, there could be more freedom in visual art than in literature. (Larry is a literature major). Larry concluded: "In this picture we have two distinctions. First, not being concerned so much with realism. Then we have it as a visual experience, something different."

Further corroboration of a changed view comes from an interview three weeks later where all of Larry's drawings over ten weeks are put on the wall for review. He feels a "divide" happened during week 7. Before that he was "attempting realism all the time, and...mainly trying to get perspective and control the pen." He was also getting progressively frustrated with "trying to present things realistically." The two exhibitions and his discussion with W (an art student who had posed for Larry for a portrait earlier) kept rolling around his mind. "I guess I loosened up a bit...I really was tight. It was getting really depressing."

Larry further supported the interpretation that thereafter his works became more symbolic to him. As he put it: "It's more of an effect. A feeling rather than just a representation." And he acknowledged he didn't really have to know precisely what it meant.

Subsequently, in the remaining sessions following week 7, Larry explored media much more freely, using brushes of all sizes, inventing new strokes, varying pressure, amount of water, and speed of execution. He also developed some free "doodles" freely rearranged parts of the still life, depicting them with rapid strokes of a large brush; did more "abstracts" in the vein of the screen of week 7; and terminated the series with a very spontaneously rendered depiction, with a one-inch brush, of an image of a standing sculptural form (a Giacometti "man" he had seen in the Philadelphia Museum).

Thus, in Larry's development, we see him moving from a tighter, more ego-controlled, regime of self-instruction oriented toward realistic representational skills, in which he could barely conceive of himself as interested in "feeling" or "expression," toward a relaxation of control and *a priori* goal, a freer exploration of media and ideas, and a willingness to let the freedom he felt in visual art speak in its own cryptic, partly ambiguous way. There is a fuller acceptance of his limited skills (preceded by depression, even though he knew he was improving his representational ability) and a recognition of his own feelings and expressive needs.[53]

In this example, as so often in the Drawing Lab, we find an extended awareness which is not only artistic but *spiritual*, in the sense of *an evolution in the state of consciousness*. As also it often happens, this evolution is a kind of transformation requiring the *symbolic death* of parts of the self which then become reintegrated at a higher level.

Larry was not a person trained inart, but he arrived at significant insights into the art process after only seven weeks of effort. Those whose lives have been devoted to art, to the degree that they have kept imagination vital and active, can speak much more elegantly about *the role art plays in the evolution of consciousness.* We believe this is clearly shown by some excerpts to follow, taken from ten weeks of participation in the Drawing Lab by a man who at the time was a dynamic head of a large university's art department. His statements will be presented in a format which will later lead to the distancing and interpreting moments of the art of qualitative thinking. This means that though the dialogue excerpts with the artist will be here given intact, they will already be loosely classified according to a *structural-existential model* (which hereafter will be called the *S-E Model*) which looks to *the structure of metaphor* as a *metaphor for the qualitative world of creating.* This usage "contains a metaphor for metaphor, for what is 'existential' is usually counterposed to what is 'structural'. In viewing acts of creation as situated (or embedded, or weakly caused) as well as spontaneous (or inexplicably novel), a proper tension is maintained between what would otherwise be warring partners, and a powerful dialectic is set up."[55]

Here an approach to understanding the qualitative world of creating is developed which allows mind, as thought, to engage that which transcends thought—as spirit and its data. This method in general is one which corresponds to Wilber's *mandalic* or *paradoxical thinking*—"it is mind (intelligibilia) attempting to reason about spirit or transcendelia."[56] In the example to follow, terms corresponding to metaphor are developed into the categories of the S-E Model, thus:

> (1) the *antecedent*, or the form and history the artist brings to his present situation; (2) the *constituent*, or the context or actuality wherein the clash or conflict with what was antecedent inevitably arises (so much so that it is impossible to say whether the past causes the present or whether the present fictionalizes and functionalizes the past); and (3) the *consequent* where spontaneity and novelty appear in the form of synthesis where metaphor itself is born as an evolutionary constellation. In adopting the S-E Model, a powerful empty analytic is set up. It is "empty" because it does not

> prejudice *a priori* the content arising from within the
> qualitative context of each act of creation.[57]

With this preparation in mind, we will now turn to the transcription of the dialogue in the Drawing Lab between the artist and us, as inquirers. The transcript is broken into cycles, each of which is broken into its antecedent, constituent, and consequent parts. The rhythm of these cycles, *showing that the clash of antecedent elements with constituent elements sets the stage for the consequents that follow*, is such that it pervades all of our *texts* of dialogues on the creation of art. We will use the symbols ANT for antecedent, CST for constituent, and CONS for consequent.

> I haven't worked for several years. What I planned to
> do was purely exercises. (ANT)
> And then I became interested in making a picture
> and (CST)
> I couldn't keep my attention on the exercises. It's
> probably due to the somewhat unnatural conditions of
> working in here (CONS)
>
> And then I got mesmerized by that little still-life
> thing, in just trying to make things stand
> out and go back...(ANT)
> but I had difficulty with control. (CST)
> So then I started thinking that rather than
> working from imagination. I'd set up a little
> still-life thing, (CONS)
>
> and then I remembered a piece I'm very fond
> of, *A Bell Ringing in an Empty Sky*, and (ANT)
> the emptiness of that started to occur to me
> which became more important than just blocking
> in, so I tried to experience the emptiness (CST)
> and I wind up having been some place
> at that point. (CONS)
>
> I was trying to feel what that emptiness was,
> sort of a life trip, (ANT)
> and then responding and then changing, (CST)
> and then finding something coming to a conclusion
> and trying to feel that with the brush. (CONS)
>
> And then I tried to go back and understand what the
> forms were which really wasn't the problem. (ANT)
> The problem was that I couldn't get myself to do that
> roundedness. (CST)
> It's hard to explain these feelings. (CONS)
>
> And then I tried to compensate by letting that
> mean something (ANT)
> And then I went back to just trying to do the
> damn thing, (CST)
> And it occurred to me that the break wasn't bad

because it allowed me to come to the next form
rather than just adhering to the shape that
was frustrating me. (CONS)

If I were to begin work again [he hadn't worked
for seven years], (ANT)
I wouldn't begin at this speed and I'd probably
force myself to remain on those exercises...(CST)
but the environment and being watched and the
performance factor came in too...the performance
factor weighed heavily on me as I was coming
over here, but then I decided to do exercises and
not worry about it. (CONS)

I had two enormous style schools pushed on me, (ANT)
and they were in conflict, (CST)
but people became more important to me, more
important than painting...(CONS)

I think that language about art...is a film loop
dealing with conceptualization that is cloaking,
deliberately cloaking...(ANT)
language about art is to me simultaneously very
difficult and quite simple...at the very same time. (CST)
If that becomes unbearably impossible for you,
you've got problems and you don't know who
you are. (CONS)
That's figure-ground language...(ANT)
You can switch back and forth very easily. (CST)
Painting is a reality in the same sense that breathing
is. Painting is part of reality, as is breathing. (CONS)

Because I am not complete...(ANT)
it isn't complete. (CST)
But painting deals with an aspect
of reality that is again...you see, you get
forced into using language which isn't adequate...
and the language has the same problems as
an empty experience in the studio has...but
that we keep trying to approach. (CONS)

Painting is a dimension that can be entered, that is,
from the painter's viewpoint, from my viewpoint...(ANT)
and from which you may not return...(CST)
and you constantly have to weigh what your priorities
are. (CONS)

Is it more important to seek experience and take the
risk (ANT)
or is it more important to protect yourself...and the
"protections" are very devious (CST)
because you may wind up empty...rather than
this other thing. (CONS)

If you accept the paradox, the betwixt or
between...(ANT)
I think that it has to be dealt with eventually and
probably most of our lives are preparation for that... (CST)

if we are alive at all as individuals...so it is
a very large thing. (CONS)

You know, *it all starts there, it starts with the
paradox...*
That's how one is caught...he must learn to accept
both poles...(ANT)
I don't know if you can unify it...I don't know
how to face that yet...(CST)
In my evolution, art education, working with people
became exactly like painting. Its characteristics,
though, were related with its form and, ultimately, to
what painting means to me. You *become* painting.
Painting is like the magnificant death. You don't
return. (CONS)

It's romantic and all of that...(ANT)
but it really isn't. It is very real to me. (CST)
So in that sense, if I were to become another person, I
would become me, in the parallel between working with
people and painting. The lure of another person being a
separate reality or a larger reality as there is
in painting is a possibility. (CONS)
Part of what I'm interested in and hopeful that I'll go
beyond is understanding through feeling what
you (the researchers) have been trying to explain
to me which I can't understand...(ANT)
When we speak there are signals we are passing
back and forth that are in root common, and while
you baffle me, the signals are clear...(laughter) (CST)
I have been trying for years to understand words and I
don't find gratification in finding out what words mean
in the way I find gratification with forms...so
That's why I'm fascinated to feel this (the Lab
experience) and understand more, *and then to
understand more about myself.* (CONS)

You know, in meditation, before it was a cultist popular
thing, I started yoga, and for about three years to the
best of my ability practiced without having available
the masters we have now, (ANT)
but just reading and studying and practicing
and trying to understand (CST)
...so I had a trip or an experience which really
specifically identified what I felt, and there was a
"form" that was attached to it and has been of
interest ever since. (CONS)

I had a visualization of a slit of light, (ANT)
and then I projected and left myself (CST)
and then I began to approach that slit of light
and was going to pass through it and become
that light and at that moment I had a choice
of becoming cosmic energy or of staying in this
form and completing this part of whatever it's
about, and I chose to return without any fear. (CONS)

It wasn't a fearful thing. (ANT)
But there is still the unknown about what the hell
happens when you go through. (CST)
To me, I would not have awakened, I would have
died. That would have been death if I had chosen at
that point to become this cosmic light. Well,
that is the choice that has to be faced in the studio,
that is the reality of painting. (CONS)

When it works and when you make contact with
it, you can become it. (ANT)
And you've got to decide whether you're going to be
that pure or whether you're going to remain in this
kind of more mundane existence and try to
find out more about it, which is my choice. (CST)
This is the kind of confrontation that you face,
that I face, in the studio. (CONS)

That is why *painting probably feeds as a*
preparation for some kind of ultimate understanding
that you have as an individual. (ANT)
So that is not fear; it is rather a certain amount of
apprehension because we are bound this way...(CST)
still though, maybe part of the choice staying
this way is fear, which the enlightened Asian·
doesn't have...but there is a level of which
I am aware that is purely a level of limit
on my part. For *you must in effect, accept*
both poles...and I am perfectly willing to
admit to limits.[57]

Here is an extremely powerful text which like the one from
Proust contains *a text within the text.* Direct mention is
made to satori, transcendence, paradoxical thinking, and
evidence is given of major and minor epiphanies associated
with painting, meditation, human interactions, and the limits
of language. This is assuredly an evolved and an evolving
consciousness. *As an expressive-descriptive historical text it
could not be more perfect for our purposes.* All of this
dialogue was set off by the *feel* of *one* brush stroke, which
was "like the old days"—that is, which opened up all of painting again to its ultimacy, its "magnificent death" from which
"you don't return," and to the significant choices of whether
to expand and grow or play it safe. As with the narrator in the
excerpt from Proust, we are left unclear of the outcome,
because we have stepped within a still-evolving life-world
aware of decision, paradox, and of the ultimate realm of
spirit. (We will return to this example again, also, in discussing distancing and interpretation.)

References like the last two transcend what is usually
meant by *case history.* It is a special kind of history that

points to qualitative events and experiences. A history in which the historian-narrator is directly involved at the event level is already an existential-phenomenological history with its own hidden autobiographical ingredient. The narrative (really a description or story of events and contexts) is therefore qualitative in base. One might try to negate or bracket out one's being-in-the-events, *but that's a pretty big bracket*, and a useless and impossible one where the qualitative and the spiritual are concerned.

Contemporary historiographer Hayden White in his book *Metahistory*,[59] analyzes great nineteenth century historians and philosophers of history. From this foundation he has developed a brilliant multidimensional analytic in which tacit stylistic, formal, political, and explanatory (metaphysical) tropisms are ineluctably operative in each historical narrative. He concludes that facts and events decidedly do *not* tell their own story. Ricoeur has also shown the remarkable correspondences obtaining between the *text* in hermeneutics, *action* in the theory of action, and *narrative* in history.[60] We will return to his insights later, for they pertain to the dialectic at work between understanding and explanation in interpretation. The crux of his position is that "the activity of analysis...appears as a simple segment of an interpretative arc which goes from naive understanding through explanation to knowledgeable understanding." As applied to history, which contains the ideas both of *story* and *action*, he says:

> History begins when we no longer have immediate understanding, and when we undertake to reconstruct the sequence of antecedents along lines other than that of the motives and reasons alleged by the actors in history. The difficulty for epistemology is precisely to show how explanation is added to, or superimposed on, or even substituted for, the immediate understanding of the the course of past history.[61]

To follow the unrolling of the scroll of creating art, especially over an extended period of time and as a history which one has been *inside* as a priviledged sharer, is to be content, however, with the child's wonder and ready acceptance in listening to a story — where "And then?" seems preferable to the adult's constant "Why?" which is always seeking for causes, reasons and motives.[62] *The motives and reasons alleged by the actors in the events are especially significant in histories of artistic creation, for these implicate hidden order, transformative process, and expansion of consciousness often more surprising to the artist than to even the most sympathetic observer-participant. But it can just as well go the other way too—the artist can make a significant breakthrough which, lying close to his path of action, takes distance to evaluate.*

Summary

We have described qualitative experiencing as equivalent to expressing, and pointed to an *art of qualitative thinking* which can be constructed on this base. This superimposes an interpretive process upon a creative process and leads to an understanding of the deep structure adumbrated through the expressive act. We have used the word *text* to indicate a surrogate symbolic of the pervasive quality of *an* experience, and distinguished between the *originary* and *dependent* quality of texts. The latter retains the usual hermeneutic meaning of an existing text, while the former refers to a text created anew as the first part of the cycle of the art of qualitative thinking. This cycle itself, though one process, can be conveniently broken into four moments or stages: (1) expressive text, (2) distancing, (3) interpreting, and (4) renewing. Expressive texts were further subdivided into expressive-artistic modes, under which we find iconic (nonverbal) and literary subdivisions; and expressive-descriptive modes, under which are phenomenological and historical subdivisions. This terminology is purely functional since the moments and modes often refuse in operation to honor conceptual boundaries set up purely for discussion's sake. Extended examples of expressive-artistic and expressive-descriptive texts were given from novels, poems, seminar exercises, phenomenological descriptions, and special case histories. The examples chosen were such that they often contain a *text* relating to the theme of this book within their text—that is, the content often refers to the evolution of consciousness.

Reference was made to steps said to lead to direct intuition of cosmic unity. These steps are *direct attention* (to what is both within and without); then *stopping* (silently remaining with what is); then *passive awareness* (operating beyond all dualisms). We found similar stages in our examples. We concluded that the hermeneutic-expressive cycle of the art of qualitative thinking sets in motion *a process whereby consciousness can become self-conscious of its own growth or evolution.* To the one expressing, God is not some unknowable entity but is rather "manifest like the sky."

An examination of phenomenological expressive-descriptive texts showed that there really is no pure subject or pure object. Rather there always exists an intimate relationship between humankind and world, between mind and matter, between person and person, and between being and time. Introspection does not reveal the nature of our lived experience, for it arises directly from the ongoing dialogue between us and our world.

When artist moves toward expression, the *I* speaks in such a way that the expressed feelings and beliefs modify the expressing being. Again, the imagination knows no boundaries where we usually draw them—between self-other, conscious-unconscious, and mind-matter. It intuitively knows its own way to the highest states of consciousness by working through what is manifest.

Special case histories of artists creating were presented from the Drawing Lab. A lived history of creative-evolution and self-evolution that touches on the mythic always arises from consideration of an artist's serial over an extended period of time. Transcribed dialogues between the special observers and the artist (reflecting on created works through the stimulated recall of in-process photographs) become in themselves historical expressive-descriptive texts for the art of qualitative thinking. A structural-existential analytic, the *S-E Method*, was introduced. Based on the tensional structure of metaphor, it allows its user to scan artists' dislogues and histories in terms of *antecedent, constituent, and consequent* elements that are taken as parts of one cohesive cycle. In this cycle the antecedent elements—the predisposing form, history, or condition—clash with constituent elements—the present context which is always other than expected—thus setting the stage for consequent synthesis transcending the clash into spontaneity, novelty and expression. *Though the S-E Model provides an analytic, it is a paradoxical one honoring both the unpredictable nature of what is existential, as a history lived forward, and the fact that what is expressed has structure and intelligibility despite its inclusion of inexplicable spontaneity and novelty.*[63] In searching for signs of the role of art in the evolution of consciousness, it is of foremost importance to look not only at the works but to share the motives and reasons alleged by the artists themselves. *The works will show, if we can read them, what has been made manifest like the sky. The self reports will show to what degree the evolution of consciousness has become self-conscious to itself.*

The importance of the expressive text, whether artistic or descriptive, is primary for the fullest impact of the art of qualitative thinking. Expressing is always enough in itself, provided it leads toward renewed desire for expressing. And expressing leads organically to the next moment or stage of the art of qualitative thinking: *distancing*.

References

1. Ponge, F. *The voice of things.* (B. Archer, trans.) N.Y.: McGraw-Hill, 1972; p. 187.

2. Bachelard, G. *The poetics of reverie.* (D. Russel, trans.) Boston: Beacon Press, 1971; p. 124.

3. Chakravartz, Amiya (ed.) *A Tagore reader.* N.Y.: The Macmillan Co., 1961; p. 339.

4. Palmer, R. E. *Hermeneutics.* Evanston: Northwestern University Press, 1969; pp. 98-123.

5. Gadamer, H-G. *Truth and method.* N.Y.: Seabury Press, 1975.

6. Dewey, J. *Art as experience.* N.Y.: Minton, Balch, 1934.

7. Habermas, J. *Knowledge and human interests.* (J.J. Shapiro, trans.) Boston: Beacon Press, 1971.

8. Harper, S. R. and Miller, D. L. (Eds.), *Interpretation: The poetry of meaning.* N.Y.: Harcourt, Brace & World, 1967; p. 51.

9. Dewey, J. *Op. cit.,* reference 6 above.

10. Eder, R. Metaphor's role at core of thought. *The New York Times,* April 15, 1980; pp. C-1 and C-4.

11. Bachelard, G. *The poetics of space.* (M. Jolas, trans.) Boston: Beacon Press, 1969; p. 89.

12. *Ibid.,* pp. 151-152.

13. Lipman, M. *What happens in art.* N.Y.: Appleton-Century-Crofts, 1967; pp. 2-3.

14. Dewey, J. Qualitative thought. Chapter 6 in *Philosophy and Civilization.* N.Y.: Capricorn Books, 1963; p. 172.

15. Heidegger, M. *Discourse on thinking.* N.Y.: Harper & Row, 1966.

16. Van Manen, M. An experiment in educational theorizing: The Utrecht School. *Interchange,* 10 (1), 1978-79; pp. 48-66.

17. Palmer, R. E. *Op. cit.,* reference 4 above, pp. 98-123.

18. Bachelard, G. *Op. cit.*, reference 11 above, p. 214.

19. Bachelard, G. *Op. cit.*, reference 2 above, p. 211.

20. Proust, M. *Within a budding grove.* (C.K.S. Moncrieff, trans.) N.Y.: The Modern Library, 1923; Part II, pp. 20-23.

21. Senior, J. *The way down and out.* N.Y.: Greenwood Press, 1968; p. xii.

22. *Ibid.*, p. xiv.

23. Krishnamurti, J. *The first and last freedom.* Wheaton, Ill.: Quest, 1954; p. 24.

24. Wilber, K. *The spectrum of consciousness.* Wheaton, Ill.: Quest, 1977; pp. 314-315.

25. Wilber, K. The problem of proof. *ReVision*, 5 (1), Spring, 1982; p. 94.

26. Krishnamurti, J. *Krishnamurti in India 1970-71.* India: Krishnamurti Foundation, 1971; p. 13.

27. Bucke, R. M. *Cosmic consciousness.* N.Y.: E. P. Dutton, 1969.

28. Anderson, J. M... Since the time we are a dialogue and able to hear from one another. *Man and World*, 1978, 10; pp. 115-135.

29. Heidegger, M. *Poetry, language and thought.* (A. Hofstadter, trans.) N.Y.: Harper & Row, 1971; pp. 213-229.

30. *Ibid.*, p. 219.

31. *Ibid.*, p. 226.

32. Pepper, S. C. *Concept and quality.* La Salle, Ill.: Open Court, 1966.

33. Gibson, W. *A season in heaven.* N.Y.: Atheneum (Bantam Books), 1975, pp. 122-123.

34. Dewey, J. *Op. cit.*, reference 6 above, p. 237.

35. *Ibid.*, p. 230.

36. *Ibid.*, p. 243.

37. *Ibid.*, pp. 215-216.

38. Van Manen, M. *Op. cit.*, reference 16 above, p. 57.

39. Van den Berg, J. H. *A different existence.* Pittsburgh: Duquesne University Press, 1972; p. 64.

40. *Ibid.*

41. *Ibid.*, pp. 33-34.

42. *Ibid.*, pp. 34-35.

43. *Ibid.*, p. 4.

44. *Ibid.*, p. 35.

45. Wilber, K. *Op. cit.*, reference 24 above, p. 314.

46. *Ibid.*, pp. 314-315.

47. Van Manen, M. *Op. cit.*, reference 16 above, p. 56.

48. Geiger, G. Paper written for a graduate seminar in art education, taught by K.R. Beittel, The Pennyslvania State University, Spring, 1982.

49. Meyer, S. Paper for same seminar as reference 48 above.

50. Bachelard, G. *Op. cit.*, reference 2 above. Quotation of J. Green (*L'aube vermeille*, p. 73), in Bachelard, p. 160.

51. *Ibid.*, p. 167.

52. Werner, H. *Comparative psychology of mental development.* N.Y.: Harper & Row, 1940; pp. 71-72.

53. Beittel, K. R. *Mind and context in the art of drawing.* N.Y.: Holt, Rinehart & Wiston, 1972.
Beittel, K.R. *Alternatives for art education research.* Dubuque, Iowa: William C. Brown, 1973.
Novosel, J. The structural existentiality of arting: Inquiry into the nature of the creative process. Unpublished Ph.D. thesis, The Pennsylvania State University, 1976.
Novosel-Beittel, J. Inquiry into the qualitative world of creating: The S-E Model. *Studies in Art Education*, 20 (1), 1978, pp. 26-36.
Novosel-Beittel, J. Where the desirable becomes existential. *Journal*, Canadian Society for Education Through Art, 9, 1979; pp. 40-44.

54. Beitel, K. R. *Op. cit.*, 1973, reference 53 above, pp. 50-52.

55. Novosel-Beittel, J. *Op. cit.*, 1978, reference 53 above, pp. 26-27.

56. Wilber, K. *Op. cit.*, reference 25 above, p. 94.

57. Novosel-Beittel, J. *Op. cit.*, 1978, reference 53 above, p. 27.

58. *Ibid.*, pp. 29-31.

59. White, H. *Metahistory.* Baltimore: Johns Hopkins University Press, 1974.

60. Ricoeur, P. (C.E. Reagan and D. Stewart, eds.) *The philosophy of Paul Ricoeur.* Boston: Beacon Press, 1978; p. 154.

61. *Ibid.*, p. 162.

62. *Ibid.*, p. 164.

63. Hausman, C. R. *A discourse on novelty and creation. Netherlands: Martinus Nijhoff, 1975.*

8

Distancing

In all faces is seen the Face of faces, veiled, and in a riddle; howbeit unveiled it is not seen, until above all faces a man enter into a certain secret and mystic silence where there is no knowledge or concept of a face.

Nicholas of Cusa[1]

Commentary in the widest sense has, however, an aspect that is external because it treats among other things of exoteric questions. Inversely, art has an aspect that is inward and profound by virtue of its symbolism; it then fulfills a different function and speaks directly to the contemplative mind: in this way it becomes a support for intellection, thanks to its non-mental, concrete and direct manner of speech.

Schuon[2]

When we understand a text, what is meaningful in it charms us just as the beautiful charms us. It has asserted itself and charmed us before we can come to ourselves and be in a position to test the claim to meaning that it makes.

Gadamer[3]

Distancing: A Reflection

From a distance it is possible to discern the total outline of something unseeable at close range. A distance with nothing friendly on the horizon plunges us within an alien land. In a foreign place we can fight distance which might prove inhospitable by keeping nearby someone or something we feel emotionally close to. We then feel centered and at home even in a strange land.

It is not distance that *causes* the heart to grow fonder, it is distance that rather provides the ground on which we can perceive the figure of fondness that was blurred at close range. The quality that overcomes us in an aesthetic experience requires distance so that its strands and textures can assert themselves. The harmony of the music that moved us profoundly on first hearing reveals in the distance of time the detail and intricacy there from the start.

Understanding is itself near and far, for from afar we can

understand all that we have understood already from the start, as though the outlines set up by understanding now receive their sub-headings and their words. Love, said Shakespeare, does not alter where it alteration finds, for it is a totality where all things belong to the whole as parts in which farness supports nearness. Where distance does not support and deepen nearness, we have changed our love or understanding. Then we have not only stepped back but outside the primary magical circle altogether, forgetful that the universe as a whole has but one center at a time.

In this sense there is no meaningful distance without relationship to a center—only aimless wandering where near and far become not only relativized but meaningless terms, where even "freedom's just another name for nothing else to do." Our historicality means that truth has many circlings around its center—means that truth of meaning is that centering-circling phenomenon of understanding that we only know within the general relativity theory of the spirit. We only know there is a distancing related to understanding because we know there is a centering. Distancing is to centering as expressing is to experiencing. The one gains its meaningful existence reciprocally from the other.

It is often said that we learn to ice skate in the summer and to swim in the winter. Tensional opposites are poles of one thing. When we place a jar in Tennessee, we make the landscape be. The jar gives the landscape a center and grants understanding by creating a distance-in-unity between them.

Though the deeds of the hero are great in the doing, they are greater still in the singing of them. Tall tales are not false but heroic exaggerations that are the work of imagination. Custer's last stand becomes "truer" than the historic facts. Demystifying, though essential against a freezing of spirit into inaction, always breaks into too vast a distance away from true center. "Let the circle be unbroken" is the song not just of faith but of understanding.

Descartes' *cogito* led to the fatal and false distance of modern scientism, as though all that exists is the circle drawn around the thinker who, through a sickness of doubt, strives indirectly to know through manipulation that which in itself is unknowable. The circle drawn by the *cogito* includes only the center of a limited "thinking"—a partial and alien unsure universe—which infects and tries to destroy the *cogito* of dreamer and mystic, of poet and saint, who permit us to see the universe as whole, friendly and purposive.

The romantic lover would like to keep two centers. Doing so creates an illusion of fantastic distance and simultaneously of related closeness. But at base this stance is false, for no unified figure and ground occur—only a shifting one in which the idea is preferred to the reality. Only a center in common to differing radii symbolizes love, art, dialogue, and mystical experience.

"May the Lord watch between you and me while we are absent one from the other," says the Mizpah benediction. The psalmist asks "Where shall I go to escape from Thee?" Whether in ocean depths or alpine heights, God is already there. A truly relational center permitting the "meeting" to occur across vast distances and separations defines cosmic at-homeness.

Yet distance distorts, too—neither more nor less than the necessary experiential closeness on which it depends. Both are differing moments of a unified process or cycle. There is a shock of going and returning and of the negational element in all experiencing, for, as in the clash of antecedent and constituent in metaphor, our best predictions and preparations are contradicted, and we are rudely thrown into the need for transcendence.

The truth of experiencing depends on distancing as well as on closeness, although the order requires closeness to come first. Distancing is in the dependent relationship because it limns out features, textures and strands of an aesthetic and physiognomic whole intuitively grasped from the start.

Even our dreams have lag time built within them. We dream of Pennsylvania while we are in Kyoto and of Kyoto once we return to Pennsylvania. Writers are aware of this phenomenon. The setting taking place in London moves forward as the writer settles in Boston. Distancing allows the absent quality to come forward in imagination and strips away habituation—even as phenomenology permits us to see the ordinary as extraordinarily strange.

In movies, novels and real life, parted lovers are always impelled into each other's arms across a space that echoes the temporal band separating them. Distance is poignancy, like Christmas carols in the snow of an alien city. But it is also the generous wind resuscitating fading embers. It creates a gap for mental closure, a shadowy silhouette for meaningful details. It encourages the artfull game called history, as though we were *there* and *then,* forgetful that we do not know what it is to be *here* and *now*. Distance is an ancient dialectic known well to the poet and the dreamer: the *then* that goes with *now*, the *far* that says *near*, the *moon* that suggests *sun*, the *mountain* that yearns for *ocean*.

Distance moves the art of qualitative thinking forward. It is the interval where wholes start to fall into parts so that later they can fund back into richer wholes. It is the second push of "the cradle endlessly rocking." Through it we hear the wood thrush in January because we heard one in May.

Distancing in Relationship to Reduction and Expansion

We have been suggesting that we can only distance what we have stood in the heart of and that we cannot lose our tie to that center. A kind of cooling off, a taint of reductionism, enters in nevertheless. Reduction to simplicity of outline, however, is different from reductionism. To say that Joan of Arc had some schizophrenic characteristics already does something to our grasp of the heroine, but to say that she was *nothing but* a schizophrenic is completely reductionistic.[4] The example is faulty if it goes no further. A good paraphrase acceptable to one's dialogue partner is, to Ott,[5] a positive aspect of the phenomenology of dialogue. Further, it is one which can permit the dialogue to move forward, for a good paraphrase gives the one whose meanings are being reflected essential distance and understanding permitting thought to open anew.

Thinking, reflection, and qualitative thinking already imply distancing. Imagination and expression may be said to be basic or primary thought, always an expanding and changing but unified whole, while other thought could be called secondary. That is why Ponge disclaims *ideas* for *things*. His *things*, finding words, lead to new *ideas*. If art supplies us with a *concrete universal*, it is nevertheless a universal that leads to further thought and reflection. Qualitative thinking struggles to remain true, even at the secondary more intellective level, to the pervasive quality from which it springs.

The artist is centered on direct attention to inner and outer happenings, to stopping the world, to passive awareness—all of which allow the imagination to dream itself on so that new being can come forth freely. The artist's love-gnosis is a paradoxical one: attachment as detachment, silence as the manifest. It is the potter's sphere: inside of nothing, outside of form.

Insofar as distancing means *freezing*, it should be avoided. Better to spin mindlessly from one pot to the next and let some one else figure out what is going on. But the potter has a suspicion that greater depth comes from greater understanding, deeper living and deeper insight. It is not a matter of repeating that same form over and over. Bachelard urges us to avoid reduction at all costs and to work at deepening imagination at its source:

> ...and how should one receive an exaggerated image, if not by exaggerating it a little more, by personalizing the exaggeration? The phenomenological gain appears right away: in prolonging *exaggeration*, we may have the good fortune to avoid the habits of *reduction*...The dialectics of the dynamisms of reduction and exaggeration can throw light on the dialectics of psychoanalysis and phenomenology. It is, of course, phenomenology which gives us the psychic positivity of the image. Let us therefore transform our amazement into admiration. We can even begin by admiring. Then, later, we shall see whether or not it will be necessary to organize our disappointment through criticism and reduction.[6]

But there can also be a positive dialectic between reduction and exaggeration – or expansion as we will call it, for Bachelard's *method* is to allow his dreaming, exaggerating mind to bring together a community of kindred exaggerating voices. Curiously, we *reduce* by such exaggeration, coming to feel a clarity of meaning to that which avoids reduction.

In still another sense, we keep alive what we distance. In turning our original experience and expression to differing lights at arm's length, we savor its facets. We begin to sense the deep structure that brought expression into being. Though we create something, we are never fully conscious of this deep structure. Distancing allows that dim awareness to infuse us and partially clarify itself. The consciousness, not just the mind, can examine what is qualitative.

Many so called realized or enlightened masters would not pay great attention to intellective reflection, finding it detrimental to dwelling in the here and now. The mind, they say, should be like a reflecting pond. The flight of geese, the passing of the moon, are reflected dispassionately. Consciousness is taken to be greater than mind by most people who reflect on the matter; but it is nevertheless rare that the one blessed with satori does not again and again find mind coming back to that experience in an effort to be true to it. *Though the mind be destined to fail, it can nevertheless serve the freer and expanding consciousness insofar as it remains a part of that greater whole and insofar as consciousness itself does not corrupt itself by breaking its tie with the qualitative center of what it seeks to further intuit.*

By keeping thought qualitative and by dealing with its thinking as an art, we hope to evade any academic cast of thought. There must be more than we can do than say, "It cannot be said," true though that is and important as it is to say it. After all, our expression, though implicating deep structure, even with the greatest genius is *never* sufficient for the mystery it wishes to symbolize. In that sense all expression itself is a reduction, and one of the functions of our distancing is to restore the greater ground to the figure of expression itself and to lead to renewed expression so that our creating energy can return to the universe in new and deeper celebration.

But there is still another way out of our mental impasses. If distancing and interpreting conspire together to show not only the ground and the textures of the quality of expression, but also its weak causation and its limits, we then encounter constituent elements which clash with antecedent elements, and this clash leads toward transcendence, for a leap into synthesis, speculation and renewal. For what expression rightly ignores reflection will not, so an inevitable clash results. We saw earlier that Coleridge called for a superindividual reason to come to an intuitive resolution which restores to consciousness its rightful scope above the paradoxes of the imagination. Paradoxes are but an on-level view of what from above may be one whole. Every artist knows that the whole contains tensional and even conflicting parts which nevertheless are harmonized into one. This is that unity in "multeity" of which Coleridge spoke. It is Heidegger's unity of the revealed and the concealed in the heart of being. It is the way things may be "held apart together."

Also, consciousness as we have been discussing it, will never be content to return to the more pedestrian levels of mind once implicated in imaginative constructions of cosmic overtones. As Hegel and all the lineage of the esoteric tradition know, *consciousness in becoming self-conscious prepares itself for its own transcendence.* Distancing is a stage of becoming self-conscious for a consciousness already deeply involved in expression. A modern mystic, Gopi Krishna, said:

> ...the human brain, as the result of evolution, has now the capacity to exhibit another kind of consciousness which can know itself or, in other words become conscious of consciousness, look beyond Space and Time. What is more surprising, instead of arriving at a conclusion by reasoning, as every normal mind does, it can dive into an Ocean of Knowledge in which all that is knowable is known, and all the problems awaiting solution are solved. From this ocean droplets of fresh knowledge trickle down into normal consciousness, according to the degree of attunement with the brain, and it is these droplets of rare knowledge, not possible to recognize by empirical methods, which have always been honored as Revelation.[7]

There is no reason why distancing and interpreting should not be moments where we become conscious of consciousness, where major and minor epiphanies are experienced or prepared for, where revelation itself may burst through. In any event, *qualitative thinking is an art where paradoxical language and direct intuition take on their necessary consciousness-expanding function.*

Expansionist, Associationist Modes

But let us focus on actual examples. In what follows, Bachelard applies his expanionist and associationist poetic reverie method to demonstrate "the reality of poetic sound miniatures":

> Poets often introduce us into a world of impossible sounds, so impossible, in fact, that their authors may be charged with creating phantasy that has no interest. One smiles and goes one's way. And yet, most often, the poet did not take his poem lightly, and a certain tenderness presided over these images.
>
> Rene-Guy Cadou, who lived in the Village of Happy Homes, was moved to write:
>
> On entend gazouiller les fleurs du paravent (You can hear the prattle of the flowers on the screen.)
>
> Because all flowers sing and speak, even those we draw, and it is impossible to remain unsociable when we draw a flower or a bird.

Another poet writes:

Son secret c'était
D'écouter la fleur
User sa couleur.

(Her secret was
Listening to flowers
Wear out their colors.)

Like so many poets, Claude Vigée
hears the grass grow:

J'écoute
  Un jeune noisetier
Verdir.

(I hear
  A young nut-tree
Grow green.)

Such images as these must be taken, at the least, in their existence as a *reality of expression,* and this being would be diminished if we tried to refer them to a reality, even to a psychological reality.[8]

As he continues in this section he quotes Theophile Gautier and Rimbaud. Then he examines the word *mandrake*, which in French is *mandragore*, saying: "And for ears that dream, what a noise of syllables there is in its name. Words are clamor-filled shells. There's many a story in the miniature of a single word!"[9] He then continues his exploration of "how shall we see without hearing?" by quoting Pericle Patocchi then immediately picks up a forceful concluding example from Milosz:

...Here we have the silence of the distant world concentrated in one line:

Au loin j'entendais prier les sources de la terre
(Far off I heard the springs of earth praying.)

Some poems move toward silence the way we descend in memory. As for instance, in this great poem by Milosz:

Tandis que le grand vent glapit des mortes
On bruit de vielle aigre sur quelque route
Ecoute—plus rien—seul le grand silence—écoute.

(While the high wind yelps the names of women long dead
Or the sound of bitter old rain on a road
Listen—now there's nothing—but complete silence—listen.)[10]

Here *prolonging exaggeration avoids reduction.* Through this extension we begin to "listen to everything in nature that is unable to speak,"[11] an expansion which Bachelard deepens still further through quoting a conversation which "reaches down to unplumbed depths, establishing in a few words the ontological link between invisible and inaudible."

> Violane (who is blind) – I hear...
> Mara – What do you hear?
> Violaine – Things existing with me.[12]

And as though this were indeed an exercise in expanding consciousness, in direct attention to what is within and without, a stopping, a passive awareness, he ends this section with a verse from Max Picard:

> Écoute bien pourtant. Non pas
> mes paroles, mais le tumulte qui
> s'élève en ton corps lorsque t'écoutes.
>
> (Yet listen well,. Not to my words,
> but to the tumult that rages in
> your body when you listen to yourself.)[13]

Here the poetic reverie of Bachelard develops from an imaginative core, from the speech of what does not speak. Then around that center, through admiration and exaggeration gained from his well selected poetic fragments, the theme rolls on and on so that it finally embraces the entire cosmos. This is an art of qualitative thinking which never breaks into parts. Text, distancing, interpreting, and renewing roll back and forth over one another. And through it all consciousness becomes conscious of its imaginative expansion. We become the happy one engaged in the self-formative process that Bachelard says lies hidden in poetic reverie. We begin our examples here to remind ourselves not to let any intrusive movement of thought tear apart the unified art of qualitative thinking.

The Paraphrase

Poets and dreamers resist the paraphrase. The content, the subject-matter, the meaning and the form of a poem are only in experiencing them in and through the poem. The meaning does not float from the poem of which it is an integral part. Yet, as a *part* of the whole which is a dialogue, paraphrase can be helpful.

Here is an example from the Utrecht School of phenomenological pedagogy, in the form of a piece of writing by a workshop participant who focused on *fear of the dark*.

> When I return home from work in the evening, I usually take a shorter route. The short cut is at least ten minutes faster. I leave the well-lit street and ride my bike toward a dark hollow road. The dark road has a high shoulder on the sides, and it lies in front of me like a gaping mouth. I enter the road with a feeling of anxiety and uncertainty. As soon as the last street-light and house disappear behind me, I feel as though I am digested by the darkness. It totally encapsulates me and is everywhere. I feel afraid of something that doesn't want to identify itself. This fear is different from fear of dogs for example. You know dogs, and can arm yourself against them with a stick or by taking another road to avoid them. Darkness is a different adversary. I feel threatened from all sides at once without knowing exactly what direction it comes from. As I hastily continue along the dark road my eyes pick up any sign of movement. I try to ascertain the meaning of every sould I hear. When I feel nothing unusual, I feel somewhat relieved: that was only a bird suddenly taking flight, that is the wind whistling through the treetops. Identifying sounds and naming them calms me down. But no matter how I train my eyes and sharpen my hearing, my back always feels unprotected. "It" can come from behind and yet I don't look behind me. By pushing extra hard on my bike pedals, I try to make my back feel secure. I cycle on and stay on my guard. Then, suddenly I stiffen with fright; as if my legs are paralyzed. Is someone standing there? A shape looms up ahead of me, a human figure. As I come closer I sigh with relief; it is nothing, only a bush. I am immediately inclined to recognize a human form in anything. And the worst it seems that can happen to me here is to meet another person. If I happen to pass someone in this darkness, I will keep my eyes firmly fixed on him, watching him guardedly. I cannot help but distrust him. Any person who is found in this desolate location cannot mean well. In the distance the first streetlights become visible and I see the signs of the first houses again. I sigh deeply and a feeling of "all is well" comes over me. If I meet someone now I won't feel afraid. I will look at the person and say "goodnight" even if I don't know him.[14]

After this, a reductive paraphrase to "structural elements" occurs. The above author found the following:

> 1. Darkness is a threat which does not have a definite location: it is everywhere;
> 2. Darkness is an unidentifiable threat — it has no identity, no concreteness;
> 3. There is increased sensory alertness, especially the perceptual and auditory senses;
> 4. What is behind one — the "unprotected flank" — is experienced as most vulnerable and threatened;

5. There is an inclination to see human faces and shapes in everything;
6. One has the physical sensation of increased breathing, more rapid heartbeat, feeling of weakness in the limbs, etc.;
7. Passersby are distrusted;
8. Darkness is a challenge—albeit a frightening one, it has elements of adventure.[15]

At this point the author of this description and its reduction to structural elements can follow several routes into interpretation and understanding. Here we will take up only the matter of distancing and save what it may lead to for later discussion.

In the earlier example from Proust we performed a paraphrase of the alternative explanations which the three trees might possess. These reductions were laid out originally by the narrator himself. We also found van den Berg doing some reduction and interpretation of the text of his lonely, disappointed evening when his friend could not come.

Reduction and Paraphrase of Case Histories of Expression

In the case of Larry (the student artist in the Drawing Lab who went through a sudden transformation in his work) we can illustrate a kind of *selection and paraphrase* of his history in the Lab over the two and one-half years he worked there. The case history is far too voluminous to deal with in any but an illustrative manner. But taking that material in its original text narrative, we can put some questions to it and allow the text to answer.

What were his conceptualizations about making art, those which he himself constructed and shared in the inquiry sessions? How did he modify and extend these over time? What changes in drawing processes seem to accompany them? Twenty-six self-guiding conceptualizations Larry made about making art were abstracted from the text to answer such questions. Here follows not the complete list but selections from the complete history:

Early Period

1. Larry tries to invent "pen figures" which are equivalent to discriminations he perceives in nature. He wonders how to show light with black pen lines. He seems to conclude: "I can invent medium-tool devices tentatively equivalent to my visual impressions." He

develops the concept that the artist can be master of the world out there which he is trying to represent. He can change sizes, tilt objects, leave items out, etc.

2. Concept: "Pen figures" can represent *simultaneously* more than one visual impression—e.g., "If I use wriggly lines which vary in weight and density-darkness I can represent *both* the texture of a tree trunk and the degree of light and shadow present at the same time."

3. Concept: Technical mastery, basic discipline, as in a craft, precedes satisfactory representation, which in turn is the basis for "expression." "If I can use the hammer and saw I can build something I want to."

5. Concept: The right texture and form can be represented by direct pen strokes if one visualizes the whole first. Forms in nature need not be represented by a bounded outline. "I can organize a lot of complexity if I remain open and keep my eye on the whole I am after. Techniques within a given drawing must be consistent. I can't, for example, draw the lips with a tight outline if nothing else is."

9. Concept: The world of art is much broader, much more exciting than the problems of representational mastery. "*Guernica* blew my mind. Then I saw two vastly different exhibitions (Flavin, Montenegro). The idea of art cannot be restricted. Yet all of these experiences were pleasant."

Middle Period

12. Concept: Reflection on the analogical, metaphorical quality of visual impressions aids one's efforts of expression. "I wanted to have them look like they are tumbling. It didn't look like a ramshackle house but as kind of opposed to a solid brick house...like an old wooden shack that was half crushed in...kind of bent out of shape."

14. Concept: Ideas will come without forcing them and will come while working. "It was the mood way. I was doodling and all of a sudden there was something there. Everything kind of went around it from there."

15. Concept: Exploration of media, tools, and the textures and spaces of a page are interesting in and of themselves, without guidance of a mood or visual impression beforehand. "I used a swirling kind of stroke and played around with the brush. I tried to get interesting spaces in between as I went along, to catch the eye and give movement. It was not just exploring the form but the medium too."

Late Period

23. Concept: It is possible to conceptualize what is "purely visual" in art. Larry's explanation: "When I think of some of the great art, it gives you such a strong visual sense in one way or another. They were so aware of what they were seeing." Different example: "You might be driving along in a car or walking along, or just sitting, and happen to glance at something...It just somehow, I don't know, falls together. Almost by accident." Further example: "I think it is a combination of mood and physical condition...*Not going around in a half-ass way, at a lower level of awareness, not being fully alive, not being all that perceptive. I used to think of it as a kind of animal-like awareness. It is just a superhuman awareness. You are just kind of really alive in a human way; you are seeing things and not just letting things go by.*"

24. Concept: One can perceive himself as an artist—not a "professional" but an artist nevertheless. Larry's reasoning: "I'm an artist...Maybe not, quote, like Picasso—but I think everyone can be an artist, in their own way...in the kind of expression they can work on. I think that raises a question...That everyone should have the kind of experience, you know, of trying to...of expression. A kind of good thing...for a human to do...It affects the total life this way. You know [laughs], I look at these [drawings]...I don't know if I'd hang them in my apartment or not. Among you I could feel open, but maybe someone would look at them and 'Ycchh'...You know its *nothing* but to *me* I can say it's bad but still there is something."

26: Concept: The art of drawing is its own intense reality. Said Larry: "When you're in there, you are face to face with the visual problem, You can't just have some vague undefined thoughts. You've got to get right to it. You can't evade...I don't know what you are doing when you are drawing—your feelings, your perceptions, you have to be more aware of them."[16]

The above selected eleven conceptualizations from the twenty-six originally chosen from the entire history of Larry's work in the Drawing Lab provide some appreciation of this artist's changing consciousness of how drawings are made. Certainly here we also find consciousness becoming self-conscious of itself and slowly evolving to greater complexity and depth. The twenty-six conceptualizations abstracted from the history already represent a selection guided by questions put to the basic text. In that sense they are useful reductions. Language in the drawn-out discursive form of these selections is still too verbose to lead easily to interpretations, so these were paraphrased in still briefer form. We present the paraphrases corresponding to the originals above:

Early Period

1. The artist is the source of invention, selection, and mastery.

2. Drawing elements cognized separately interact, producing higher-order principles.

3. Skill is the basis upon which to build expression.

5. Visualization of the whole can lead to sensitive handling of complex ideas and usher in a principle of consistency.

9. Art is pluralistic; many different qualities can be enjoyed.

Middle Period

12. Visual phenomena have implicit meanings which, teased out as metaphors, guide expression.

14. Ideas must not be forced; with patience they come, in-process.

15. Medium and process without regard to representation and mood are intrinsically exciting.

Late Period

23. The dialogic, transformational nature of the art process is accepted and preferred.

24. One can see oneself as an artist (though not a professional). This perception of a special artistic self is good for everyone.

26. The act of drawing is an intense experiential encounter which one cannot evade.[17]

All of this reduction must not break faith with its qualitative source. Distancing must not lose the center. In the example we are asking questions of the quality of Larry's life as an artist. We begin there and if after distancing, we go on to interpreting, we return there with ever more understanding of the mythic consciousness-expanding overtones of this unique history.

It is also perhaps obvious that distancing when elegantly done can in itself almost supply interpretations, for *any reduction that reveals structural elements seems to point automatically to the meanings immanent in the qualitative base from the start.* If we further reduce through paraphrase the longer transcript of the dialogue with the mature artist that followed Larry's example in the previous chapter, we arrive at, following the terminology of the S-E Model, antecedent complexes, constituent complexes, and consequent complexes— *the antecedent history the artist brought to his work, how it clashed with the moment of work, and what that clash gave birth to.* We can then further summarize and reduce these complexes to get a distanced grasp of the lively and qualitative content of the dialogues themselves. The material here abstracted comes from a slightly longer dialogue of which the given example was the greater part:

Antecedent Complexes

Tangible Facts and Feelings, Historical and Present	Conceptual Elements Both Harmonious and Dissonant	
	Clear, Positive, More Absolute	Ambivalent, Negative, More Relevant
2 style schools in conflict pushed on him in youth	Early mystical experience; forces esistenial choice	Choice of more mundane existence, present form over satori
Hasn't painted for several years	Painting a special reality; forces existential choice	Working with students becomes more important than painting making him love painting all the more
Performance factor a concern		
His intention is to do exercises not pictures in the Lab		"Talking about" painting a possible path to insight but not as gratifying as painting
		Teaching art in institutions today an "impossibility"

Constituent Complexes

The Lab Atmosphere as a Catalyst for Change	Artist as Agent for Change: Emergent Spontaneity
Somewhat unnatural conditions, public but not strange and alone like studio	Makes one stroke which is its "own reality" like at times "in the good old days"
"Signals" of understanding pass between researchers and artist	This "one mark" stops his world of teaching and administration and takes him back to when he was "only" an artist, an artist alone
The Japanese music "takes over" the artist and be begins to use the environment like media	The "mark" increases his conflict over the "impossibility" that he sees as the mystery of painting
The Lab lets the "hiddenness" of the artist's deepest thoughts on making art surface and "be"	
The Lab atmosphere suggests play, not seriousness, but yet a "kind" of seriousness, nevertheless	
The clicking camera must be accepted then forgotten	

Consequent Complexes

Outcomes That Deal With Working	Outcomes That Deal With Thinking or Conceptual Re-circulation
Gives up exercises, becomes interested in making a picture.	Aware of "some king of block" that he's got established, is probing that to himself as a result of the "one stroke" which "took him back" and disrupted his job for the rest of the day
Japanese music strikes associations, and he tries to flow with the "emptiness"	
A "nice little trip" occurs	Says he can't study or teach art in an institution except in some way like the Lab which "lets be" and sustains the presence of the state of being of the artist
He plays at play, full well realizing the seriousness of what he is engaged in	
He observes his vacillation, both suffers and enjoys his frustrations and is appalled by his "un-imagination" and what he has forgotten of "technique"	Realizes he must sustain himself, either "go through" his devices or become them
	He wants to do with people what he is doing through painting, and he feels he has "fallen into a strange thing"

Reductions of the Complexes

Antecedent Complexes

The artist feels his "time-lapse"; he is cautious, rusty and concerned about performance. Painting and the mystical are both reality at its best. Working with students in art school and "talking about" art are hassles, but challenging ones with great potential.

Constituent Complexes

The Lab is somewhat "public" but paradoxically allows the artist's private world to be; it is not taken completely seriously, yet very seriously; making art is a continual dilemma, a recurring conflict and an irreducible paradox, but like breathing in and out, all a part of the artist's life.

Consequent Complexes

The artist's intentions change as play becomes serious and art and spontaneity emerge as a "separate reality"; the absolute and the mundane interpenetrate and the ambivalent becomes positively charged.[18]

Once paraphrase and reduction are pushed this far they begin to sound almost like interpretations. In one sense they are; for as we will soon see, in interpreting, *the interpreter and the interpreted meet in a dialogue which reveals significant aspects of both through the engagement of both in the "subject" of the text.* For our purposes here it is sufficient to point out that paraphrase followed by still another paraphrase highlights structural elements immanent in the text as perceived by the one doing the paraphrase. Within the phenomenology of dialogue, the text, as dialogue partner, must accept such paraphrases.

Expansion Through Circumlocution

As part of the search for meaning and understanding, paraphrases do not have to be quantitatively reductive — that is, they do not have to eventuate in less words. There is almost a rule of thumb here: short text equals long words in paraphrase; long text equals short words. For a poem, for example, can have the concentration of a three line poem of Basho's or the expansion of Ponge's sixteen page (in print) "The Shrimp in Every (and All in a) State." Here the contrasting examples of poetry remind me of the distinctions I made about pottery between two kinds of decoration: spontaneity through containment and spontaneity through dispersion.

In any case, with poetry and other art works as texts, the method of distancing is often one of expansion by words and into words — a circum-locution, literally talking circles around the center of the work — setting it afloat in a sea of words. Critics usually work this way. Philosophers also talk of *unpacking* the meaning of a word, phrase, or concept, as though miles of yarn were being drawn out of a locked chest. "Critics can be obsessed with tidying things up. When they interpret a particularly difficult poem, the urge to clean can result in a poem that looks like it has never been lived in. Like a bank at night, the poem becomes an empty and severe attempt to be friendly."[19] The same critic who said these words, David Seal, does not so much tidy up parts of Robert Bly's "Sleepers Joining Hands" as engage in a series of circumlocutions which extend the reader's — and even the poet's — associative meanings. Seal writes 150 to 200 lines on a four line excerpt from Bly's poem.[20] Such circumlocutions can be apt, even loving and insightful expansions which extend qualitative immersion in the poem by giving our eyes added clarity in examining the poem's strands, textures and overtones so that we can eventually fund these back into the whole. It was all there from the start anyway if it is an expansion that really keeps us looking and receiving.

The method is sufficiently common in good criticism that we will not give examples here. But the very word *criticism* should be expunged of any of its visual judgmental overtones if it is to be of use in an art of qualitative thinking. The many words of criticism pose still more of a problem for interpretation than for distancing, so we will come back to this issue later.

In responding to painting, it would seem possible to qualitatively extend the duration of one's immediate attention through the "grey, anonymous language" of phenomenology. Foucault does just this throughout 14 pages of type as he patiently describes Velasquez's *Las Meninas*. We have the very real problem of how to find words for the silent voices of painting and the wordless voices of music. In the example that follows, after six pages of phenomenological description of the painting Foucault begins anew. Whereas before he talked about what appeared in general terms, in his new start he pins down the proper names of the figures represented in the painting:

> These proper names form useful landmarks and avoid ambiguous designations; they would tell us in any case what the painter is looking at, and the majority of the characters in the picture along with him. But the relation of language to painting is an infinite relation. It is not that words are imperfect, or that, when confronted by the visible, they prove insuperably inadequate. Neither can be reduced to the other's terms; it is in vain that we say what we see; what we see never resides in what we say. And it is in vain that we attempt to show, by the use of images, metaphors, or similies, what we are saying; the space where they achieve their splendour is not that deployed by our eyes but that defined by the sequential elements of syntax. And the proper name, in this particular context, is merely an artifice: it gives us a finger to point with, in other words, to pass surreptitiously from the space where one speaks to the space where one looks; in other words, to fold over the other as though they were equivalents. But if one wishes to treat their incompatibility as a starting-point for speech instead of as an obstacle to be avoided, so as to stay as close as possible to both, then one must erase these proper names, and preserve the infinity of the task. It is perhaps through the medium of this grey anonymous language, always over-meticulous and repetitive because too broad, that the painting may, little by little, release its illuminations.[21]

Here we sense an extended struggle to force words to relate to the silent world of painting. Language works when it "gives us a finger to point with" that travels from speaking to looking; but it must "preserve the infinity of the task," the inexhaustible source of words from that silence, and through its plodding, slow-burning character hope that the painting, like a light in this fog of grey words, "may release its illuminations." At the least, words here say *keep looking* as well as *keep talking*.

Digressions and Interludes in
the Heart of Expression

Poets and composers sometimes offer digressions and asides to give us distance within the work itself, as though to expand the attentive eye and ear as well as to refresh them. Ponge in his longish proeme "The Prairie" (it takes six pages in print) has included within the work itself just such a digression—almost in a different voice from the work proper. An entry in Ponge's journal refers to an experience five years before completing the proeme. He was walking with his wife through a pine grove when he saw a prairie with strollers on it beside a little river. "That was all. Nothing more...I was, I don't know why, taken with a kind of enthusiasm, secret,. calm, pure, tranquil. I knew immediately that this vision would remain as it was, intact in my memory. And that I had to try and tell it. To understand it? Understand is not the word. To try and hold to its promised delight and to penetrate it, comunicate it. Why?"[22]

> Later, he answers his own question: The prairie, then, is hope, resurrection, in its most elemental, unique, ingenuous sense, but stretched horizontally before our eyes for our relaxation, our repose. It is the field of our rest prepared (préparé)—past participle comprising all elements, all past action, and memory, the remembrance of the totality of past actions. Totality, the field into which have entered the remains of the three kingdoms. Accumulation of past days and principle of today's day.[23]

Parenthetically, the above two quotations also suggest a dialectic of expansion and reduction in the preparatory phases of creation, an assimilative, digestive, gestatory time. They also serve to give some of the flavor of the work to come, important here because space does not permit inclusion of the work as a whole.

For our purposes it is the distancing and the digression within the work, as part of the work, which is our focus. Ponge sets off the long paragraph of this part by two long lines of dots that further signify its role within the larger whole. We will pick up lines before and after this paragraph to give some sense of its context:

The prairie [pré] lying there like the ideal
  past participle
Is equally rever(d)end as our prefix of prefixes,
Pre-fix within prefix, pre-sent within present.

No way out of our original onomatopeias.
In that case, back into them.

No need, furthermore, to get out,
Their variations being adequate to account
For the marvelously tedious
Monotony and Variety of the world.
For its perpetuity, in short.

Yet must they be pronounced.
Spoken. And perhaps parabolized.
All of them, told.

. . . .

(Here a long passage should intervene—somewhat
like the interminable harpsichord solo of the 5th
Brandenburg Concerto, that is, tedious and
mechanical, yet at the same time mechanizing, not so
much because of the music as the logic, reasoning from
the lips, not the chest or the heart—in which I shall try
to explain, and I mean explain, two or three things: to
begin with, if pré, in French, represents one of the most
important and primordial of logical notions, it holds
equally true for the physical (geophysical), since what
is involved is a metamorphosis of water which, instead
of evaporating, at the summons of heat, directly into
clouds, chooses here—by clinging to the earth and
passing through it, that is, through the kneaded remains of the past of the three kingdoms and particularly through the finest granulations of the mineral
kingdom, ultimately re-impregnating the universal
ashtray—to renew life in its most elementary form,
grass: element-aliment. This chapter, which is *also* to
be the music of the prairies, will sound thin and
elaborate, with numerous appoggiaturas, so as to end
(if it ends) both accelerando and rinforzando, in a kind
of thunderclap which makes us seek refuge in the
woods. The perfecting of this passage could easily take
me a few more years. However it turns out...)

. . . .

The original storm spoke at length.

. . . .

Did the original storm not thunder so long within us
precisely so that
       for it rolls away, only
       partially filling the lower
       horizon where it lightens still—
Readying for the most urgent, rushing to the most
  pressing,
We would leave these woods,
Would pass between these trees and our remaining
  scruples,

> And, leaving behind all portals and colonnades,
> Transported suddenly by a quiet enthusiasm
> For a verity that might today be verdant,
> Would soon find ourselves stretched out on
>   this prairie,
> Long ago prepared for us by nature
>   —where nothing matters any
>   more but the blue sky.[24]

This beautiful passage takes us in and out of the prairie, in and out of poetry through a prose interlude. Such distancing changes, highlights, and finally strengthens our mood. These are poetic prose digressions in defense of the poetic, occurring in the heart of it—like the woods nearby the prairie for the thunderstorm. Such qualitative distancing in support of the quality itself is a model for distancing. *And so our distancing must be within the internal moments of the art of qualitative thinking, if it is not to disrupt the "art" and the "qualitative."* So said we could envision the art of qualitative thinking thus, all due credit to Ponge:

Expressive Text

· · · · · · · · · ·
(Distancing
Interpreting)

· · · · · · · · · ·
Renewal

Dangers in Distancing

"Thinking" is the dangerous part. The thirst for too sure a knowledge, too "thin" an explanation—these are the dangers to be fought in the heart of distancing. *There is a need to distance distancing itself,* and that is partly what the above interlude signifies.

The parenthetical moments of distancing and interpreting, as the thinking part of the art of qualitative thinking, play a role here inversely proportionate to the role they are assigned in much of hermeneutics. The "thinking" part must remain "qualitative" and subservient to one complete "art." *Besides, the role is that of rendering self-conscious the artistic consciousness so that it can further evolve.* Many of our examples from art include, symbolize and commemorate the epiphany, the numinous, the satori-like illumination striking within the everyday and within the heart of things. Here we have transcendelia, the data of the spirit. We must be especially sensitive in any effort to "reduce" or distance the realm of spirit, so that we do not leave that realm altogether through a retreat to the level of mind and its data, in-telligibilia. *Transcendelia are by definition non-intelligibilia.*

The internal moments are always a step behind and a step preparatory to expression. We know well from the Drawing Lab that: "Poets will always imagine faster than those who watch them imagining."[25] And when we deal with originary texts from our own hands, that imagining expressing part of us will always be faster than our thinking part. But a proper movement of consciousness that renders it self-conscious to itself may liberate still further that poetic consciousness within us.

> How, then, without "dephilosophizing" ourselves may we hope to experience the shocks that being receives from new images, shocks which are always the phenomena of youthful being? When we are at an age to imagine, we cannot say how or why we imagine. Then, when we could say how we imagine, we cease to imagine. We should therefore dematurize ourselves.[26]

The state of qualitative thinking *must* retain some of the quali-ty of poetic reverie, some of the characteristics of exploratory thinking rather than of coldly directed thinking. "The com-munication between the dreamer and his world is very close in reverie, it has no 'distance,' not that distance which marks the *perceived world,* the world fragmented by perception."[27] *Think-ing,* here, must be an appreciative, receptive and meditative one to deserve to be called *qualitative.* This is perhaps even more crucial when we approach our own expressions. Introspection, psychologism, or reductionism will not do. If a poet tells us: "The poplars tremble gentle in their mother tongue;"[28] then our words must tread lightly so not as to disturb the text in its har-mony and stillness. We must prepare to answer in kind or to fall into receptive silence in kind.

> The poet no longer describes; he exalts. He must be understood by following the dynamism of his exalta-tion. Then one enters the world by admiring it. The world is constituted by the totality of our admiration... admire first, then you will understand.[29]

There is a distance and strangeness in turning to any kind of thought from within poetry and art. This strangeness is again and again encountered when the mystic returns from il-lumination to the everyday. Poets, like Whitman, after their most inspired writing, are apt to reason as he did: "Compared to the flash, the divine illumination from which they had their origin, how poor and worthless [my] poems are."[30] If that is true of art, how much more will it not be true of qualitative thinking about art? Still, the parenthetical parts of *this* art, of *qualitative thinking*, are at least as important as that useful interlude in Ponge's *The Prairie.* Such interludes fund back into the base experience and expression, and they point toward renewal in experience and expression.

It took Gopi Krishna seventeen years of long disciplined meditation to arrive at a state of bliss and unity. Von Weizsacker summarized Gopi Krishna's progress thus: "Nature seeks unity with God through man and in the particular man who does not look towards her but only towards God. The man who opens up that path for her is blessed by nature with the torrent of her bliss, with the realization of a new sphere of consciousness."[31] But significant for our present perspective is the fact that twelve years after Gopi Krishna realized this blissful union, and after which he felt severe estrangement from his culture and world, he finally established "a stable consciousness, open to, yet not dependent on, the outside world."[32] Then suddenly one day, on a bridge thronged with people, he says there flowed "past my eyes like a radiant writing in the air, which vanished as fast as it had come...two lines of a marvelous poem in Kashmiri...like a mighty presence rising from nowhere, embracing me and over-shadowing all objects around me...like an ocean of life moving from within."[33]

Here a *divine possession* occurs which recalls the ancient usage – now largely lost – of inspiration. What strikes us so important in this example is that a more or less stabilized state of mystical union and illumination is visited by the voice of poetry. And this is a case, so he tells us, where there was formally no interest in poetry or its creation. Even at this high level – and let us accept the record as it is given – after an interlude between illumination and its steadier achievement, an interlude lasting twelve years, that steadier state speaks through revelation as poetry. Renewal in expression is no less the aim of the parenthetical interlude, the "twelve years" of distancing and interpretation, which form an organic part of the art of qualitative thinking. Like Gopi Krishna, all of one's life up to that point is preparation for expression, even for a minor "illumination." To stabilize that state at even a higher level, such an interlude may be essential. Even satori is not a finished or constant state.

Distancing, then, is capable of extending meaning, but it is just as capable of diminishing it by too intrusive an entrance of thought. It is at the uncertain boundary between distancing and interpreting that a clash between qualitative thinking and explanatory thinking is prone to arise.

References

1. Nicholas of Cusa. *De visione.* (E.G. Salter, trans.) N.Y.: E.P. Dutton, 1928; pp. 25-27.

2. Schuon, F. *Language of the self.* (M. Pallis and M. Matheson, trans.) Madras, India: Ganesh, 1959; p. 110.

3. Gadamer, H-G. *Truth and method.* N.Y.: Seabury Press, 1975; p. 446.

4. Frankl, V. E. *The will to meaning.* N.Y.: New American Library, 1970; p. 152.

5. Ott, H. *Hermeneutics and personhood.* In Hopper, S. R. and Miller, D. L. (eds.) *Interpretation: The poetry of meaning.* N.Y.: Harcourt, Brace & World, 1967; pp. 23-25.

6. Bachelard, G. *The poetics of reverie.* (D. Russel, trans.) Boston: Beacon Press, 1971; p. 219.

7. Gopi Krishna. *The secret of yoga.* N.Y.: Harper & Row, 1972; p. 181.

8. Bachelard G. *The poetics of space.* (M. Jolas, trans.) Boston: Beacon Press, 1969; pp. 176-178.

9. *Ibid.,* p. 179.

10. *Ibid.,* p. 179.

11. *Ibid.,* p. 178.

12. *Ibid.,* p. 180.

13. *Ibid.,* pp. 181-182.

14. Van Manen, M. An experiment in educational theorizing: The Utrecht School. *Interchange,* 10 (1), 1978-79; p. 57.

15. *Ibid.,* p. 58.

16. Beittel, K. R. *Alternatives for art education research.* Dubuque: Iowa: William C. Brown, 1973; pp. 59-62.

17. *Ibid.,* p. 63.

18. Novosel-Beittel, J. Inquiry into the qualitative world of creating: The S-E model. *Studies in Art Education,* 20 (1), 1978; pp. 32-33.

19. Jones, R. and Daniels, K. (Eds.) *Of solitude and silence.* Boston: Beacon Press, 1981; p. 219.

20. *Ibid.*, pp. 223-225.

21. Foucault, M. *The order of things.* N.Y.: Pantheon Books, 1971; pp. 8-9.

22. Ponge, F. *The voice of things.* (B. Archer, trans.) N.Y.: McGraw-Hill, 1972; pp. 177-178.

23. *Ibid.*, p. 178.

24. *Ibid.*, pp. 180-182.

25. Bachelard, G. *Op. cit.*, reference 6 above, p. 25.

26. Bachelard, G. *Op. cit.*, reference 8 above, p. 236.

27. Bachelard, G. *Op. cit.*, reference 6 above, p. 174.

28. *Ibid.*, p. 189.

29. *Ibid.*, p. 190.

30. Bucke, R. M. *Cosmic consciousness. N.Y.: E. P. Dutton, 1969; p. 234.*

31. *Gopi Krishna. The biological basis of religion and genius. N.Y.:* Harper & Row, 1971; p. 15.

32. *Ibid.*, p. 18.

33. *Ibid.*, p. 19.

9

Interpreting

Any interpretation which is to contribute understanding, must already have understood what is to be interpreted...What is decisive is not to get out of the [hermeneutic] circle but to come into it in the right way ...[for] in the circle is hidden a positive possibility of the most primordial kind of knowing.

Heidegger[1]

Two vocabularies should be organized to study knowledge and poetry. But these two vocabularies do not correspond...The language of the poets must be learned directly...

Bachelard[2]

I can only, in effect, approach a text if I hear it as it speaks to me, if I am seized by what is said through the text. It is in this sense that it is necessary to believe in order to understand, but I cannot grasp what it has told me unless I first decipher the text.

Ricoeur[3]

All understanding is interpretation, and all interpretation takes place in the medium of language which would allow the object to come into words and yet is at the same time the interpreter's own language.

The hermeneutical experience is the corrective by means of which the thinking reason escapes the prison of language, and it is itself constituted linguistically.

Gadamer[4]

Overview

Language, at its best, can cope with the difficult task of interpreting only by escaping from its own prison. Language has a particularly difficult task bringing expressive texts to words, since these were fashioned out of a hidden order, under a metaphysics akin to progressive organicism, and under an attitude through which play transforms into structure. In addition, the coming of the new into expression exceeds the artist's conscious intention, so that spirit may be said to be operating as artist through the artist. And though this path may be one of love, gnosis is implicated thereby, as the creating consciousness begins to be self-conscious of spirit moving through it. So we have said that *image-work is indirectly self-work*. More surprising still, as the artist turns toward the thick of matter he or she finds that releasing the voice of things *simultaneously* opens up the mystery of being anew. In the simple art pottery we then saw how easily it wants to move from tradition into community into selflessness.

Distancing as paraphrasing permits us to grasp anew the power of an expressive text as it speaks directly to the contemplative mind, for "in this way it becomes a support for intellection, thanks to its non-mental, concrete and direct manner of speech."[5] Insofar as the expressive text rests, as it often does, on some major or minor epiphany, we have implicated within it the range of meanings from across the centuries which are embodied in the esoteric tradition, within the perennial philosophy. Out of interpretation we hope not to "explain" the text away or psychologize it or its maker, but to enlarge our understanding, to renew our faith, and to guide our action. The esoteric tradition and the art of qualitative thinking assume that the norms of understanding and action are implicit in epiphany and expression. We need not posit ideal universals, essences, or hierarchies *a priori*: love, dialogue, art, and revelation are their own energy and life, dealing most vitally with what is other and thus with that which enlarges us. Experience is indeed, in this sense, greater than scriptures.

We saw that only by first standing in the heart of something can we profitably distance it, and that only without a loss of center. Then whether we use the knife or the harvest basket, distancing can have the same healthful function.

Interpretation as a Dialectic of Explanation and Understanding

We earlier presented Ricoeur's notion that there is a hermeneutic arc which moves from naive understanding through explanation to a knowledgeable understanding.[6] The art of qualitative thinking, however, throws a different accent on *explanation* than does philosophical hermeneutics. As an *art* it does not assume a philosophic stance, and thus it is more content with the pre-symbolic, revelatory, world-making and world-revealing function that art is willing to assume. Art knows it can get us into trouble faster than our minds.

Still, interpretation always carries with it the connotation of a crisis stage. It seems to tease out from hiding our hidden motivations, our personal causation, even our partial awareness of cloaking things in what they are not. *We interpret to make clear what eluded us in our intuitive understanding even though we there caught the shadow of it.* We wish also to enlarge our self-awareness and to bolster our everyday self-acceptance as vital, existential, expressive beings through which spirit moves into form.

And while the mind can help to extend us through alternatives, *as creatures of Eros we choose existentially.* At the crossroads of alternatives, we incur an unavoidable existential fault: we can follow only one path at a time, and an attracting force, a charm within the event itself constrains us to go this way rather than that.

Even so, the drift toward *an* interpretation is not arbitrary, and it does get a true view of its object, though from its own perspective. When we are on the path our chocies seem destined. We pointed out that in the story of the three trees from Proust, the narrator, after going through six alternatives, *chose to believe* "that they were phantoms of the past, dear companions of my childhood, vanished friends who recalled our common memories."[7] From within Proust's life-world, or at least the life-world projected by the novel, the choice seems fated.

Interpreting, as the third moment of one artistic process of qualitative thinking, does not take well to a search for cause or explanation outside its own movement. To do so would be as useless as leaving a painting three-quarters on the way to seek external counsel for the finish. For *the clues for the end of the painting are implicit in the first three-quarters.* So, too, text and distancing are the ground for interpretation, and these three are the ground for renewal. In this sense, an artistic view of interpretation sees it as part of one total artistic effort, and thus subsumes it under a progressive organicist view. The end, the total, are implicated in a hidden order where all the fragments are meaningful.

In the heart of the art of qualitative thinking interpretations become inevitably stained, even as with the narrator in Proust's novel, by our existential projects and concerns. For when the mind has opened up a lull in our understanding through uncovering alteratives and providing explanations, then our deep structure and our autosymbolic tendencies begin to enter in so that we may dream the myth onward. There is a surfacing of interest which is an unavoidable concomitant of human knowledge and action. Until we express it in interpretation in such a way that we can assimilate it, we cannot move toward renewal. So seen, a dynamic movement of interpretation advances our interest and self-awareness toward a higher stage of consciousness.

Even when our explanations take on a more objective flavor—for example, by the physical plotting of structural elements that distancing has laid bare—what we choose to believe about these takes on an existential flavor. The quality is not in us nor in the text but *between*. The text addresses us even as it itself was addressed in its formative process. *It questions us so that we may learn something of the questions it answers.* Explanation is inevitable in the development of qualitative thinking, but it is a descent preparatory to a final ascent. It teases out, under the guise of mind—but of a mind straining toward transcendelia—what is at stake for us, so that our total understanding of the meaning of the text can move forward, absorbing our crisis of self-interest and self-understanding into one total rounded-out artistic episode.

Understanding makes the first move in interpreting. In its initial naivete it is nevertheless on the way to the knowledgeable understanding to come. Explanation helps clear away what is hidden from what is misunderstood, so that true revelation of the expressive text can carry within its light the shadow of what is concealed inside its deep structure. Explanation then serves less a logical than a depth hermeneutic one. It is less a matter of "because of" than of "why?" In the artistic, we are even well advised to accept the more childlike "and then?" as a story unfolding before us, guided by interests intrinsic to the story itself. An interpretation then becomes like a more distanced expression, an imaginative "fiction" which bears within itself self-healing and self-revealing properties congruent with its qualitative source in the expressive text, returning eventually to that quality that which originated through our interaction with it and under it. For we find again and again that not concepts but *rapture* is called for. With Bachelard we retain a child's sense of wonder, of delight, and of excitement. We have no need to criticize. Exaggeration is met with exaggeration. Thereby we can by-pass reductionism and renew faith in the human condition as fundamental happiness. This allows clarity in observation.

Expressive Texts Do Not Distort but Reveal

Even Bachelard felt that he was being automatically psychoanalyzed as he engaged in poetic reverie. This suggests a negative or demystifying function to interpretation sometimes stated as "all texts are distorted," implying the need for a depth hermeneutic. We prefer to emphasize the affirmative side of this issue: *expressive texts do not so much distort as reveal.* And without that unconcealment automatic to expression we could not claim art's central role in the evolution of consciousness. Expression, which is about otherness, leads to an enlarged self. *That which requires selflessness in its functioning renders consciousness capable of self-conscousness in the service of its own transcendence.*

Expressive texts can indeed reveal self-distortion. They can reveal something we are perhaps partially conscious of hiding from ourselves. But there is no need to psychologize ourselves or to reduce ourselves to mechanical explanations based on psychic defenses.

> Why does an individual hide communication from himself? He hides those aspects of communicative exchange *which appear to threaten the death of the ego or verbal self-concept.* He substitutively sacrifices those aspects, "kills" them, tosses them out, alienates them, in order to preserve his egoic immortality project. That is, the shadow is a substitute sacrifice of the mental-egoic form of the Atman project [the desire to move toward the ever-present and ultimate Wholeness].[8]

This quotation from Wilber was taken from a context where what he calls the mental-egoic stage was under discussion. Similar forms of distortion occur at all the postulated levels of consciousness arranged on a hierarchy. This hierarchy is roughly equivalent to the great chain of being earlier discussed, and it finds its support generally in the literature of the esoteric tradition.

The positive side of such unconcealment from expressive texts is that by acknowledging them as distortions of our expressive intent, we may come to assimilate them so that we can symbolically "die" at one stage of consciousness toward transformation to a higher stage. The task of a depth hermeneutic is then life-affirmative, not reductive.

There is something troubling, however, about making the connection between distorted communication within the self and expresion too exact. To the degree that art cannot be selfless, the self intrudes to distort; and in so doing, it shuts itself off from an enlargement of consciousness. It shuts itself off from becoming self-conscious through expression, which can lead to transformation of consciousness to higher levels. "Spiritual nourishment, like material, becomes part of the man who imparts to the product of the exchange the qualities he receives from it." *The expression of art is a matching of spirit with spirit that occurs at the cross-roads of spirit and matter.* It is that uniquely special dialogue between artist and medium. The ego self does not control this encounter, but rather stands in the service of the higher self.

It seems best not to grade into vertical hierrarchies what is more likely one horizontal extension of spirit as artist, while allowing for the differential potential for self-revelation that varying texts can possess. As the left hand of scriptural revelation:

> ...art will be more inward and more profound than verbal expositions, and this explains the central function which a sacred image, such as that of the Buddha, can assume. There is a highly significant connection between the loss of a sacred art and the loss of anagogy, as is shown by the Renaissance: naturalism could not kill symbolism—sacred art—without humanism killing anagogy and, with it, gnosis. This is so because these two elements, anagogical science and symbolical art are essentially related to pure intellectuality.[10]

In a time when even twofold vision is rare, let alone threefold and fourfold vision plus revelation, expressive texts have foremost as their positive function the affirmation of soul and spirit through the integrative working of matter, body and mind, and secondarily their self-revelatory, therapeutic and educational functions. The former implicates the latter to remove the restrictive force upon its greatest potential for wholeness. The expressive text releases its self-transcending properties through its wholeness and its self-revealing properties. *The work in transcending its maker liberates its maker.*

Art will team up with scriptural revelation and anagogy only as these occur at their source, at their highest level. It withdraws instinctively from mere morality and over-institutionalized exoteric religion, because the spirit has fled.

This rhythm of closeness and withdrawal we find throughout recorded history. The horizontal extension of art, paralleling nature herself, can accommodate the highest vertical extension of consciousness as spirit, but so can it accommodate all levels of consciousness wherever spirit is manifest, *because Spirit itself is artist.* The lower reaches point upward, but even the highest falls short, so art's unconcealment aids the pilgrimage of even the most advanced consciousness.

We are saying that so-called "distortions" — a term applied by an external eye — are really part of the revealing and affirmative nature of expression. A further exploration of this function will be made later under the discussion of expressive therapy. Suffice it here to say that the interpretive moment brings into the open self-limiting influences encumbered in expression. The writers of the book *Yoga and Psychotherapy* present a clear idea of how this happens:

> The artist is one who allows the better part of himself to have its say. He gives his underlying consciousness a means of expressing itself that is relatively uncontaminated by his ego-oriented thoughts and concerns. He stands aside, in other words, and lets the inner voice "speak." Therefore, the artistic achievement is not merely to create art but to transform one's personality. For it is by the symbol that has been outwardly created that one is able to reintegrate and reach a new level of awareness. Hence, the act of creation and the act of being created are part and parcel of the same phenomenon. By contrast, when art becomes ego-entangled, creativity stagnates. It is then that an artist comes to "imitate himself"; his symbols no longer evolve and his personal growth ceases.[12]

It is the ego-entanglements that limit expression and cause self-imitation, and these entanglements are subtle and often nearly or completely unconscious because of fear and repression. Externalizing them gives opportunity to the artist to move away from self-imitation and to break through to new insights.

As with distancing, *one of the functions of interpreting is to show the greater ground from which expression sprang and which our intruding ego-self unconsciously limited.* This, we repeat, is an affirmative function. For if all expression partially fails, it is expanding to seek awareness of what that expression would express without its incompleteness. "Incompleteness" is here not as an aesthetic but a spiritual term.

This search turns up for our amazement the limits of our creating self so that our own self-formative process may be released from these limits.

In expressive therapy and in a vital art education, the presence of a teacher (of one who nurtures what is already there and in progress) leads toward a depth interpretation of the artist's self-formative process. Thus the unconcealment within an expressive text has a clear function: to keep expression open and vital, to enlarge our admiration and appreciation of expressions of others and of ourselves, to lead toward renewed expression, and to render ourselves and others aware of limitations and fears within the self which impede the evolution of consciousness. So-called "distortions" are then no longer regressive or reductive but urge us to move in a transcendent direction.

Interpretation as a Thinking Dialogue

Expressive texts, thus, are no more distorted than privileged, but in either way they require a depth interpretation which challenges the interpreter just as much as the text. In confronting expressive texts, we sink into a dialogue with a dialogue, with an effort to understand our understanding. But this is no infinite regress. We come to a rock bottom which is life, experience, the disclosure of being. So seen, *the art of qualitative thinking is basic inquiry into the disclosure of being.* In Bergson's terms, interpretation is a minding of intuition, a "going-around" an "entering-in."[12]

We are back again to circum-locution, first introduced in the discussion of distancing. But here we pick it up more from the perspective of Heidegger's *thinking dialogue* and *meditative thinking*. Bachelard, in his distrust of concept and thinking where images are involved, does, however, mention "reveries which think." These are those which "welcome images and ideas, contemplations and experiences at the same time."[13] To him, such reveries are "impure."

Heidegger, however, to our view steps within that circle where images and ideas *co-exist*. Some might call his language paradoxical—as mind struggling to cope with transcendelia, the data of spirit—but we feel it is also direct intuition of spirit, approaching originary and poetic speech itself. To call it criticism or even interpretation seems insufficient. It is doubtlessly closer to anagogy, taking the poetic fragments from which he begins as high examples of the art, as revelation.

An excellent example of this mode is to be found in Heidegger's fifty page meditation on *What Are Poets For?* which begins from Holderlin's line "...and what are poets for in a destitute time?"[14] Heidegger sets his task in choosing poetic fragments to illustrate and answer this question thus:

> It is a necessary part of the poet's nature that, before he can truly be a poet in such an age, the time's destitution must have made the whole being and vocation of the poet a poetic question for him. Hence "poets in a destitute time" must especially gather in poetry the nature of poetry. Where that happens we may assume poets to exist who are on the way to the destiny of the world's age. We others must learn to listen to what *these* poets say — assuming that, in regard to the time that conceals Being because it shelters it, we do not deceive ourselves through reckoning time merely in terms of that which is by dissecting that which is.[15]

Heidegger finds in Holderlin and Rilke such poets. He is not afraid to "misuse" poetry "as a rich source for a philosophy," for there is "the sole necessity, by thinking our way soberly into what his poetry says, to come to learn what was unspoken. This is the course of the history of Being. If we reach and enter that course, it will lead thinking into a dialogue with poetry, a dialogue that is of the history of Being."[16]

Thus Heidegger sets his profound hermeneutic task and route. He turns to a late improvised poem by Rilke as his focus, conscious of the need to move slowly in his effort:

> Who today would presume to claim that he is at home with the nature of poetry as well as with the nature of thinking and, in addition, strong enough to bring the nature of the two into the most extreme discord and so to establish their concord?[17]

Parenthetically, Heidegger here touches on the delicate task of an art of qualitative thinking and also indicates the paradoxical nature of interpretation within it. Here possibly transcending Bachelard, we must bring art and thinking "into their most extreme discord and so...establish their concord." The improvised verses of Rilke which follow then become Heidegger's expressive text:

1 As Nature gives the other creatures over
2 to the venture of their dim delight
3 and in soil and branchwork grants none special cover.

4 so too our being's pristine ground settles our plight;
5 we are no longer dearer to it; it ventures us.
6 Except that we, more eager than plant or beast,
7 go *with* this venture, will it, adventurous
8 more sometimes than Life itself, more daring
9 by a breath (and not in the least
10 from selfishness)...There, outside all caring,
11 This creates for us a safety—just there,
12 where the pure forces' gravity rules; in the end,
13 it is our unshieldedness on which we depend,
14 and that, when we saw it threaten, we turned it
15 so into the Open that, in widest orbit somewhere,
16 where the Law touches us, we may affirm it. [18]

This becomes the basis for Heidegger's "exercise in poetic self-reflection." We certainly can in no way present to the reader this poetic self-reflection, except to say that it remains for us a model of where interpretation can go, in its breadth and depth, within an art of qualitative thinking. Note that it is *poetic* self-reflection, implying that we recover ourselves, our meaning, our action in this movement between poetry and thinking. In the course of the forty-three pages to follow the giving of the poem, Heidegger presents twenty-two poetic fragments, parts of letters, and reflections from Rilke which help further extend the meaning of the improvised verses. For example:

> But when, in the creation of a safety, man is touched by the Law of the world's whole inner space, he is himself touched in his nature, in that, as the being who wills himself, he is already the sayer. But since the creation of a safety comes from the more venturesome, these more venturesome ones must dare the venture with language. The more venturesome dare the saying. But if the precinct of this daring, language, belongs to Being in that unique manner above which and beyond which there can be nothing else of its kind, in what direction is that to be said which the sayers must say? Their saying concerns the inner recalling conversion of consciousness which turns our unshieldedness into the invisible of the world's inner space. Their saying, because it concerns the conversion, speaks not only from both realms but from the oneness of the two, insofar as that oneness has already come to be as the saving unification. Therefore, where the whole of all beings is thought of as the Open of the pure draft, the inner recalling conversion must be a saying which says what it has to say to a being who is already secure in the whole of all beings, because he has already accomplished the transmutation of what is visible in representation into that which is an invisible of the heart. This being is drawn into the pure draft of one side and the

other of the globe of Being. This being, for whom
borderlines and differences between the drawings hardly exist any longer, is the being who governs the
unheard-of center of the widest orbit and causes it to
appear. This being, in Rilke's *Duino Elegies*, is the
Angel. This name is once again a basic word in Rilke's
poetry. Like "the Open," "the draft," "the parting,"
"Nature," it is a basic word because what is said in it
thinks the whole of beings by way of Being. In his letter of November 13, 1925, Rilke writes:

> The Angel of the *Elegies* is that creature in whom
> the transmutation of the visible into the invisible,
> which we achieve, seems already accomplished.
> The Angel of the *Elegies* is that being who
> assures the recognition of a higher order of reality
> in the invisible.[19]

Finally, Heidegger returns to Rilke's poetry *as* poetry as
the place to find the answer to his initial question. But he
returns us to the silence so that the poem can sound out of its
stillness and so that we can hear it as though for the first
time. Heidegger says:

> Rilke arrives at the poet's question: when is there song
> that sings essentially? This question does not stand at
> the beginning of the poet's way, but at the point where
> Rilke's saying strains to the poetic vocation of the kind
> of poet who answers to the coming world era. This era
> is neither a decay nor a downfall. As destiny, it lies in
> Being and lays claim to man.
>
> If Rilke is a "poet in a distitute time" then only his
> poetry answers the question to what end he is a poet,
> whither his song is bound, where the poet belongs in
> the destiny of the world's night. That destiny decides
> what remains fateful within this poetry.[20]

Heidegger sets for us the model of a thinking dialogue with
an expressive text, for his interpretations probe "the
mysterious process of disclosure whereby being comes into
manifest existence."[21] The expressive texts he turns to are
chosen with the utmost care to answer the most profound of
questions. With him we go behind the text to what was not
said but needs saying, and to the question to which the text
itself is an answer. This disclosure indeed enlarges our consciousness toward a grasp of Being's trace in the manifest.
Interpretation here lays out our plight and our glory, implicating our very destiny.

Interpreting Phenomenological Expressive-Descriptive Texts.

Since they lie closer to thought to start with, expressive-descriptive texts offer up their structural elements to interpretation more easily than do expressive-artistic texts. Even so they too will not tolerate our wrenching parts away from the whole they belong to. In phenomenological expressive-descriptive texts the "investigator remains true to the facts as they are happening" for "an accurate description of an incident necessarily involves a judgment concerning the incident, according to a theory of the incident."[22] The quality of events, of situations, reflects our mood, our attunement, our relationships with things, others, and time. In the example from van den Berg the bottle of Medoc wine changes when he knows that his friend will not come. The silence, the snow, even the temperature of the room change. *Theory and incident become one.* Seer, seeing, and seen become one. Any interpretation of these must not psychologize or objectify them at the expense of their essential qualitative oneness. A "closer inspection" does not inspect the same situation if the power which bound it together is broken. If we put ourselves in the place of the person describing, we see the events and incidents differently. Not only the artist sees differently, so does the phenomenologist in taking the qualitative aspect of things seriously.

Van den Berg first presents then interprets an incident from a novel:

> When the mother of the Jewish girl, the central character of "Het Huisje aan de sloot" (the Cabin at the Ditch), by Carry van Bruggen, on the morning of the sabbath, takes from the table the daily red and black cloth and puts the gleaming white one in its place, then, writes Carry van Bruggen (no doubt from her own experience), there is always one undetermined moment in which "it" happens, a moment one always misses. As long as the black and red cloth remains on the table, there is nothing; mother comes, and there is nothing extraordinary about her, either. She takes away the black and red cloth; the bare table is old, full of stains and scratches. Now the white cloth flutters in mother's hand, by the lamp, almost touching it. Now it is lowered, it is on the table and—another miss. "It" has come and no one has seen "it" arrive. Mother suddenly has another face; and every chair and the cabinet and the stove—they all look different. No one has been able

> to see the actual change, no one has been able to catch
> that moment. But next time, the little girl decides
> again and again, she won't be looking at the cloth; but
> she'll watch her mother and the cabinet, the chairs and
> the stove, for one day she wants to catch this wonder-
> ful moment in which all things change their ap-
> pearance.[23]

Van den Berg then goes on to interpret this incident "according to a theory of the incident," that is, remaining true to the
quality of the experience itself.

> In which all things change their appearance? What
> does the author mean to say? That the objects change
> their appearance? Their shape? She speaks of the
> *change in themselves* of the objects. Yet this kind of
> change has never been observed. The observation of
> the change is a difficult-to-establish fact. The change in
> itself is a fact. Are things capable of change, then? Of
> this, the author is entirely convinced, as we are when
> the same sort of incident happens to us. Each one of us
> has a memory similar to the one of the girl in the story.
> An experience. Or is it more correct to say that every
> day each of us lives in the reality of this kind of ex-
> perience? Objects are changing their appearance daily,
> continuously and never without reason.
> ...Things change to such an extent that they disap-
> pear and return. The house, the sky, the tree, the chair,
> the cabinet, the stove, everything changes. But
> nothing ever changes without sense or reason. Objects
> change on special occasions. When someone arrives or
> leaves. When the day begins, or when the evening falls.
> On Sunday, things look different from their apperance
> on workdays.[24]

This is why a "new self" shrivels in the light of "old eyes." This
is why, as Scheler shows, the adolescent, like the one in love,
does not see nature differently but *seens a different nature.*[25]
This is why the lover does not see the beloved as others do,
for "love knowledge" is truer — it sees the beloved as a whole of
which potential and destiny are a part. Not to see something
or someone as whole is decidedly to see a different thing or
person. *If a cold eye were to say, "A white tablecloth now
replaces the black and red one, that is all," then that eye is not
in that home — is, in fact, a homeless eye.* Then the incident is
not being observed according to a theory of the incident. Objects are not being seen in a way that brings them into unity
with seer and seeing. They are being reductively thingafied
into meaningless pieces of an alien world and our language is
that of strangers for we have accepted "a philosophy of

epistemological loneliness."[26] To use even "thingafied" is an act of discrimination, for it implies that we do *not* know things, or we would know that they are one with us, and we one with them.

In the example from the Utrecht School of phenomenological pedagogy, "fear of the dark," which was then shown in its reductive paraphrase, further steps would continue what adherents to this School call "situation analysis." This proceeds as follows: (1) life-experience material is gathered, as in the example given; (2) this material is then examined for its structural elements or main themes; and (3) interpretations and recommendations for practical action are the made.[27] Interpretation proceeds much as in the examples from van den Berg, who is a psychiatrist belonging to this School. The goal is to understand a situation or incident through exhaustive description and imaginative variation:

> Exercises...are further experimented upon by varying the examples or by thinking through analogous experiences. This is an attempt to look at the same phenomenon using different perspectives which may be only slightly different from one another. Next, the field of intersubjectivity is expanded by complementing personal life-world material obtained from such sources as existentialist or phenomenological literature, poetry, novels, diaries, interviews, folk wisdom, observations, and art.[28]

The Artist's Way of Interpreting

The methods of Bachelard and Ponge are close to art and phenomenology simultaneously. Bachelard exploits the variational nature of the image as his poetic reveries expand to interpret themes of vast scope: intimate immensity, universal childhood, the tree, and roundness itself as equated with being. His works on concrete metaphysics and the material imagination are extended interpretations of the way we have our being with things and they with us:

> It is an honor to be the wind
> It is a happiness to be the stone.[29]

With Bachelard's phenomenology of the imagination, interpretation becomes intra-textual. It fills in the gap between images and poetic fragments, like mortar between bricks.

An artist cannot explain or interpret his or her works any more than a mother her child. Instead, it seems that the artist turns toward discussion of artistic methods in the act of interpreting. But what is this if not describing and interpreting the creative incident according to a theory of the incident itself? Says Ponge: "Could it be that the fact that a poem cannot be explained by its author is not to the shame of the poem and its author, but rather to his honor?"[30] So in the Drawing Lab we do not have drawings explained to us. Rather the artist talks about what led to what, how and why it was done, what unexpected things happened, and what the mood and guiding feelings were.

Ponge wrote an eight and one-half page poem on *The Pebble*. He also talks about a pebble, "any old pebble," within the long series of entries under *My Creative Method*:

> Monday, January 5, 1948(2)
>
> Well, let me say it finally, for the reader will soon realize than I begin by the end, so let me say it to begin with: any old pebble, for example *this one* that I picked up the other day on the bed of the Chiffa river, seems to me capable of giving rise to fresh remarks of the *highest interest*. And when I say *this one* and higher interest, what I mean is this: this pebble, since I consider it a unique object, arouses in me a particular feeling, or perhaps it is rather a complex of particular feelings. First I have to become aware of it. At this point, the reader shrugs his shoulders and disclaims any interest in such exercises. For, he says, there is nothing of man in that. And what else could there be? Only it is man until now unknown to man. A quality, a series of qualities, a composite of qualities, unwritten, unformulated. That is why it is of highest interest. We are talking about man of the future. Do you know anything more interesting? I am completely taken with it. Why am I so taken with it? Because I think I can carry it off. On what condition? On condition of being single-minded, and obeying *it*. Of not being satisfied with too little (or too much). Of saying nothing that is not exclusively suited to it. It is not so much a question of saying everything; that would be impossible. Only what is suitable to it alone, only what is valid. And to the limit: all that has to be said is a simple valid thing. That is quite enough.
>
> So here I am with my pebble, which intrigues me, arouses in me untapped resources. With my pebble which I respect. My pebble which I want to replace by an adequate logical (verbal) formula.
>
> Fortunately, 1) it persists; 2) my feeling at the sight of it persists; 3) the dictionary is not far, I have the feeling the right words are there. If not, then I will have to create them. But words that can communicate, be conductors of thought (as one says conductor of heat or

> electricity). After all, I have the syllables, the onomatopeias, the letters. I'll get along just fine!
> And I really think words will do...
>
> This pebble won the victory (the victory of existence—individual, concrete; the victory of coming into my sight and coming to life with the word) because it is more interesting than the sky. Not quite black, dark gray rather, the size of half a rabbit liver (a rabbit has nothing to do with this), nice in the hand. The right hand, to be precise, with a hollow in which the outside (when someone else looks at me) of my median finger's last joint fits comfortably...[31]

The aesthetician and the philosopher turn all too quickly to the form, the context, and especially to interpretation of the *meaning* of the work of art, unless they are guided by a meditative thinking dialogue, almost a poetic philosophical reverie of its own, as did Heidegger in the earlier example. *The artist, in contrast, directs his or her ongoing consciousness not toward the meaning but toward the doing, for doing and meaning are one to the artist.* in the presence of works the artist is content to be still and receptive, "hearing" the work—doing the receiving or doing the creating—often in silence. Doing encircles meaning through the expansiveness of action, through the patience before a hidden order, through an active dialogue that transforms into a structure, just as doing opens up the creating consciousness in the thick of action. Brush in hand the wedding of color, form, and meaning occurs and the fragments progressively become a whole. Brush in hand expression extends itself anew. What was not understood in this painting will have to be understood in making a new one. From this point of view, distancing and interpreting are interludes, trial dreaming grounds, to be bracketed between expressing and the renewal of expressing. To an artist, willing though he or she may be to share methods, interpreting is only useful *if* it permits one "to dream the myth onward." *The winged centaur seeks release and evolution through the interpretive pause. It is not an end or art in itself. There are other paintings and pots to do. It is in that form of active meditation that consciousness finds the means toward its own evolution.* Reflection on method thus serves well the end of rendering the artistic consciousness self-conscious so that it can move on. So interpreting for the artist often centers playfully on creative method, as in the example from Ponge.

Songs of Innocence

The artist here leads the way for us again. He turns "into the Open" to arrive at meaning; he sees the present of interpreting as "an invitation from out of the future to gain mastery over bygone times"; and he can see it thus because his past, as found in expression, counts for more than all of the rest of his life; and because the past, as expression, is a well-ordered one, he has an accesible future.[32] *So for the artist, meanings come as reflections on past expressions which lead to intuitions of future ones.* What greater interpretations toward action and application could there be? The artist takes the side of the past in letting the expression come to tell its own story according to the theory within it—often appearing as a reflection on creative method—and also takes account of medium toward new expression. There you have much of interpreting for creating consciousness.

Much of art is not only prereflective, pretheoretical, and presuppositionless, as is phenomenology ideally, but also presymbolic. Its meanings still have the newness of the Silence, of things "whose seal has not been broken." It is in this sense that we headed this section *Song of Innocence*, for this attitude extends to a general distaste for interpretation, except in an open and playful way, or as an emphasis upon it as a bracketed interlude between two expressions, that interlude itself being seen foremost expressively. What should we expect from a singer of songs but songs and more songs or preparations for singing?

Simple and naive expressions can take on mythic proportions in our consciousness. In the Christmas song *Do You Hear What I Hear*,[33] the night wind asks a little lamb if it *sees* a bright star dancing. The little lamb then asks a shepherd boy if he *hears* a song that sounds like the sea. Then the shepherd boy asks the great King if he *knows* a special child was born. Then the King *says* to the people all around: "a newborn child has come to bring us peace and light."

This song parallels an insightful interpretive path: a special *seeing* comes to one of nature's creatures; when this is shared with the shepherd boy a unique *hearing* occurs; this leads to special *knowing* as the shepherd boy alerts the King; and the King's *saying* to his subjects everywhere goes out as a decree for action.

In the delightful book, *The Tao of Pooh*, [34] Pooh, the bear of little brain, is found to have characteristics remarkably akin to the ancient Chinese sages. Among all the creatures, Pooh just *is*. He solves problems by not trying too hard, finding solutions already at hand. He accepts others as they are, letting their potential unfold through their very idiosyncratic limitations. 'Roos bounce, tiggers pounce, owls pontificate, rabbits are preoccupied and in a hurry, while Pooh Bear looks at the sky, stretches out and sings "Cottleston, Cottleston, Cottleston pie."

We find in such *song of innocence* the same paradox that Ricoeur found in listening to the Parables of Jesus: the *extraordinary is like the ordinary*. They are like the pebble in Ponge's hand. In the Parables we are shocked into reversal and decision. The chain of three steps set off by the Parables is not unlike the directed attention, stopping, and passive awareness which lead to fullness in the eternal present: "letting the Event blossom, looking in another direction [reversal], and doing with all one's strength in accordance with the new vision [decision]." [35]

In the Parables, listening is focused on metaphors, on images, what the Kingdom of Heaven is *like*. "The power of this language is that it abides to the end *within* the tension created by the images." These images "taken all together... say more than any rational theology." [36] Further, says Ricoeur—and here they share much with Bachelard's approach to the material imagination—the Parables do not teach in any ordinary way, but engage in a language of exaggeration which disorients us prior to reorienting us. Says Ricoeur:

> To listen to the Parables of Jesus, it seems to me, is to let one's imagination be opened to the new possibilities disclosed by the extravagance of these short dramas. If we look at the Parables as at a word addressed first to the imagination rather than to our will, we shall not be tempted to reduce them to mere didactic devices, to moralizing allegories. We will let their poetic power display itself within us. [37]

And then, because, like Heidegger, he has preserved the "saying power" of the text, Ricoeur ends his interpretation thus:

> Listen, therefore, to the Parables of Jesus (Matthew 13:31-32 and 45-46):
> And another parable he put before them, saying, "The

Kingdom of heaven is like a grain of mustard seed which a man took and sowed in his field; it is the smallest of all seeds, but when it has grown it is the greatest of shrubs and becomes a tree, so that the birds of the air come and make nests in its branches.

"Again, the Kingdom of heaven is like a merchant in search of fine pearls, who, on finding one pearl of great value, went and sold all that he had and bought it."[38]

Reversal and decision follow listening, just as in the carol hearing was followed by seeing, knowing, saying and doing. The impact of disorientation on reorientation is commonplace in literature of the esoteric tradition. Artful simplicity, dwelling with the images themselves, prepares the way for change and renewed action. The experience of epiphany says "you must change your life" just as the archaic torso of Apollo talked to Rilke. Reversal comes when the extraordinary is like the ordinary:

For years, in all seasons, weather and light permitting, I have loosed my dog and taken a daily walk in the woods adjoining my home and studio. These woods are not part of my real estate, but certainly they are mine in proportion to the use to which they are put. It is a walk, ordinarily, of only fifteen or twenty minutes. Without reasoning about it, until now, I have always veered to the right where the path forks and begun through the lighter, hardwood forest of oaks, hickories, maples, and wild cherry trees and circled back through the darker, hemlock woods via what would be the left fork in setting out.

Today, for no premeditated reason conscious to me, I took the left fork first. The territory was the same, but I scarcely recognized the familiar landmarks. My reasons for walking daily over the same route are many, and it is a habit from youth, when I wandered along the Susquehanna River banks. For adequate perception, one must be alone although I enjoyed sharing the walk then and still do. Yet, perception of nature's changes can hardly be the motive, for I am often lost in thought or have a problem tucked away in my mind. It is as though the solitude, the familiar path with its change in constancy, sets ideas freely circulating. The unexpectedness of sights like Mayflowers pushing up, three-score jack-in-the pulpit plants, several deer or grouse, the miraculous unfolding of the hickory bud, or a new kind of mushroom is not lost because of this state of consciousness. Rather it seems symbolic of the discovery my mind is preparing for. And moving from the lighter woods, into an open stretch of park-like grounds, then to the darker, hemlock woods where I must duck and twist among rocks and branches, symbolically seems like the

> security and protectedness I associate with a return to childhood. The cycle done, I return refreshed.
>
> To reverse the path today seemed strangely appropriate and symbolic. The territory, I repeat is the same, but my experience and the meaning of what I meet along the path are changed. True, these change even if I follow the same path habitually. They lead me on and I ordinarily have no desire for reversing directions. But now that I have, the issue will be upon me each day at the fork. I will doubtlessly take the left path for a while, to probe its strangeness further. But then I will likely fluctuate.[39]

Interpreting songs of innocence should have an influence like taking the left fork for the first time, for these songs mean to *disorient toward reorientation*, toward laying bare the extraordinary at our very feet without removing us from the territory.

Interpreting Case Histories of Artistic Creation

If we turn once more to the two artists working in the Drawing Lab we can push their histories one step further into interpretation. It should be reiterated here that phenomenological and historical expressive-descriptive modes, despite the inevitable contribution of the describer, distancer, and interpreter, nevertheless attempt to *remain true to the events as they happen in their context*. These are special histories, because the *historians* were present while the events described occurred.

In Larry's case we collected together and then paraphrased twenty-six items selected out of his own recorded comments in which he gave evidence of conceptualizing about making art. If we place these items along time line covering two and one-half years of work in the Drawing Lab, we can see how Larry's self-consciousness of how to make art changed from his early to middle to late periods. Here are some of the questions we could ask of these twenty-six items, and possible answers to them:

> 1. How conscious is Larry of his own drawing series or drawing history, and how does this consciousness enter into his conceptualizations about making art? A search of the twenty-six items turned up six clearly touching on this question, all of them, as we might expect, in his middle and late periods in the Lab, and the more "subtle" ones in the late period.

> 2. How conscious is Larry of an emerging artistic self-identity? Here thirteen items seem supportive, six of these merging with the first question above. Two of these fall in the early period, four in the middle, seven in the late, again showing a cumulative effect upon his consciousness.
>
> 3. How aware is Larry of in-process thinking? Here we find eight items, all but one in the middle and late periods. If we merged the items from questions 1 and 3 – that is, drawing series effect and in-process thinking – these would merge almost perfectly with the items under question 2, which deal with Larry's emerging artistic self-identity. This play with items and questions suggests that Larry's artistic self-identity is composed of the influence from the series effect – the build-up of meaning over a long working period – and in-process thinking, or the ability to be absorbed into the play and hiddenness of making art.[40]

We are not making a strong case for this play with selected and numbered items ranged along a time line, for it is not a statistical game at all. Rather it is a systematic way to attend to a greater number of concepts than the mind can easily manipulate simultaneously. In any event, it appears that Larry's *emerging artistic self-identity* is related to *a cumulative effect of the history of his own drawings* (the "series effect," through which he is able to reflect upon, interconnect, and evaluate what he has done so that he can conceptualize that series in terms of qualities of drawings, strategies of drawings, his feeling of freedom or its lack, and the like) and of his consciousness of "in-process thinking." More as a valid conclusion than a reduction, we can say that for Larry his artistic self-identity is comprised of consciousness of an evolving history of making art and a movement toward the confidence to engage in and actively welcome in-process, in-the-medium thinking.[41]

We could interpret other outcomes by examining these twenty-six self-conceptualizations about making art as these reflect upon a time line. We would find toward the middle and late periods Larry's awareness of art-life connections; his own nascent theory of art; idiosyncratic meaning; and inner drawing or drawing in the imagination without touching the paper. Certainly if Larry can cognize his own drawing history, can begin developing an open theory of art, can be aware of mood and feeling and of idiosyncratic meaning, can see art and life as transactionally interdependent, and can tend toward in-process working habits, then he is construct-ing a viable artistic self-identity.[42]

In becoming self-conscious of his artistic consciousness, Larry participates actively in his own evolution in and through art. He positively reinforces and expands his capaci-ty to feel, to see, and to act; and be becomes conscious of *a separate reality which art has opened up for him.* He had to transcend his self-limiting ideas. He moved beyond represen-tation toward symbolized feeling, toward the purely visual, and to the dynamic aspects within the medium and the form-ing process. He utilized himself as an instrument responsive within an encounter. *And he knew that he was an artist and when he was an artist.*

We could not interpret in this way had we not entered into a special relationship with this artist, and had we not record-ed this history and asked of it one big question and a number of sub-questions. The big question reveals a primary intuition guiding not only the above inquiry but also this book as a whole: *art making is a subtle esoteric discipline toward the evolution of consciousness. Its extensions into education and therapy are organic applications growing out of this insight.*

An interesting aspect to interpretations of such case histories lies in the fact that distancing and reduction true to the phenomena seem to clarify essential immanent meanings to the point where the history seems to interpret itself. In the example of the mature professional artist, we arrived at inter-pretive insights through selected dialogue transcripts and their further reduction into antecedent, constituent, and con-sequent complexes, according to the categories of the S-E Model (structural-existential model). Let us pick up this case again, this time focusing on:

Zones of Conflict Educed from Dialogue

1. The Lab atmosphere interacted with his initial inten-tions and helped change them.
2. The dialogues plunged the artist deeply in touch with his true feelings about painting and its powerful relationship to his life.
3. He was a highly trained professional artist who hadn't painted for several years. He wanted to share his re-beginning with us even though he heavily felt the "performance factor" and was concerned about the "publicness" of the Lab context.
4. He had originally planned to do only exercises but saw this intention break down almost as soon as he

picked up his sable brush. He was confused and con-
flicted by this.

5. Soft Japanese music in the Lab took him on a "nice
little trip" and from that point on, creative emotionali-
ty, mood, and intuition completely won out over his
disciplined intention to do only exercises.

6. He tried to experience the "emptiness of the music"
as it suggested and brought back many associations
which demanded paintings rather than exercises.

7. The startling differences in approach of the two style
schools that were "pushed on" him in his extensive
training in art reappeared and presented a major problem for him.

8. While he deeply wanted genuine dialogue and interaction about his work with artists and his paintings,
he saw "language about art" as "conceptualization that
is deliberately cloaking."

9. This conflict with language allowed conceptualizations about paintings or any phenomena of reality to
have "no more or no less insight" than "all the other
methods we have of insight."

10. For him painting was the "ultimate reality," yet the
"almost reality" of "talking about painting" became increasingly desirable.

11. He spoke strongly of the existential choice that
painting is for him and how working in the studio is a
lonely venture that can be frightening at times.[43]

Here we arrive at a kind of summary which is interpretive in
its very form, as it explores an artist's significant statements in
light of the major forms of conflict surrounding them. Since
clash does indeed often set the stage for the creative act, finding
zones of conflict is fundamental to its understanding. These
clashing constituents then guide the interpreter in staying close
to the nature and the context of the creative act, while also
facilitating understanding of the *how* and *why* of the art-
making event.[44] *Clash areas* can guide those in a helping-
sharing relationship with the artist, as researchers, art teachers,
and art therapists—those concerned with a depth hermeneutic
of the artist's self-formative process according to a common
tradition and according to the evolution of consciousness.

Just as a historical approach can lead to interpretive insights, so *the S-E Model can become a scanning device that
allows one to look at the qualitative world of creating with an
understanding akin to that which presents itself for
understanding—that is, according to the nature or
characteristics of what is to be understood,* or according to
the *structure* revealed through the *existential* record. The S-E
Model can:

1. Show the relationship of structure to change and the components of movement within a given process.
2. Present in juxtaposition zones of time (past, present, and future) and their interacting potential for the artist's forward creative movement.
3. Permit one to retrace the evolution of the art work and explore after-the-fact the "what," "how," "when," "where," and at times "why" of the arting event, revealing what pushes and pulls the artist and what resolutions and consequences emerge.
4. Show clashes which may set the stage for the work to follow.
5. Disclose self-concepts, "significant others" as well as relationships to researchers and the art-making context as they effect and influence the creative act itself.
6. Clarify the artist's existential relationship to his very own acts of creation, in other words the reflective and reflexive components within creating itself.
7. Effectively reduce "the event surrogate" so that understanding is enriched by interpretations arising effortlessly from the unique structures of content, clash, and synthesis laid bare within the qualitative world of the act of creation.[45]

Both of the examples above, of Larry and of the skilled professional artist, remain *true to the qualitative wholeness of the expressive-descriptive texts they interpret.* They take on themselves the active protection of that wholeness in all that is said. They are direct efforts at *deciphering* the text, through an examination of its strands and textures, its conflicting but unified fragments, its structural elements seen as variety within its unity. But *we can perform these operations only insofar as the text "speaks" to us, only insofar as we "understand" because we also "believe."* Then the dialectic between understanding and explanation is set in motion so that we may arrive at a more knowledgeable interpretation of what we more naively understood from the start. *As artists studying and interpreting artists, we are believers of the artistic path toward a more evolved consciousness and we are inclined to talk about how the play of process, medium, and method upon the impelling subjects and images sets this almost mythic evolution in motion.*

Where Language Prepares to Fail

Our focus on the artist's way of interpreting and on songs of innocence, as well as our tendency to bracket off distancing and interpreting as interludes between expressions, reveals a lingering suspicion we have with any fixation on these moments. Yet, even as interludes, as in the example from Ponge's "The Prairie," these moments are parts of one whole of qualitative *thinking* which we are calling an *art*. As such, they have a primary function and one which is all the more important as we focus on art's role in the evolution of consciousness. They are like the trough between waves which becomes successively higher and higher until a near tidal wave sweeps into a separate reality and the ocean of consciousness becalms, as it were, at higher tide.

It is by extending experiencing, expressing, and understanding as far as we can that these lead toward deeper experiencing, expressing, and understanding. All experience, through the negational clash wherein our expectations are always countered and exceeded, makes us sadder but wiser. Our interpretations of expressive texts lead us to what the texts themselves express. *The being of the expressive text is the meeting ground for Being itself,* for that which comes into being through our qualitative experience. An inevitable clash occurs between the expressive text and interpreting. Out of this clash renewal and liberation are born, and the art of qualitative thinking moves toward final integration in a return to wholeness.

Mind, at the level of interpretation, produces feasible alternatives, provides explanations within the gaps in our understanding, detects the drift within selection and paraphrase, reveals that though playful and relaxed we perforce participated in taking this path and not that as we distanced, and helps us articulate our perspectivity on our origins. At this level we acknowledge our participation *through language* in the various fictions and explanations we produce in distanced dialogue with the text.

For Ricoeur, interpretation is "where language prepares to die." We arrive at a reflexive level of thought where we begin to question how, in our process of quanlitative thinking up to and through this stage, what we have done relates to the comprehension of self and its evolution. And we learn that the death of one language relates to the resurrection of another. In the language of faith—and this art is such a language in its positive belief in guidance through qualitative experiencing as expressing—the very failure of thought gives rise to an "in spite of" which keeps us turned toward expressing and then strengthens into a "thanks to," while both of these refusals of a dying language become positive in action by the "how much more"—constructions which Ricoeur[46] borrows from the Scriptures. Implicit faith and the art of qualitative thinking are alike life-affirming, upward surging. They say "still the worst is never sure"[47] and bargain with the wind to "go abroad and start anew...to build again a better life and song.[48]

Spirit Is Artist

Spirit moves through and beyond the most that thought can do, absorbing it back into one art of the Spirit. It is important to see the interpreting of qualitative experiencing and expressing this way. *Artistic-expressive texts require a thinking dialogue which clears the way for a deeper "hearing" of what the text has to "say" and of what is revealed behind the text itself.* We are returned to a meditative silence where the poem speaks out of its own stillness. In expressive-descriptive texts we remain true to the event as the incidents occur, according to a theory of the incident. *In neither case do we break the spell, no matter how much mental activity we engage in.* Our speech appropriately borders on paradox and intuition, the outposts of creative imagination itself. The artist, often maligned as last in thought, becomes the first. The artist prefers songs of innocence to heavy thought. The artist is inclined to speak of the reality and vitality of the path of expression itself, gathering together toward new adventures. *The failure of mental language is the victory of expressive language. It is humility and thanks for the state of grace which grants us vision and revelation and the sure knowledge that if we are open, selfless and ready they will return in renewed expression.*

Reference

1. Heidegger, M. *Being and time.* (J. Macquarrie and E. Robinson, trans.) London: SCM Press, 1962; pp. 194-195.

2. Bachelard G. *The poetics of reverie.* (D. Russel, trans.) Boston: Beacon Press, 1971; p. 15.

3. Ricoeur, P. *The philosophy of Paul Ricoeur.* (C. E. Reagan and D. Stewart, eds.) Boston: Beacon Press, 1978; p. 222.

4. Gadamer, H-G. *Truth and method.* N.Y.: Seabury Press, 1975; pp. 350, 363, 446.

5. Schuon, F. *Language of the self.* (M. Pallis and M. Matheson, trans.) Madras, India: Ganesh, 1959; p. 110.

6. Ricoeur, P. *Op. cit.,* reference 3 above, p. 154.

7. Proust, M. *Within a budding grove.* (C.K.S. Moncrieff, trans.) N.Y.: The Modern Library, 1924; Part II, pp. 22-23.

8. Wilber, K. *Up from Eden.* Garden City, N. Y.: Anchor Press/Doubleday, 1981; p. 276.

9. Faure, E. History of art. Vol. V. *The spirit of the forms.* (W. Pach, trans.) N.Y.: Harper & Brothers, 1930; p. 267.

10. Schuon, F. *Op. cit.,* reference 5 above, pp. 110-111.

11. Swami Rama; Ballentine, R.; and Swami Ajaya. *Yoga and psychotherapy.* Glenview, Ill.: Himalayan Institute, 1976; pp. 261-262.

12. Bergson, H. An introduction to metaphysics, from Barret, W. and Aiken, H. (eds.) *Philosophy in the twentieth century.* Vol. 3. Contemorary European Thought. N.Y.: Harper & Row, 1962.

13. Bachelard, G. *Op. cit.,* reference 2 above, p. 211.

14. Heidegger, M. *Poetry, language, thought.* (A. Hofstadter, trans.) N.Y.: Harper & Row, 1971; pp. 91-142.

15. *Ibid.,* p. 94.

16. *Ibid.,* p. 96.

17. *Ibid.,* p. 98.

18. *Ibid.,* p. 99.

19. *Ibid.,* pp. 133-134.

20. *Ibid.,,* pp. 141-142.

21. Palmer, R. E. *Hermeneutics.* Evanston: Northwestern University Press, 1969; p. 161.

22. Van den Berg, J. H. *A different existence.* Pittsburgh: Duquesne University Press, 1972; pp. 63-64.

23. *Ibid.,* pp. 60-61.

24. *Ibid.*, pp. 61-62.

25. Scheler, M. *Sympathy.* (P. Heath, trans.) Hamden, Conn.: Anchor Books, 1970.

26. Bakan, D. *On method.* San Francisco: Jossey-Bass, 1967.

27. Van Manen, M. An experiment in educational theorizing: The Utrecht School. *Interchange,* 10 (1), 1978-79; p. 56.

28. *Ibid.*, p. 58.

29. Bachelard, G. *Op. cit.*, reference 2 above, p. 165.

30. Ponge, F. *The voice of things.* (B. Archer, trans.) N.Y.: McGraw-Hill, 1972; p. 98.

31. *Ibid.*, pp. 94-95.

32. Van den Berg, J. H. *Op. cit.*, reference 22 above, pp. 91-92.

33. Perry Como Christmas album. N.Y.: RCA Records, 1968.

34. Hoff, B. *The Tao of Pooh.* N.Y.: Penquin Books, 1983.

35. Ricoeur, P. *Op. cit.*, reference 3 above, p. 241.

36. *Ibid.*, pp. 242-243.

37. *Ibid.*, p. 245.

38. *Ibid.*, p. 245.

39. Beittel, K. R. *Mind and context in the art of drawing.* N.Y.: Holt, Rinehart & Winston, 1972; pp. 203-204.

40. Beittel, K. R. *Alternatives for art education research.* Dubuque, Iowa: William C. Brown, 1973; p. 64.

41. *Ibid.*, p. 64.

42. *Ibid.*, pp. 64-65.

43. Novosel-Beittel, J. Inquiry into the qualitative world of creating: The S-E model. *Studies in Art Education.* 20(1), 1978; pp. 26-36.

44. *Ibid.*, pp. 33-34.

45. *Ibid.*, p. 35.

46. Ricoeur, P. *Op. cit.*, reference 3 above, p. 58.

47. *Ibid.*, p. 58.

48. Tagore, R. Quoted in Swami Ajaya (ed.) *Living with the Himalayan Masters.* Honesdale, Pa.: Himalayan Institute, 1978; p. 240.

10

Renewal

But the imagination
 knows all stories
  before they are told

William Carlos Williams[1]

The dragonfly
Perches on the stick
Raised to strike him.

Kohyo[2]

When we perceive the incongruity between theories about life and what we feel intuitively to be true on the nonverbal, nonjudging plane, there is nothing to do but laugh.

Zen tenet[3]

And I plucked a hollow reed
And I made a rural pen,
 And I stained the water clear,
And I wrote my happy songs
 Every child may joy to hear.

William Blake[4]

The Second Coming of Song

When the qualitative thinker breaks out of the bracketed thought-full interlude of distancing and interpreting, the language of faith arises anew as the poet's voice. The bracketing of thought is part of nature, part of this art, but the winged centaur shakes it off like the snow of winter. The most distanced view, the cooler eye, gets but an ironic grasp of the whole, sees how it broke into parts and how parts reassemble into the whole; *but it is wholeness rising to wholeness — before and after — that reaffirms qualitative thinking as experiencing, as renewed expressing.* The art of qualitative thinking is a great work of conceptual art. By losing yourself in it, you can see yourself in it, and you can free yourself through it. The loss precedes the seeing, and the seeing must yield to a renewal of freedom — or the cycle dies out. The bracketed mental interlude at mid-cycle is necessary to free consciousness from mind at the end of its tether.

We will deliberately play down the more mentalistic and philosophical expressions of this moment, for there is a vast literature on these. Having come this far, evaluator, critic, and judge, if they are true to an art of qualitative thinking, will have cause for fear and trembling and turn expectantly toward renewal. The political will have been sorted out. The healthful wholeness of the qualitative clashes headlong with any conceptual or political *a priori*. For power and thought presume to decide what shall be encouraged to come into existence. It is almost a case of cultural eugenics. From the side of experience, it is fair to ask a series of questions: Where does any notion of standard come from? What is the politics of experience which it supports? How does it limit the freedom of the experiencer? Who are those who have access to the system as reward seekers?

In all such questions the experiencer is a passive object. Judgment becomes merely a match between experience and pre-existent ideal. But what is originary exceeds origins:

> If one pushes the dreaming philospher to polemics, he will declare that the idealizing values do not have any cause. Idealization does not belong to the realm of causality.[5]

And we do not seek to sum up in concepts what is qualitative and is an art, even though it deals with "thinking." Images come to us in expression as though on their own mission, so that we intuitively feel "the essential difference between an absolute image that is self-accomplishing, and a post-ideated image that is content to summarize existing thoughts."[6] Thus the renewal to which this art of qualitative thinking leads rests on the "innate optimism" native to all works of the imagination. "In its germinal form...all of life is well being."[7] In making us self-conscious of the springs of expression and meaning, qualitative thinking opens us to active celebration of experience anew:

> in the end,
> it is our unshieldedness on which we depend,
> and that, when we saw it threaten, we turned it
> So into the Open that, in widest orbit somewhere,
> where the Law touches us, we may affirm it.[8]

The interludes of distancing and interpreting lay open our limits and our unshieldedness. But it as a return to origins, always on a new level and toward a higher state of consciousness, that we strike out into the Open, expressing in affirmation that new insight of our consciousness "where the Law touches us."

This return is not a U-turn. It is as though our consciousness struggles upward while our expression does its leaping wherever it finds its place on the horizontal extension of nature and art. *"Return" then means "reversal" and "decision" in the sense of a strengthened resolve to act.* That action is a new "song of innocence." Spirit is artist, a wind that blows away the interlude of thought:

> ...provoking an intensification of the true, authentic,
> unadorned nature of beings and things;
> nothing but awaiting it, awaiting that very moment[9]

A true rebeginning is indeed "a madness of life,"[10] the only madness really supportive of life that extends simultaneously beyond life, the only "thoughtless" madness that paradoxically learns from a kind of self-conscious thought.

The Range of Intellect in Relation to Mind and Spirit

Art, as a concrete discipline in unknowing, works through a hidden order. It calls forth a unification of body-mind which moves toward oneness with the cosmos; it descends into matter to ascend beyond body-mind to soul and spirit. It operates toward the higher reaches of intellect, in touch with transcendelia:

> Intellect, which is One, presents itself in three fundamental aspects...namely, first the divine Intellect, which is Light and pure Act; secondly, the cosmic Intellect, which is a receptacle or mirror in relation to God and light in relation to man; and thirdly the human Intellect, which is a mirror in relation to both of the foregoing and light in relation to the individual soul.[11]

The thinking, bracketing interludes struggle on the level of human intellect; but expressing and creating yearn for the level of cosmic intellect. Human intellect helps sort out what was contingent from what was cosmic in the expressive text. Its function is toward the revealing-guiding aspect of textural distortion. But this light is dim, and it serves its role well if it clears the way for a reappearance of the brighter cosmic light of expressing. Philosophers who stand in a dependent relation to cosmic intellect and thus to art as revelation, are like adoptive fathers who would tear the babe away from the mother. All this noise of human intellect, when it serves some role other than in the interlude of thought (for self-insight) bracketed between vital expressions, is in large part only masculine show, for it is the creating *anima* or "valley spirit" which rules over reverie and image.

Art as Truth and Knowledge

In following Gadamer's argument against modern *aestheticism* and his effort to see art as a *non-differentiated whole*, as we did earlier, we found the problem of *truth* and *knowledge* in art brought back to the center of our artistic experience. The modern tendency to separate feelings from the intellect is then called into question. The three kinds of intellect referred to in our quote above help us reflect upon how this dichotomy occurred. In restricting itself to positivistic, scientific and logical thought, human intellect has cut itself off from cosmic intellect. The imaginative thought, paradoxical thinking and intuition of the cosmic level then become something other than intellect in its reductionistic distortion, and a debilitated, partial art is left to titillate feelings and is exiled altogether from the provinces of truth and knowledge. Traditionally, as a form of rhetoric, art as been considered as knowledge:

> Thomas Aquinas says that "beauty relates to the cognitive faculty," and "since knowledge is by assimilation, and similitude is with respect to form, beauty properly belongs to the nature of a formal cause." And Augustine says, "Beauty is the attractive poewr of a perfect expression." And Dante did not write the Divine Comedy in order that we should have delicous sensations but "to remove those who are living in this life from the state of wretchedness, and to lead them into the state of blessedness." Though it sounds almost facetious to proclaim it, Plato, Aristotle, Dionysius the Areopagite, Augustine, Thomas, Dante, Sidney, Shelley — the list could be longer, though scarcely more luminous — all agree that the idea and the poem are one, that though prettiness may charm aesthetically, beauty is the radiance of truth.[12]

The idea and the poem are one as intuitive knowledge at the level of cosmic intellect, as "mirror in relation to God and light in relation to man." Human intellect, which at its best can serve the light of self-consciousness in the human soul, expresses itself as language of the descent preparatory to an ascent toward cosmic intellect. The individual must lose self to participate in the cosmic and reflect the divine light, but the individual then recovers self from this inspired otherness. The bracketed interludes of distancing and interpretation prepare the way for this transcendence of the individual soul on its divine path. The last moment of the art of qualitative thinking, as a rhythmic movement from cosmic to human and back to cosmic intellect under the light of divine intellect, leads organically to renewed expression and selfless action. It does not lead to thinking as we usually mean it, unless we call it a renewed art of qualitative thinking.

> Art is an activity, an exteriorisation, and thus depends by definition on a knowledge that transcends it and gives it order; apart from such knowledge art has no justification: it is knowledge which determines action, manifestation, form, and never the reverse.[13]

But this knowledge is that of an intuitive, imaginative, and concrete grasp of Spirit itself, as transcendelia, as cosmic intellect in touch with the reflected light, "manifest as the sky."

The Art of Qualitative Thinking as an Esoteric Spiritual Discipline

Such an art of qualitative thinking as we propose here is an organic one that takes a long view of the human condition and its tangible opportunities for self-transcendence and self-evaluation. This occurs by means of immersion in it as an esoteric discipline, as a spiritual science, which in-vokes and ex-presses what was e-voked and im-pressed in *experience,* moving through the deepest involvement to an evolution by way of *expression,* to an *understanding* that flowers anew into song and selfless action. To envision such an esoteric discipline apart from the world's aging and parochial traditional esoteric disciplines requires some courage, but our planetary plight urges its feasibility. If it were something invented on the spot, it would be indefensible. But it is rather a generalization provided organically from the fusion of spirit as artist, the esoteric tradition across the ages, hermeneutic philosophy, and the common need for self-evolution in consciousness, for selfless service and action in a severely politicized world. Its character makes it anti-establishment, anti-structural, not just toward our scientistic and technological culture and its institutions, but toward the organized art world as well.

On a communal scale, such a discipline can occur only in transient buffer institutions, where anti-structure can be temporarily tolerated. On an individual basis, it can exist wherever it finds fertile ground and receives encouragement from those who have experienced it within themselves. For there is a desire for communion and community in such a discipline.

It is on the ground of such an emergent planetary artistic esoteric spiritual discipline that we move naturally at this point into more meaningful and liberating applications to education and therapy. Application then becomes the living forward of meaning as impassioned actions in the world. The world needs changed perhaps, but only if we work slowly at changing ourselves can we open the world to change. Such an esoteric tradition through art as here envisioned is neither elitist nor popular. It occurs when through the un-shieldedness of the artist within us we are able to turn toward the Open, moving with courage into new expressive action.

Where thinking has painfully redeemed its political en-tanglements with self and culture, has seen its autosymbolic tendencies at work within the deep structure of qualitative experience, wholeness of thought returns as more vital and mysterious than ever — it has refused to die under the worst that self, culture, and analysis can do to it. In acknowledging the direct link between interest and knowledge, thought takes a stand consciously and responsibly, saying: "Here am I, and for this purpose." The ethical component arises as we find human vitality wanting to be reflective of divine and cosmic intellect. Though limited and finite, our actions show us as new beings creating a new planet.

Just as all modes of texts are expressive, so are all forms of renewal also expressive. At the end as at the beginning, some modes are more expressive than others. Renewal means simultaneously return and advance. The whole returns to the whole, the whole implicates the Whole. And throughout the entire cycle only *-ing* forms count:
   (1) text as expressing, celebrating
   (2) distance as selecting, circling
   (3) interpretation as explaining, understanding
   (4) renewal as again expressing, celebrating — in act,
       in thought , and in art

This art is a circle dance in four parts around the qualitative immediate present, the eternal Now. It is itself qualitative throughout—that is, quality lived forward. It is one grand art form, a cycle, two waves as one with the Great Ocean, moving toward high tide. The second coming of song is that renewal of inspiration that opens us to receive life-sustaining energy from the universe.

> Wholeness before and wholeness after...
> The end is nearest the beginning...
> The circle of Hermes is Love.
>
> —K.B.

References

1. Williams, W. C. *The selected poems of William Carlos Williams.* N.Y.: New Directions, 1962; p. 172.

2. Holmes, S. W. and Horioka, C. *Zen art for meditation.* Rutland, Vermont: Charles E. Tuttle, 1973; p. 86.

3. *Ibid.,* p. 96.

4. Yeats, W. B. (ed.) The poems of William Blake. Cambridge: Harvard University Press, 1969; p. 47.

5. Bachelard, G. *The poetics of reverie.* (D. Russel, trans.) Boston: Beacon Press, 1971; p. 91.

6. Bachelard, G. *The poetics of space.* (M. Jolas, trans.) Boston: Beacon Press, 1969; p. 153.

7. *Ibid.,* p. 104.

8. Heidegger, M. *Poetry, language, thought.* (A. Hofstadter, trans.) N.Y.: Harper & Row, 1971; p. 99.

9. Ponge, F. *The voice of things.* (B. Archer, trans.) N.Y.: McGraw-Hill, 1972; p. 187.

10. Bachelard, G. *Op. cit.,* reference 5 above, p. 124.

11. Schuon, F. *Language of the self.* (M. Pallis and M. Matheson trans.) Madras, India: Ganesh, 1959; p. 232.

12. Senior, J. *The way down and out.* N.Y.: Greenwood Press, 1968; p. xx.

13. Schuon, F. *Op. cit.,* reference 11 above, p. 128.

11

Expressive Therapy

Cows are of many different colors, but the
Milk of all is of one color, white;
So the proclaimers who proclaim the truth
Use many varying forms to put it in,
But yet the truth enclosed in all is One.

Upanishads

The day wears on to night when all things rest.
Out of the timeless black night a new day emerges.
This is the cycle of the Chinese yin and yang.
In psychotherapy, all action is the day and all
of the holes are the fertile void of night. The
fertile void of night comes into psychotherapy
so that we might dissolve a little and come
out a little changed into a new day. I no
longer fear the fertile void for either my
patient or myself. The way to day is through
the night. The night or the void is the no-mind
of Zen. It is not nothing nor is it something.
It is a fertile emptiness.

Wilson van Dusen[1]

The neurotic aspect is the counterpart of wisdom,
so you cannot have one without the other. In
the ideal case, when enlightenment is attained,
the neuroses are still there but they have become
immense energy. Energy is the euphemism for
neurosis from that point of view.

Chogyam Trungpa[2]

Once your purpose is established, then you have
surely dealt with problems such as self-
indulgence and the need to be like someone
else. So the external noise is not so loud
anymore, not so negative. This gives you a
chance to make your commitment to Art, which
is ultimately the path of devotion, balance,
creativity and love. What deeply moved me is
sitting in the pottery studio at night, listening
to the rhythm of my breathing, meditating,
thinking of only the clay, and then of
nothing at all—absorbed in my thoughts and
actions, and then coming away from it all,
exhausted, but with a special feeling. A
feeling of being calm. Not wanting anything.
Just being one with the earth.

Anonymous student reverie
on a beginning pottery course[3]

The Scope and Nature of Expressive Therapy

We work at expressive problems and ourselves simultaneously through a formula as old as man. Dogen-zenji said it like this: *"To study Buddhism is to study oneself. To study oneself is to forget oneself."*[4]

The art of qualitative thinking *all by itself* leads to expressive self-therapy and self-education. But when we focus on a general art therapy through this cycle, it is necessary to add the art therapist as change agent. Then, to see how this process brings forth both new forms and personal growth through the hidden order of art, it is helpful to focus in more detail on its stages. This cycle moves from *aceptance of the way things are,* to *what is desired,* to *awareness of certain limitations,* to *affirmation and visualization,* and finally to *taking action.* As a general formula, this sequence actually allows you to begin to create whatever you want.

It is through the therapist's ongoing dialogue with the artist that the stages of this cycle enter into the artist's actions and consciousness. And these stages lead to more than the creation of art because, as already suggested, they represent the general way that newness comes into being through human action. What is so wonderfully therapeutic and positive about this particular art setting is the complete independence of the art work from both the artist and the therapist. Attention is directed to the unfolding of the creative process itself and not toward the interaction between the artist and therapist. Therefore internal processes have an external focus. This sets the stage for the enigmatic self-transcending nature of art to become the true subject matter of the therpeutic dialogue.

Through this dialogue, attention can be directed naturally to the stages of the cycle. It is concentration on these stages that brings about growth, newness and change. And the general focus on the creative process arouses a deep passion and dialogue for the meaning of whole art within the wholness of life itself.

It is like the charismatic power of a Pavarotti who can charm several hundred million Chinese people with his extremely disciplined but richly spontaneous and impassioned singing. His whole life is a song. An artist of this stature speaks to the heroic proportions and power of the human at a time forgetful of its origins. The cyclical and upwardly spiraling processes of creation empower the artist with a similar vision. Art cannot be practiced within this cyclical model without probing the heights and depths of human consciousness.

Pavarotti is by total orientation a master teacher. A master teacher is *always* a student. A master therapist is *always* undergoing change for the purpose of growth. To express his passionate relationship with life Pavarotti has to be alive and aware every moment. That means that his art is practiced *all* the time. This is the very same attitude the great art educator Viktor Lowenfeld expressed when he told me: "Kenneth, even when I dance in my nightshirt I am an art educator."

And that is the difference between a Pavarotti and a person who sings just occasionally. It is a matter of a total unrelenting focus and commitment. The same is true in practicing and learning *any* art. It is true in taking up the art of pottery as an esoteric spiritual discipline:

> When I teach beginners, there is much I cannot show them in their first and second years. In the third year, there is much for which they are preparing. In the fourth year, good students can sense something of what I cannot say, and in the fifth, inner vision begins to awaken. A tension develops between thought and action in the sixth year, and during the seventh year, despair sets in at the passage of time. In the eighth year, students are lost in clay, and by the ninth year, they are ready to take up their apprenticeship within the Great Tradition.[5]

We have been presenting art as an esoteric spiritual discipline in its own right. We have struggled to set forth, through example and through poetry something of the metaphysical basis of art as a science of the soul. Now it is our purpose to focus on and to recapitulate some of the spiritual remedies which art has at its disposal.

The unfolding of consciousness in therapy through art does not take place in any single systematic way. It is for this reason that expressive therapy is often distorted by any effort to connect it too closely with any specific school of therapy. *Art serves the whole of consciousness through its wholeness.* On the horizon between earth and sky, art moves within the middle range of existence without ignoring the below or denying the above. Since its mode is a transmutation of baser into higher, it can be seen as synonymous with transformation of the self as well. And here another important general principle is advanced: *though each school of psychotheraphy serves some specific problem area within the various levels of consciousness, art as expressive therapy serves all levels.*

Poets and artists who have attained the highest levels of consciousness speak humbly and even apologetically about how insufficient their expressions are. In this they are no different from saints and mystics. Nevertheless, Whitman speaks of "The rare, cosmical, artist mind, lit with the infinite, [which] alone confronts his manifold and oceanic qualities."[6]

It is often the custom to limit art, poetic reverie, and creative imagination to the level of consciousness where mind first struggles to transcend its limits in order to move toward soul and spirit. The transmutation and transformation effected by art are seen as *only* a way station, albeit a most important one, toward the highest levels. The mistake here is to limit image-work to a specific kind of image-work, applicable to only one level of self-work. The usage which Coleridge and Bachelard make of creative imagination, however, far transcends this limited view. As Bachelard points out, the imagination which leads to cosmic images in all their immediacy, believes in its exuberance, that "it is telling the whole of the Whole."[7] It is in this sense that various *imaginations* may be distinguished from one another, just as Blake distinguished between twofold, threefold, and fourfold vision. Trungpa says that theory, conceptual study on the path, gives way eventually to imagination. This might be called imagination[1]. Through it intuitive knowledge begins to open up, and dualisms are partially ignored. Step by step this leads slowly to imagination[2], "which is more real than merely imagination, though it is still colored by imagination."[8] In much the same way Blake suggests that analogies yield to archetypes, these then yield to direct images, and these, finally, to visions. The point to emphasize here is that all of these are kinds of imagination to be found within expressive art therapy as it plays upon the transcendence of one or the other of the levels of consciousness.

In this sense, the higher levels of imagination are drawn forth by higher levels of spiritual need. Artists give evidence of this. Rilke said:

> Works of art always spring from those who have faced
> the danger, gone to the very end of an experience, to
> the point beyond which no human being can go. The
> further one dares to go, the more decent, the more per-
> sonal, the more unique a life becomes.[9]

And Beethoven said:

> Speak to Goethe about me. Tell him to hear my
> symphonies and he will say that I am right in
> saying that music is the one incorporeal
> entrance into the higher world of knowledge
> which comprehends mankind but which mankind
> cannot comprehend.[10]

But the fascinating thing about the unfolding of consciousness through expressive art therapy is that it works equally well for the child, the novice, the neurotic, and the genius.

In an earlier chapter we saw how Larry, an undergraduate literature major untrained in art, arrived at ever-deepening insights through his conscious conceptualizations about making art. He found himself caught up in the "purely visual" aspects of experience, leading to a kind of "superhuman awareness" which was nevertheless a non-thinking "animal-like awareness." In trying to express such feelings in drawing and painting, he had to come "face to face with the visual problem." He found "You've got to get right to it — you can't evade." In daring to do this, he finds that he is an artist and thinks that "everyone *should* have this kind of experience...It affects the total life this way."[11]

The professional artist whom we earlier discussed, had characterized painting as being "like the magnificent death — you don't return." It is, for him, "a separate reality, a larger reality." This same artist, one day in the Drawing Lab, underwent a transcendent and transformative experience:

> I made one mark that felt like the "old days."...
> It was the first time that I was not trying to catch
> up with the mark that was being made by the brush,
> and I was ahead of it or at least with it...And
> thinking about that mark while away from the Lab
> interrupted me the rest of the day...*The
> seriousness that interrupted me that day wasn't
> related to anything except the making of that
> one mark, and that mark wasn't play in my mind.
> That mark was a distinct change in the kind of
> reality. It was a religious experience.*[12]

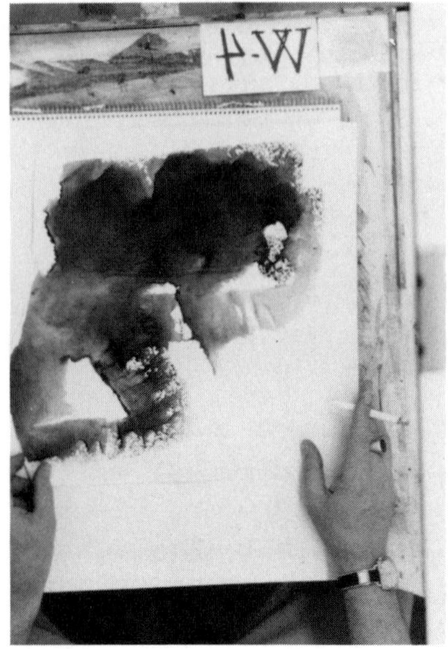

a.

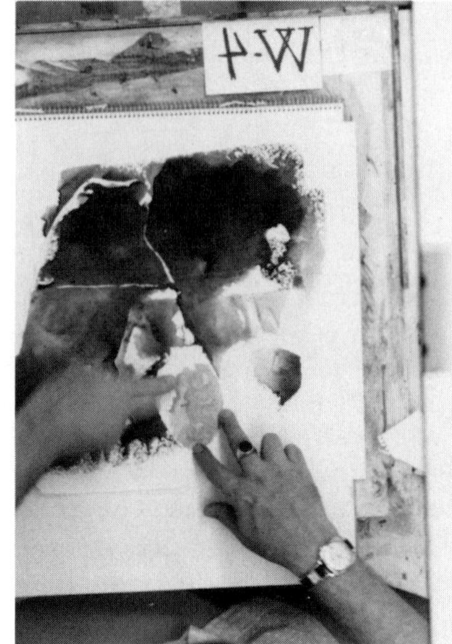

b.

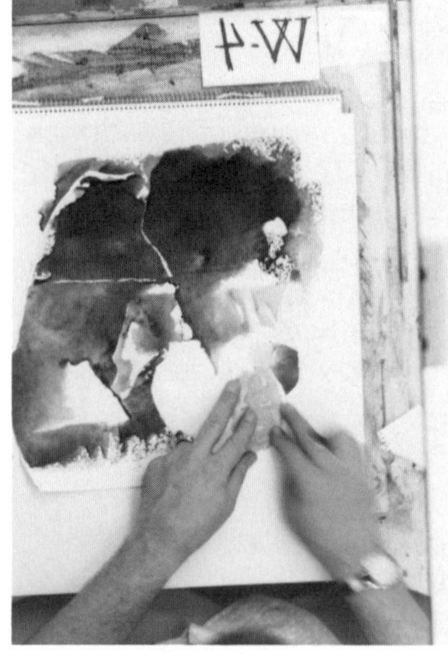

c.

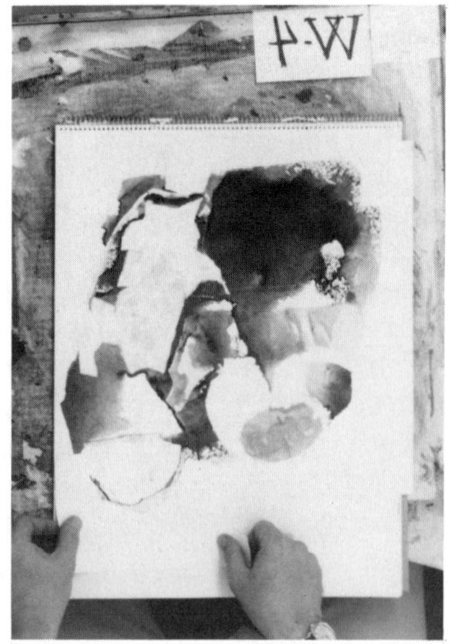

d.

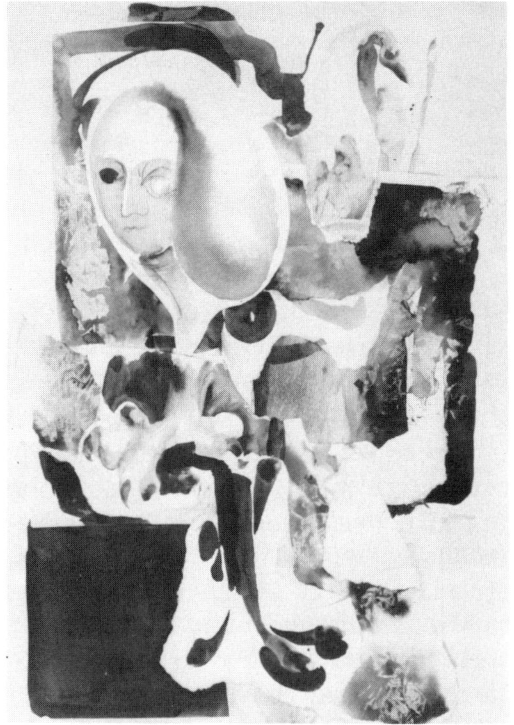

e.

Examples from Case Study I.
The Drawing Lab, Penn State.

a. Colloge in Process, Stage I.
b. Colloge, Stage II.
c. Colloge, Stage III.
d. Colloge, Stage IV.
e. Colloge II: Beyond Time, Beyond Space.

Such changes in consciousness are effected through art as it engages the antecedent stage of consciousness of the artist, clashes with it in the constituent or present stage of action in the work, and ushers in a consequent, transformative, separate reality. Any broad view of therapy sees this process repeated on many levels, all potentially a part of the evolution of consciousness. The authors of *Yoga and Psychotheraphy* confirm this view as being a cyclic one of observation, control and synthesis:

> ...growth is always based on the attainment of
> some degree of disentanglement from attachments,
> which allows one to observe something about himself
> and his world to which he was previously blind. This

> is the expansion of awareness. As awareness grows,
> one inevitably discovers within his new definition of
> himself a new ability to control. What he was pre-
> viously blind to and controlled by is now within his
> power to regulate. Increased capacity for observation
> leads to increased capacity to control.[13]

Thus the basic cyclical mechanism of transcendence of limits through heightened awareness leads to greater control and to transformation to still higher levels of observation, control and awareness. The words in the various descriptive systems vary, but the three-stage cycle leading to renewal on a higher level is common to them all. The art of qualitative thinking is our effort to treat this cycle in a way which renders consciousness self-conscious so that transformation and renewal can ensue.

Our purpose here is to deal with this cyclic expressive process in its most general way so that its operation across the entire spectrum of consciousness can be grasped. This is a general, not a technical work. At another time it would indeed be challenging to lay out the details of this expressive evolutionary cycle as it is engaged in each specific level of consciousness and in relation to traditional systems of psychotherapy operating at these various levels. It is important to reiterate, however, that *we are presenting a generic expressive therapy which accelerates the evolution of consciousness on all levels and which is not merely an adjunct to existent therapies.*

From the therapeutic standpoint, this process begins with *acceptance.* For the artist this is equivalent to strengthening the ingredient of self-love. Whatever one creates is *just what it is* — not something to be critically judged or turned away from. There are no mistakes. There is only learning. You can't really mess up! It is all part of a history that is moving forward in the best way it can. By accepting *all* of your history and then *letting go of it,* the wholeness of its nature comes forward. Such a focus allows the artist to focus on what is really desired. And the clash between acceptance and desire directs attention to self-imposed limitations and core beliefs no longer serving growth. When the artist focuses on what she or he really wants, then affirmations and visualizations follow naturally. They arise in imagery anytime, anywhere that specific desires or needs are thought or felt.

The focus of the setting of the Drawing Lab made it possible to take action within a supportive non-judgmental climate. The cycle was then repeated. What is, is. It is accepted and even valued. It is a rite of passage to further change, growth, creation and renewal.

The Special Nature of the Helping Relationship in Expressive Therapy

Chogyam Trungpa says that neurosis is like the counterpart of wisdom. They come together. Enlightenment transmutes neuroses into "immense energy."[14] This suggests a valuable insight applicable to all levels of development: the warring elements that are transcended do not disappear, but are rather assimilated, along with their opposition, into the dynamic harmony of the higher unity. Thus mind, which had to forge its existence through transcending and separating from the body-nature or body-matter split, must be transcended to bring about a higher order body-mind integration to open up consciousness toward the spirit level, where body-mind and the cosmos are capable of a new, higher unity. The transcended elements, as neuroses of the way, are transmuted into immense energy as they become parts of the new unity. It seems that whatever has been attained must be transcended because the limits within each level eventually impede further progress. Wilber would say that at each level only temporary renewal is possible, in the form of translation from one to another form within the level. This he likens to a struggle between Eros and Thanatos in which the latter slowly gains ascendence. Thereafter a symbolic death of the self at the achieved level is necessary for transformation, which is a movement toward pure spirit and superconsciousness. Lacking this transformation, a contraction of consciousness is possible. And this is equivalent to involution, or the manifestation of consciousness at the next lower level.[15]

Therefore not to grow in art is to repeat oneself to the point where an involution or a contraction of consciousness is likely rather than an evolution. But the cyclical dynamic of consciousness we have been discussing spins toward evolution naturally within its healthy exercise and function without loss of the transcended stages or parts, although these take on new meaning in the new unity. Thus an "enlightened" person does not give up the ego, but rather has a new relationship to it and a freedom from its constraints. The so-called *corrupt consciousness* is involved in not only a forgetting but in a decline in which the negative connotation of neurosis takes over and designates a loss of energy.

The making of art is an expressive therapy to start with, even without a helper or therapist involved. The othering of the self in the making of art already leads, *by itself*, to a self-consciousness permitting and encouraging self-transcendence. Reductive theories have it that the expression is an acting out of neuroses, whereas it is preferable to see it as a conversion of them into immense energy. Thus Bachelard can claim that "...a man's work stands out from life to such an extent that life cannot explain it."[16] But further than that, it is possible to say that in the evolutionary sense his work is his true life. Thus Beethovan's outward circumstances are of small concern to a person who can reach the ultimate level of consciousness represented by the "C# Minor String Quartet." Outward circumstances of life are of no more use here than they are in observing a Himalayan master in rapt meditation in his cave.

We have numerous examples of primitives like Grandma Moses, who have developed artistically and spiritually in isolation, without teacher or therapist. In fact, as with the famous saying by Montaigne about doctors, in art no teacher is better than a bad one. This is why, in our earliest studies in the Drawing Lab,[17] our "search for the teacher" took the form of removing the teacher at first altogether. We thus strove to "counter-intervene," to "non-instruct," as an *active* and conscious aim. The artists who came to work knew they would receive no instruction and that they would only be interviewed between working sessions in an effort to share and understand their creating stream of consciousness. But it turned out that this very effort to share their *idiosyncratic meaning*, their *artistic causality* and autonomy, and their *intentional symbolization*, represented the best of all possible instructors, for it helped them to a *self*-consciousness through unfettered communication and sharing which encouraged their evolution through and in art.

We learned that there were very special conditions necessary for truthful and authentic disclosure of the artist's world:

> The nature of the creative act...can be disclosed to anyone who assumes the proper attitude. This attitude requires that he stands outside himself in openness, responsively, as he enters the interior meaning of an interpersonal world. The artist must also be in the proper

> attitude. He must be "there" as a fully autonomous creative agency, not as a research subject, not as a student, not as anything else but as an artist who is in his creating world. Under these two necessary conditions for disclosure, the making of art is seen as a primary dialogue and is honored as such...The artist is free to seek his own form, to use his own intentionality and creative intuition to give meaning to his symbolic transformations. The ethics of disclosure preserves the artist as "other" in all his radicality, for as the researcher becomes "self-less" the artist becomes "self-full." Through these conditions they find a common language where two worlds can meet. They are led by an authentic search for the truth of the artist's world, and when they find that "truth," the co-sharing of creating moves community toward communion within the reciprocity of the I and Thou. This can only occur...where there is no artistic end in sight and no research method which attempts control.
>
> These conditions for disclosure come out of an atmosphere of care. As researcher I see the artist entrusting his world to my view. This demands that I be "there" for him, authentically (my thoughts, feelings and actions are congruent). He is a sovereign being who engages me in dialogue. Our dialogue becomes a moment of disclosure of possibilities for being of some essential content between us. These possibilities are moments of authentic existence where self and art are located in existential truth. Existential truth lies in our becoming aware of our freedom to be.[18]

We become deeply interested participants, co-sharers, of the artistic path. We become not authorities, although the authority of belief in evolution must have shone through, but encouraging witnesses, keepers of a vital history, "spirit instructors" helping the artist to *distance, see, interpret,* and *renew* what he or she had expressed. I suppose it would be possible to construe our role as close to teacher, therapist, even guru – in the most positive connotations these roles can have. "Obedience to the guru" would here mean "daring to believe in my own evolution in and through art." Naranjo defines guru, simply, thus: "A guru is somebody closer to God than the disciple; therefore obedience to him is the closest approximation to an obedience to God."[19] The word does not therefore precisely fit here, except by extension to mean *someone who believes more in the self-transformative and evolutionary power of art than the artist.* By saying thus we have defined the therapist in expressive therapy. We would also insist, for authenticity, that this person be much experienced in art *and* at struggle with the self-transformative power of art in his or her own life. This additional criterion rules out many well-meaning psychotherapists, who not knowing art in terms of deep self-evolution cannot stand authentically before an artist setting out on that path. If one is not a potter in the deepest sense one cannot mediate pottery as an esoteric spiritual discipline.

Expressive therapy, then, need not proceed by way of the many methods of other forms of therapy, for *the ritual of making art encloses the essential seed of evolution,* not the interaction with the therapist. Artist and therapist do not turn toward each other foremost; rather *both turn toward the evolutionary reality of the art process.*

Among other virtues of this relationship we can underscore *patience,* for art-making is out of time, within its own qualitative immediate time, a state of indefinite qualitative duration which stops time. No "hidden agenda" is appropriate, and that means setting aside prediction, evaluation, or any efforts at control. A nurturant, expectant, encouraging atmosphere arises, a place "where the desirable becomes existential."[20] In this atmosphere we find affirmation, care, respect for the "artist within," and a general attitude reflecting *empathy, congruence, unconditional positive regard,* with an *absence of external evaluation.*[21] This does not mean that authentic encounter cannot and does not arise, for *congruence* can mean that too, just as Ott reminds us that we can disagree with our dialogue partner and, in so doing, move the dialogue forward.[22]. The art therapist, having experienced the evolutionary cyclic nature of art making and having also become sufficiently reflective concerning it to develop some theory about it, is in a position to encourage his or her own imagination to envision ways in which this potential can be evoked in ways which often elude the artist. The process of making art is so demanding that no one would be beyond the help of a nurturant art therapist capable of operating at a stage of development commensurate with the artist's need.

Examples of Self-Consciousness and Self-Transformation in Expressive Therapy

We are fortunate in not having to remain theoretical about expressive therapy, for sixteen years of on-going experience in the Drawing Lab provided the readiest base for examples illuminating this discussion. Our first example reveals unusual self-discovery set off by an ideational change, a reversal, in working attitude and method. The artist is a visiting scientist from Sydney who had painted for several years on his own, mostly portraits in oil. "Good art" for him meant extreme realism, with a slavish effort to copy precisely what was in front of him. A "cool analysis," taking no expressive liberties on the artist's side, was his ideal of a good portrait painting.

In spite of this view, one day as he was doing a painting of T. S. Eliot, with whom he strongly identified, his preconceptions broke down. He is not satisfied with the placement of the head, so he tries it twice, and then again, meaning these as "corrections," but all on the same page. He becomes, however, fascinated with the resultant multiple images and the meanings they suggest. Already, his intention to paint realistically begins to break down. A shift in attitude sets in and persists. In another drawing he takes details of Eliot's head apart and rearranges them. In still another, a huge " + " or cross-shaped division cuts through Eliot's head, which shifts apart into planes not neatly coming together behind the divisions created. Later on further details become centered-on: the eye and the ear of the poet by themselves, and the "necktie" connoting Edwardian propriety slowly turns into a hangman's noose. Brush strokes begin to define a dancing figure, sometimes represented as a

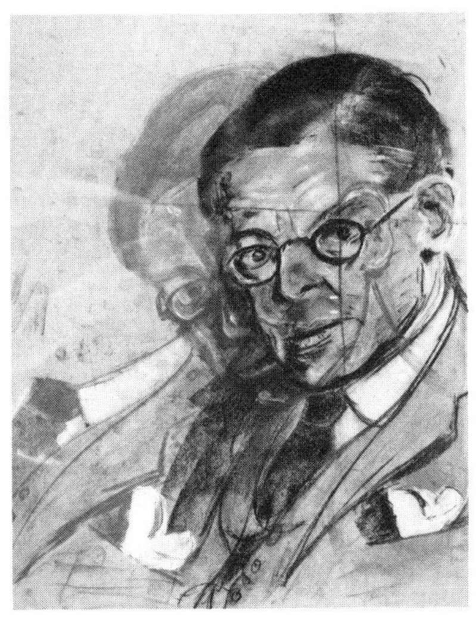

a.

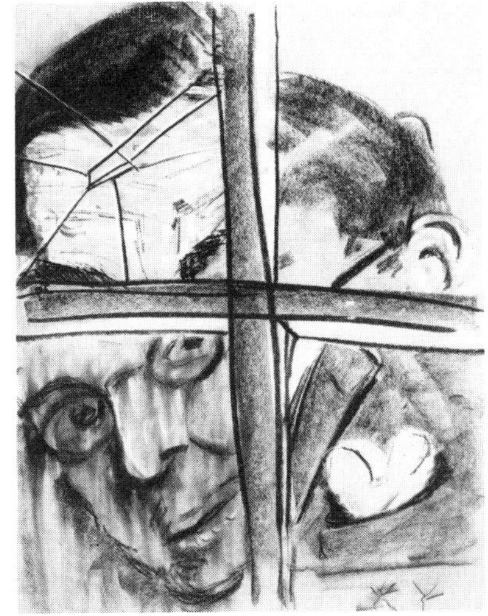

b.

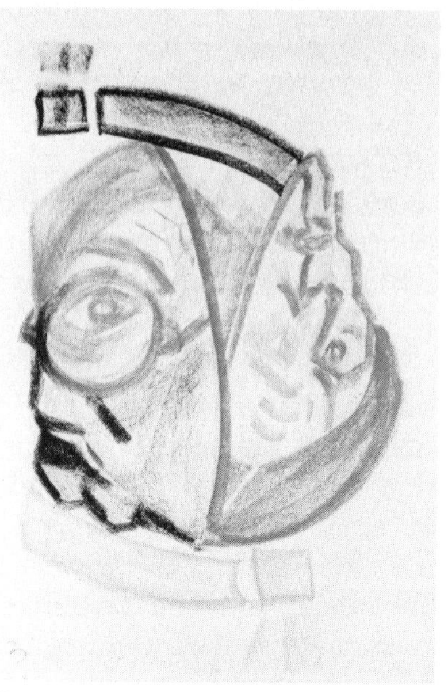

c.

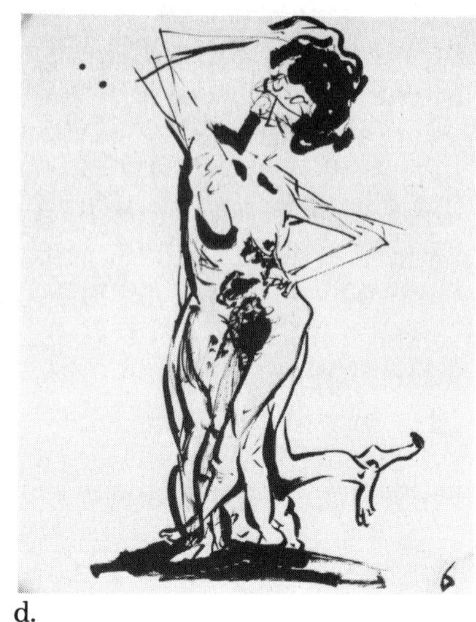

d.

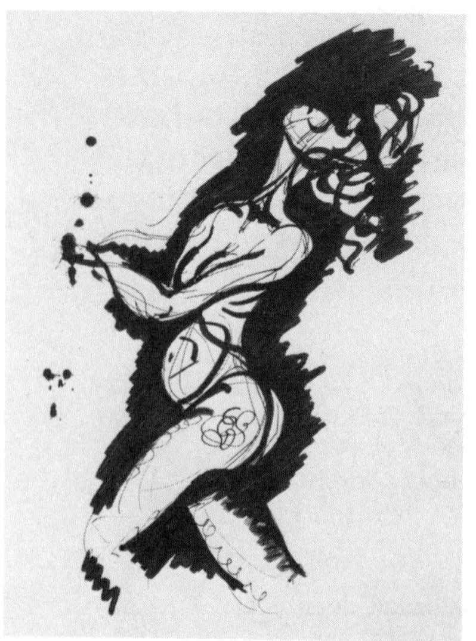

e.

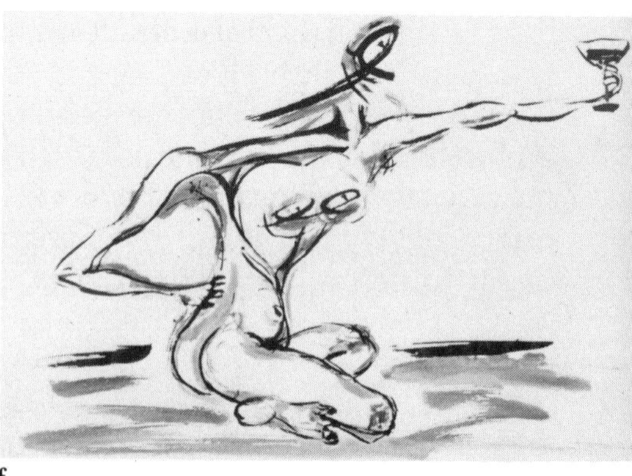

f.

Examples from Case Study II.
The Drawing Lab, Penn State.

a. Beginning Series: Portrait of the Poet.
b. Beginning Series: Deconstructing the Poet's Image.
c. Beginning Series: Intentional Symbolization.
d. Advanced Series: Unpremeditated Spontaneity.
e. Advanced Series: Unpremeditated Spontaneity.
f. Advanced Series: The Wine of Art and Poetry.
   An Invitation to the Dance.

gesture arising from a single, dynamic stroke. Expression and symbolism join together in a great outpouring. The artist/researcher is represented as a teacher, as the feminine, holding out in her hand the wine of poetry to the artist. A conflict is set up between life-enhancing and life-detracting forces, literally between Eros and Thanatos. A Dionysian, frenzied, earthy dance, full of *joie de vivre*, breaks through. It is countered by the Apollonian, the classical, the cognitive, by a questioning of this run-away emotionalism, by a fear of headless action and of the "shadow side" of the intellect. Finally, the life-enhancing values take over: joy, spontaneity, and dance follow the acceptance of the proffered glass of poetic intoxication. The artist represents himself as dancing with abandon, half-god, half-man, his head turned toward the sun, his body-mind one, a surprising symbolization equivalent to the centaur. Here is what the artist says about his change in attitude and approach:

> I am searching for the significance of symbolic detail. The eye and the ear overlap in the head of a poet, and all overlap has to serve a double purpose, so I choose out significant details and chop them up and put them in some kind of order....To me, the colors were suddenly more interesting than the shapes, the chalks more fascinating than T.S. Eliot.
>
> As to the cracks across the forehead of Eliot, are they symbolic? Hell, I was just thinking...It was the crucifixion cross, I was nailing him to the cross of cruelty and pain; and the cracked glass, well, it is a rather adolescent image in a way, but I associate pain and suffering with Eliot, and that came out very strong when he was slashed. Things were bugging me subconsciously— like, where else do I want to go? What else do I want to do, other than just paint naturalistically?...I want to go beyond that. I'm not any longer simply trying to make it look like a head...I've got to break down that whole copying kind of thing...and this is a new approach for me. It has been in my head...with chalks I can't overlay and make it look like it is...but I like my problem.
>
> One of the good things about this is that I don't even care if it looks like T.S. Eliot anymore, or anyone, even. Each piece reads whatever way it is to read; that's my solution—let it do what it will do is the better solution. That's quite a change from my "stage-to-stage."
>
> *I do have the distinct feeling that this is all leading up to something rather good which I'm not aware of—*yes, these are all pieces which seem to be making sense, one by one. Curious, I used to be very concerned to be able to draw well, and now it doesn't seem to matter any more—at least, it's only temporarily frustrating. What I'm doing here is more important than getting it naturalistically sound. I'm rather pleased with myself.[23]

Such examples could as easily be shown under education as under therapy. In fact, we aim to draw no sharp line between them. From the point of view of art as an esoteric spiritual discipline, the terms are interchangeable—it is merely a matter of emphasis. In the above example, the sharing of these changes visually and verbally accelerates the process of change by means of the self-consciousness encouraged through making art, which is then underscored by verbalization concerning it, where it is leading and where it came from. The feeling of change and new direction is reinforced by its open acceptance and by the fact that the achievement of change was witnessed; and this becomes quite an exhilarating affair.

In the third example, we see the drama of a deaf artist who slowly turns from the darkness of isolation and cultural repression, as both deaf and a woman, towards the light of open expression, self-acceptance and love. As with the first example, early gains bring in a vacillating period which must eventually be overcome in order to evolve. Early drawings illustrate the beginning condition: mechnaical mouths and improvised hands gain one acceptance within the dominant hearing world, but at the cost of self-destruction through hands that cannot talk expressively and words that cannot be spoken. Teachers of the hearing world do not understand the deaf world. They are shown as speaking machines and demonic jailors. The deaf artist is represented as a woman pregnant beyond her time whose meanings cannot be delivered, accompanied by a sly cat who knows her unspeakable secret. Then life breaks over this repressive condition by a positive focus on hands gesturing in expressive speech. The life of feeling arises, the sensitive touch of one hand on another is shown, and an honest release of emotion, even rage, occurs. This tender beginning toward open expression arouses a potential which has the shadow of fear and depression still upon it, but this slowly retreats under a growing affirmation and self-esteem. The contest between depression and expression leads toward the elevation of the hand, as symbol of sharing and meaning. A true, not mechanical, smile appears between two expressively drawn hands. The hand becomes a person walking on two fingers on the road of expression. The joy of open expression takes over, as the artist has her first vision of a *garden of growth*—a depiction symbolized through many arms shooting up from the fertile ground toward the sky in the expressive sign for *growth* where the open hand

and stretched out fingers represent reaching toward sun and nourishment. This *garden of growth* is later to symbolize her vision of a community of deaf artists of all kinds united in expression and sharing of their inner worlds. And this eventually becomes a reality through her labors.

Up to about the fifth week in the Drawing Lab this artist always worked from sketches made *prior* to coming in. The following dialogue reflects a new level of security and confidence in her working processes:

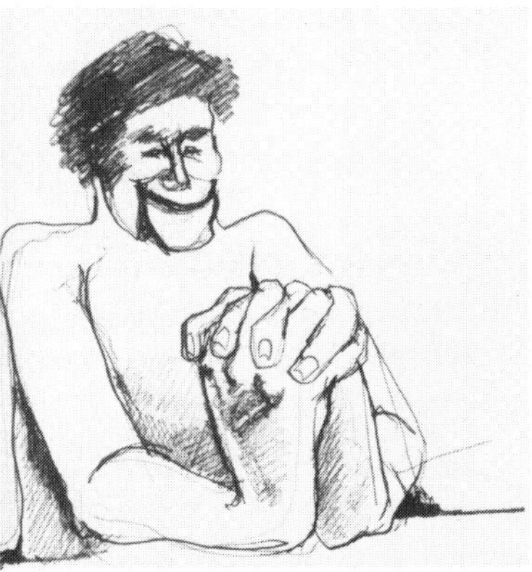

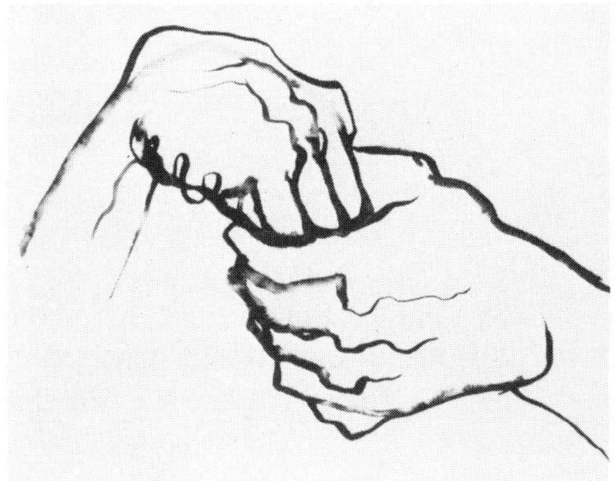

b.

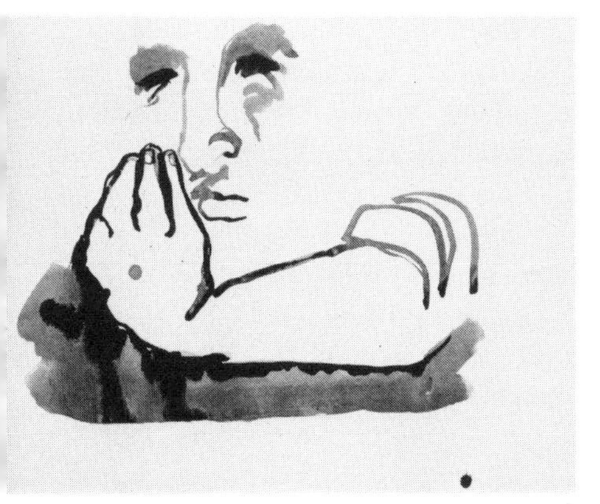

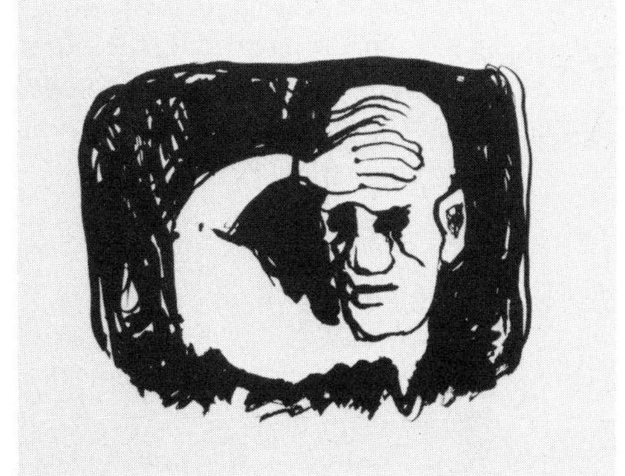

d.

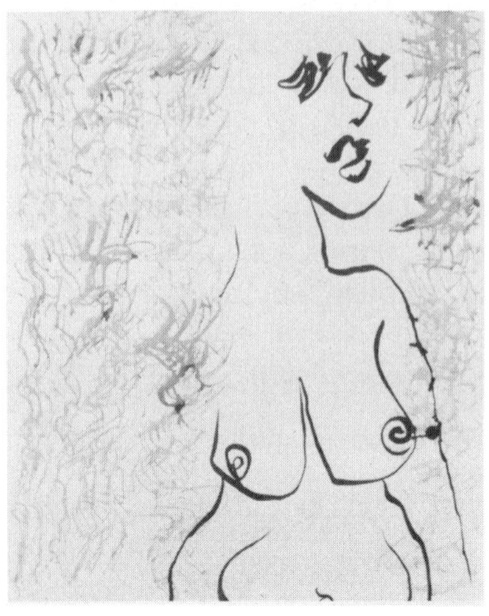

e.

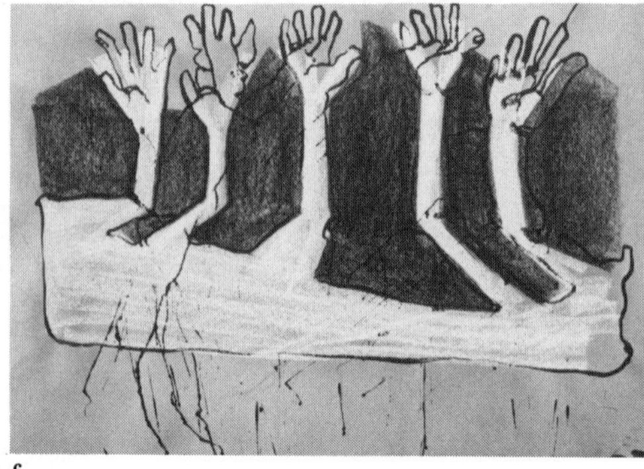

f.

Examples from Case Study III.
The Drawing Lab, Penn State

a. Constrained Expression.
b. Agony of the Deaf Artist.
c. Openning Out onto Understanding.
d. Looking for a Way Out.
e. Pregnant Hope.
f. Garden of Growth.

> I came to the realization of what was happening. As you remember, I mentioned how I told my students not to be afraid of mistakes. I found out that I was doing exactly the same thing...and with that realization, I worked from that time on to *make* mistakes...and it gives me a better insight of what was happening to the other students, too. It feels great to allow myself to make mistakes. The controlled approach is my feel of things, in a sense, you know. You grow up to this phase level where you're not supposed to be making more mistakes.

When asked who said she was not supposed to be making more mistakes, she laughingly replied: "*I* said." She adds: "*I see now that what you do is what you do, and you accept it.*" She then admists that she is not yet satisfied with this newly found freedom and that she will undoubtedly fall back on control, but a basic insight has nevertheless been won which makes her more congruent and more honest in both her work and teaching. In her own words: "I guess I am really concerned about changing my thinking on drawing and painting, *about how to make more mistakes and be myself.*" She speaks excitedly about her work in the Lab and her desire to provide others the same opportunity: "My experience here is such a joy that I feel tremendous. This is something that I have never experienced...and it never occurred to me that I should."[24]

The last example is about a psychotherapist who came as artist to the Drawing Lab. He is a good one to conclude this section with because this awareness of his own mental processes allowed him to verbalize feeling states usually inaccessible to conscious sharing. We get a graphic image of how he thinks in the following interview concerning work he had done at the end of his twentieth week in the lab. In this case he has worked in Maine, away from the Lab, but the Lab has gone with him:

> ...there was a certain eeriness about the whole thing
> ...like, this is just too big and too much [the Maine
> landscape and the ocean]. Who the hell am I to assume
> that I can capture any of this?

He then describes how he tried to do a pastel of a small inlet, with sheds, rocks, and boats:

> I *fought* with it...I don't know how else to describe it. I
> fought with it. It's not part of my body, it's something
> other, something "out there." The clash is "me-other." It
> is how much of "me" can be without disrupting the
> "what is." There is a sense that I am me and I'm part of
> what's happening here and I'm not as awed anymore.
> There's a real shift in awed-ness. I think: I can say back
> to it what I want to say. It's like: "Hey, I can lay on it
> some of my own stuff...and it didn't cry. It didn't cry!"
> You know? [laughing] It really didn't!

Another time he talks about self-actualization, boredom and self-limiting ideas and how these relate to his own work in the Lab and to his professional work as a therapist:

> I recall very vividly the day I said I was feeling bored.
> I was feeling at a plateau where I didn't experience
> anything new really happening inside me and I was
> feeling kind of dissatisfied. I was saying to myself:
> "What am I doing?" I wanted to see something else
> happening. I feel trapped by my own success. Now,
> what else is there that I am not allowing myself to ex-
> perience? It's kind of like in Maslow's sense, where *you
> create a tension for yourself to push yourself to try new
> things which are not demanded by the environment,
> but come from wanting to move beyond yourself,* to
> create new meanings, to give new meanings. I'm sure,
> too, that there is a very strong interplay between mood
> and cognition. I was reading some of Viktor Frankl's

original things about meaning, about meaning that doesn't come at you, but which you create for yourself...and when you do this you are dealing with existential structures. I mention this for I think I was coming to the place where meaning wasn't happening, and rather than sit around waiting for something to happen next, I began to pull something around me that would pique my interest, that would really involve me and pull me into it.

I was allowing the work I was doing to be in a very personal state, a very personal state of myself, *taking off from wherever I was, and just allowing the internal stimuli to be the primary focus.* Then there came the sense of attitudinal, almost cognitive realizing that I've said and done for the time being, most of what I thought was relevant about me. And *now I was being prodded by another voice in my own head—something was now saying to me that I didn't have to stay in my own head all of the time, in my own being.* In fact, there was a lot of tension there. In our discussions, I've talked a lot about play. I think the kind of intense analytic processing of one's own present history [referring to the Lab ritual of stimulated process recall] is still a very heavy kind of thing, a very "un-playful" thing, and I think there was a sense of: "Let's get some fresh air in here. Let's get out of this hermetically sealed world!"—that I was getting trapped in, and beginning to realize that the trap is one's own creation. There are obviously many other options that you can entertain.

What I also like is the breaking up of plateaus, of existentially probing the range of alternatives, choices, a sense of deciding, *not being just defined by your history at any given point in time, but rather using your history and going on.* After my period of boredom, there was decidedly a cognitive shift, out of my frustration, in the sense of breaking out and not just doing anything, not just "fun," "doodling," or enjoying the sense of movement. *The shift was a very heavy time for me in a way.*

You see, I define boredom as "in-here." Because there is no way in hell that you're going to be able to do anything about it if you put it "out-there." O.K.? That would be self-limiting. If that's as far as I can take it, I am doomed to feel that feeling. Let me put it another way. *If I identify boredom as my own feeling, this boredom is me here and now feeling it. Then I can do something about it.* But if I say I am bored because of this thing, then I am trapped. I am stuck.

I have control over changing my attitude. I can let myself try other things, to take different shots at the problem. Just as I could say that I am really disappointed in not technically capturing all the planes or whatever on my [Maine] picture of the boats, and I could hate myself for that attitude, but in hearing myself say that and then saying to myself, "Now wait a minute! Do I have to be caught up with that? Is that all that's here? Is that all that's possible?" *In a sense, I've got to kick myself into the future.* I've got to see that what I've captured in the boats is more than a technical rendering, *in that it opens out and leads me to so many new possibilities.* So with boredom, I can do something about that. *My self-limiting statement is followed by alternatives.* Do you understand what I mean by self-limiting? I mean in Ellis's sense, where you define it as if it were at the level of truth or belief, that is incontrovertible, and there is just no disputing. The important thing is that one must move beyond that and use it as a reasoning principle. It is not just that I am bored, I am boring, I am bound to be bored, I am a bored person, a boring person, and so on—where boredom almost and at times in fact does become an attribute of personality, rather than viewing boredom as one feeling among a whole set of feelings. And you can do something about these if you will open yourself to trying out some other options—like kicking yourself into the future.

You know, I was trying in that drawing to get the situation clear enough, through a kind of dispute or self-confrontive statement, a reasonable statement where I say: "*O.K. Things aren't too great right now, but it's not the end of the world, and I have some resources to make this world or this experiencing different.*" That's a kind of formula which you can plug most anything into, in that I have resources to do this or that. It is a positive optimistically oriented statement. It moves you into saying: "Yes, I am in charge of what I am feeling." And you begin feeling differently within that very process of experiencing. *You begin immediately to experience control over feeling,* if not in the external world, at least in the internal one, and as a consequence of the confrontation, there is often a shift in attitude, in cognitively looking at what's possible, a shift as a result of talking to oneself differently, of feeling oneself differently, and, in effect, acting differently in the world.

I was very aware of finally confronting myself and saying: "What the hell! There is no reason for me to experience boredom, except by my own hand. Now what am I going to do about it? I have the capabilities to go beyond what I am doing now. I know that I have sketched other things and have been very pleased about them in the past. What would it be like to try sketching some things now, differently?" *And I am very aware of cognitive statements that moved me toward where something might happen.*

If one gets boxed-in in their own work, and in my experience this happens very often, the boxing-in involves first a plateauing, and maybe frustration, and then they have got to have a regrouping of their sense of skills and capacities. There are any number of things that people have to present to themselves to get themselves off of first base, so to speak. And this means confronting a set of things or experiences. I find in the midst of therapy *something comes up where they can really see themselves doing something different, experiencing themselves differently.*

And there again, just yesterday, a person was saying that everything came together for her in the midst of an experience. I was just so aware of that person's potentiality for caring, for softness, for also being firm, you know, a whole range of hasslings which had been downing and dinning her, cracking her up, negatively self-limiting all over the place—and I tried to break that up and see her vision of the possible opening up. *The very critical thing is the way in which one makes statements about oneself.* The "bad" or "wrong" or "terrible" labels. The whole set of self-limiting statements which in the case of the client yesterday just began to melt away.

It was really like participating in making something creative happen—that is, it was an interplay of the situation and what one brings to it. *It is in a sense a convergence of a lot of skills, a lot of potential...all of which were there, just waiting to happen.* There is something very humbling about tapping into things that were already there, which were stifled, often suffocated. Events like this are very important phenomenologically—like, how does one see it and express it and experience it? How will they set it up? This is very potent, and *as one opens out the possibilities of seeing differently, the springs are renewed,* and that is really humbling.

But the point I want to get back to very rapidly is that I do have significance in the process. I couldn't do what I am doing, otherwise. I view therapy and education as an opportunity to speed up, through my facilitation, a process that may well occur later in time, under different events and conditions. It may well not happen either. People must make it happen for themselves, really, and I am participating in that process, taking the position of alter-ego, *the self juxtaposed to the self in a never-ending awareness of not getting boxed into a system. I am participating in something that is possible but hasn't had a chance to happen yet.*[25]

In this last statement, the artist conveniently summed up a basic concept for therapy in and through art as it works toward the unfolding of consciousness.

Method of Expressive Therapy.

The very word *method* takes on the connotation of technique, of step-by-step means-end control, but:

> ...technique is a somewhat misleading term to apply to
> the various psycho-perceptive methods used. It sug-
> gests a more or less automatic functioning. Actually
> the constructive technique is in the main a matter of at-
> titude. This is not to suggest that the methods
> employed are in any sense unimportant. On the con-
> trary, for most people they are indispensable. But
> unless the basic attitude behind them is right, they will
> not work.[26]

We have tried to set forth the basic attitude which a
sharer/witness/therapist must bring to therapy in and
through art. We have also commented earlier on Jung's
hermeneutic method where he extends the dreams or symbolic works of his clients into myth and other symbolic
material in an effort to prompt their imaginations to insight
and interpretation. We have also engaged in selective processes—such as the historic tracing of an artist's self-
conceptualizations on making art; and such as the S-E Model,
which examines *clash* statements and events which lead the
artist from conflict to resolution—which reduce a mass of
material so that it can yield up its insights and potential for
guidance. What aids in interpretation can aid in therapy, for
both processes attempt to understand what lies *hidden,
distorted, misunderstood.* The conscious utilization of the
hermeneutic cycle of the art of qualitative thinking follows,
we feel, most closely the self-formative process hidden within
the art process itself, just as it echoes the famous
hermeneutic formula: experience, expression, understanding—and we have added renewal of experiencing-expressing
and application to changing one's life.

Attitude and belief are implicated in this work over technique and method. The therapist's long dialogue in our example does, however, suggest an old principle: *luck favors the
trained hand.* In that sense the search for method again provides the *theory* that can give way to *imagination* and eventually to *intuition.* Certainly, if belief is implicated in the interpretation of an expressive text, how much more is it implicated in intuitively understanding an expressive-text
which "hasn't had a chance to happen yet."

We find then the same irony in considering *method* that
Gadamer unfolds in his book on hermeneutic philosophy,
Truth and Method,[27] for truth in hermeneutics, despite the
clarity of its cyclic path as we have extended it in an art of
qualitative thinking, evades the methodic man. "Method,

Method," said Jules Laforgue, "what do you want from me?/You know that I have eaten of the fruits of the subconscious."[28] The artistic imagination, having eaten of those same fruits, will not submit well to even so-called *hermeneutic method.*

We have sufficient guidance through our efforts to define an art of qualitative thinking which has much of the clarity of the steps in other esoteric spiritual sciences, and in the valuable experience in the Drawing Lab which has defined the special role of the therapist. We repeat, the process is first of all laid down *within art itself* and *within the workings of the creative imagination.* We have merely bound together what was already there toward expressive therapy.

Developmental Levels in Expressive Therapy

As in our discussion of method, so here the emphasis runs against categorizing into levels where expressive therapy is concerned. The levels of most concern in our perspective are those of the expansive cycle of the creative imagination at work. "The problem...is not to examine men, but images. And the only images that can be examined phenomenologically are transmissiable ones; they are those we receive in a successful transmission."[29] Thus both artist and therapist begin by facing the work. Sharing the artist's creating stream of consciousness helps the therapist sharpen his or her vision to be receptive to the widest range of "transmissable images."

We focus on *what changes in the art,* for it is there that changes in consciousness are revealed – and revealed often *before* the artist has explored their meaning reflectively. We cannot therefore say that attitude shift precedes change, for it works the other way around as well. Sometimes the change follows a pervasive broadening of attitude, as in the sessions preceding Larry's shift from his hang-up on realism and technical control as preconditions for feeling and expression. As often happens in other forms of therapy as well, blocking, conflict, or depression precedes a significant change in one's art. But the unexpected feel of a single brush stroke can also stop time, usher in "a different reality" and "a religious experience." The courage to change can follow despair or exhuberance. It can seem almost predictable or be set off by what appears to be a trivial incident or seem to have no obvious antecedent whatsoever. Historically seen, a weak causality—or at least a *structure* to the *existentiality*—is discernible. But as lived forward in creation, causative and motivational factors recede, and the sudden and spontaneous emergence of vision takes precedence over will. Then a phenomenology in touch with what unfolds must proceed by way of a "theory of the incident."

"An artist," said Jean Lescure, "does not create the way he lives, he lives the way he creates."[30] But there is no need to take sides. We can hold to an inclusive definition of art, not a narrowly aesthetic one, and still turn first toward the work and the making of the work, taking our departure from the view: "The image is formed in the words which dream it."[31] We do not wish in therapy in and through art to psychologize or "explain" the artist, but to understand and follow the artist's evolutionary path. *For while art does not evolve, artists do. They evolve in and through their art.* We agree with Bachelard:

> Doctrines that are timidly causal, such as psychology, or strongly causal, such as psychoanalysis, can hardly determine the ontology of what is poetic. For nothing prepares a poetic image, especially not culture, in the literary sense, and especially not perception, in the psychological sense.[32]

It is the ontology of what is poetic and artistic that opens the potential for consciousness to expand through that which is radically other than the artist. Whatever dim antecedents there may be are best intuited functionally through the ongoing work and dialogues close to the creating artist's stream of consciousness. No prior case histories, no diagnoses are necessary. In fact they are injurious unless they are considered as hypotheses to be disconformed—as prejudices that drop away as we come to understanding. The series of works and the intensive dialogues related to them are active definers of clash, transcendence and transformation. Changes are traceable in the art and in the thought of the artist in relation to the art.

Comparatives are of little use in this therapy. True, there is a *lawfulness* to the evolution of each single artist, but that is like the thread of an artistic *telos*, a superordinate artistic myth of the particular path. "Comparison of inspired poets would soon make us lose sight of inspiration. Any comparison diminishes the expressive qualities of the terms of the comparison."[33]

In short, developmental levels in this therapy are those of the developing individual, determined through the way they are revealed in the work itself, not in general categories. The horizontal character and extension of art is capable of exposing the positive shift in consciousness of individuals on all levels of theorized hierarchies of consciousness. As a love-gnosis, *the way of art is not that of the royal road, not that of step by step according to clear stages and definite practices. Art is the democratizing magnanimity of Spirit. Spirit is artist, and as artist Spirit visits us all. Its manifestation, wherever, is our concern. Through that we serve the common good and the general evolution of humankind.* The step-by-step paths of the spiritual sciences have a masculine ring about them, while the creative imagination is under the *anima, the archetype of creation.* This horizontal vagueness, this patience and receptivity to enthusiasm is anathema to system builders. "The purest intelligence," said the poet William Carlos Williams, "can never become official. Either the power is lacking to the ability or the ability is lacking to the power."[34] In that sense art seems erratic and powerless, and certainly is suspect to the official, but it is the readiest means for the visitations of spirit to become manifest for our guidance.

Our training and our successes do not set us forward. Art cannot be taught, must be learned all at once, always from the beginning.[35] Art is a concrete discipline in unknowing. It works through a hidden order and through the things themselves. Although the artist's works give

> evidence of wide culture and knowledge of all the dynamic expressions of space, they are not applied, they are not made into recipes...Knowing must therefore be accompanied by an equal capacity to forget knowing. Non-knowing is not a form of ignorance but a difficult transcendence of knowledge. This is the price that must be paid for an oeuvre to be, at all times, a sort of pure beginning, which makes its creation an exercise in freedom.[36]

Therapy in and through art takes on the witnessing and nurturance of this delicate process, content to know that wherever it is encouraged spirit is becoming present and consciousness is evolving. *The therapist must be an artist in a continuing movement of evolving consciousness permitting him or her to enter into this nurturant, witnessing, admiring, believing relationship, for it is sure to test the therapist just as much as the artist.*

Reference

1. Van Dusen, W. Wu wei, no-mind, and the fertile void in psychotherapy. In Welwood, J. (ed.) *The meeting of the ways.* N.Y.: Schocken Books, 1979, p. 221.

2. Chogyam Trungpa. A dialogue with psychotherapists. In Welwood, J. (ed.) *op. cit.*, reference 1 above, p. 193.

3. Anonymous student reverie. Beginning pottery course taught by K. Beittel, The Pennsylvania State University, Spring, 1982.

4. Suzuki, S. *Zen mind, beginner's mind.* N.Y.: Weatherhill, 1970.

5. Beittel, K. *Zen and the art of pottery.* Tokyo: John Weatherhill, 1989; p. 127.

6. Whitman, W. *Complete prose works.* Section on Democratic vistas. Philadelphia: David McKay, 1892; p. 215.

7. Bachelard, G. *The poetics of reverie.* (D. Russell, trans.) Boston: Beacon Press, 1971; p. 175.

8. Chogyam Trungpa. *Meditation in action.* Berkeley: Shambala, 1970; pp. 28-29.

9. Rilke, R. M. *Lettres.* Paris: Stock; p. 167.

10. Sullivan, J. W. N. *Beethovan.* London: Penguin Books, 1949.

11. Beittel, K. R. *Alternatives for art education research.* Dubuque, Iowa: William C. Brown, 1973; p. 62.

12. Novosel, J. The structural existentiality of arting: Inquiry into the nature of the creative process. Unpublished Ph.D. thesis, The Pennsylvania State University, 1976; p. 155.

13. Swami Rama, Ballentine, R. and Swami Ajaya. *Yoga and psychotherapy.* Glenview, Ill.: Himalayan Institute, 1976; p. 283.

14. Chogyam Trungpa. *Op. cit.*, reference 2 above, p. 193.

15. Wilber, K. *The Atman project.* Wheaton, Ill.: The Theosophical Publishing House, 1980; p. 168.

16. Bachelard, G. *The poetics of space.* (M. Jolas, trans.) Boston: Beacon Press, 1969; p. xxix.

17. Beittel, K. R. *Mind and context in the art of drawing.* N. Y.: Holt, Rinehart and Winston, 1972.

18. Novosel-Beittel, J. Where the desirable becomes existential. Annual *Journal*, Canadian Society for Education Through Art, 9, 1979, 40-44; pp. 43-44.

19. Naranjo, C. *The one quest.* N.Y.: Ballantine Books, 1972; p. 115.

20. Novosel-Beittel, J. *Op. cit.*, reference 18 above.

21. Rogers, C. R. *Learning to be free.* In S. M. Farber and R. H. L. Wilson (eds.). *Conflict and creativity.* N.Y.: McGraw-Hill, 1963; p. 275.

22. Ott, H. Hermeneutics and personhood. In *Interpretation: The poetry of meaning*. N.Y.: Harcourt, Brace & World, 1967.

23. Novosel, J. *Op. cit.*, reference 12 above, pp. 223-238.

24. *Ibid.*, pp. 238-268.

25. *Ibid.*, pp. 423-454.

26. Martin, P. W. *Experiment in depth: A study of the work of Jung, Eliot and Toynbee*. London: Routledge and Kegan Paul, 1955.

27. Gadamer, H-G. *Truth and method*. N.Y.: The Seabury Press, 1975.

28. Bachelard, G. *Op. cit.*, reference 7 above, p. 1.

29. Bachelard, G. *Op. cit.*, reference 16 above, p. 174.

30. Lescure, J. *Lapicque*. Paris: Galanis, p. 78 (quoted in Bachelard, *op. cit.*, reference 16 above, p. xxix).

31. Bachelard, G. *Op. cit.*, reference 7 above, p. 187 (quote is of E. Jabes).

32. Bachelard, G. *Op. cit.*, reference 16 above, p. xx.

33. Bachelard, G. *Op. cit.*, reference 7 above, pp. 6-7.

34. Williams, W. C. *The embodiment of knowledge*. N.Y.: New Directions Paperbooks, 1977; p. 114.

35. Beittel, K. R. Perceptions of the artist about the affective domain. In Berman, L. M. and Roderick, J. A. (Eds.) *Feeling, valuing, and the art of growing: Insight into the affective*. Washington: Association for Supervision and Curriculum Development, 1977 Yearbook; pp. 111-126.

36. Lescure, J. *Op. cit.*, reference 30 above, p. 78 (quoted in Bachelard, *op. cit.*, reference 16 above, pp. xxviii-xxix).

12

Educating for Higher Consciousness

You know, Ken, art education
is about spirit, what else?

Viktor Lowenfeld

To participate in the relationship of artist-to-other in-
volving physical media and metaphysical reality is to
humble and fill with awe one who would help artists
dream myths onward.

J. Novosel[1]

Inside the creative imagination, spirit and matter co-
mingle like the dance of elemental energies. Evolutionary change and higher consciousness are the
natural fruits of practicing art as an open and joyful
self-formative process.

Ken Beittel

What is really needed now is *passion* — and lots of it. All
I can offer you is just an invitation to the dance... it's
your choice to accept it or not. But some of you need to
question your assumptions about what you *believe* is
aesthetic and explore deeply your feelings of what is
ecstatic. I'd like you to *feel now, really feel* with every
cell of your being the bodily sense of happiness, the
most wonderful and delicious feelings you can
imagine... what really turns you on and makes you feel
so good and *so* alive. Stay with this and focus on what's
happening in your body. This will open you up
energetically to the creative process and enhance your
life in extremely exciting and powerful ways. You've
got to get out of your heads, for you all *know* it don't
mean a thing if it ain't got that swing. *To make art is a
great adventure...live it with passion.*

Joan Novosel-Beittel[2]

The Ground of Educating

Though the relationships between art and consciousness are vast, there is one point that stands forth from all others: the creative imagination demands absolute freedom as its birthright. Alone free in a world of limitations and contingencies, the imagination ignores all boundaries. Its desire is to burst through all thought forms, all fears, and all self-limiting beliefs. It knows that to do otherwise is to be swamped by thoughts and systems not of one's own making—to be enslaved.

I believe that we have all come to this earth plane as spirits inhabiting a body, and as such we are all inspirited by the great mystery, by the Divine. And a spark of that divinity is in us all. I see the divine as the Great Creator—the most famous Artist of all. Since we are direct descendents, we have inherent powers of creativity—inherited powers to create. We are co-creators of our lives, our years here, our days—each moment of our time-space on this planet. And in that sense, we are all evolving toward higher consciousness. Even if we suffer involution—a decline on the scale of consciousness—that decline itself eventually serves our evolution, for spirit is everywhere on the great chain of being, and all experience brings with it some learning, seen from the highest level. There is no way down that is not part of the whole process up.

It then appears that we'll be evolved somehow, sometime, even if we choose not to create and evolve now—so why not now? We have the choice. That is the artist's way, and that is the only way in the art of life: to create moment by moment the absolute uniqueness of our individual days. Our body is an instrumentality granting us the *choice* to do things. That choice is miraculously ours. The great mystery gives us the capacity to create our world anew with each new thought.

That's what the Drawing Lab was really about. When we put art back squarely into the hands of the artist, the choice to be, to create, to change, to step by step unfetter the imagination came automatically. We did not know that we had set up conditions that were a microcosm of the great plan that gives us all our ultimate evolutionary freedom: the ability to be co-creators of the universe.

The major insights from the Drawing Lab are all related to the privotal point of our universal freedom to create and how that freedom, once it leads to action, educates us for higher consciousness. The art of qualitative thinking flows naturally from this center as a method to allow consciousness to become conscious of itself through its creations so it can evolve.

The reciprocity between freedom and nurturance sets the stage for this evolutionary drama. There were only three rules: participating artists could not harm themselves, the researchers, or the environment. Everything else was wide open. The choices and decisions were completely theirs. This nurturant setting become a place for imaginative desires that were looking for a place to happen — where the desirable could indeed become existential. We did not have to chant "OM" or set up special practices, for the freedom to choose and act set a tone, a climate for artistic freedom that demonstrated again and again that art means to be an esoteric spiritual discipline available to *all*.

We found that for us to share the creative act with another we had to become co-creators. In accepting the willingness to allow the other to be we had to set aside our egos sufficiently to listen. We had to suspend all disbelief toward both the artist and the art that person was making.

As we observed and felt that *every thought and every action* had weight in the creation of a person's reality, we developed a sense of awe and wonder at the lawfulness of each person's special evolution. *We provided no answers.* Instead we held up a mirror in the form of time-lapse in-process feedback of the artist's own creative acts. *The self got reflected back to the self.* The small self made contact with the larger self. Self-limiting thoughts could be *safely* examined. Once artists saw how core beliefs were limiting them, they could accept them where no judgments were imposed. They could relax and even feel good about them. They could act and change. They could begin to take pleasure in whatever they did. It was O.K. to feel that your art is wonderful.

There was tremendous motivational power in the pleasure artists felt in changing their approach. In the Drawing Lab it became pleasureable to take a lot of risks and to make big changes. If an artist felt it absolutely necessary to work in a proper stage by stage realistic manner and then found it possible *to play with that belief*, great energy and enthusiasm typically followed. If an artist felt there should be no mistakes whatever in procedure, the ability to risk and to set out *to deliberately make mistakes* brought great release with it.

The outcome was not what counted. What counted was the expansion of consciousness that came with the pleasure of relaxing boundaries and inhibitions. A success loop was often established as artists became clearer on what they really wanted, felt safe to take action, reflected on the results, and then went on to appropriate changes and new actions. By opening up their *core beliefs* more and more of their creative potential was engaged in those new actions. And the success of these actions, however partial they may have seemed, further questioned the basic core beliefs, releasing still further potential, and so on. In this sense creative visualization of desired outcomes is a natural part of constant engagement in art processes. And when to this foundation is added the open future of all art processes creatively engaged in, our expanding consciousness is almost assured. *The hidden order of art parallels the hidden order of our own evolution. Image work is indeed self work.* Creative art is a self-formative process under these conditions.

So it is that we claim that the method of the Drawing Lab and the method of the art of qualitative thinking that grew out of it constitute an extremely powerful foundation for educating toward higher consciousness through art. Taken together, these mirror the self-formative nature of the creative process for the artist. Taken more broadly, they mirror an education toward higher consciousness that can operate in any free and nurturant setting where the creative actions of participants are the total focus. It need not be in art. But art is a privileged path because of the limitless freedom it demands for the creative imagination and *because expressions result in tangible form for self-reflections.*

Still further, when creative and tangible outcomes persist through time, our evolutionary path, the parabalic curve of our spiritual destiny, becomes strongly implicated. The imagination then projects no limit to what we can become, if we so choose and act according to the faith and intuition that can take us there step by step.

It was the desire to move closer to the artist's creating stream of consciousness that led to the Drawing Lab. It had become obvious to me that this could only occur through the privileged access granted the artist. But artists do not know what they do through introspection, nor even through general recall. It seemed necessary to watch that stream *in action, in choices along the way to creation,* and to record the outer signs of that stream so that recall could be relived in terms of those actions and choices, not just thoughts, beliefs, and intentions only. In taking that step, *I unknowingly stepped within the stream itself.* More than that, I got carried along with it. So when recall was stimulated by a replay of the time-lapse records of action, the stream was recreated jointly by the artist and me, whether I intended to do so or not. For the stream remained a mystery for artist and me alike.

The metaphor is apt. Walk deep within a woods with me, on beyond the pines, down past the hemlocks, and on the other side of the rhododendrons to where a mountain stream clear as the upper air takes its musical path onwards. See how it circles almost back on itself, forming a miniature island here, a quiet deep pool under the shade of the high bank there. Feel peace as Renoir-like sun circles illumine woods and stream in the most delightful random fashion. Smell the deep moss-green, blue-green, Hooker's-green mingled sweet scents of water and forest floor. Hear the tintinabulation of a thousand water bells, never repeating a rhythm or harmonic. See the signs of other living creatures—perhaps a bone, a feather, a footprint. Perhaps hear the haunting solo song of a hidden woodthrush that suddenly overpowers even all this richness.

Find the right spot, your spot, your *power spot*, to sit by this stream. Allow the world to stop and just be. No need to strain for cosmic consciousness. *Let go of everything.* Then everything around you in all seven directions can come forward on its own: north, south, east, west, above, below, and within. Everything within your universe—the universe—is there. Be in touch with it. Feel how silly it is to speak about it; how little need there is. But playfully a line, a metaphor, an image may come to you as a gift. All consciousness is there. *All is possible.*

This is a metaphor for a metaphor. *The artist's creating stream of consciousness is like that pure mountain stream deep within the sun-spotted sweet-smelling woods. You must quiet yourself to sense the universe there. In that one stream is the link with all streams, the great river and the unbounded ocean of consciousness itself.*

To educate for higher consciousness is a great privilege. To nurture the absolute freedom of the creative imagination *is a sacred calling.* To follow the stream of expanding consciousness brings exhileration and joy for student and teacher alike.

Disciplined Spontaneity

The metaphor of the mountain stream has still other dimensions to it. It suggests the infinite richness and expansiveness of the creating stream of consciousness and of all consciousness. In our approach to it, however, we also encumbered *discipline* and *exclusivity of will and attention*. These were also apparent in the Drawing Lab, and they are central to our notion of art as an esoteric spirtual discipline leading to higher consciousness.

Art Power

Take *any* experience, anything singled out of the flux of being that constitutes consciousness in daily life. The experience singled out can be inner or outer, real or imagined. What matters is that that experience becomes your *exclusive* concentration. Savor it. Play with it. Hold it in your hand, close to your eyes, close to your nose. Now impose silence on all else and commit your full attention to it.

Already that experience shows itself in its illimitable meanings, in its individuality and uniqueness—like nothing else that ever was or will be. Images and feelings and thoughts constellate automatically around it. If you relax sufficiently, letting it go so that it can be, it will come forth on its own to guide you to expression. That's the secret of Ponge turning the pebble over and over in his hand. That's the secret of thinking only "clay" while you're kneading it for the wheel. *A guiding image comes forth as though self-empowered.*

If then the same exclusive concentration is transferred to the pen or brush in hand, to the medium and tool, the same guidance appears. In this sense we are all *channels* for the free becoming of art. True, practice helps in these matters, but it is not enough on its own.

The power I am speaking of would be equally apparent if you singled out one grape from a bunch of grapes, if you examined it, felt it, smelled it, saw it against the light—if you dwelled with it in an extended qualitative present with no concept whatsoever of clock time. Then if you were to eat it, you would find it to be the most phenomenal taste experience you ever had.

The artist within us knows this kind of concentration of the total body-mind intuitively. The ways of the artist, like the "laws of God," are written on our inward parts. They only need to be awakened under the right circumstances. The sleeping artist within us is like the magical child within us – always there whether our conscious mind acknowledges it or not.

Can this special education occur without special teachers and special circumstances? Can motivation, confidence, love and passion develop without these? To envision an education for higher consciousness we must envision an inspired teacher, one who is in spirit, inspirited. We need a whole person who can move and act with radiance and magnetism – one who can inspire people of all ages. That person will have to be in love with self, with subject, with others, and with the universe. The happier, more evolved, more nurturing, more satisfied – in the Taoist sense of being an integral part of all that is, that comes and goes – the better. Instead of hanging on to all the negative conditioning we all inherit as part of our earth walk, such a teacher moves continuously toward the positivity of unstoppable confidence, feeling totally loved, and exudes humor, happiness, and joy.

Such teachers will speak with the body, not just with the head. The heart and the spirit will manifest in spontansity, playfulness, in mastery and discipline. Disciplined spontaneity exists in teaching as well as in decorating pots. The original discipline and training of such teachers must be superceded, so that they are able to take the very basics of their discipline back to origins in our common needs and our common humanity.

Students usually come with a desire to learn. Where that has been damped, it needs to be rekindled by contact with teachers who serve as exemplars and models. Modelling is an art that's been around for ages but is just now coming into its own. It says: anything another human being has learned I can learn by paying sufficient attention to the specific process involved. Where desire exists or has been rekindled, an organic matching up of natural aptitude with that desire lets learning unfold exuberantly and spontaneously.

In terms of the total educative process, we greatly need to hold firmly to a vision that educates body, mind, and spirit simultaneously. A strong physical basis does this best, starting at an early age with music, dance, pottery, carpentry, martial arts, nature skills, swimming, cooking and hiking, for example. These should be combined in a way that follows the child's interests and aptitude to provide the richest learning experience possible. Poetry needs to be balanced out by carpentry, voice training with nature skills, violin-practice with the martial arts so that each child's natural inclinations are not only encouraged but also expanded and deepened. Also areas where a child appears less skilled need to be taken into account in educating for wholeness so that a child not physically inclined is nevertheless given opportunity to participate in some individual sport, for example, where she or he can feel good. The opposite is equally true for the physically endowed child, who may need the balance of music, art, or dance. To be sure, the very notion of a truly well-balanced person is often an abstract ideal. Excellence in any area usually occurs only where there is extreme commitment, passion and concentration — and to the average person these may well seem like an imbalance. Whatever choices are made they are in the spirit of assisting the child in confidence in being and doing — as well as in daring — and to cultivate an art of appreciation for the gift of life and for all living things, so that gratitude is spontaneously expressed for the unique opportunities of each new day.

Contemporary culture conspires to rob many of us of powers and capacities we had naturally as children. It's interesting that no baby ever needs to be taught to breathe diaphragmatically. Babies can cry powerfully loud and clear all night long on the same note and not hurt their throats. Yet not one out of a hundred children gets reinforced for using the breath and the voice in natural and intuitive ways.

Life educating should take into account the healing power of color, light and sound. Children know about these intuitively and if they are raised in nurturant environments where these natural forces are honored for all their health-giving benefits, then they will not forget them as they get older.

The same is equally true of energy. Through breath, movement, live food, and play — as well as color, light, and sound — it is possible to learn to preserve and master the seemingly inexhaustable supply of energy available from the universe. We can learn, wherever we are, to pay careful attention to energies in ourselves, in those around us, and in the environment, rather than focusing on the *content* of what is said or the external emotions that often come in on us. Many sages have said: "Pay attention *only* to the energy — nothing else." In like manner, if we could really see that the ingestion of dead or over-processed food actually burdened the body, *requiring more energy to digest than it gave us,* then we would organically and naturally turn toward life-giving nourishment.

The connection between breath and energy is so well established that it is astounding that it has not been more central in early education. Overstimulation from sugar, soda pop, and junk foods, as well as from the media with their emotional and pychic manipulative intent—these first affect the breath, then the emotions and energy.

The primary connection to the earth is as basic a need as that of breath and energy. All of these are *constantly* interacting. We are meant to *feel* and *be aware* of the *power* and *presence* of the rain, the sun, the moon, the tides, the wind—*all the great natural forces.* American Indians and Chinese Taoists can teach much about the fundamental relationship with the earth and with all its panoramic changes. If you are really in tune with these, all the artificial enticements can't get in. They are just too pale by comparison.

Children are natural healers, for they are in touch with primal energies and are open to feeling. They can easily learn how to heal a cut or to soothe a pain. They can also take care of animals beautifully.

We are just beginning to learn how the mind and its total orientation can heal or destroy the body. Those who have worked at reversing the ravages of our most feared diseases say that the first thing most sufferers need is self-acceptance and self-love— *totally and unconditionally.*

Children need to know how their bodies function in relation to various common foods, especially readily available commercial fast foods. They need to become aware, for example, of the common behavioral mood swings associated with sugar ingestion.

One of the biggest problems in education is a lack of dream time. Everything is programmed, on-schedule according to clock time. Children know the magic of snowflakes and the excitement of the sunrise. At a very fundamental level they are in touch with natural elements and cycles. For the health of the creative imagination and of the whole body-mind, it is essential to keep these innate poetic capacities alive.

The greatest mastery that any education can give is represented in our theme: how discipline in and through art according to the absolute freedom of the creative imagination—all the while loving oneself and finding joy in one's expressions—is an education toward higher consciousness. Through this commitment, healing and unification of body-mind-spirit are available to everyone.

Such disciplines as here envisioned teach one great lesson: *how to control and direct our minds and emotions so there is harmony between us and the unimpeded energies of the universe.* The cutting edge of mind/brain research reveals how we already direct our thoughts and emotions—often mostly through unconscious conditioning and social inhibition— and how we are all really doing as well as we can but are stuck in loops without *sufficient choices.* It now appears that the same brain cues that unconsciously limit choices can be used to open up, expand, and unlimit—to go completely in the other direction by will and by choice. Where there are plenty of choices, where people are happy about themselves and having lots of fun, there is no room for negativity and depression.

It is possible that we can control our internal representations and therefore our behaviors using the same brain that seems to limit us. For example, we can personally orchestrate and control certain internal sounds so that we feel inspired, confident, motivated, and loved. A very powerful and humorous therapist recently said, in referring to the drabness of most people's internal auditory representations: "I don't need no big thing on my shoulder...but at least those people are trying!" The point of all this is to raise the important goals of controlling and directing energy, of self-direction, and of becoming masters of love, happiness and gratitude.

For discipline, whatever the student engages in needs to be done daily, naturally, ritually, and communally. Some form of meditation—active and passive—balances and centers disciplined activity. We need centering and quieting as part of the rhythm of life, and we need the Zen of the simple act which brings the fullest attention and joy to even washing the dishes. All disciplines, at bottom, need to be disciplines in our own well-being and in that of our planet.

Since we are social persons, the communal aspect is vitally needed. Early on we need to know more than one language. We also need to serve others as ourselves and to serve and conserve our sacred planet. We are all like great chefs, seasoning with salt and pepper the good soup of life.

It is important that what we have called the art of qualitative thinking be assimilated and internalized as a natural discipline toward self-formation into expanded consciousness. But even beyond that it is important to underscore how this manifests: as the Springtime of spontaneous ever-renewing expression, welling up like sap into the early buds for contantly new flowering.

Passion! Living with passion! *That is the vital ingredient!* Not an angry voice yelling from your subconscious at 7:55 a.m.: "Get to work!" But jumping out of bed at 6 a.m. because you can't wait to get started! That is the greatness of the beginner's mind. *That is the daily art of living that is like the daily cycle of the sun.*

The absolute freedom of the creative imagination cannot be nutured without discipline. Here the various traditions within art provide a ready basis, but only insofar as they do not become ends in themselves in the traditional or professional sense. Professional artists also, as we learned in the Drawing Lab, equally with beginners need nurturance permitting exploration of higher consciousness. The various art disciplines like pottery or painting are indeed consummatory experiences, ends and not merely means towards some other end. But they stand within the purposes of this chapter much as the local traditions of pottery stand within a great planetary tradition that is only emergent at present.

Educating for higher consciousness and practicing an artistic discipline are symbiotically intertwined. There is no pure or content-free education for higher consciousness. There is no pure artistic discipline serving the absolute freedom of the creative imagination that fails to take the education of higher consciousness into account. *Immersion in both is wanted, then discipline and spontaneity go hand in hand.* Then the creating stream of consciousness serves the evolution of consciousness in general. Then one stroke of the pen can be more daring than flying your private helicopter over a live volcano in Hawaii.

Spontaneity practiced within a discipline is like change within the context of expected sameness. The heroic, the novel, the playful, the highly idiosyncratic — all gain meaning against the common contextual ground *against which* they appear. Change can then occur suddenly, through the clash of opposites, through intrusive novelty, or even through chance or accident. The idea that change must be slow or even painful, that it can emerge only after reliving and catharsis, was *not* upheld in the Drawing Lab. *Change occurred in all the forms possible:* sometimes slowly and even somewhat painfully, but more often suddenly, unexpectedly, without clear steps and progressions. After the fact, understanding can always find ways to rationalize and assimilate what has come about as change. And change always provided an education toward higher consciousness.

Again, it is best to return to our metaphor of the stream. Artist and nurturer or researcher or teacher can only follow the mystery of that stream with humor, compassion and wonder. It has its own course within its own unique terrain and with its own particular destiny.

Of Directions, Cycles and Seasons

The risk and the change that occur when more and more of the self's potential is opened to the absolute freedom of the creative imagination are like so many shamanic deaths preceding re-membering of the spirit's purpose in the body. Various versions of the native American and South American medicine wheel add further insights to our quest for an education for higher consciousness through art. Here I wish to liken the stages of the art of qualitative thinking to the directions of the medicine wheel and to the cycle of the seasons.

But first, let me say that the art of qualitative thinking itself will doubtlessly undergo changes as it is directed toward education for higher consciousness. The word *thinking* — even *qualitative thinking* — most likely will merge with harmonious feeling. *The heart of the mind will gradually shift to the mind of the heart,* for no longer do intuition, spontaneity, and right action need to be in opposition to thought.

Because the unified body-mind is ruled by the heart center and is integral with in-dwelling spirit, it easily acquires wings for the highest flights of the creative imagination. Body-mind-spirit, subconscious-conscious-superconscious are one in that flight.

The four stages of the art of qualitative thinking — expressing, distancing, interpreting, renewing — find their metaphoric parallels in what follows. These parallels have behind them the intent to enlarge as far as possible the meanings of these stages for educating for higher consciousness through art.

Expressing is like the full flowering of being in *midsummer.* On the medicine wheel it is the *north,* ruled by the *horse*, by spiritual strength. Distancing is like the fruitful *autumn* when meaning is first harvested. It is the *south*, the *snake*, the autobiographical self that is preparing to shed its skin again. *Interpreting* is *mid-winter* where quiet detachment allows understanding to come forward. But on the medicine wheel it is the *west*, the sunset, ruled by the *black panther* of death. *Renewing* is the exuberant energy and pure joy of *spring*. It is the *east*, the sunrise, the *eagle* capable of the highest flights of imagination and inspiration.

But take one last look at the *black panther* of the *west*. In shamanic lore to face the black panther of the west is to face death itself, fear itself, in its biggest form and in all the forms present in our daily lives. Once that fear is faced, the black panther lies down and can be crossed over to the other side. The black panther miraculously transforms into a rainbow bridge to higher realms.

Facing the fears, the self limitations, the restricting core beliefs that we bring to the creative process, changes the black panther into a rainbow bridge. The infinite colors on the artist's palette play out the full range of the spectrum of consciousness. Their curving arc of energy forms a rainbow bridge to higher consciousness. It is always there, inviting us to cross over and bring into our art and lives more and more of the absolute freedom of the creative imagination. If black panthers come, can eagles be far behind?

References

1. Novosel, J. The structural existentiality of arting: Inquiry into the nature of the creative process. Unpublished Ph.D. thesis, The Pennsylvania State Unversity, 1976; p. 321.

2. Beittel, J. Statement made in a gallery talk given at a West Virginia Art Education Association Conference, Marshall University.

13

Celebration and Thanksgiving: The Dancing Butterfly

Ho! This is good. Thank you
Great Spirit.

Sun Bear

deep most dark of forest night
it's morning, come.
center flame of light moon
fevers cool.
Born dawn drops dew gently now
and I smile with the sun
    ont of the wilderness of my mind

Joan Novosel[1]

new wine
no bottles
how absurd
let us rejoice

Joan Novosel[2]

The butterfly counts not months
    but moments
and has time enough.

Rabindranath Tagore[3]

"Gerry, Gerry — we are *alive* Gerry. . ."

J. Novosel[4]

I am the necessary angel of earth,
Since, in my sight, you see the earth again.

Wallace Stevens[5]

An aimless joy is a pure joy

. . . .

And wisdom is a butterfly
and not a gloomy bird of prey.

W. B. Yeats[6]

But only the dance is sure!
make it your own.
Who can tell
What is to come of it?

William Carlos Williams[7]

All streams flow on. This book too is a stream. If you follow it now you will see that it has taken a turn into a different landscape.

Here the air is heavy with the fragrance of wild roses. You can feel the warmth and hear the sounds—the bee-loud hum of the fertile earth, the song sparrows, the wind on the shiny new aspen leaves.

This is the state of mind I'm in while writing this now. The dancing butterfly is in mid-air and there is no longer any need for explanations.

Once all the concepts quiet down, I am left where I began: *in celebration and thanksgiving*. It's all about how art and consciousness embrace each other. How each sees the other as pure creative potentiality and lets be what is so that it may be more. The reciprocal love of art for higher consciousness and of consciousness for embodiment through art is what makes practicing an art an ideal education for higher consciousness. One draws out the best of the other.

The dancing butterfly, that being who lives but moments yet has time enough, is poignantly suggestive of the artist. Both suggest self-transformation as celebration, for spirit is latent in every cocoon and is destined for flight and dance. Friends of sun and flower and wind, both engage in an unpredictable mid-air dance. Here we have a truly Zen flicker of spirit, inimanent and transcendent, both at the same time. All we need to do is to celebrate the freely granted choice to live in this way and enter into thanksgiving for it.

This book was a pleasure to do—now it's a pleasure not to do. I am thankful that I have had the time and opportunity to gather these thoughts together and to share with you my feelings about art and consciousness. I have had great company throughout this venture—a vast community of artists, philosophers, writers and poets.

Perhaps some of you will hear the call and will read between the lines—"between the bread...between the wine."[8] Perhaps you will find the unspoken questions behind this work itself. Perhaps you will move toward a deeper interpretation of your own self-formative process in this journey.

I have been in a good space in a good time. I have many, many reasons for thanksgiving. I have seen art and education come and go. It has been my special privilege to play a formative role in many innovations in teaching, in art, and in research. I have enjoyed not only the great company of writers and artists I have met in my research, but also the motivation and enthusiasm that have constantly arisen from my unusual day to day roles: among undergraduate and graduate students, teaching studios and graduate seminars, engaging in basic research into the creative process, guiding doctoral students and their theses, interacting with interesting colleagues and supportive administrators, and finding those strands of freedom — often hidden — essential to institutional vitality. The stars have given me every indication that mine is a mission important to fulfill. In this lifetime I have been meant to be a pointer, not a way station.

I want to make it very clear here, however, that my "priviledged path" was not one lined with primroses. Adverse politics, bitter struggle and severe frustration were also mine to endure. When I espoused a phenomenology of the creative imagination that operated from within the center of the creating stream of consciousness, I became a threat to the core beliefs of many of the established people and institutions holding power. Also, for years, I had to work with less than adequate equipment, especially in teaching pottery, because funds were just not available to provide something as small as a bisque kiln. And equally often these very limitations led to improvisations that added to the vitality of teaching and learning. So taken from a higher view, all of these were but failures and frustrations along a way that eventually led to success.

There is never an end to opportunities for new actions and new discoveries. I have no doubt that the practice of art in the spirit set forth in this book will be a prime force in educating for higher consciousness in the years just ahead.

How this will come about I cannot tell you. There are no megatrends published for the life of the spirit. But let no one tell you it cannot be done. Art in education in the manner of this book is a great calling. Whenever the vision of this great calling — to educate for higher consciousness through art — is truly received, *nothing* can prevent it from manifesting.

Already the seeds are planted, but the faith that supports step by step action against all odds has not yet found expression. There is no failure on such a path — failure is just one step along the way, something that teaches what *not* to do. *Massive failure* has always been the way to great achievement. I remember building experimental live flame high-fire pottery kilns in the early fifties. I tried one after the other, trying to relearn what the Chinese knew several thousands of years ago. I used to say that each kiln I improvised was a better failure. Even beyond all judgment, it appeared that each kiln, whatever its problems, imparted its own unique artistic quality to the pots fired in it.

I am convinced that we are here on this earth plane precisely because it's not easy. If we knew it all ahead of time, we wouldn't be here. Yet the way is not all painful, not just one damn thing after another. Rather each situation can provide us with the possibility of eventual pleasure and success if we can but assume the right attitude and savor each moment as a rare privilege to learn. It is more and more clear to me that if we live fully in the moment, then the next moment will come already prepared to guide us.

I do not want to sound like a coach at half-time trying to motivate his or her players to reverse the odds against them. It's all in the playing, and though the stakes seem high, there's no real losing. Consciousness will evolve whether we get behind it and help it along or not. But to do so is to be on the side of the gods. And we have the opportunity to do so through the practice of art according to its universal self-formative freedom.

In a real sense, art has come full circle for me. When I turned toward it in early adolescence, I already knew it was a sacred summons, that it would be my kind of "work" in a world whose institutions did not make much sense to me. When the creative process and the freedom of the creative imagination became apparent, I felt a bridge between childhood and the adult world. I had no idea how things would work out. For some years I felt that, like Walt Whitman, I would take some job to supply my basic needs but really live for art.

The one big thing I knew was that art was a call to higher consciousness...although I wouldn't have called it that then. It was more like a religious fervor. It was the clear realization that *simple things, simple acts* had to be performed with *love and full commitment.* Art alone seemed to allow that. Even religion, as I saw it growing up in a minister's family, did not conpare with art in this regard. There were no parishioners or official boards to please, only that feeling of celebration and thanksgiving that came with fullness of artistic expression.

I was fortunate in many ways, for my circumstances provided me early in life with a nurturant ground for my art. Now I see that it was an interactive, transactional phenomenon. My more solitary ways and my inner quest granted me a vision and a faith which others sensed. They either supported it as best they could or left me alone, and both actions helped me. Concrete events stand out as I look back: when my father helped me set up an attic studio, complete with improvised skylight; when my brother bought me a book on art history at a time I was sick in bed; when my high school art teacher turned over the "back room" to me as my private studio; when my academic prowess won me the scholarships that got me away to art school. Even when World War II interrupted my college art career, it granted me the time to mature and the timing to discover Viktor Lowenfeld and Herbert Read. They opened up for me a second vocation: educating for higher consciousness through art. Again, those weren't the words used in the mid-forties, but that's what was meant. Lowenfeld's comment to me in the mid-fifties, at a time that the National Committee on Art Education of the Museum of Modern Art was meeting at Penn State, was prophetic in that regard: "You know, Ken, art is about spirit, what else?" What else indeed?

When I think about educating for higher consciousness through art, I also think of what an extremely individual affair it is. The few autobiographical details I've included underscore that. My own awareness of the idiosyncratic but essential features surrounding every artist undoubtedly come through my own history. It was important that I could sketch the pulse of life from the large parlor dormer window seats in the old Victorian brownstone parsonage I grew up in. It was important that the sunday ritual changed the atmosphere and the vision that partook of it. It was important that in three short city blocks, I could walk along the banks of the broad Susquehanna River and see the changing seasons and lights, especially those on the mysterious and perfect far shore. It was important that I met Lowenfeld and that he chose me to be on his staff.

The Drawing Lab itself, which existed at Penn State from 1968 to 1984, materialized out of these biographical details as they interacted with my challenging role in art education and the dawning realization that art itself constituted a natural way for educating others toward higher consciousness as long as the absolute freedom of the creative imagination and the unique destiny of each soul was honored.

It is not really such a long time from that beginning 55 years ago. What is new now is that I have had the opportunity to explore and write about art as an esoteric spiritual discipline directly. What continues is that same feeling of celebration and thanksgiving that attends the imagination's full engagement in the free becoming of art. All the examples that follow reflect that beginner's mind, that Zen of the simple act of making. They do not need to be "high art," for the calling to art is already high, moving to higher, all by itself.

So at this point I want to celebrate and give thanks through art works themselves. To take on a topic of the magnitude of this book, I have had to live the life of dialogue to the best of my ability in teaching, in art, and in research. By practicing art throughout my life, I have been able to feel the celebration, thanksgiving, and expanding awareness of which I write. By teaching art I have been able to explore how others could learn in their own individual ways what I have learned in mine. By engaging in basic research, I have been able to enlarge, verify, share and question all that I have learned and that others have taught me through their learning.

I will not provide extensive commentary with the works that follow — only something of the context from which they have sprung. They are to be experienced as stepping stones into the fuller garden of art and consciousness. Only that.

It is important to my sense of authenticity and congruence to show these examples. I must allow for my creative journey what I allow for others. Through these you may be able to form some idea of how the creating stream of consciousness runs for me and not think of it as an abstract concept only. Where imagination leads the artist is as much a mystery to the artist as to the observer.

Once after a clinging *Early Spring Snow*, I was moved to capture something of the quiet, timeless unity of whites on the bushes, trees, and grasses right outside my windows. Ever so slowly, with dots of black ink — like a negative of the beautiful dots of falling snow — I allowed myself to become a snowfall. Yes, I did pour love into them — a friendship going back to childhood. Whenever I picked up my pad and made more dots, nothing else mattered. The snowfall slowly settled unto that surface.

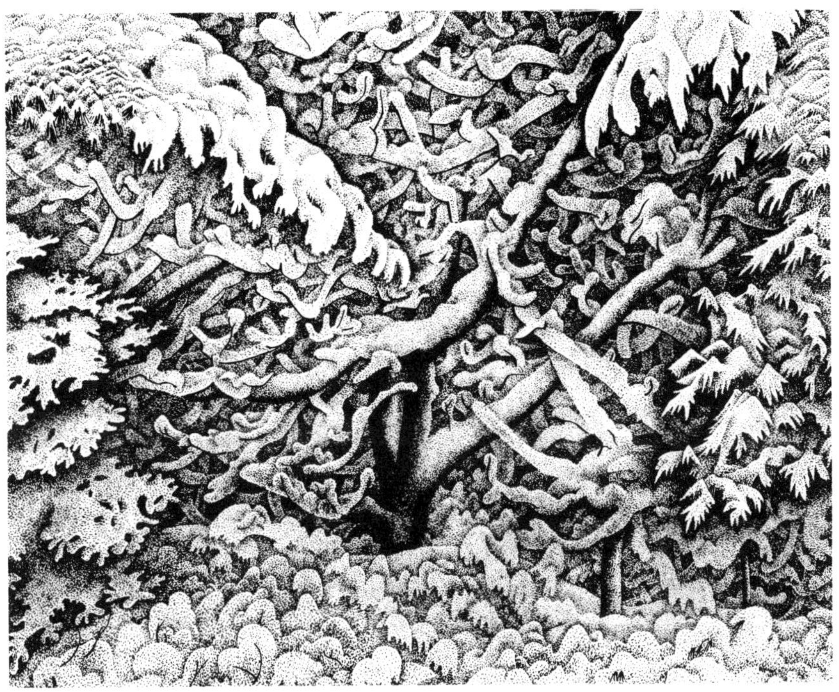

Early Spring Snow.
Pen and ink. By the author.

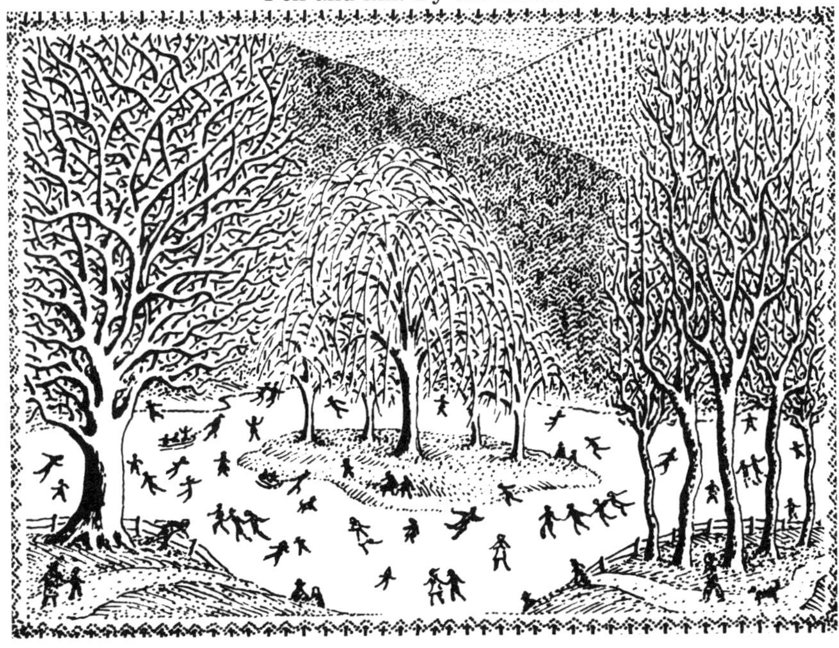

The Skating Pond.
Pen and ink. By the author.

The Skating Pond celebrates one of the festive faces of winter. It captures something of the feeling I early acquired when I drew and painted crowds of people at Eastertime in the Sunken Garden along the banks of the Susquehanna River in Harrisburg. The joyful interaction of nature and the human is its real theme.

The rolling hills of central Pennsylvania have become indelibly impressed on my imagination. They appear again and again on my pots, where their curved spaces fit magically onto the curvature of clay spheres. In my drawings these hills become like music, as though you could *hear* the landscape, not just see it. It's a music of swelling curves and rhythmic encirclements, of theme and counter-theme, of repetitions with variations, of over-arching settings for meandering detail—of the face of nature in smiles. They speak of farming that is neither scientific nor organic, but rather poetic.

Two such drawings are shared here: *Huntingdon County of the Mind: Winter,* and *Down Home on the Farm: Spring.*

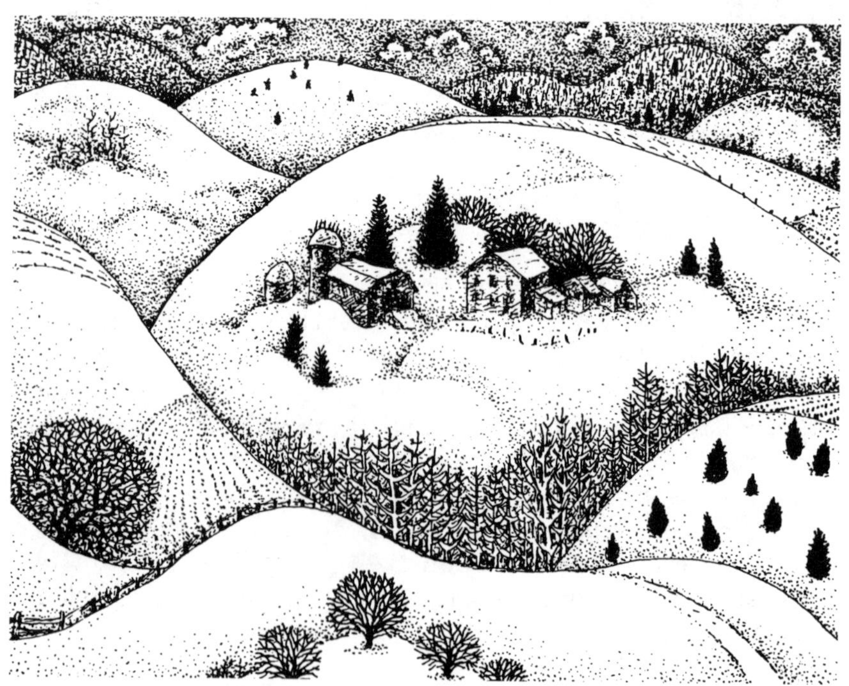

Huntingdon County of the Mind: Winter.
Pen and ink. By the author.

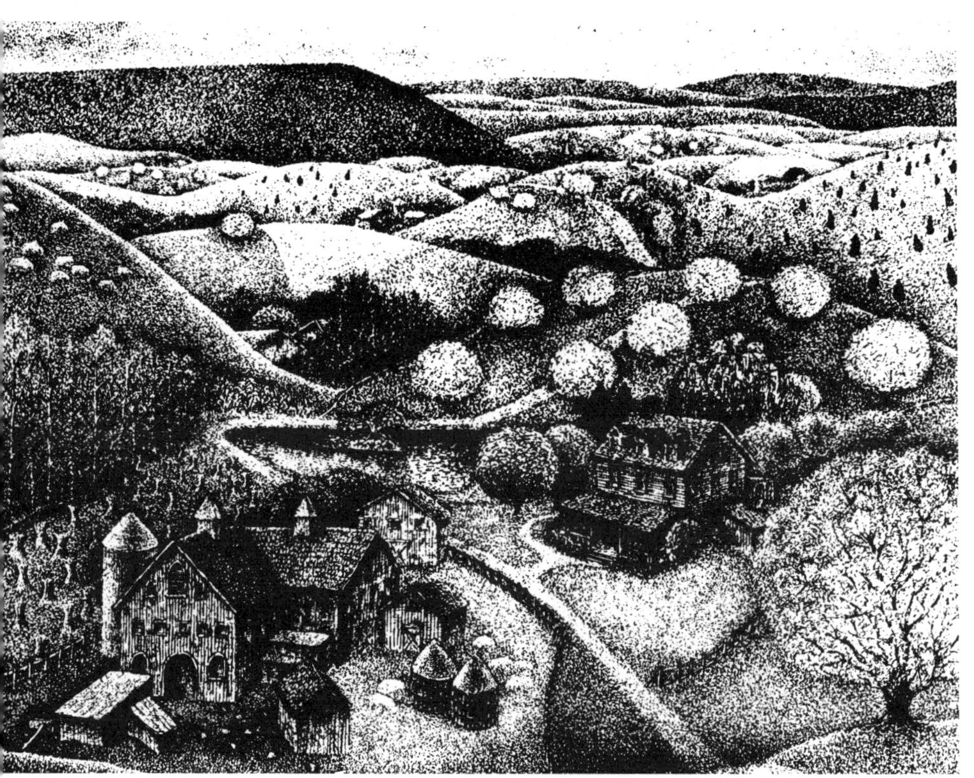

Down Home on the Farm: Spring.
Pen and ink. By the author.

These are like seasonal landscape archetypes — hinting at big forces which pervade all the individual things. That affective magnetism is also like music to me.

I am including here a working photo showing the construction of a large jar. The physicality of making art — especially in an art like pottery — *is extremely important to me. The expansion of consciousness is often best served by such challenging and concentrated work.* And curiously enough, large jars are very, very responsive to the *slightest changes* in pressure. Their forms want to fall into massive classical unadorned simplicity.

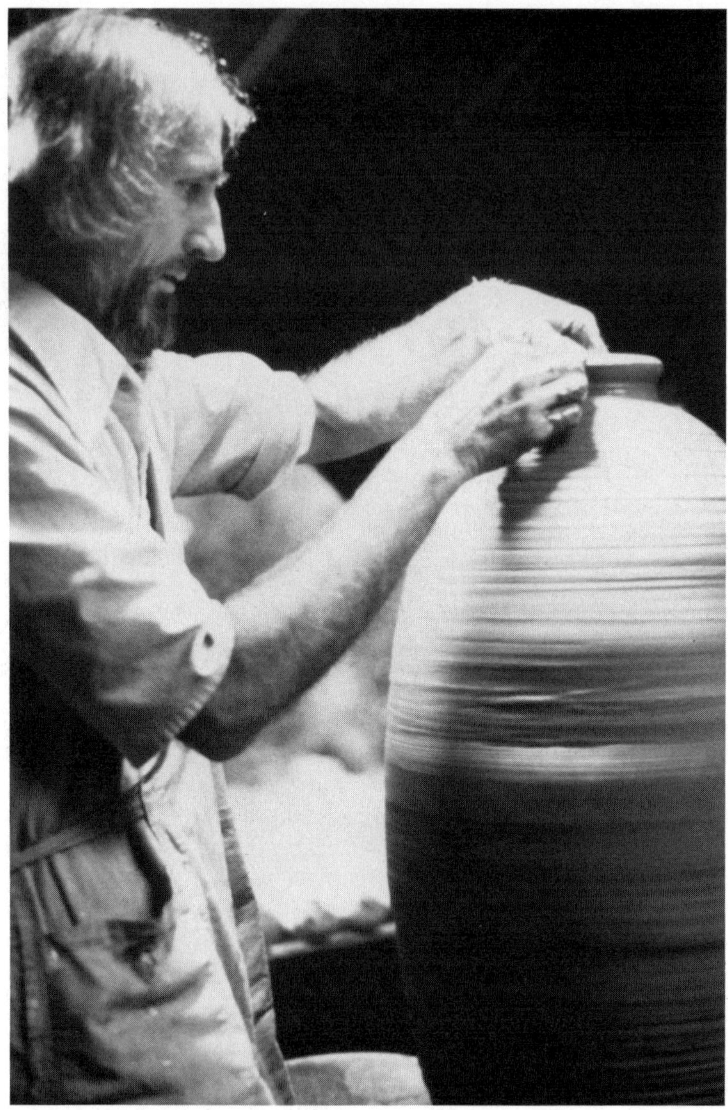

The Author Working on a Large Jar.

Following this there are two larger decorated jars. These give evidence of the range of poetic themes that come into imagery for translation into the simple clays and oxides of pottery. Painting on pottery is like no other act of painting I know: it is freer than watercolor on the one hand but as solid and enduring as painting a fresco.

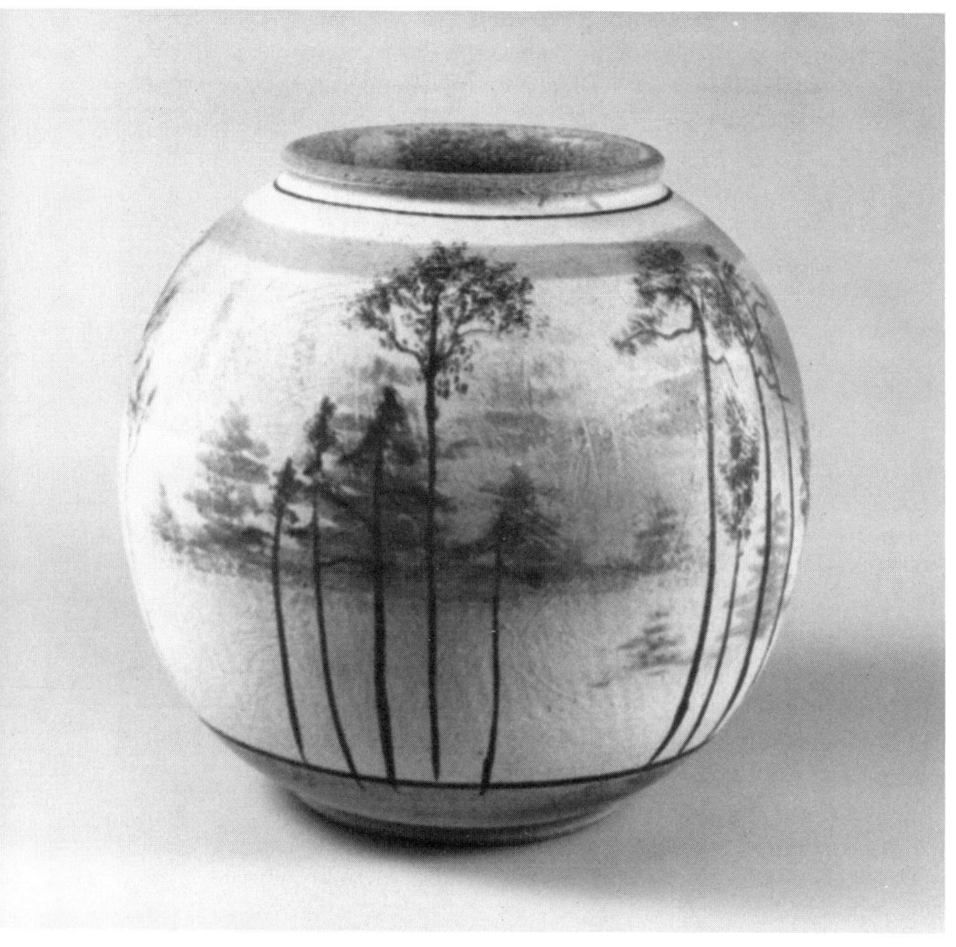

Jar of the Summer Fog.
Stoneware. By the author. Collection, Dr. Yasuro Kamachi, Arita, Japan.

The first, *Jar of the Summer Fog*, explains exactly what it is through its title. So does the second: *Homage to the Alps III: The Rhineland, The Castle.* What continues to fascinate me is how such fragile and exotic themes can materialize through clay and fire in the most concrete manner on a ceramic sphere.

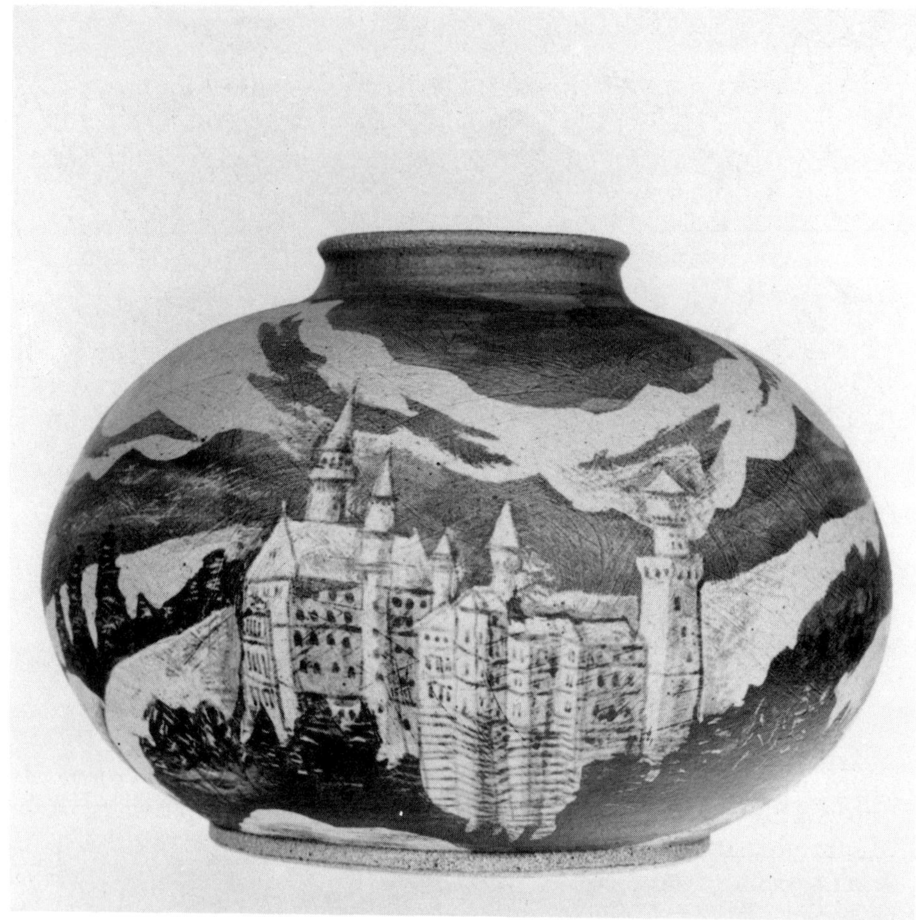

Homage to the Alps, III: The Rhineland, the Castle.
Stoneware. By the author.

Several years ago, animals wanted to appear in my land-scapes. I had never included them in my art before. But one Spring they showed up — first an eagle, then, in order, a lion, an elephant, a giraffe, a hippopatamus, a mountain goat, a dolphin, and a gorilla. Not only did they appear in my draw-ings, but they often appeared in decidedly non-jungle set-tings — in aspen groves and among the rolling hills of central Pennsylvania.

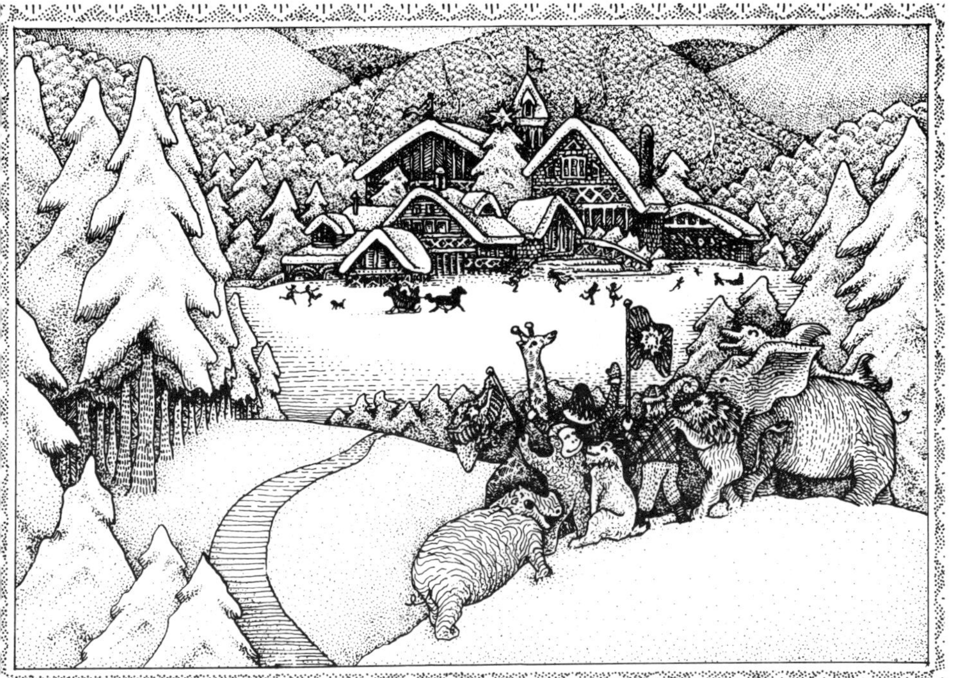

The Winter Resort.
Pen and ink. By the author.

In this first drawing with the animals, they are just catching sight of a special resort — perhaps in Vermont, perhaps in Colorado, perhaps in the Alps. The air is electric with excitement as the resort comes into view.

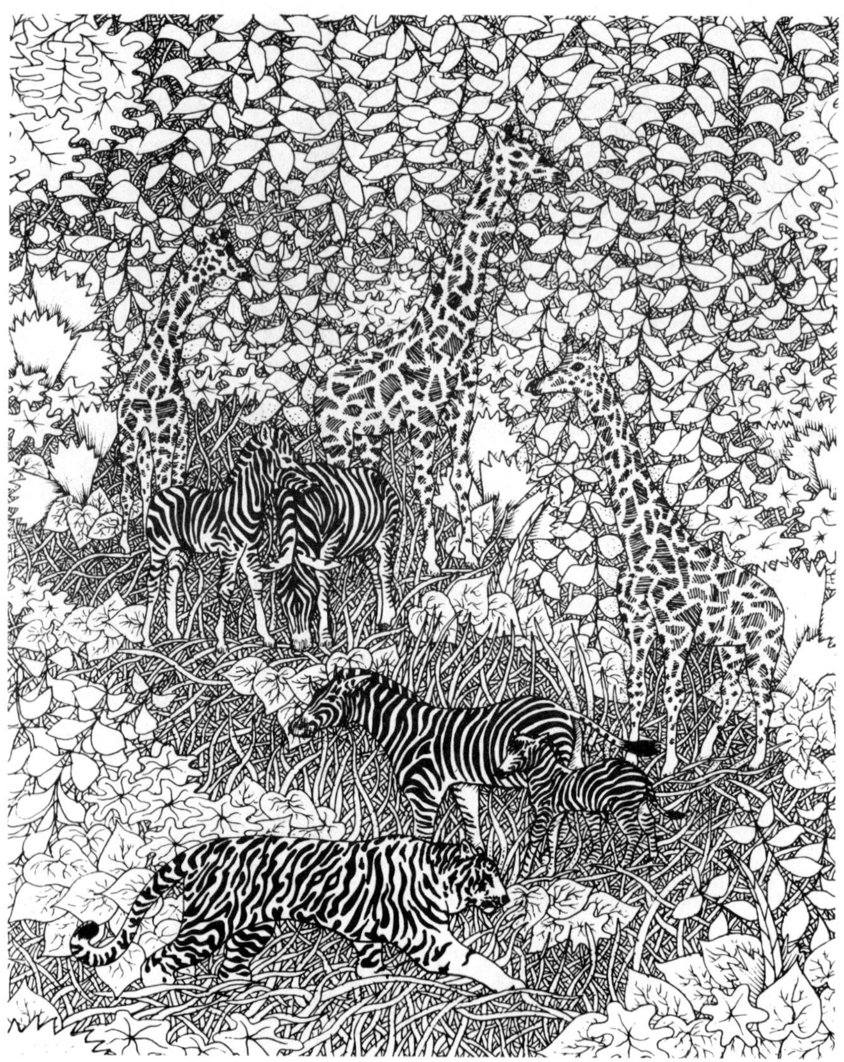

Pattern Valley.
Pen and ink. By the author.

Each of these animals has acquired a name and a personality. They all now appear in several illustrated children's stories that Joan and I are writing.

This is a drawing I call *Pattern Valley*, a special place that exists in the imaginal jungle.

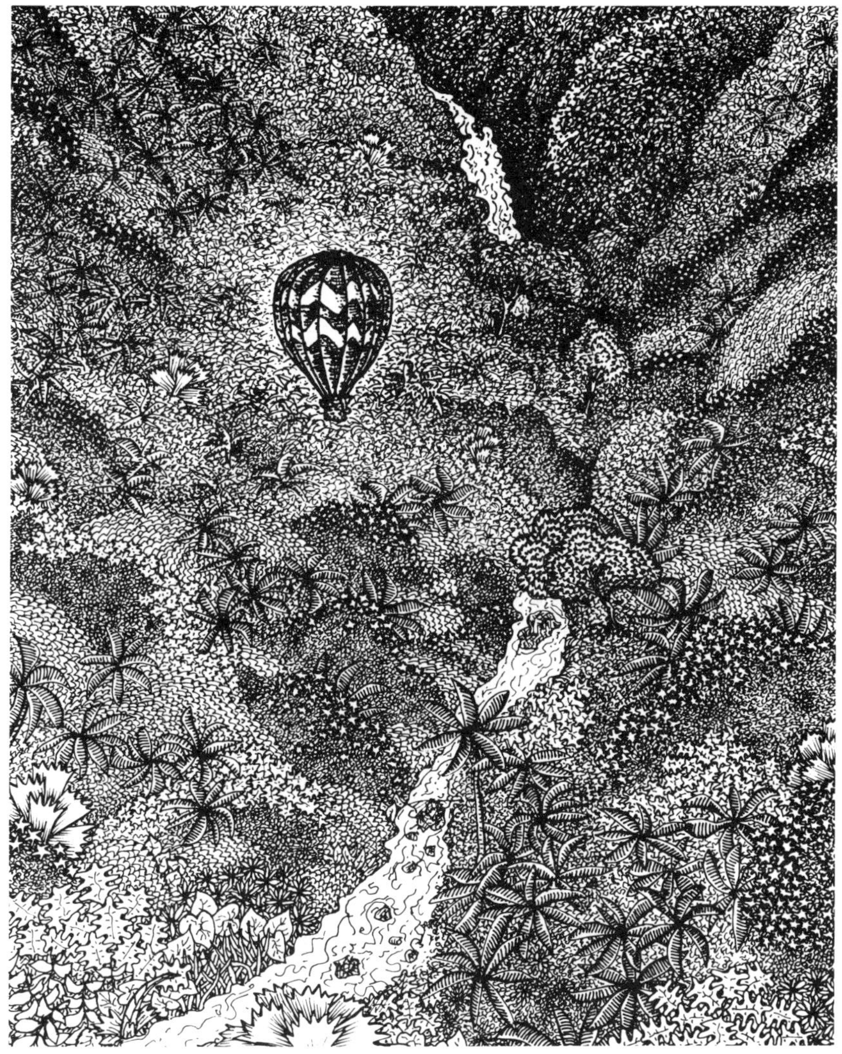

The Balloon Ride.
Pen and ink. By the author.

Here the animals go for a *Balloon Ride* that takes place in the tropical mountains high above the waterfalls, much like in Kauai.

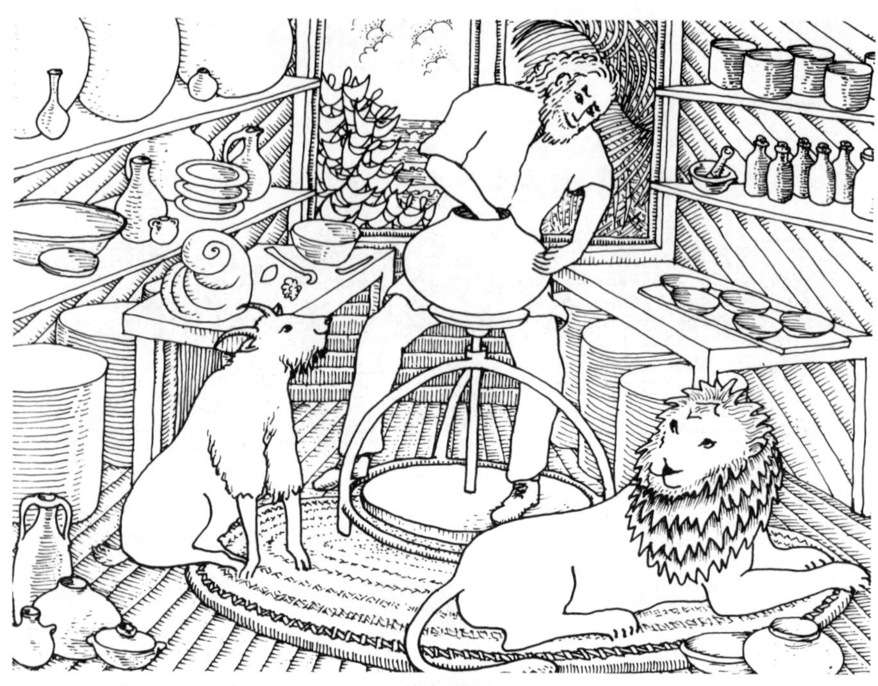

John the Artist in the Studio of Stelmo the Mountain Goat.
Pen and ink. By the author.

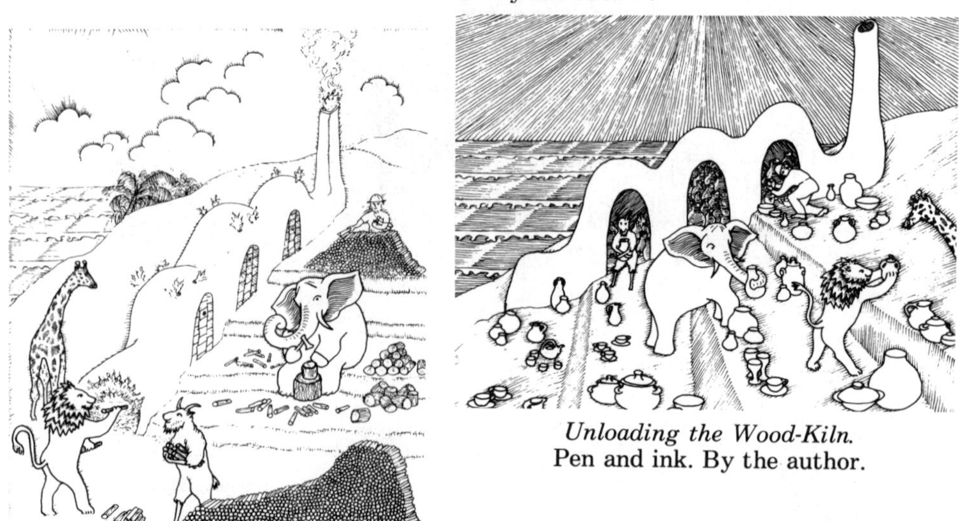

Unloading the Wood-Kiln.
Pen and ink. By the author.

Firing the Wood-Kiln.
Pen and ink. By the author.

John the Artist in the Studio of Stelmo the Mountain Goat,
Firing the Wood Kiln, and Unloading The Wood Kiln were
fun to do.

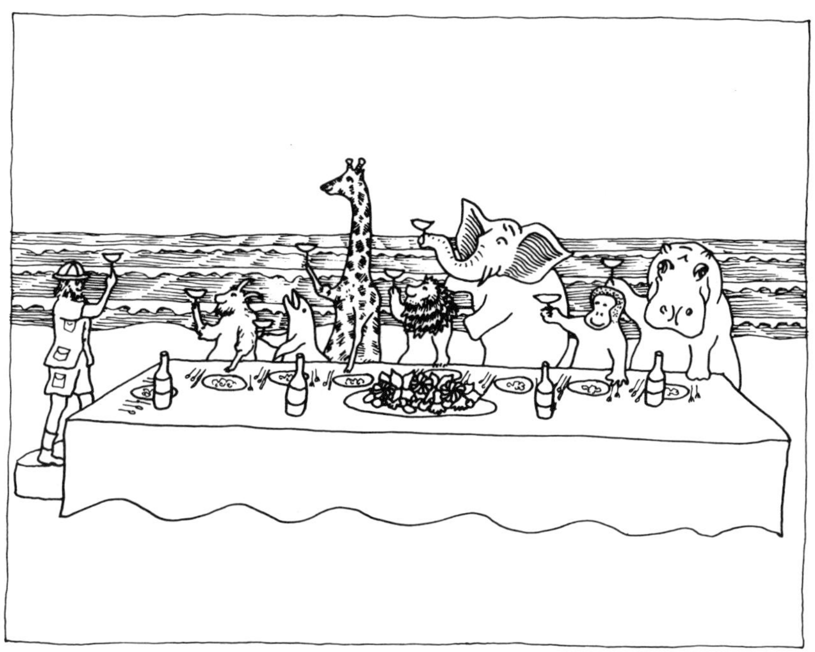

The Toast.
Pen and ink. By the author.

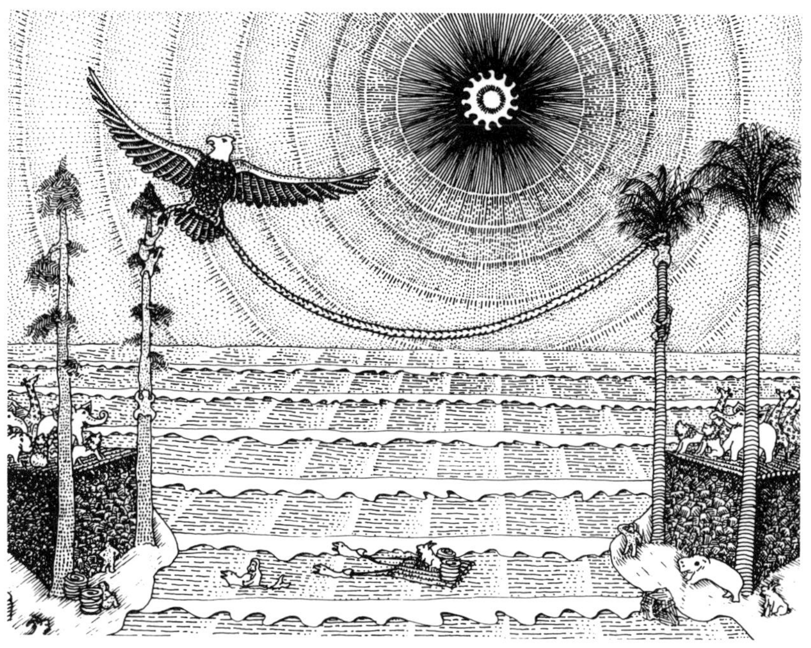

Securing the Cable.
Pen and ink. By the author.

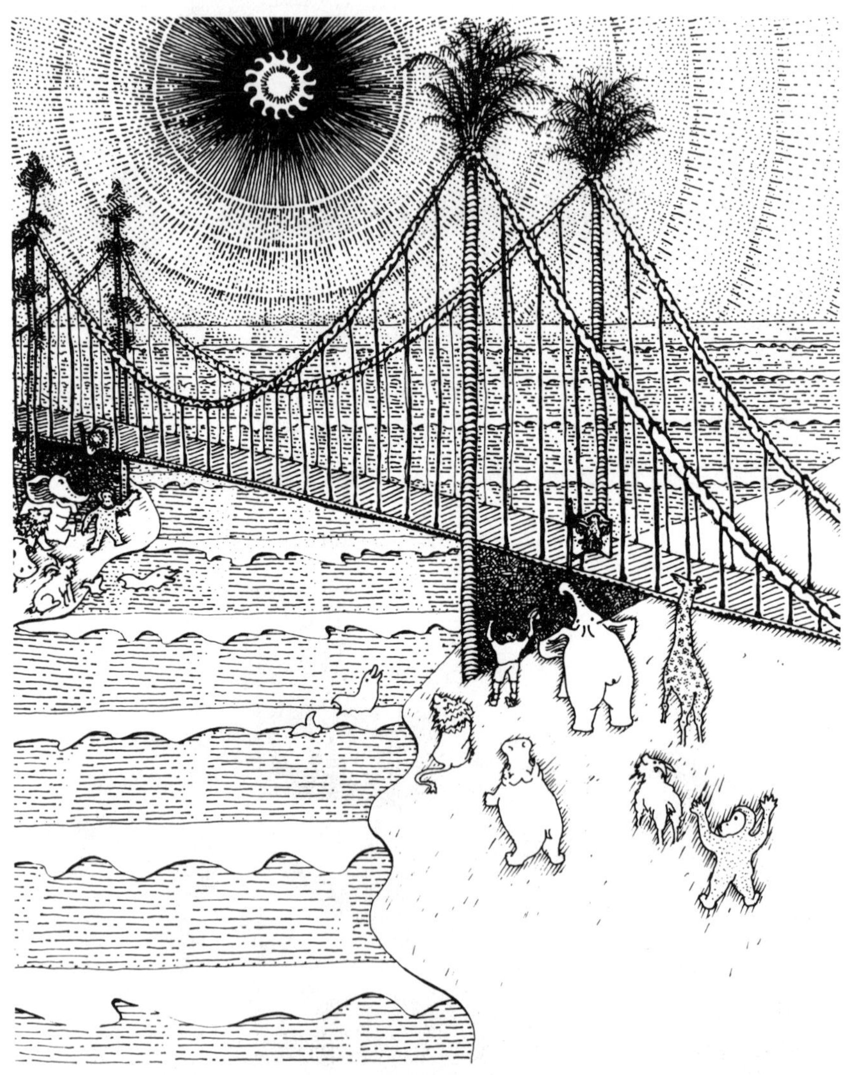

The Completed Bridge.
Pen and ink. By the author.

In *The Toast*, John and his friends are at a seaside banquet
that celebrates the beginning of the construction of a special
bridge together. *Securing the Cable* shows that bridge in progress. This is followed by *The Finished Bridge.*

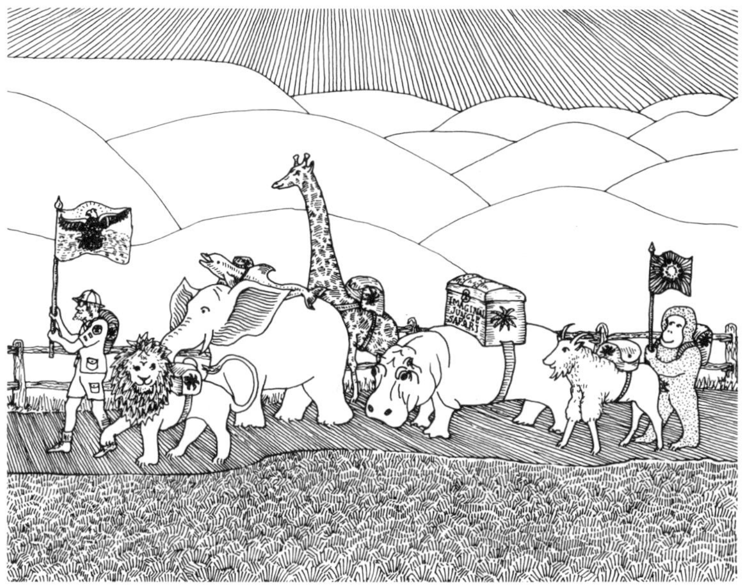

The Safari.
Pen and ink. By the author.

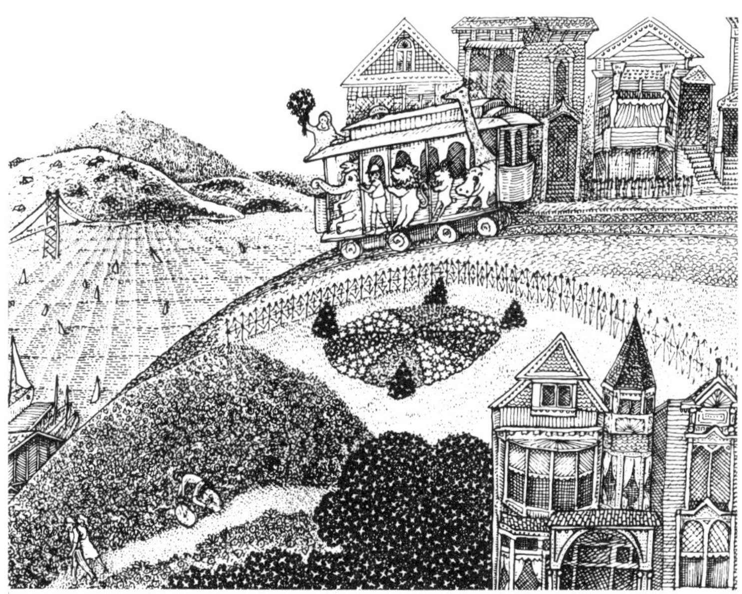

Cable Car Ride Over Nob Hill.
Pen and ink. By the author.

In the *Safari*, John takes his seven animal friends off on an expedition.

Here the animals take a *Cable Car Ride Over Nob Hill* in San Francisco.

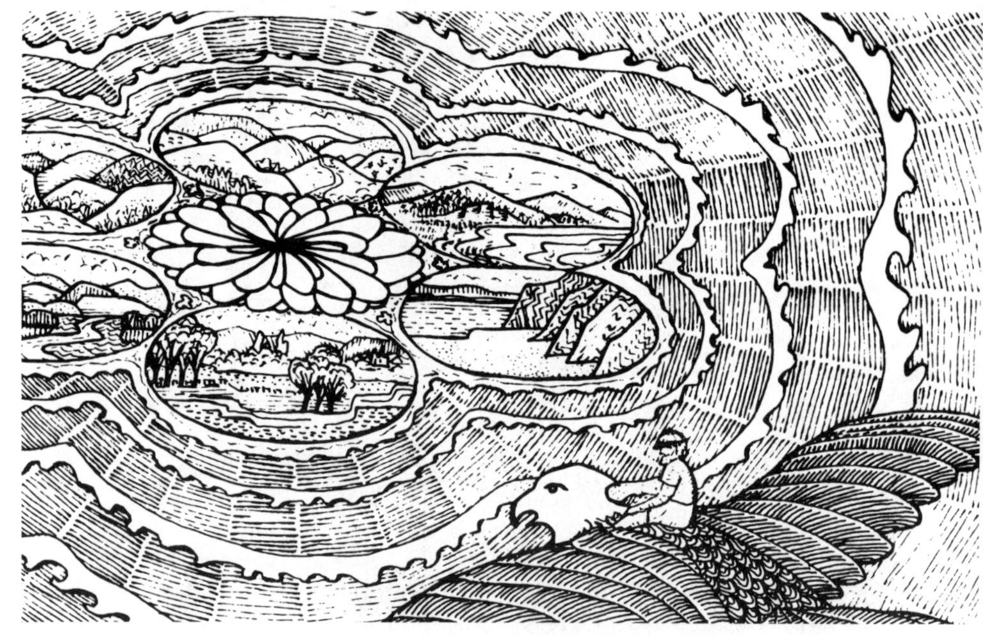

The Seven Imaginal Continents Afloat in the Cosmic Ocean.
Pen and ink. By the author.

John sees *The Seven Imaginal Continents Afloat in the Cosmic Ocean*, high in flight, carried on the wings of E. Pluribus.

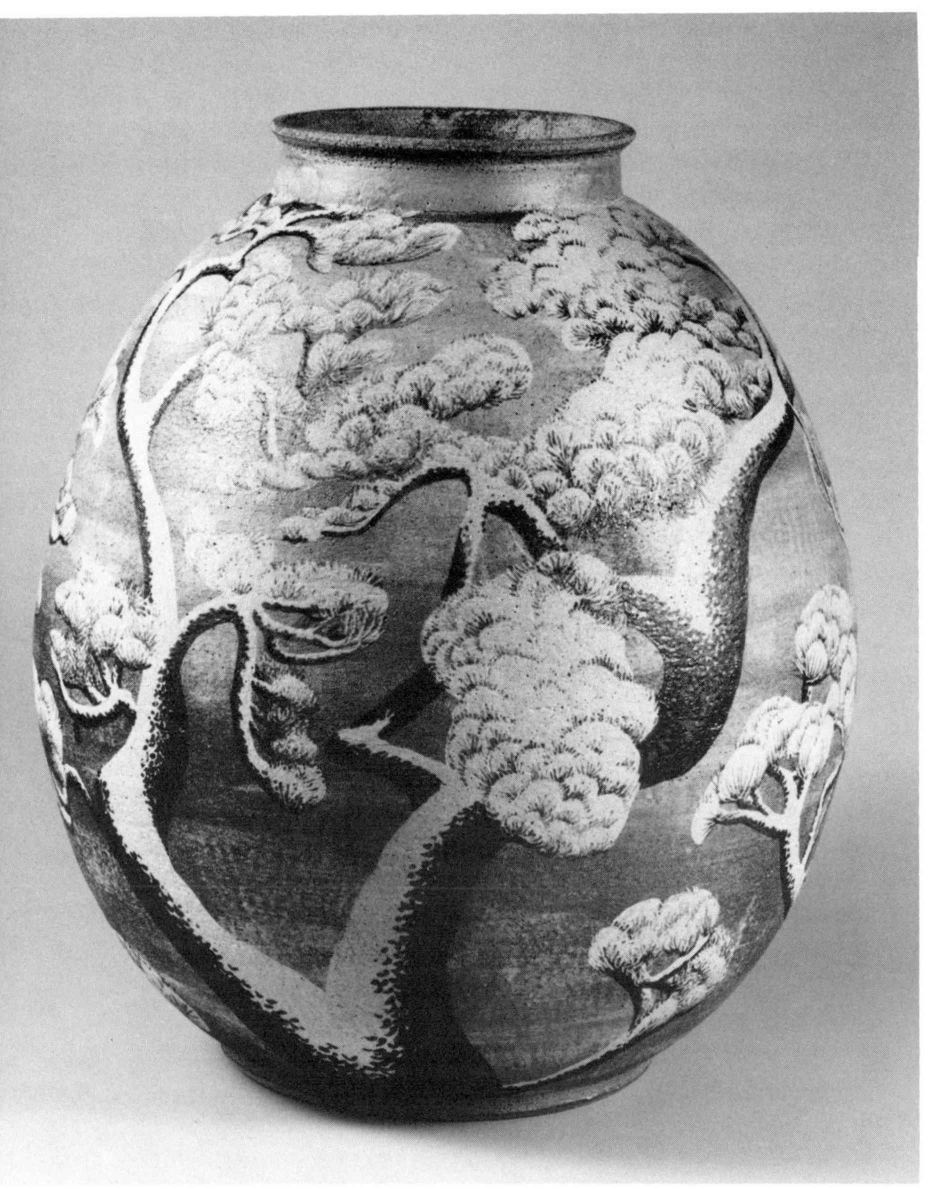

Snow Pine Vase.
Stoneware. By the author. Collection, Saga Prefecture Museum of
Procelain and Ceramic Arts, Arita, Japan.

Now it is time to become silent again. Suppose we place a
jar in the new-fallen snow. Let the departing words become
snowflakes settling quietly on a twisted old pine. *Snow Pine
Jar.*

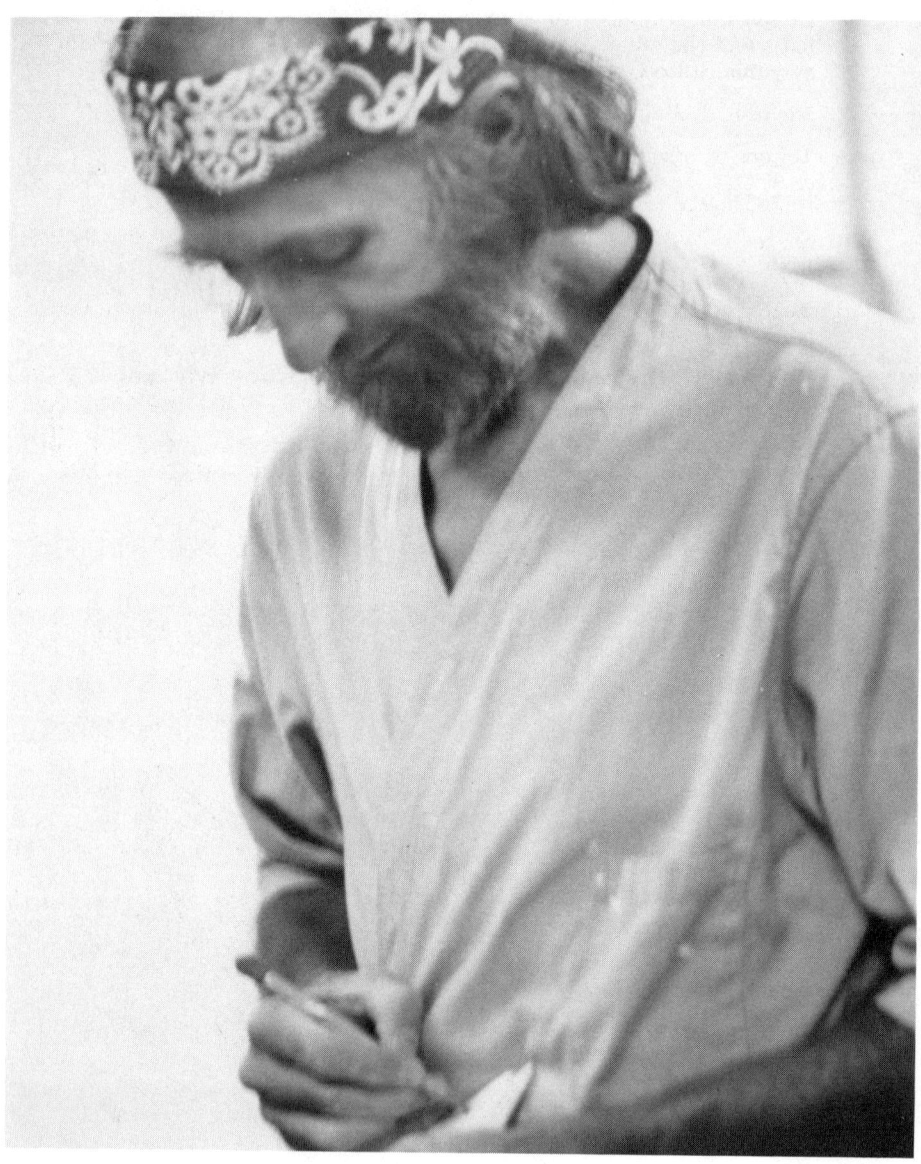

It is time to return to action and to the physicality of being. Time to wedge clay and kick the potter's wheel again. Time to pick up the brush and dance with the colors. Time to walk on the beach. Time to just be. Time to take the rainbow bridge to the only dance there is.

References

1. Novosel, J. The structural existentiality of arting: Inquiry into the nature of the creative process. Unpublished Ph.D. thesis, The Pennsylvania State University, 1976; poem entitled *born dawn*, p. 371.

2. Novosel, J. *Ibid.*, poem entitled *aesthetic necessity*, p. 366.

3. Tagore, R. *Fireflies*. N.Y.: Macmillan, 1976; p. 13.

4. Novosel, J. In conversation with a friend, Paris, France, 1969.

5. Stevens, W. *The necessary angel.* N.Y.: Vintage Books, 1942; forepage.

6. Yeats, W. B. *The collected poems of W.B. Yeats,* N.Y.: Macmillan (seventh printing), 1955; from *Tom O'Roughly*, p. 139.

7. Williams, W. C. *The selected poems of William Carlos Williams,* N.Y.: New Directions Paperbacks (second printing), 1968; *The Dance*, p. 167.

8. Beittel, J. From the poem *And to Think I Came to Penn State to Find the Answer.*

Epilogue

Out of the depths of the Earth a faraway sound arose. It was the sound of beings preparing to do Art again. It was not new beings and a new Spirit, yet it was new beings with a new Spirit, for Spirit never manifests in the same way twice. The winged centaur knows both the summit of pure Spirit and the valley of pure Matter – and it moves toward that unity through Art. *Spirit is Artist.*

Let there be Light.
　Let there be Art.
　　Let the butterflies dance.